Baedeker

IRELAND

Hints for using the Guide

Following the tradition established by Karl Baedeker in 1844, buil
ings and works of art, places of natural beauty and sights
particular interest are distinguished by one ★ or two ★★.
  To make it easier to locate the various places listed in the "A to .
section of the Guide, their co-ordinates are shown in red at the head
each entry: e.g., Connemara C 1/2.

Coloured lines down the right-hand side of the page are an aid to findir
the main heading in the Guide: blue stands for the Introduction (Natur
Culture, History, etc.), red for the "A to Z" section, and yellow indicate
Practical Information.

Only a selection of hotels, restaurants and shops can be given; no refle
tion is implied therefore on establishments not included.

In a time of rapid change it is difficult to ensure that all the informatior
given is entirely accurate and up-to-date, and the possibility of error car
never be entirely eliminated.

Although the publishers can accept no responsibility for inaccuracies and
omissions, they are constantly endeavouring to improve the quality of their
Guides and are therefore always grateful for criticisms, corrections and
suggestions for improvement.

Preface

This guide to Ireland is one of the new generation of Baedeker guides.

Illustrated throughout in colour, they are designed to meet the needs of the modern traveller. They are quick and easy to consult, with the principal places of interest described in alphabetical order, and practical details and useful tips shown in the margin. The information is presented in a format that is both attractive and easy to follow.

The subject of this guide is the whole of Ireland, both the Republic of Ireland and Northern Ireland which forms part of the United Kingdom.

The guide is in three parts. The first part gives a general account of the country, its topography, climate, flora and fauna, population, religion, language, state and society, education, economy, history, famous people as well as art and culture. A brief selection of quotations and some suggested routes lead into the second part, in which the principal places of tourist interest – towns, villages, landscapes, lakes and rivers – are described. The third part contains a variety of practical information designed to help visitors to find their way about and make the most of their stay. Both

The picturesque landscapes of White Park Bay and the attractive little town of Kinsale reflect Ireland's charm

the sights and the practical information sections are listed in alphabetical order

The new Baedeker guides are noted for their concentration on essentials and their convenience of use. They contain numerous specially drawn plans and colour illustrations; and at the end of the book is a large map making it easy to locate the various places described in the "A to Z" section of the guide with the help of the co-ordinates given at the head of each entry.

Contents

Baedeker Specials

The Eme

Green in all its many shades dominates this country with meadows, fields and trees as far as the eye can see. Rambling fuschia hedges and rhododendron bushes together with glorious parks and gardens set the tone. The main attraction for the visitor to Ireland is its natural beauty. It is at its best in the sunshine but it would be a mistake to think it is always fine – it frequently rains. There is a saying that every day encompasses all four seasons.

Following a heavy shower the sky soon clears up and the gentle Irish sun breaks through to bathe this hilly country with its many rivers in sunlight.

Along with the countryside Ireland also has its cultural history. The unique beauty of the strange shapes and forms from Celtic prehistory is striking. High points of a journey looking at Irish art are the monastery sites and tall crosses. The ruins harmoniously buried into the landscape exert a powerful effect.

Holidays in Ireland can also be active. Top of the list of favourite sports is golf. The Emerald Isle has about 250 golf courses and new ones are constantly being

Lough Erne
Lake district in Northern Ireland with innumerable little islands

Quin Abbey
One of Ireland's picturesque partly ruined abbeys

ald Isle

created. The numerous clean rivers and lakes contain shoals of fish which make the island an angler's paradise. Many visitors explore the country on horseback or by bicycle. But you need to be fit – there are lots of hills to cycle up and down. Boating holidays on the River Shannon and its tributaries are popular – no licence is required to steer your own boat on Irish waters. There is no more picturesque way to see the countryside.

The Shannon–Erne Canal now connects Ireland's longest river

with the beautiful Erne lake district of Northern Ireland. However, crossing the border from the Republic of Ireland to Northern Ireland is still difficult and not just by boat. Although in the autumn of 1994 the bloody troubles of the Northern Ireland conflict came to an end, the ceasefire only lasted until February 1996.

The best way to get to know the Irish is in a pub. Here, over a Guiness, the locals tell stories, discuss life, sing songs or simply chat. Often the visitor is drawn into the conversation. The first word of Gaelic that the foreign guest learns to understand is nearly always "Fáilte" – it means "welcome".

Advertisement
for the Irish national drink

Pubs
Imaginative façade decoration

Dublin
Ireland's undisputed capital

Facts and Figures

Note

The old Celtic language of Ireland is known as Irish or Gaelic. Since there are variations in the spelling of place-names and personal names, in both their Irish and English versions, the forms adopted in this guide are those used in the publications of the Irish Tourist Board.

General

Location

Ireland (Eire in Irish) is politically divided into the Republic of Ireland and Northern Ireland. Together with the main island of Great Britain and various smaller islands and groups of islands it forms part of the British Isles – a term of purely geographical significance. It is separated from Great Britain, to the east, by the North Channel, the Irish Sea – which can often be rough – and St George's Channel; the west coast is open to the Atlantic, with numerous rocky offshore islands and islets.

Area and population

The total area of the island is 32,600sq. miles/84,403sq.km, of which 27,100/70,283 are in the Republic of Ireland and 5500/14,120 in Northern Ireland. From Malin Head in the north to Mizen Head in the south-west is 301 miles/486km and the widest point from east to west coast is 180 miles/290km.

© Baedeker

Republic of Ireland
Northern Ireland

Location: from 51°30' to 55°30' N and 5°30' to 10°30' W

Area: 32,600sq. miles/84,403sq.km of which 5500sq. miles/14,120sq.km is Northern Ireland

Population: 3.5 million (Republic of Ireland) 1.6 million (Northern Ireland)

Capital of the Republic of Ireland: Dublin

◀ *Cliffs of Moher on the west coast of Ireland*

Topography

Interior

Only in the east, around Dublin, do the Central Lowlands reach the coast. The interior of the island is a landscape of extensive limestone plains with expanses of moorland, innumerable loughs (lakes) large and small, and here and there low ranges of hills; the Shannon system of rivers and lakes covers about a fifth of Ireland.

Mountains

Near the coasts the pattern is different, with ranges of hills of some size and varying geological structure. The ranges in the south of Ireland are built of folded red sandstone, separated by river valleys, which are usually well wooded. The highest peak, at 3147ft/1041m, is Carrantuohill (Macgillicuddy's Reeks) in the south-west of the island. In Connemara, Mayo and Donegal the predominant rock is granite, sometimes overlaid with quartzite. Characteristic of these areas are the isolated bare conical hills which rise abruptly out of the plain. A basaltic plateau covers most of north-eastern Ireland. In the Wicklow Mountains granite again predominates. An area of particular interest both to geologists and to botanists is the karstic landscape of the Burren, near the west coast in Co. Clare.

Ireland went through at least two Ice Ages, which have left their traces in polished and striated rock surfaces and dark hill loughs, in the course of many valleys and in numerous morainic deposits of debris. The drumlins – elongated whale-backed mounds of boulder clay – which occur in swarms across a wide swathe of northern Ireland, broadly between Sligo and Belfast, are deposits of this kind.

Coastline

Round Ireland's much-indented 1988 mile/3200km coastline, with its many wide bays and narrow inlets, will be found numbers of beautiful beaches, offering ample scope for long walks or rides in the pure and bracing sea air, even when the weather is not inviting for bathing.

The coastal region around Donegal

View of the lakes at Killarney

In comparison with other European countries Ireland has so far had few ecological problems to contend with. That is partly because industrial development has not advanced so much and partly because agriculture is primarily restricted to organic cattle farming. The strong south-west winds also limit the effects of air pollution. A relatively low level of population density is also influential on the ecosystem.

Ecology

However, environmental problems are beginning to arise on the "Emerald Isle". The capacity of purification plants is insufficient, in many places industrial effluence and sewage from private houses flows untreated into the sea. The destruction of the bog country, the draining of some of Europe's unique moorland, has met with strong protests from environmentalists. In the cities of Dublin and Belfast smog, caused by heavy traffic and burning coal for fuel, is a problem.

Climate

Ireland lies in a region of mild south-westerly winds, subject to the influence of the warm water brought by the Gulf Stream. Since no point on the island is more than 70 miles/110km from the sea, the whole country has a relatively temperate climate, with mild winters and cool summers. Rain and wind are regular features of Irish weather, but snow is rare except in the hills and never lies long.

Oceanic climate

Seasonal fluctuations in temperatures are small. While the temperature in the coldest months – January and February – ranges between 39°F/4°C in the north-east and 45°F/7°C in the south-west, the thermometer rises to 57–61°F/14–16°C in the warmest months – July and August – and very seldom exceeds 77°F/25°C. The sunniest months are usually May and June, and in general the south-east of the island gets most sun.

Temperatures

11

Climatic table Dublin	Temperature in °C			No. of hours of sunshine per day	No. of days of rainfall	Rainfall in mm
	Air		Sea water tempera-ture			
Months	Average maximum	Average minimum				
January	7.6	1.3	9	1.9	13	67
February	8.2	1.6	8	2.5	10	55
March	10.4	2.6	7	3.4	10	51
April	12.7	3.7	8	5.0	11	45
May	15.4	5.9	9	6.2	10	60
June	18.4	9.1	11	6.0	11	57
July	19.6	11.0	13	4.8	13	70
August	19.4	10.6	14	4.9	12	74
September	17.3	8.9	14	3.9	12	72
October	13.9	6.3	13	3.2	11	70
November	10.3	3.8	12	2.1	12	67
December	8.4	2.6	10	1.6	14	74
Annual	13.5	5.6	10.7	3.9 (1435)	139	762

Rainfall

Rainfall is higher in the west of Ireland with an annual average, away from the mountains, of around 43in./1100mm, while in the sheltered east, it is around 32in./800mm. The rainfall rises dramatically on the peaks of the mountains, the maximum in the west being 118in./3000mm in Macgillycuddy's Reeks in Kerry and 79in./2000mm in the east in the Wicklow Mountains. The west of the island lies under the direct influence of Atlantic winds. The moisture-laden air masses are forced upwards by the coastal hills, and the cooling of the air at the higher levels brings down the rain in heavy downpours. Showers of this kind can frequently be seen coming, as they appear on the horizon and move past or draw rapidly closer. When a strong wind whips against the wall of rain it is blown horizontally rather than falling from above. In these conditions good rainwear is of more use than an umbrella.

The moisture content of the air is generally high, with the highest levels in the west.

Changeable weather

The weather of Ireland is very changeable. After a rainy day the sky will clear towards evening, with fine light effects and frequently also rainbows.

Flora and Fauna

Flora

Variety of species

Overall the variety of flora of Ireland is particularly narrow. During the last Ice Age almost the whole country was covered in a layer of ice. Only a few Arctic plants were able to survive. When the ice melted Ireland was at first still connected to Great Britain and the continent by a land bridge. With the increase in sea level about 8000 years ago it became separated, but the post-glacial migration of plants was far from complete. For example, not even half the number of flowering species of plants which exist in Great Britain can be found in Ireland.

However, most visitors are not aware of this lack of variety. After all the island is covered in every conceivable shade of green – dependent

To be found in Ireland: foxgloves . . .   *. . . cotton grass . . .*

. . . tall fuchsia hedges . . .   *. . . and gigantic rhododendron bushes*

on the weather, cloud formation, amount of rainfall, wind direction and soil condition – which earns it the name of the "Emerald Isle" and attracts many visitors.

Forests

Of the forests which gradually covered the country after the Ice Age only a few remnants survive. The original tree cover consisted of oak, holly, birch, ash and hazel. Today only a small proportion of the country consists of forest and the Government has made efforts to remedy this by extensive afforestation schemes. Most of the plantings have been of Sitka spruce, which has not in fact done particularly well in Ireland. Deciduous trees do, however, flourish, and fine single specimens with wide-spreading, regular branches can frequently be seen.

Bogs

About 16% of the land area of Ireland is covered with bog. There are different varieties of bog: moor (about 4%), which reaches a depth of 23ft/7m, blanket bog (about 11%, depth of 12ft/3.5m) which covers both upland and valley floor and lowland bog. Various types of sphagnum moss flourish on all types of bog, on moorland and surface bog heather, cotton grass, broom and bell heather are also found.

Sub-tropical-Mediterranean and Arctic-Alpine vegetation

Tropical and sub-tropical species originally planted in the parks and gardens of country houses have spread beyond these, particularly in the warm south-west where palm trees and evergreens are found.

Giant broom and rhododendron bushes together with flowering fuchsia hedges provide splashes of colour among the greenery. In the nature parks, however, these are not welcome as they choke the original indigenous vegetation.

In the mild Irish climate many familiar flowering plants flourish luxuriantly and develop vigorous new forms, such as the foxglove and a bluebell with an unusually long stem and deep blue colour.

Surprisingly in the south-west and in the Burren sub-tropical plants and Arctic alpine plants are found side by side. Owing to the cool summers they were able to survive after the last Ice Age.

Fauna

Variety of species

As with its flora Ireland is also relatively poor in native fauna. There are only 56 mammals (89 in Great Britain), no snakes at all and the only reptile is the upland or bog lizard.

Birds

There is, however, a wide variety of birds. In addition to the 135 indigenous varieties there are about 250 species which overwinter in Ireland or rest here on their migratory flight. Hawthorn hedges provide nesting places for songbirds. In moorland places the cry of the curlew and the snipe can be heard, and the song of the soaring lark. Oystercatchers leave their haunts on the coast and move far inland wherever they find sufficient water. Gulls and guillemots nest on crags off the Atlantic coast, and

Puffin

puffins with their gaudy beaks can occasionally be seen. Cormorants patrol the coasts, and gannets, flapping their great wings, plunge down from a great height to seize their prey. Such seabirds as the stormy petrel and fulmar are more rarely seen.

Fish, sea creatures

The water of Irish loughs (a term applied both to inland lakes and to major arms of the sea), rivers and streams is frequently brown and peaty, but it is almost always unpolluted and supports an abundant fish population. Salmon and trout are the most sought-after species; pike and rainbow trout are relatively recent introductions.

The seas around Ireland are home to 250 species of fish. Herring, sprat, cod, mackerel, plaice, haddock, sole and monkfish are of chief importance for commercial fishing. Round the coasts of Ireland various species of seal can be encountered.

Population

With 3.5 million inhabitants to an area of 27,136sq. miles/70,283sq.km Ireland is one of the most thinly populated countries in Europe. To the visitor travelling around the country this impression is reinforced by the fact that almost one in three Irish people live in the area around Dublin (Pop. of Greater Dublin: 1.1 million). Northern Ireland has about 1.6 million inhabitants and a population density of 116 per sq.km.

Numbers

In the first half of the 19th c. Ireland was one of the most densely populated countries in Europe. During the 18th c. a prolonged period of peace and intensive agricultural activity resulted in a sharp population increase; in the second half of the century the population was increasing by 15% every ten years. By 1821 the population numbered 6.8 million, by 1845 it had reached 8.5 million (figures relate to the whole country). The Great Famine between 1845 and 1850, caused by successive failures of the potato harvest, halted this trend. By 1851 the population had dropped to 6.5 million Almost 1 million people had died and another million had emigrated. Over the following decades unfavourable living conditions contributed to a decrease in population. In 1961 only 2.8 million people were living in the Republic of Ireland.

Population trends

At the beginning of the seventies this trend began to change. A sharp natural growth in population and improved economic factors resulted

The Irish enjoy discussions and debates

Population

in a population increase between 1971 and 1981 from 3 million to 3.8 million (growth of 15.6%; in Northern Ireland the figures for the same period were only 1.7%). Recently, however, despite a high birth rate in European countries, growth has been slow.

Emigration

In the second half of the 19th c. a wave of emigration gradually began which grew considerably in strength with the Great Famine of 1845. During the 19th c. about 3.5 million Irish people left their homes to try and build a new life in the United States or in Great Britain.

Following the Second World War emigration began again (between 1951 and 1961 over 40,000 emigrated annually). In the seventies this trend reversed but the high unemployment of the eighties led to further emigration. In the past it had been poorer farmers and unskilled labourers who left the country but in recent years the number of educated Irish leaving has drastically risen.

Irish in the USA

The Irish who emigrated to the USA settled in the large cities of the north where they soon dominated the market for unskilled labour (building sewers and railways). They grew into a political force to be taken seriously. Between 1870 and 1920, in every town in the USA which had a sizeable Irish population, there was an Irish politician, often an Irish mayor and a large Irish contingent in the police and fire brigade. In spite of this considerable influence it was 1960 before an American of Irish descent, John F. Kennedy (1917–63), was elected president. Kennedy, leader of the Democratic Party, was the first Catholic president.

Also of Irish descent was the American dramatist Eugene O'Neill (1888–1953); his plays have been performed since 1916 and in 1936 he received the Nobel prize for literature.

Travellers, tinkers

The "travellers" or "tinkers" (this last term is considered derogatory) are an underprivileged minority. Like the gypsies (with whom they are

Traditional cottage

not related) they are persons of no fixed abode who in the past earned their living as tinkers and had a secret argot-like language. It is accepted today that the travellers did not come from elsewhere but are of Irish origin. They have long since exchanged their colourfully painted horse drawn vargos, in which they used to travel the country and which today are a tourist attraction, for modern caravans.

Those families are described as Anglo-Irish whose forefathers from the mid-17th c., either as members of the lower English aristocracy or as former officers, were rewarded with expropriated Irish lands for their services. In contrast to earlier English settlers who learnt to speak Gaelic and accepted the lifestyle of the local population, these new arrivals kept to themselves. They continued to speak English, kept their religion and shut themselves away behind high walls from their Catholic and Irish neighbours. In the worst cases they used their lands as a source of income, seldom coming to Ireland and appointing agents to collect the rent from the people living in mud huts on their property. Later the "Anglo-Irish Gentlemen" as ruling class became upholders of cultural life. They built castles and laid out large parks where many tropical plants flourished thanks to the mild Irish climate.

Anglo-Irish

The Anglo-Irish were responsible for the spate of building activity in 18th c. Dublin which has been described as a windfall for European architecture. They built their own university, Trinity College, from which many important men have graduated: politicians and philosophers as well as poets and writers.

In the 18th c. several cultural organisations were established by the Anglo-Irish. The Royal Irish Academy collected early manuscripts (including the famous Psalter of Columcille) and published a Gaelic dictionary extending to several volumes. The Royal Dublin Society, known today for organising the Horse Show, was also dedicated to promoting cultural life. Its collections formed the foundations of the National Library and National Museum.

In the course of time the Anglo-Irish settled into a casual, rural lifestyle. With the larger part of the island becoming an independent state they became less influential. Some of the former estates were destroyed by the Irish.

In Ireland it is customary to own your own house (no matter how modest) but in the cities more and more people are having to rent a flat. The traditional house is the cottage with a yellow straw roof but living in one is not particularly pleasant. Usually the cottage consists of a central large room with a smaller room on each side. Families of six or more still live in an area of 654sq.ft/60sq.m. Not all the cottages have electricity and running water, so it is not surprising that there are few left which are inhabited except in the extreme barren region in the west. Those who can afford it have exchanged their cottages, which tourists find so romantic, for a comfortable bungalow or simple farmhouse.

Living conditions

Religion

Celtic Christianity

During the 5th c. the Celtic population of Ireland adopted the Christian faith as it was taught by St Patrick. There were no martyrs. Frequently the old Irish groups went over en masse to the monastic life: the head of the clan became abbot and his family, retainers and servants followed him. Nunneries were established for the women. As a result there was a great flowering of religious houses and the number of monks grew rapidly; and just as the kinship group had previously lived in a ring-fort, so they now sought safety within the enclosing walls of the monastic precinct. The Penitentials and Monastic Rules that have come down to us bear witness to the hard conditions of life in the early monasteries.

St Patrick is believed to have received part of his training on the Iles de Lérins, off the Mediterranean coast near Cannes, and it seems likely that while there he met representatives of some of the Eastern churches. This may be how the idea of the "religio arctior", the strictest ascetic life, came to Ireland, where it was enthusiastically received.

Green martyrdom

Since the faithful were deprived of the opportunity of "red martyrdom", at the cost of their own blood, many of them sought the "green martyrdom" of voluntary exile to remote places. While the hermits of the Near East withdrew to the desert, their Irish counterparts retired to a solitary life on very small inaccessible islands off the Atlantic coast.

A typical example of a monastic settlement of the 8th c. is provided by the tiny churches and beehive-shaped stone cells still to be seen on the upper terraces of the treeless little islet of Skellig Michael (see Art and Architecture, Early Christian Period).

Monasteries

In addition to one or more churches and the cells for the monks a monastery would have a refectory and a guest house, scriptoria and craftsmen's workshops. Students from England and the Continent and men and women fleeing before the upheavals of the Great Migrations sought refuge in the Irish religious houses, some of which grew to become real monastic cities. Latin as well as Irish was spoken in the monasteries, and not only religious works but the writings of Virgil, Cicero and Ovid were read. There are records, too, of monks who knew Greek.

White martyrdom

At the same time there was a movement in the opposite direction. Side by side with the "green martyrdom" there developed the "white martyrdom", the "peregrinatio pro Christo", the pilgrimage for Christ's sake. In frail boats made of animal hides on a timber framework Irish monks ventured out into the "pathless sea" and made their way as itinerant preachers by way of England and France into other European countries. With them they took not only their austere faith but also a humanist education, carrying in leather pouches their precious manuscripts, including copies of the Scriptures which perhaps were already illuminated. The traces of their journeys and their settlements can still be followed today. In regions devastated by war and the passage of armies they established new religious and cultural centres. Later, from the 9th c. onwards, when the process of conversion to Christianity was complete, Irish monks still found their way to Europe as scholars and as advisers to various European rulers. Thus Ireland was able to repay to the Continent, many times over, what it had earlier received from it.

Among the saints of the Early Celtic Church there are some names which will constantly be encountered by visitors to Ireland.

St Patrick

St Patrick, who came to Ireland in 432, tells us in his "Confessio" that in him "the spirit glowed". He travelled through the country with a large retinue and treated the High King as an equal, baptising his daughters and lighting the Paschal fire near Tara. Around his life, the exact dates of which are unknown, numerous legends have grown up. He is the national saint of the Irish.

St Enda

St Enda was one of the first to withdraw, in the year 490, to a remote and solitary place in order to devote himself to a life of study and renunciation on the model of the desert hermits. Soon so many disciples followed him to his retreat on Inishmore, one of the Aran islands, that a large monastic settlement grew up, the fame of which spread to the Continent.

Many of the monks who gathered round St Enda themselves founded monasteries and gained a reputation for sanctity, including St Ciarán, who in 548 established the monastic settlement of Clonmacnoise on the Shannon. The learning of the Clonmacnoise monks soon earned it the style of the "University of the West".

St Ciarán

Equal to Clonmacnoise in size and importance was Glendalough in the Wicklow Mountains, to which St Kevin, followed by numerous disciples, withdrew to lead a hermit's life.

St Kevin

The leading female saint was St Brigid, who founded a large double monastery for monks and nuns in Kildare in 490. In her "fire house" there burned a perpetual fire – perhaps the continuation of some pre-Christian cult – which was extinguished only at the Reformation. A "St Brigid's cross", woven of straw or reeds and regarded as a protective symbol, is still found in Irish houses, and also on cars and tractors.

St Brigid

St Brendan, who founded a monastery at Clonfert and gathered round him a host of monks, became the model for all those who left home for Christ's sake and ventured on to the open sea, sailing they knew not whither. The "Navigatio Sancti Brendani Abbatis" (Voyage of St Brendan the Abbot), the account of which survives in numerous medieval copies, is said to have lasted nine years.

St Brendan

St Columba (521 or 543–597) is known in Irish as Columcille (The Dove of the Churches) and in Latin as Columbanus (the Elder, to distinguish him from the other Columbanus). Columba, who was born at Gartan and, like St Kevin, came from a royal house, went into exile to atone for his guilt. He had secretly made a copy of a psalter belonging to St Finian, who guarded his books jealously and demanded that Columba should give him the copy. When the two could not agree Finian brought the matter before the High King, who held that the copy belonged to Finian, on the grounds that a copy should go with the original book, as a calf goes with a cow. Columba and his supporters refused to accept this verdict, and thereupon fought a battle with the High King on the slopes of Benbulen, north of Sligo. Columba was victorious but left 3000 of his men dead on the field, and by way of penance left home and went into exile. In 563 he landed with twelve companions on the Scottish island of Hy (now Iona), where he founded a monastery. From there he carried on missionary work, mainly among the Picts and Angles. For all the strictness of his faith he is said to have been a kindly man and a lover of nature, particularly of animals.

St Columbanus the Elder

St Columbanus the Younger, born in Ireland in 540, was of a less amiable temperament than Columba. About 590, when a disciple of St Comgall in the celebrated Monastery of Bangor and already of advanced years, he resolved to go on pilgrimage. With twelve companions he travelled to the Continent and gained great influence at the Burgundian Court, founding monasteries at Annegray and Luxeuil. He is described as powerful in the faith but uncompromising and irascible.

After a dispute with the Burgundian King he and his companions made their way up the Rhine Valley to Lake Constance and crossed the Alps into northern Italy. The rules he laid down were an influential contribution to Western monasticism, and the disciples whom he gathered round him were thus given a definite pattern for the monastic life.

St Columbanus the Younger

Other Irish saints who propagated their faith on the Continent were St Gallus, one of Columba's companions, who founded the Monastery of St Gall in Switzerland; St Kilian, Apostle of the Franks, who suffered martyrdom at Würzburg; and St Virgil, now Patron Saint of Salzburg.

St Gallus
St Kilian
St Virgil

Religion

Learned monks

In later times, when the Vikings were already harrying Ireland, many learned Irish monks found employment at European Courts, and "Scotus", or "Irishman", became a term of honour. Clemens Scotus succeeded Alcuin as head of Charlemagne's famous Palace School, at which Dicuil, described as a grammarian, geographer and astronomer, also taught. Sedulius Scotus, a scholar of outstanding quality, moved from Metz to Cologne. Johannes Eriugena ("Irish-born"), one of the leading spirits of his day, is recorded as having been at the Court of Charles the Bald about 845.

Scottish houses

The influence of Iro-Scottish missionaries reached far into eastern Europe, as is shown by the existence of "Scottish houses" (in German Schottenklöster) at Regensburg, Vienna and Kiev. Thus the Early Irish Church was able to transmit to other countries far afield the treasures of its faith and its learning, and its foundations became "the store cupboards of the past" and "the cradles of the future".

The Church and the tradition of the faith

More than in any other country in Europe, the tradition of the faith has been maintained unbroken among the Roman catholic population of Ireland, in spite of the oppression to which they were exposed in past centuries. When Catholic worship was forbidden Mass continued to be celebrated in secret in the open air, at "Mass rocks" in remote places. Those who wanted to become priests had to seek training and ordination abroad, mainly in France and Spain. When the building of churches was again permitted they had at first to be unobtrusively sited in side streets.

The influence of the Roman Catholic Church, to which some 94 per cent of the population belongs, makes itself felt in all areas of life in the Republic. On Sundays the numerous services are attended by crowded congregations. Children are commonly baptised with the names of early Irish saints.

Marriage and the family

Marriages are celebrated in church in the presence of the whole family; registry-office weddings are rare. Divorce is prohibited under Irish law, although this may change as the result of a referendum scheduled for late 1994.

Abortions are also illegal, except in cases where the mother's life is in serious danger. In a referendum in 1992 the majority voted for freedom of information in questions of abortion and for freedom of travel for pregnant women, but voted against a change in the existing law.

Priests are part of everyday life in the Republic. Irish priests and nuns are found in many countries, particularly in the Third World, as teachers, nurses and social workers. In the field of private charitable work within Ireland itself the Irish put the inhabitants of wealthier countries to shame.

There are, of course, more negative aspects, including the strict censorship of plays and books – a reflection of the influence exerted by the Church until quite recent times over the whole range of culture in the Republic – which led writers like James Joyce and Sean O'Casey to leave the country, though O'Casey was already living in London before he became a victim of it.

Pilgrimages

Some of the pilgrimages which are still popular among Catholics in Ireland indicate that the ascetic aspirations of the Early Celtic Church have persisted into our own day.

Croagh Patrick

On the last Sunday in July every year tens of thousands of people climb Ireland's holy mountain, Croagh Patrick, in memory of the 40 days of penance which St Patrick imposed on himself on the summit of the hill in the year 441. The ascent of this bare cone of quartzite with its steep slopes and sharp-edged scree is exceedingly strenuous. The pilgrimage is not performed in a well-ordered procession: people go singly or in groups e.g. school classes, sports clubs, military units; many are non-Catholics or foreigners. Some pilgrims go barefoot. Until some years ago the hill was climbed on the night of Saturday to Sunday, but when, with increasing numbers of pilgrims, the number of mishaps also increased, the Church authorities moved the pilgrimage to the following day.

An island in Lough Derg, near the frontier with Northern Ireland, is also associated with St Patrick. In pre-Christian Ireland a cave on the island was thought to be the entrance to the Underworld; and in medieval times the place became famous throughout Europe as St Patrick's Purgatory, when a travelling knight claimed to have seen the fires of Purgatory in the cave. The pilgrims who make what has been called "the hardest pilgrimage in Christendom" are now almost exclusively Irish. They spend three days on the island performing the numerous penances prescribed, mainly vigils and fasting, as well as attending Mass. During the pilgrimage season in summer visitors are not allowed on the island and photography is forbidden. *Lough Derg*

Knock, in Co. Mayo, the scene of a 19th c. apparition of the Virgin, also attracts large numbers of pilgrims, including sick people seeking a cure. Few foreigners find their way to Knock. *Knock*

In addition to the major pilgrimages there are many local ones on a particular saint's day ("pattern day"). Thus, for example, on Inisheer, the smallest of the Aran Islands, the Church of St Cavan, which is in danger of disappearing under drifting sand, is swept clear so that Mass can be celebrated on June 14th. *Pattern day*

"Lourdes grottoes" are often set up at crossroads or in natural rock formations. Occasionally visitors will encounter a well surrounded by a wall, round which rosaries or coins or sometimes everyday objects have been deposited; and bushes or posts near the well are hung with rags of clothing. Such "holy wells" are credited with the power of healing particular ailments. *Holy wells*

Just as monks were the first to record the ancient popular legends and thus helped to perpetuate them, so the Celtic Church tolerated and thus preserved beliefs that attributed some form of life to nature. Hence the various forms of spirit which survive in Irish tradition, such as the fairies or "sidhe" who dwell on tree-clad hills, and the "little people" or leprechauns who live under hawthorn bushes. To destroy a hawthorn bush, it is believed in the west of Ireland, brings bad luck. There, too, lives a black beast known as the "pooka" which scares lonely travellers, and the "banshee", whose wailing cry foretells the death of a member of one of the old-established families. *Belief in spirits*

The Irish Language

The Irish or Erse language, also called by the philologically incorrect name of Gaelic, belongs to the Celtic group of languages and, within that group, to the Insular Celtic languages. Gaelic in the wider sense includes Scottish as well as Irish Gaelic. Another insular Celtic language is Breton, which was taken into north-western France by immigrants from the British Isles.

References to the Irish language in this guide are to be taken as meaning the Old Celtic language, not the regional variant of English spoken in Ireland.

The Irish Language

Celtic

Originally Celtic was spoken all over the British Isles. The Germanic peoples who began to settle in Britain in the 5th c. brought their Germanic languages with them, and the Anglo-Saxon and later English which developed out of those tongues displaced the old language so effectively that it survived only in remote regions without contact with the outside world – and Ireland in those days was such an area. In later centuries, during the period of English rule and the United Kingdom of Great Britain and Ireland – that is, until the establishment of an independent Irish State – the speaking of the Irish language was not only a means of communication but also a declaration of national identity. The latter part of the 18th c. saw an enthusiastic and almost romantic interest in Old Celtic, which prepared the ground for the appearance of such a celebrated literary fraud as MacPherson's "Ossian". Like many languages, spoken by minorities, which have never attained the status of a national or even an official language (e.g. Breton and Provençal), Irish enjoyed a regular renaissance in the late 19th c. – a recollection by the Irish people of their own language, culture and history which involved not only a stock-taking of their inheritance but also a purposeful concern with the old language as a living spoken tongue.

Ogham Script

From the 4th to the 7th c. the language was written in the ogham script. Although based on the sounds of the Latin alphabet, ogham is quite different from the latter in origin and characteristics. The 25 letters of the ogham alphabet take the form of points or horizontal or oblique lines, in groups of from one to five, set on a long vertical line (which often runs down the edge of a stone slab). Later the Latin alphabet was adopted.

Although the Irish language may seem strange and different to one accustomed to the Germanic and Romance languages of Europe – with no parallels to familiar structures, no immediately obvious relationships in the vocabulary – it nevertheless belongs to the great Indo-European family of languages which spans so much of the globe. Having developed independently of other European languages from an early stage, it has evolved grammatical patterns which have no direct equivalents in those languages. There is the additional difficulty, for those seeking to understand or learn Irish, that it has no "received standard", merely a series of local variants which have equal validity and status.

All official papers are required to be presented in both Irish and English, since both languages have equal status. Members of the Irish parliament, the Dail, generally begin their speeches with a few words in Irish. Even road signs are in the two languages. Normally communication is conducted in English, for it is only in a few restricted areas in the west and south of the country that Irish is the mother-tongue of the people. These linguistic islands are collectively known as "Gaeltacht"; they have their own governmental minister and the inhabitants enjoy certain tax advantages. Whether these and other measures and the efforts of an Irish-speaking elite will be sufficient to ensure the survival of the Irish language remains to be seen.

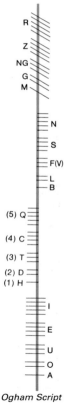

Ogham Script

Gaeltacht

Irish-language areas in Ireland

Londonderry

NORTHERN

BELFAST

IRELAND

Sligo

REPUBLIC

Athlone

Galway OF DUBLIN

IRELAND

Limerick

Waterford

Killarney Cork

© Baedeker

State and Society

Northern Ireland, created a self-governing State within the United Kingdom by the Government of Ireland Act 1920, was brought under direct rule by the United Kingdom Government in 1972, when the Northern Ireland Parliament was suspended as a result of political difficulties within the province. Subsequent attempts to re-establish some form of self-government having failed, Northern Ireland remains under direct rule as part of the United Kingdom.

Northern Ireland

The Republic of Ireland (Poblacht na hEireann), established in 1949, succeeded the Irish Free State which came into being as an independent State in 1922. Under a constitution adopted in 1937 it is a parliamentary democracy governed by a House of Representatives (Dáil Eireann) and Senate (Seanad Eireann), with executive power in the hands of the Prime Minister (Taoiseach) and his Ministers. The Head of State is an elected President (Uachtarán na hEireann), whose official residence is in Phoenix Park, Dublin.

Republic of Ireland

The flag of the Republic is a tricolour, green-white-orange. The national emblem is the harp, together with the three-leaved shamrock, a symbol recalling St Patrick and his interpretation of the Trinity.

The National Anthem is the "Soldier's Song" — written in 1907 by Peadar Kearney, with music by Patrick Heeney and Peadar Kearney — a marching song harking back to the fight for independence.

Ireland

- Republic of Ireland
- Northern Ireland

National frontier ━━━━
Provincial boundary ────
County boundary ────
(in Northern Ireland district boundary)

© Baedeker

DISTRICTS IN NORTHERN IRELAND

1 Moyle
2 Ballymoney
3 Coleraine
4 Limavady
5 Londonderry
6 Strabane
7 Omagh
8 Fermanagh
9 Dungannon

10 Cookstown
11 Magherafelt
12 Ballymena
13 Antrim
14 Lisburn
15 Craigavon
16 Armagh
17 Newry
   and Mourne

18 Banbridge
19 Down
20 North Down
21 Ards
22 Castlereagh
23 Belfast
24 Newtownabbey
25 Carrickfergus
26 Larne

The two main parties in Ireland "Fianna Fáil" (founded in 1926) and "Fine Gael" go back to the Irish independence movement "Sinn Fein". Both parties which have alternated in government since the state was founded, have conservative aims. In the November 1992 elections they suffered heavy losses but with Fianna Fáil gaining most seats with 68 representatives. Since a government shuffle in December 1994 there has been a three-party coalition consisting of Fine Gael, the social democratic Labour party and the Democratic Left.

Parties

The law of the Republic is based broadly on the principles of British law. The old Irish Brehon law (Law of the Judges), based on traditional Celtic conceptions, was abolished by the British authorities in the 17th c.

Legal system

The army of the Republic is a volunteer force – there is no compulsory military service in Ireland – which has shown its mettle in United Nations peace-keeping forces in many parts of the world. The Army School of Equitation has demonstrated on an international level the high qualities of Irish competition horses.

Officially the Republic is bilingual. All official documents must be presented in both Irish and English, since the Irish national language (see p. 21) has equal status with English. Representatives speaking in the Dáil usually begin their speeches with a few words in Irish. Road signs, etc. are bilingual. Throughout the country as a whole, however, the language generally spoken is English: Irish predominates as the mother tongue of the inhabitants only in a few areas in the west and south. These islands of Irish, known collectively as the Gaeltacht, are the responsibility of a special Government Minister, and the people of the Gaeltacht enjoy certain tax benefits. Whether these and other measures, and the efforts of those concerned to promote the use of Irish, will be successful in preserving the old language remains to be seen.

Bilingualism

Gaeltacht

The Irish are great talkers, delighting in argument, and gifted with the liveliest imagination. Even in a difficult situation an Irishman will rarely fall into despondency but – if necessary with the help of alcohol – will seek refuge in a world of dreams. In dealing with strangers the Irish are friendly, receptive and ever ready to help.

The Irish character

The Irish pubs, which are subject to licensing laws controlling their opening hours, play a considerable part in social life.

Education

Northern Ireland

As in Great Britain education is compulsory until the age of 16. The public education system, other than the universities, is the overall responsibility of the Department of Education. In addition to state schools there are many privately run voluntary schools which are grant-aided.

Schools

Northern Ireland has two universities, the Queen's University of Belfast and the University of Ulster. Queen's was founded in 1845 as a non-denominational institution, but the University of Ulster dates only from 1984. In addition there are more than a score of institutes of further education.

Universities

Republic of Ireland

From time immemorial the Irish have held the spoken and the written word, and indeed all knowledge, in esteem, and those who teach are

"Hedge-schoolmasters"

Education

also held in high regard. This respect was accorded even to the "hedge-schoolmasters" who travelled the country during the period of the penal laws and taught the country children for a penny a week in the shelter of a hedge. It is said that they carried their ink-well on a chain round their necks and stuffed a Virgil as well as a Gaelic reading-book into their pockets.

When the Irish were again allowed to have schools education was mostly in the hands of the teaching Orders and the secular clergy. The Christian Brothers played a particularly important part in educating the children of the poorer classes.

National Schools

Today education is compulsory from the age of six to fifteen. There is a State system of national schools with a uniform curriculum, in which some of the staff are ecclesiastics. As a rule children go to these schools in their fourth or fifth year.

Secondary Schools

Later they go on to secondary schools, which are not State-run but are grant-aided and inspected by the Department of Education.

Leaving Certificate

The Leaving Certificate at the end of the school course is issued by the Department. In recent years some comprehensive schools have been established. The school day is from 9am to about 3pm. The yellow school buses which take children to school are a familiar sight in country areas.

Technical Colleges

For the further education of pupils aiming at a practical trade there are vocational schools – which also provide further education classes for adults – and a number of technical colleges.

National Institute for Higher Education

There is also a technologically orientated college in Limerick, the National Institute for Higher Education, opened in 1972. A similar college with the same name was opened in Dublin in 1980.

Trinity College

There are two universities in the Republic, Trinity College in Dublin and the National University of Ireland. Trinity College, the oldest university in Ireland, was established by Elizabeth I, exclusively for the sons of the Protestant Anglo-Irish. Irish students were admitted for the first time in 1793, and Roman Catholics were excluded from fellowships and scholarships until 1863. Nevertheless Trinity College has played an important part in the intellectual and political life of Ireland. Among its students have been writers including Oliver Goldsmith and Jonathan Swift, Oscar Wilde and J. M. Synge, the philosopher and statesman Edmund Burke, and also men such as Theobald Wolfe Tone and Robert Emmet, both of whom died for the cause of Irish independence.

National University of Ireland

The National University of Ireland, which can trace its origins back to a college founded in 1845 of which Cardinal Newman was the first Rector, was established as such in 1908. It now consists of three colleges in Dublin, Galway and Cork. Associated with it is St Patrick's College at Maynooth, a seminary for priests which also admits lay students; it has a department of Celtic studies. The National University has over 8000 matriculated students in Dublin, 4000 in Cork and 3500 in Galway.

While Trinity College is housed in fine classical buildings in the heart of Dublin, the three colleges of the National University are situated in suburban surroundings. Galway in particular has a fine campus on the banks of the Corrib, with handsome modern buildings. Originally all teaching in the Galway college, including that of science, was in Irish, but English is now also used. The college still sees itself, however, as the intellectual and cultural centre for the Irish-speaking areas in the west of the country, and seeks to bring fresh impulses to this long-neglected region.

Trinity College, Dublin

Efforts are also being made in the rest of the Republic to preserve the old national language from extinction. Irish is a compulsory subject at all schools, and in 28 secondary schools the teaching is wholly or partly in that language. Classes of city children are taken during the summer holidays to places in the Gaeltacht, where they stay with Irish-speaking families. Adults who want to improve their Irish can go to one of the Irish Colleges in the Gaeltacht; and their regular courses are also attended by foreigners, usually of Irish origin.

Preserving the Irish language

Economy

After the establishment of the Irish Free State in 1921 most of the country's capital remained in the hands of wealthy Anglo-Irish and the native Irish had little share in the profits. When Eamon de Valera's Fianna Fáil Party came to power in 1932, however, it followed a policy of economic self-sufficiency and fostered the growth of productive industry by protective tariffs. When the new Irish Government refused to pay the "land annuities" – the interest on capital originally advanced to enable Irish farmers to buy their land – as the 1921 Treaty required, an economic war developed between Britain and the Free State. The British Government imposed a 40 per cent duty on Irish goods, which led to a drastic decline in Irish exports. A compromise was reached under which the quota for the export of Irish cattle to Britain was increased on the understanding that the Free State would purchase all its requirements of coal from Britain. The economic war finally came to an end in 1938 when Britain withdrew from its naval bases in southern Ireland.

In the years before the Second World War the Irish Government promoted the country's economic development by a variety of means,

Developments up to 1945

including the establishment of partly State-controlled institutions such as the Agricultural Credit Corporation and the Electricity Supply Board. The Republic's withdrawal from the Commonwealth in 1949 gave it greater economic independence.

Economic
performance

In recent years the economic situation in Ireland has strengthened not least because of supportive measures by the EU. With low inflation a relatively high growth rate has been possible. In 1993 the inflation rate was only 1.4% and the gross national product increased by 2.7%. Yet Ireland still ranks as one of the poorest countries in the EU. Income per capita is about 70% of the EU average. Its unemployment rate is the highest in the European Union after Spain at 16.9%. The outlook for the next few years is not optimistic.

Minerals

Although Ireland is relatively poor in minerals, the working of metal ores has been increased in recent years – principally lead, zinc and silver (at Tynnagh, Co. Galway, Navan, Co. Meath and elsewhere), but also copper, mercury and pyrites. Deposits of natural gas have been found at Kinsale.

Industry

Foodstuffs, drink, tobacco and textiles are traditional Irish industries, but since the late 1950s the Government has promoted the development of new industries and the establishment of foreign firms in Ireland, manufacturing machinery, electrical and electronic apparatus, pharmaceuticals and chemicals as well as textiles and foodstuffs. Attracted by tax advantages, relatively low wages (the average wage in Ireland is 40% lower than in the USA or Germany) and low living costs, about 1000 foreign companies have established subsidiaries in the "Emerald Isle". A quarter of the working population have a foreign employer. From Germany 200 or so companies have dared to branch out to the edge of Europe together with mainly British, American and Dutch firms.

Cattle on the edge of the Burren

Many fishing boats are somewhat old-fashioned

Some 70 per cent of the country's total area is devoted to agriculture, the great bulk of it as pasture. In Central Ireland cattle are reared for beef, while in the south dairy-farming predominates. After cattle, the most important types of livestock are sheep, pigs and poultry. On good grazing land racehorses are bred for export.

Agriculture

The predominant agricultural crop is barley, which is used in the brewing of beer as well as for fodder. The production of potatoes, sugar-beet, wheat and oats is also of economic importance.

The fishing industry has long been neglected, the fishing fleet is clearly obsolete. The particularly clean rivers, lakes and bays are one of the country's assets. In recent years fish farms have sprung up breeding high quality fish.

Fishing

A third of the Republic's energy needs is met by hydro-electric and peat-fired power-stations, rather more than 60 per cent by imported fuels, namely coal and oil. The largest of the hydro-electric stations on the country's numerous rivers is the one on the Shannon.

Energy

Much of the Irish central plain and extensive areas on the north-west, west and south coasts are covered with moorland and bog; and peat has been from time immemorial, and still is, the domestic fuel of Ireland. Since the beginning of industrialisation it has been increasingly worked by mechanical methods for use as industrial fuel, and in 1946 the Government established Bord na Móna, an organisation concerned with all aspects of peat working, processing and use. There are now several peat-fired power-stations; peat briquettes, factory-made from milled peat, provide domestic and industrial fuel; and peat is increasingly being used by gardeners to improve their soil. There is a peat research institute at Droichead Nua, Newbridge, Co. Kildare. Gradually the dangers inherent in the continued digging of peat on the moors are being realised. Every year some 14sq. miles/36sq.km of

Peat bog – a gradually disappearing sight in the countryside

moorland are destroyed and it is feared that by the end of the century this land will have disappeared.

Exports

Britain is the principal customer for Irish exports, though the British share of the total has fallen from two-thirds in the 1960s to under a half today. Over the same period exports to the other EU countries have risen to some 30 per cent of the total. The principal exports are cattle, meat, machinery, textiles and chemicals. For some years the value of exports has exceeded that of imports.

Tourism

Despite its many ancient Irish monuments, castles and mansion houses, its picturesque scenery and its charming people Ireland has, for a long time, been an attractive holiday region for just a handful of individual tourists.

Not until 1988 were any efforts made to attract a significant number of visitors to the Republic. A five-year plan is aimed at improving the infrastructure both quantitively and qualitively. Since 1993 a marketing plan has been in force which is expected to increase tourism by 60% by 1997. However, there is no intention of giving the country the image of a destination for mass tourism, but rather to improve facilities at the quieter times of the year. It is hoped that these measures will create an additional 25,000 jobs in the service sector.

About 85% of the 3.5 million international visitors to the "Emerald Isle" come from Great Britain, France, Germany, Italy, Holland, USA and Australia.

Tourism in Northern Ireland was badly hit by the outbreak of the troubles at the end of the Sixties. After 25 years of decline an upturn is hoped for. At present Northern Ireland has no more than 7500 beds but that could quickly change. Primarily in coastal regions owners of pensions and small country hotels are hoping for wealthy foreign clientele.

History

The first settlers reach Ireland and bring the land into cultivation. They construct large megalithic tombs.

Stone Age
(c. 7000–2000 B.C.)

From this period date the earliest identifiable traces of human activity in Ireland. The first settlers are believed to have come from Scotland, first establishing themselves in what is now Antrim, in the north-east, and moving on from there into the interior of the island. They live by hunting and fishing.

About 7000 B.C.

After a second wave of incomers the clearance of forest and scrub land begins, and the population turns to farming and herding.

About 4000 B.C.

The first megalithic tombs are constructed.

About 3000 B.C.

Implements and weapons begin to be made of metal.

Bronze Age
(c. 2000–500 B.C.)

Metal axes, daggers and swords are produced, and – towards the end of the Bronze Age – large pots, shields and horns.

About 700 B.C.

The Gaels, a Celtic people, come to Ireland. Numbers of forts are built. Rule by kings. The new iron weapons are superior to the old bronze swords.

Iron Age
(c. 500 B.C.–A.D. 400)

Various peoples, including the Gaels, move into Ireland from the Continent and subjugate the native inhabitants, the Druid-ruled Tuatha Dé Danaan (People of the Goddess Danu). In the prevailing insecurity, with constant warlike raids and cattle-stealing, the people of the island seek safety in strong forts.

Migrations:
From 500 B.C.

A division of Ireland into four provinces develops. Society is split into three classes – priests (druí), warriors and peasants. The king (rí) owes allegiance to an over-king (ruirí), who in turn is subject to a king of over-kings (rí-ruirech), or high king.
Below the king are the nobles of the warrior caste (flaithí), who are patrons of the aes dána, men of art and learning, including poets, doctors and jurists. The family unit is the deb-fine, a four-generation family which possesses land and rights of succession.

Social system

Many of the Irish are converted to Christianity and numerous monasteries are founded. Viking raids on the island are repelled.

Early Christian period
(c. 400–1170)

St Patrick, captured by Irish pirates and brought to Ireland as a slave, escapes but later returns to Ireland and converts its people to the Christian faith.

About 432

After Patrick's death numerous monasteries are founded, which during the 6th c. grow in size and influence. Many monks leave home and spread the Christian faith in Scotland (Columbanus the Elder, d. 597) and England and on the Continent (Columbanus the Younger, d. 615).

5th–9th c.

Viking raids. The Vikings establish settlements on the east coast of Ireland which later develop into towns (Dublin, Wexford, Waterford, etc.). They teach the Irish the art of shipbuilding.

About 800

In the Battle of Clontarf, near Dublin, the Vikings and their allies are defeated by the Irish under their High King, Brian Boru, who is killed in the battle. This defeat puts an end to the Viking conquest of Ireland.

About 1014

History

Norman period (1170–1534)	The descendants of the Normans who had come to Britain with William the Conqueror in 1066 attack Ireland from bases in Wales and seize much land.
	King Henry II of England (1154–89) grants fiefs in Ireland to Norman barons and receives the homage of the Irish clan chiefs. The Normans, leaving the Irish only certain areas in western and northern Ireland, occupy the extensive territory which becomes known as the Pale and build mighty castles to defend it. They found numerous monasteries for the new monastic orders (Cistercians, Dominicans, etc.), to which they appoint English abbots. Inland, towns come into being as market-places and centres of authority.
1261	The Battle of Calann, near Kenmare, is one of the first signs of success-ful Irish resistance to the Normans.
1348–50	Norman power is weakened by the Black Death which ravages the country.
15th c.	Decline of Norman rule. A new Irish national feeling emerges – fos-tered, paradoxically, by one of the great Norman families, the Ger-aldines. They and the Butlers, another Anglo-Norman family, dominate Irish political life in the second half of the century.
English (and later British) rule (1534–1782)	Ireland is still more closely bound to Britain, and the condition of the Irish people grows steadily worse.
1534	Execution of "Silken Thomas", a Geraldine.
About 1535	Henry VIII (1509–47) breaks with the Pope; Dissolution of the Monasteries.
1541	Henry VIII assumes the title of King of Ireland.
Second half of 16th c.	Elizabeth I (1558–1603) continues the political and religious oppression of the predominantly Catholic Irish.
1598	After many years of resistance Hugh O'Neill defeats the English in the Battle of the Yellow Ford.
1601–03	In the Battle of Kinsale the Irish are defeated.
1606	The traditional Irish system of Brehon Law is abolished by the British authorities.
1607	"Flight of the Earls": the three leading figures in Ulster – O'Neill, O'Donnell and Maguire – flee to the Continent.
1608	The central and western areas of Ulster, the last bastion of Irish resis-tance, are settled by Scottish and English Protestants, who are given land confiscated from the native Irish: an event which many see as the root of present-day troubles.
1649	Oliver Cromwell ruthlessly represses an Irish rebellion (1641 onwards) against the Protestants.
	The Roman Catholic King James II (1685–88), whose attempts to re-establish Catholicism in Britain have met with fierce resistance, seeks to restore his position by a campaign in Ireland.
1690	Battle of the Boyne, in which James is decisively defeated by the Protestant William of Orange (King, as William III, from 1689).
18th c.	There follows a time of severe political and religious repression in Ireland. Penal laws discriminating against Roman Catholics are in-troduced. Many Irish people emigrate to the United States.

Battle of the Boyne (1690)

The poverty of the native population is in stark contrast to the prosperity of the Anglo-Irish, who possess fine houses and great estates.

A brief period during which Ireland has a Parliament with a measure of independence.	Relative independence (1782–1800)
After several rebellions against the repression of Catholicism Britain recognises an Irish Parliament with a greater degree of independence, in which the leading figure is Henry Grattan. The Parliament does something to improve the plight of the poor. Its membership, however, is entirely Protestant.	1782
The United Irishmen led by the Anglo-Irish lawyer Theobald Wolfe Tone, influenced by the French Revolution, call for the establishment of a republic in Ireland.	During the 1790s
A rising supported by France is defeated.	1798
Britain proposes a union of the British and Irish parliaments. Influenced by the offer of financial compensation, offices and pensions, the Irish Parliament dissolves itself; it meets for the last time on August 2nd.	1800
More than a century of efforts to secure equal rights for Catholics and national independence for Ireland end with the establishment of the Irish Free State.	Religious freedom and Irish nationalism (1800–1922)
The Act of Union provides for the establishment of a single Parliament of the United Kingdom of Great Britain and Ireland, meeting at Westminster. Ireland is represented in both the House of Commons and the House of Lords.	1800

33

History

In Dublin the Irish Members of the British Parliament establish their own Parliament, the Dáil Eireann, declare Irish independence and set up a Provisional Government headed by Eamon de Valera (1882–1975).	1919
The British attempt to block Irish independence leads to civil war, in which the leading part on the Irish side is played by the Irish Republican Army (IRA).	1919–21
Parliament passes the Government of Ireland Act, which provides for two self-governing areas in Ireland, one in the six northern counties with their Protestant majority, the other in the rest of the country.	1920
The British Government and the moderate leaders of the independence movement (Arthur Griffith, Michael Collins) sign a treaty establishing an Irish Free State (Saorstát Eireann) within the British Empire. The six northern counties remain part of the United Kingdom.	1921 (December 6th)
The Dáil Eireann ratifies the treaty.	1922 (January 7th)

Irish Free State and Republic of Ireland

Arthur Griffith (b. 1871) becomes first Prime Minister of the Irish Free State in January, but dies in August. He is succeeded by William Thomas Cosgrave (1880–1965), who holds office until 1932.	1922
Armed resistance to the Government by opponents of the treaty. The Government wins the day, but at the cost of many lives.	1922–23
Supporters of the Anglo-Irish treaty form the Cumann na nGaedheal, which later unifies with a number of smaller groups to form the Fine Gael (Family of the Irish) Party.	1923
Opponents of the Treaty, led by Eamon de Valera, form the Fianna Fáil (Comrades of Destiny) Party.	1926
After Fianna Fáil's election victory over Fine Gael Eamon de Valera becomes Prime Minister, a post which he holds until 1948 (with two later periods of office).	1932
A new constitution comes into force declaring Ireland to be "a sovereign, independent, democratic state" under the name of Eire. The constitution provides for the election of a President.	1937 (December 29th)
Ireland remains neutral during the Second World War.	1939–45
In a general election Fianna Fáil is defeated, and the Fine Gael leader John Aloysius Costello (1891–1976) heads a coalition government.	1948
Ireland becomes a republic, the Republic of Ireland (Poblacht na hEireann) and leaves the British Commonwealth.	1949
Ireland becomes a member of the United Nations.	1955
President J. F. Kennedy of the United States visits Ireland and is given an enthusiastic reception.	1963
Ireland joins the European Union.	1973 (January 1st)
In Ireland, with its high rate of population increase, just under ten per cent of all workers are unemployed. During his visit to Ireland Pope John Paul II calls for an end to violence.	1979

1984   United States President Ronald Reagan visits Ballyporeen, the parish from which his ancestors are said to have come, known here as O'Reagan.

1985   In February the Irish Parliament decides by a small majority in favour of permitting the restricted use of contraceptives: the first time in the history of the Republic that a government has successfully resisted the influence of the Roman Catholic Church.
On November 15th the British and Irish Prime Ministers (Mrs Thatcher and Garret FitzGerald) sign the Hillsborough Agreement, arrived at after long secret negotiations, which provides for the establishment of a secretariat in Belfast and for regular meetings between Irish and British ministers and officials to discuss questions concerning Northern Ireland and particularly the fight against terrorism.

1986   A public referendum results in a clear "No" to a Government proposal to amend the constitution by legalising divorce.

1987   The growth in the rate of unemployment to almost 20 per cent results in the largest wave of emigration from Ireland for many years.

1988   Parliament passes the Extradition Bill, a prerequisite to Ireland's membership of the European Convention in the Fight Against Terrorism.

1990   Lawyer and novelist Mary Robinson becomes the first woman president (in office until 1997).

1991   The European Community names Dublin Cultural Capital of Europe for one year.

1992   A majority of the Irish people approve in June the Maastricht Treaty for the foundation of a European Union.
In November 65.5% of the Irish vote against a government proposal to permit an abortion in the case of serious risk to the life of the mother. At the same time 62.6% approve unopposed travel abroad of pregnant women (at the beginning of the 90s some 5000 Irish women annually undergo an abortion in England).
The early elections in November bring a defeat for the Conservative parties. However, Fiana Fáil remains the strongest party with 68 seats.

1993   The British Prime Minister John Major and the Irish Prime Minister Albert Reynolds sign a declaration on December 15th which is intended to bring about the peace process (further developments in Northern Ireland on the following pages).

1994   Following a government crisis and the resignation of the Prime Minister a government reshuffle is necessary in December. John Bruton, leader of the former opposition party Fine Gael, is elected head of the government. He forms a three-party coalition consisting of Fine Gael, the Labour Party and the Democratic Left.

Northern Ireland

1920–60   The six counties of Northern Ireland (Ulster), with a predominantly Protestant population, form part of the United Kingdom of Great Britain and Northern Ireland. Northern Ireland has its own Parliament, at Stormont, and its own government.

1969   Tensions between the Protestant majority and the Roman Catholic minority lead to major outbreaks of violence. The mainly Catholic Irish Republican Army (IRA) becomes increasingly active, and the Protestant Ulster Defence Association (UDA) is formed.

The IRA is split into an "Official" wing, which calls for a united socialist Ireland, and a "Provisional" (nationalist) wing which seeks to achieve the incorporation of Northern Ireland into the Republic by acts of terrorism.

Britain and the Republic agree to establish an All-Ireland Council. 1973

The Women's Peace Movement, involving both Catholic and Protestant women, is launched by Mrs Betty Williams and Miss Mairead Corrigan. 1976

IRA prisoners in the Maze Prison, Belfast, go on hunger strike. 1980 (October)

The IRA activist Bobby Sands dies after a 66-day hunger strike. Other deaths of hunger-strikers follow. 1981 (May)

End of the hunger-strike. The Maze prisoners fail to gain their chief objective, to be recognised as political prisoners. 1981 (October)

The Irish Prime Minister, Garret FitzGerald, sets up a New Ireland Forum, with representatives of the main political parties in the Republic and the Social Democratic and Labour Party (SDLP) of Northern Ireland, to seek a solution of the Irish problem. 1983 (May)

The New Ireland Forum puts forward a report with proposals designed to bring about a future united Ireland; but the realisation of any such plans is evidently dependent on the agreement of the Protestant majority in Ulster. 1984 (May)

A powerful bomb, for which the IRA "Provisionals" claim responsibility, kills and injures members of the British Conservative Party in the Grand Hotel, Brighton, during the annual party conference. 1984 (October 11th–12th)

IRA activists carry out a mortar attack on a police station in Newry, Northern Ireland, killing nine people. 1985 (February)

The protestant Unionists of Northern Ireland, representing a majority of the population, express violent opposition to the Hillsborough Agreement. When the House of Commons, by a majority representing all the main parties, approves the Agreement Ian Paisley, leader of the Democratic Unionist Party in Northern Ireland, and other Unionist Members of Parliament resign their seats in protest, deliberately provoking by-elections in which fourteen of the fifteen Unionist candidates are re-elected. 1985 (November)

Thousands of Belfast shipyard workers demonstrate against the Hillsborough Agreement. 1985 (December)

Resistance to the Agreement intensifies. In March there is a 24-hour general strike and, during the Easter holiday, violent clashes between Protestants and the police.
    In November some 250,000 people protest against the one-year old Anglo-Irish Agreement. 1986

Clashes between members of the IRA and Protestant extremists continue.
    Following a shoot-out between the IRA and members of the Security Forces in Loughgall in Northern Ireland, in which several people are killed, riots break out in Belfast, Londonderry and other towns. 1987

After the SAS in Gibraltar have shot dead three IRA members who were thought to be laying a bomb, there are riots in Belfast involving the use of force against police and soldiers. 1988 (March)

37

History

On Oct. 19th the British Government prohibits radio and TV interviews with IRA representatives.

1989   More than 100 people are killed in IRA attacks in Northern Ireland.

1992   Talks break down in November after six months of consultation between the four largest constitutional parties of Northern Ireland and the governments of England and the Irish Republic in an effort to find a solution to the conflict in Northern Ireland.

1993   In October a bomb planted by the IRA explodes in a busy shopping street in Belfast killing ten people and injuring 50.

1994   At the end of August the IRA announces a unilateral ceasefire to which the Protestant paramilitary groups agree.
Life for the people improves markedly and the military and police presence is scaled down.

1995   In February the British Prime Minister John Major and his Irish counterpart John Bruton present a framework for unity between Northern Ireland and Great Britain. Central to the plan is the creation of a Northern Irish parliament and a North–South authority to deal with important aspects of Irish and Northern Irish relations.
In October the Irish poet Seamus Heaney (b.13.4.1939) receives the Nobel Prize for Literature.

1996   An explosion at Canary Wharf in London in February ends the IRA ceasefire. In spite of intense efforts this is not resumed in time to allow Sinn Fein to attend the all-party talks in June.
In July a bomb, the first in the province for nearly two years, destroys a hotel in Enniskillen. The future of the peace talks is in jeopardy.

Famous People

The following alphabetically ordered list brings together people of historical importance who through birth, residence, actions or death are connected with Ireland and have attained international significance.

Note

Samuel Beckett is the leading representative of the Theatre of the Absurd. He was born in Dublin and from 1937 lived in Paris. After studying Romance languages and literature at Trinity College in Dublin (1923–27) he taught English at the École normale supérieure in Paris. Here he was part of the circle around James Joyce who, together with Dante, Descartes and existential philosophy, exerted a great influence upon Beckett's literary work. From 1931 to 1932 he taught French at Trinity College. Between 1933 and 1936 he lived in London. He was already writing essays, stories and poetry before the Second World War. He first came to fame with his novel "Molloy" (1951). His earlier works were published in English, the later ones (including "Molloy") were written in French and translated by himself into English. After publishing more novels he turned to the theatre and caused great interest with his first play "Waiting for Godot" (1952). In all his works – novels, dramas, stories, radio and TV plays – he breaks with traditional form; action is reduced to a minimum. He pessimistically portrays – with a tendency towards the grotesque and burlesque – the absurdity of the human condition, the emptiness of an existence futilely waiting for death. In 1969 he received the Nobel Prize for Literature.

Samuel Beckett (1906–89)

Brendan Behan (1923–64) became involved as an adolescent in the activities of the Irish Republican Army and spent several years in British penal establishments. His experiences during this period are described in his autobiographical novel "Borstal Boy" (1958) and his posthumous "Confessions of an Irish Rebel" (1965). The heroes of his plays, with their fierce social criticism, are the outsiders of society – "The Quare Fellow" 1956, "The Hostage" 1958.
   The Irish are particularly noted as writers of short stories, which are concerned with the precise depiction of a particular situation or state of mind, their expressive force resulting from the tension between linguistic precision and the humour of the situation, between pessimism and cheerfulness. The subjects are mostly taken from Irish everyday life. Among particular masters of the genre are Liam O'Flaherty (1897–1984), Sean O'Faoláin (b. 1900) and Frank O'Connor (1903–66).

Brendan Behan

Who really discovered America? – The Genoese sailor, commissioned by the Spanish, Christopher Columbus in 1492? The Viking Leif Erikson in the year 1000? The Phoenicians towards the end of the 7th c.? Or was it an Irish monk?
   In the 8th c. a travel report came onto the market which became a sort of bestseller in the Middle Ages and was translated into many West European languages: "The Sea Journey of St Brendan". It tells how the Irish abbot Brendan discovered the "Promised Land" on the other side of the Atlantic in the 6th c.
   The Irish St Brendan (c. 484 to c. 578) founded several monasteries in Ireland, including Clonfert in county Galway. Driven by missionary zeal he allegedly travelled around the Scottish islands and Wales. When he heard that there was a "promised land" inhabited by saints beyond the ocean he set off, according to legend, in 540 with 17 companions and a well equipped ship and only returned seven years later.
   In order to prove that crossing the Atlantic in a leather boat, as would have been the case in Brendan's time, is not just pure phantasy the scientist Timothy Severin sailed in such a boat in 1976 from Ireland to Canada. He

St Brendan (c. 486–c. 578)

was excited by the similarity between descriptions of places in the book and actual geographical conditions on Labrador.

Chris de Burgh
(b. 1948)

In Ireland he received the award of "most successful songwriter of all time". The "troubadour of rock culture" has also enjoyed huge success abroad. Many of his singles reached the top of the record charts and received gold and platinum awards. The man in question is Christopher John Davidson, better known as Chris de Burgh. De Burgh was his mother's maiden name, one of the most common surnames in Ireland dating back to the Anglo-Norman "de Burgo" family which was rewarded by the English king with extensive lands in Connaught in the early 13th c. His parents are, however, not Irish but English. He was born in Argentina on 15th October 1948. Beause of his father's job as an official in the diplomatic service he spent his childhood on Malta, in Nigeria, the Belgian Congo and Rhodesia. He attended school in Wiltshire, England. In 1960 his parents bought Bargy Castle near Wexford and converted it into an hotel. In accordance with his parents' wishes he studied French, English and History at Trinity College, Dublin. After studying he devoted himself to music as a profession but there were no early successes. He received his first recording contract in 1974. His second LP "Spanish Train" (1977) was a great commercial success. On his fifth LP, "Eastern Wind" (1980), he abandoned for the first time the gentle, rather melancholic ballads which were often about knights and devils. He concentrated more on realism, with the first sounds of rock music appearing in this LP which he made with his own band. With the release "Don't pay the Ferryman" from his '83 album "The Getaway" he achieved the final breakthrough and it landed at No. 1 in the American charts. Since then all the albums of this father-of-two, who never had music tuition and whose repertoire stretches from heartfelt ballads to rock songs, have been successful. The recipe for success behind his instinctive feel for music is – as he says himself – his Celtic-inspired melancholy. "The Lady in Red" was a major hit in Britain in 1986, reaching fifth place in the German charts.

Roger Casement
(1864–1916)

On 3rd August 1916 in London a man was hung for conspiring with the enemy Germany and plotting an Irish uprising: Sir Roger Casement who had been knighted by Great Britain five years earlier.

At the age of twenty Dublin-born Roger Casement left Ireland and travelled around Africa. On behalf of the British government he investigated conditions in the Belgian Congo and in Peru as rumours kept persisting concerning the maltreatment of the native population by the whites. His discoveries, which were worse than the rumours, attracted international concern. His role as a lawyer helped him to international recognition and in 1911 to the nobility. As his health had suffered through the time he had spent in the tropics he left the British civil service in 1913. He then dedicated his efforts to the Irish struggle for independence from the English Crown. He had a leading role in the Irish Volunteers, a resistance movement. Soon after the outbreak of the First World War he contacted the German government in Berlin. He sought official support for the Irish fight for independence and wanted the enemy Germany to supply them with weapons. At the end of 1914 the Imperial government declared their sympathy for Irish independence. At Easter 1916 the Irish rebels wanted to rise against Great Britain; Berlin confirmed its support and sent a fishing boat carrying 20,000 rifles and ammunition towards the Irish coast. However, the boat was discovered by a British cruiser and sunk by its own captain so as not to let its dangerous cargo fall into enemy hands. Casement, who wanted to secretly reach Ireland by German submarine, was arrested on 21st April 1916 as soon as he set foot on Irish soil by the British security forces.

The news of the sinking of the German ship and Casement's arrest made it clear to the instigators of the rebellion that the uprising could not succeed. But it was already too late: on Easter Monday, April 24th 1916, the uprising broke out. Four days later it was bloodily crushed by the British armed forces. Casement, held by the British government to be the chief instigator of the rebellion, was brought before the court. Charged with co-operating with the enemy Germany and instigating an uprising against the Crown the judge and jury sentenced him to death by hanging. Not content with his condemnation to death attempts were made to destroy his reputation abroad as a lawyer for the native people in the colonies. His diaries were publicised in which alleged homosexual encounters were described. This led to the Archbishop of Canterbury and the US President Wilson withdrawing a plea for mercy for Casement. It has still not been confirmed whether the diaries were genuine or fake.

On February 23rd 1965 the mortal remains of Sir Roger Casement were transferred from England to Dublin and buried on February 28th at a ceremonial state occasion.

The dramatist Sean O'Casey (1880–1964), who began by earning his living as a labourer on the railways, joined the Irish national movement at an early age. The Irish struggle for independence is the background both to his six-volume autobiography and to his early plays, such as "The Shadow of a Gunman" (1923), most of which reflects the life of the poor and wretched. In his dramas O'Casey combines comedy and humour with tragic irony. The Abbey Theatre turned down "The Silver Tassie", a new play he offered them in 1928, but staged it some years later. The rejection is often cited as the reason he left Ireland for ever, but he had been living in London for a year when it happened.

Sean O'Casey

The writer James Joyce is remembered on "Bloomsday", June 16th, in Dublin (see Baedeker Special pp. 164/65).

James Joyce
(1882–1941)

After being educated in church schools and at University College, Dublin Joyce went to Paris to study medicine in 1902. His mother's death brought him back temporarily to Ireland before he began to live in self-imposed exile (Trieste, Rome, Zurich, Paris among other places). In 1914 "Dubliners" was published, a collection of 15 short stories influenced by Ibsen, in which Joyce depicts the ordinary life of Dubliners in its various phases of childhood, adolescence, maturity and public work. In the autobigraphical novel "Portrait of the Artist as a Young Man" (1916) he employs the technique of inner monologue and portrays the tensions between the young artist and the world about him. His most well known novel is "Ulysses" (1922). In his final work, "Finnegans Wake" (1939) Joyce is trying to capture in language the unknown. Written in a dream language "Finnegans Wake" (seen superficially it is about the dreams of an Irish innkeeper and his family on one night), like "Dubliners" and "Ulysses", retains the atmosphere of his native Dublin. Despite the many difficulties in interpreting his works the novels of Joyce have been a major influence on the 20th c. novel.

Joyce fled with his family in 1940 from Paris to Zurich where he died in 1941 after serious illness. He is buried at the cemetery at Fluntern.

Daniel O'Connell is one of the best known leaders of Irish resistance against the English Crown. In the first third of the 19th c. he was "Ireland's uncrowned king". But in the end he had to yield to harsh reality.

Daniel O'Connell
(1775–1847)

Daniel O'Connell was privileged to be the son of a relatively prosperous Catholic landowner from County Kerry and was therefore able to study in Paris. Here he experienced the turmoil of revolution, its ideals together with its violence. Perhaps these experiences were responsible for his later politics when he was prepared to seek peace. When he returned to Ireland the English laws toward the Irish had relaxed somewhat. Above a certain level of income the Irish were allowed to vote and schooling had improved. O'Connell settled in Dublin where he became famous throughout the country as a successful defence lawyer. He became increasingly involved in politics. For Ireland to break completely from the union with Great Britain which had existed since 1801 did not seem feasible to O'Connell. His politics followed two other goals: equal rights for Irish Catholics and protection for the small Irish tenant farmers against the unscrupulous

English landowners. To this purpose he founded the "Catholic Union" in 1823 whose numbers soon reached over a million. As well as the middle classes and poor farmers it was made up of Catholic nobles, Protestant liberals, churchmen and even robbers. With the help of the "Catholic Union" O'Connell was elected Member of Parliament for County Clare. But only after the English Prime Minister felt compelled to introduce a law allowing Non-Anglicans access to all offices of state did O'Connell take his place at Parliament in London. With the re-election of the Conservative government O'Connell lost his political influence. He set up a second union: its aim was Irish independence. London was becoming more irritated by O'Connell's mass rallies and his bold words of freedom for Ireland. He was spared a prison sentence when the House of Commons acted in his favour. When the Catholics tried to organise another rally before the gates of Dublin the English governor interceded and sent in troops to prevent the rally taking place. O'Connell, still disposed towards a peaceful solution, called off the event the evening before. Most young supporters felt betrayed and turned their backs on him. In addition he was not in very good health. He left Ireland and went to Italy to recuperate and died in Genoa in 1847.

Oliver Goldsmith   Oliver Goldsmith (1728–74), known as the author of a novel "The Vicar of Wakefield" (1766), poems ("The Deserted Village", 1770) and plays ("She Stoops to Conquer", 1773), describes in his works the country around Athlone, still known as Goldsmith Country. When a poor student at Trinity College, Dublin, Goldsmith wrote ballads for street singers in order to earn a few coins and would creep out at night to hear them sung.

James Joyce   Of one of Ireland's greatest writers, James Joyce (1882–1941), it could be said that in his intricate play with words and ideas he brought to literature the masterly skills of the old Celtic book illuminators. Just as the Celtic artists "abhorred a vacuum", so Joyce sought in "Ulysses" (1922) to depict the whole of one particular day in the life of Leopold Bloom, June 16th 1904, following out every convolution and ramification of events, ideas and feelings. Before "Ulysses" Joyce had published "Dubliners" (1914), a collection of short stories, and "Portrait of the Artist as a Young Man" (1916), a largely autobiographical work in which he portrays the tensions between a young artist and his surroundings.

In his last work, "Finnegan's Wake" (1939), Joyce seeks, as in "Ulysses", to give linguistic expression to the unconscious or subconscious mind. Since he employs words from more than 20 different languages and refers to a variety of esoteric myths and religions, "Finnegan's Wake" must rank as one of the most difficult works in all literature.

Grace O'Malley   No other woman in the history of Ireland won the hearts of the Irish
(c. 1530–1603)   population as much as the once feared "pirate queen" Grace O'Malley. In the song and legend of the oppressed Irish people she is hailed as an early patriot.

Grace O'Malley was the only child and sole heiress of Owen Dubhdarra (nickname: "black oak"), head of the O'Malley clan and ruler of Clew Bay near Westport. The O'Malleys lived from the sea: from fishing as far afield as Scotland, France, Spain and Portugal, and from piracy. Grace, who had an unbridled love of the sea, soon followed in the footsteps of her father. At the age of nine she managed to extract permission from her father to learn seamanship. Her first marriage was arranged by her father to Donal, the "battle-hardened", the ruling prince of the O'Flaherty clan. At first she took on the duties and role of a wife but after the birth of three children she returned to the sea. Through her trading, fighting and piracy she contributed more to the family fortune than her husband. The O'Flaherty's soon came to regard her as their natural leader and not her husbend. Following

James Joyce

Charles Stewart Parnell

George Bernard Shaw

the death of her husband she returned to her own family. In 1566 she was voted the first female head of the O'Malley clan. She decided upon her second husband herself. As the only region left to give her control of the whole of Clew Bay was the land belonging to the Burke family with the strategically important Rockfleet Castle, she chose to marry Richard Burke. According to Celtic law the marriage was limited to one year which meant that after one year either partner could dissolve the union. According to legend Grace made use of this law: from the battlements of his own castle she greeted him with the news that he could leave and the castle belonged to her. With her 20 ships and 6000 men she soon ruled large areas of the west coast of Ireland and terrorised all the trading ships in the Atlantic. The following example illustrates how little mercy she showed her adversaries: when her lover was murdered she had the entire clan from which the murderer came wiped out except for one so that he could tell the rest of the world of her terrible revenge. Yet she held nothing against England which was making renewed claims towards Ireland under Elizabeth I. She obeyed superior strength, paid homage to the English queen and received her property as a fiefdom. In 1593 she travelled to London to plead personally for the freedom of her imprisoned son. This meeting was retold in legend as showing the patriotism of the "pirate queen", of the unbroken confidence of Grace O'Malley towards the power of the English. Even though there are no deeds connected with Irish independence which can be attributed to Grace, in the minds of the Irish people this fearsome clan princess is seen, as the time since her death (1603) increases, as more of a Robin Hood type figure and a freedom fighter for Ireland.

Thomas Moore (1779–1852), a talented musician as well as a poet, sought to build a bridge between the world of Celtic traditions and the rather frivolous attitudes of the Anglo-Irish society which he admired by fitting the old sagas to traditional airs in his "Irish Melodies". With these songs, which were soon popular in English drawing-rooms and on the Continent, he won new friends for Ireland and the Irish cause.

Thomas Moore

Witty comedies were also written by the Anglo-Irish playwright Richard Brinsley Sheridan (1751–1816), best known for "The School for Scandal" (1777).

Richard Brinsley Sheridan

Typical Irish qualities – wit and humour, delight in telling stories – can be seen in the work of Laurence Sterne (1713–68), scion of an old Irish family, who spent his life as a country clergyman in England. His principal work is the humorous novel "The Life and Opinions of Tristam Shandy", in which the action of the story takes second place to the author's own personality and whimsical fantasy.

Laurence Sterne

Famous People

Charles Stewart
Parnell
(1846–91)

The statesman Charles Stewart Parnell, from a Protestant Anglo-Irish family, is a symbol of Irish nationalism in the second half of the 19th c. His political career began in the Home Rule League, a party founded in 1870, which, unlike the "Republican Brotherhood" (Fenier), broadly accepted a union with Great Britain, merely demanded a degree of independence for the Irish parliament and rejected using violence against English rule. He soon became party leader and the most powerful man in Irish politics. By peaceful means he gained compromises from the English government. He achieved popularity in the country by calling a "boycott", a word which first found its way into many modern languages through Parnell. The prime target of hatred for the Irish were the English landowners and their administrators of their Irish estates. Owing to the English settlement policy in Ireland in the 16th and 17th c. many British were able to take over the most fertile land. The estates were mainly managed by agents of the landowners who barely put a foot on Irish soil. These agents often took advantage of the tenant farmers. Such an agent was Captain Boycott. He displayed his power in the most brutal fashion. Parnell made the suggestion of ignoring him, of not trading with him, in short of boycotting him. The plan worked – Captain Boycott was forced to give in and left the "Emerald Isle" for ever.

His political efforts towards a peaceful approach to the "Home Rule" policy of the British Prime Minister Gladstone was not popular with everyone. As it became clear that Irish independence would not be won constitutionally his political opponents, even among his own party, found a suitable reason to oust him – his relationship with Katherine O'Shea who was married, yet separated from her husband, a party friend. This "immoral behaviour" was systematically exploited; more and more supporters went over to the opposite camp, including Gladstone and the Irish bishops. His marriage with Katherine O'Shea did not prevent him from being deselected as party leader. A few months afterwards he died.

St Patrick
(about 389–461)

It is said that Ireland was the only country to be converted to Christianity without bloodshed. This peaceful process was the work of St Patrick, the apostle and patron saint of Ireland. Patrick was born in what is today Kilpatrick in Scotland, the son of a deacon. At the age of 16 he was taken prisoner by pirates and taken to Ireland where he was sold as a slave and kept as a shepherd. Six years later he managed to escape back home where he had a vision telling him to convert Ireland to Christianity. Until then there were only a few isolated Christians. In Gaul he trained as a priest and in 431 he returned to the island of his imprisonment as a bishop. He founded a string of schools, churches and monasteries and established the bishop's seat in Armagh. With much skill and empathy – he was familiar with the Irish mentality from his time as a captive here – he succeeded in converting the princes and kings, who still followed the Celtic religion, together with their subjects to the Christian faith. Unlike many other countries there were no Christian martyrs on the "Emerald Isle". At the time of Patrick's death Ireland had been completely converted to Christianity.

Ireland's most successful missionary is surrounded by numerous legends. In the Middle Ages the "purgatory of St Patrick" was famous, a cave in Ulster (Northern Ireland) where Patrick is said to have seen purgatory and many knights experienced visions of the next world. Erasmus, Rabelais, Dante and Calderón were inspired by him. The cult of St Patrick became part of the Irish national and religious legacy. Since the 17th c. at the latest there has been a St Patrick's Day in Ireland. It is said that whenever at least three Irish people meet abroad they celebrate this day. In New York they celebrate St Patrick's Day with a big parade along Fifth Avenue.

George Bernard
Shaw
(1856–1950)

Cynicism, satire and humour made George Bernard Shaw famous – not only with regard to his literary works.

George Bernard Shaw was born in Dublin. His father was English, his mother Irish. In 1876 he moved to London. At first he tried his hand at being an estate agent before beginning to write theatre, music and art criticism which was both admired and feared. In 1884 he founded the "Fabian Society" with like-minded people: a society of intellectuals, who advocated non-Marxist, non-revolutionary, progressive socialism. In 1891 he began to write plays. With jokes, quick-wittedness, cynicism and satire he poked fun at conventions and overused clichés; he employed witty paradoxes, polished dialogues and outstanding punchlines. His most famous plays include "Pygmalion" (1912) and "St Joan" (1923). In 1925 he received the Nobel Prize for Literature, but turned down a title.

In his private life as well as on stage there was no lack of intelligent humour and biting satire. On one occasion a famous society beauty remarked to him "Just imagine, Mr Shaw, a child with your intelligence and my looks!". To which he rather ungallantly replied "And what if it had your intelligence and my looks?!".

The only one of his works which shows any feeling towards his native Ireland is "John Bull's Other Island" (1904) in which he says that Ireland, both good and evil, cannot be compared with any stretch on earth; and nobody can walk upon its green meadows or breathe in its air without feeling either better or worse for it.

On hearing of "Gulliver's Travels" one cannot help being reminded of one's childhood. The first two books of this adventure story are among the most read children's books of world literature. And yet "Gulliver's Travels", written by Jonathan Swift in 1726, is definitely not a children's book. Swift described the adventures of the hero Gulliver in the kingdom of the Liliputians, in that of the giants, in the land where immortality is possible and in the kingdom of the rational horses who have succeeded in forming an ideal society and whose servants are people made like animals. It is a furious satire on contemporary English society, on human stupidity, malice and wrong-doing. Ridicule, for example on the properties of the various denominations in "The Tale of a Tub" (1704), was the hallmark of Swift's literary works. He is regarded as the greatest English satirist, even as one of the greatest satirists ever. He was at the disposal of political groups, first for the Whigs, a group in the English Parliament, which he began working for in 1689. After a few years he changed over to the opposition, to the Tories, when he felt his political and moral views to be betrayed by the Whigs. After the Tories lost power to the Whigs he returned to Dublin where he held the deanship of St Patrick's Cathedral until his death. In 1729 he received the freedom of the city of Dublin. Following the death of his closest friend Stella, whom he never wanted to marry, and possibly as a result of a pernicious illness which he had suffered from for a long time, his writings became increasingly cynical and gave his contemporaries the impression he was mentally ill. He lies buried next to Stella in St Patrick's Cathedral, Dublin.

Jonathan Swift (1667–1745)

The writer John Millington Synge came from an Anglo-Irish lawyer's family and studied at Trinity College in Dublin before travelling around Germany and Italy. Between 1893 and 1898 Synge spent most of the time in Paris. There he met William B. Yeats, upon whose advice he went to the Aran Islands to study the life-style and language of the inhabitants. At first he only stayed for six weeks on the islands but returned for several weeks at a time over the following years. He describes the land and its people in his work of prose "The Aran Islands" (1907).

John Millington Synge (1871–1909)

Synge, who had settled in Dublin, was appointed director of the newly founded Abbey Theatre in 1904, a post he retained until his death.

Not only in the "The Aran Islands" but also in his plays he portrays the lives of Irish farmers and fishermen. One of his most important

Famous People

Jonathan Swift

Eamon de Valera

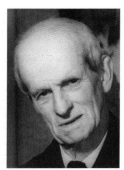
Jack B. Yeats

works is "Riders to the Sea", which depicts the tragic life of fishermen on the west coast of Ireland and is based upon their actual experiences facing the inevitability of death at sea. Also particularly well known is the comedy "The Playboy of the Western World" (1907), in which the vigorous and yet at the same time delicate language of the islanders finds full expression.

Eamon de Valera
(1882–1975)

Eamon de Valera is the most important person in 20th c. Irish history. For six decades (from 1913–73) he exerted a definitive influence on the politics of the "Emerald Isle". He was Prime Minister three times (1932–48, 1951–54, 1957–59) and President once (1959–73). The creation of the Republic of Ireland is primarily his work.

De Valera was born on October 14th 1882 in New York, the son of a Spanish father and an Irish mother. Following the death of his father he went to Ireland with his uncle where he lived with his grandmother. He studied mathematics in Dublin and entered the teaching profession. His political career began in 1913 when he became a member of the "Irish Volunteers", who demanded greater self determination for Ireland. He was one of the leading figures in the Easter uprising in 1916 and commander of the batallion based in Boland's Bakery. After the defeat of the rebellious Irish he was thrown into prison by the English; the death sentence he had received was not carried out. Free again he stood as a candidate for the British Parliament and was elected. In May 1918 he was arrested again by the English government and interned in England; however, he managed to escape to the USA. At the end of 1920 he returned to Ireland. Meanwhile in 1918 the Sinn-Féin party, standing for Ireland's independence, of which de Valera had been president one year earlier, won the majority of all Irish mandates to the House of Commons. The new MPs refused to enter the House of Commons. Instead they formed the Irish Council (Dáil Eireann) in January 1919 with de Valera being elected president of this illegal Irish parliament.

When the Dáil Eireann ratified the free-state treaty negotiated with England on January 7th 1922, Valera left parliament. He was not satisfied with the status of British Dominion for the new Irish free state; he sought the complete independence of Ireland and the unification of Ulster with the free state. After the bitter civil war (1922/23) between the opponents and supporters of the new republic, which ended in victory for the republic, and after one year in prison (1923/24) Valera's position towards the new state became rather more conciliatory. In May 1926, with opponents of the treaty, he founded the relatively moderate "Fianna Fáil" party (comrades of fate). They won the 1932 election against the government party "Fine Gael" (family of the Irish)

46

and de Valera became Prime Minister. He and the party quicky set about cutting the remaining ties with Great Britain. According to law his government abolished the oath of allegiance of the Irish Parliament to the British king. In 1937 a new constitution was introduced. Some of the paragraphs were wriiten by de Valera. From now on the Irish free state was a real republic (it officially came into existence in 1949). The government took over foreign policy and nominated its own diplomats. Great Britain vacated the naval bases on the west coast of Ireland. In the Second World War Ireland remained neutral. De Valera took his neutrality so far that on May 2nd 1945 he sent his condolences to the German ambassador in Dublin on the death of Hitler. In 1948 after the defeat of his party in parliamentary elections he handed over power to the opposition. Later he was to be head of the government twice more (1951–54; 1957–59). In 1959 he transferred office from Prime Minister to President, which he retained until 1973. Eamon de Valera ("Dev", as he was known to his followers) died on August 29th 1975 at the age of 93.

Oscar Wilde, full name Oscar Fingal O'Flahertie Wills, was first introduced to literature in the parental home. Both his father, a doctor, and his mother were interested in literature and surrounded themselves with artists and Bohemians. During his studies in Dublin and in Oxford his interest in classical culture, art and cultivated life-styles was awakened. In 1879 he moved to London and tried his hand at being a poet and art critic. His novel "The Picture of Dorian Gray" (1890) was a great success. The foreward to this novel and some of his essays (1891) vividly reflect his aesthetical viewpoint of "l'art-pour-l'art" (art for art's sake). In his satirical salon comedy "Lady Windermere's Fan" (1892) and "The Importance of Being Earnest" (1895) he gently criticises the sham morals of late Victorian society. Wilde ranks as the leading representative of fin-de-siècle literature in England.

*Oscar Wilde
(1856–1900)*

On the one hand Wilde ridiculed society in his comedies, on the other he sought recognition from high society. He tried to live his life according to his aesthetic ideals: his flat was richly decorated and he liked to dress ostentatiously. He married an attractive woman and had two children. He was at the height of his success in 1895, worshipped by society, but then he was mercilessly rejected. Since 1891 Wilde had had a passionate relationship with the young Lord Alfred Douglas. Rumours soon emerged that the two were having a homosexual relationship which sent Lord Alfred's father, the violent and choleric Marquess of Queensbury into a rage. After a few confrontations between Wilde and the Marquess Wilde sued for libel. He lost the case and was himself prosecuted and sentenced to two year's hard labour for "immoral behaviour". Public opinion turned against him, his publisher stopped the sale of his books. On the publication of the judgement prostitutes danced in the streets because a "troublesome competitor" had been removed. During his imprisonment he wrote the confession addressed to Lord Alfred "De Profundis" (published 1905). Two years of prison and the humiliation he suffered there made him into a broken man. His wife and two sons left England, he himself emigrated to France. He turned increasingly to alcohol and died in a Paris hotel on November 30th 1900.

The brother of the Nobel Prizewinner for Literature, Willian Butler Yeats, dedicated his talent to painting not writing. Jack Butler Yeats was born in London. After his childhood in Sligo, Ireland he returned to study in London. But in his paintings he was captivated by the land of his fathers with subjects from the Irish countryside, the life of the pubs, the music halls and the race track. He favoured dark colours on which he applied bright spots of colour with a spatula. His works include "Sailing, Sailing Swiftly" (1933) and "The Careless Flower" (1947).

*Jack Butler Yeats
(1871–1957)*

47

Famous People

The poet William Butler Yeats was the leading light in the Celtic Renaissance, a movement to preserve and revive the Irish-Celtic tradition in art and culture and closely linked to the Irish people's desire for independence from Great Britain.

His childhood was spent in Dublin, London and Sligo. He was absorbed by the scenery of Ireland's west coast, with its legends and folktales, throughout his life. From 1884 to 1886 he attended the academy of art with the intention of becoming a painter. However, from 1886 he turned to literature – poetry, drama and story-telling. Gradually he became involved in the Irish independence movement. Together with Lady Gregory, G. Moore and E. Martyn he founded the Irish National Theatre in 1899. Following the declaration of the Irish free state he became senator. In this office (from 1922 to 1928) he proposed decorating Irish coins with the animals that appear in the Book Of Kells: hares and dogs, fish and birds.

The chief influence on Yeat's early work was that of the Pre-Raphaelites, later the influence of French symbolism and *fin-de-siècle* aestheticism became noticeable, but his preoccupation with magical and occult phenomena is apparent. In his early poems his symbolism is relatively clear whereas the later poems are mystical and obscure. A characteristic of all his poetry is the inclusion of Irish-Celtic legend, fairy tale and myth. His plays resemble dramatic poems, the action is symbolic, the characters are types. His later dramas are reminiscent of Japanese Noh plays; in which he tries to combine drama, dance, masks and ritual acts. There is such deep symbolism in his final major works that they go beyond the scope of theatre. In both volumes of poetry "The Tower" (1928) and "The Spiral Staircase" (1933) are many of his most beautiful poems. Yeats was awarded the Nobel Prize for Literature in 1923.

Ardmore: reliefs on St Declan's Church and the Round Tower ▶

Art and Culture

History of Art

Note
Ancient monuments and other features of interest scattered through-out the country are usually indicated by signposts, which in the Repub-lic are green and white. Many of these places are under State protection as National Monuments. They are usually open and un-guarded, and visitors are asked to treat them with the respect they deserve.

Foreword
Since the Roman legions never came to Ireland the Celtic inhabitants of the island were able to develop their own distinctive culture and art without influences from outside, and as a result Ireland offers visitors the opportunity of discovering the characteristic forms and figures of Early Celtic art in unique beauty and abundance. Monastic sites and high crosses, metalwork and book illumination are the most impres-sive manifestations of this Early Irish art; but after this great heyday the late medieval period saw an artistic decline, since the country lacked a wealthy middle class with an interest in art. It was not until the 18th c. that the well-to-do Anglo-Irish ruling class began to build their great country houses, usually in Neo-Classical style, and the elegant Geor-gian houses to be seen in the towns, particularly in Dublin and Limerick.

While elsewhere in Europe it is possible to date old buildings by reference to developing styles, in Ireland the style of building in earlier centuries showed little change. The country is littered with the ruins of the past, fitting picturesquely into the landscape; and it has often been possible – as at Ballintubber Abbey and Bunratty Castle, for example – to bring an old building back into use by giving it a new roof and inserting new doors and windows in the gaping holes in its walls.

Stone Age
During the Stone Age (c. 7000–2000 B.C.) megalithic tombs, built of huge slabs of undressed stone, were constructed all over Ireland. The term dolmen is generally applied to the earliest megalithic chambered tombs, with a chamber formed by a number of upright stones (orthos-tats) which support a capstone weighing many tons and sloping down towards the rear of the tomb. A good example of this type is the gigantic dolmen on Browne's Hill near Carlow.

In the passage grave the chamber is approached by a passage formed of orthostats. The stones are decorated with spirals, zigzags and other forms of ornament, and the whole structure was origi-nally buried in an earth mound. In some of these tombs there are three side-chambers opening off the main one, giving them a cruci-form plan. The passage graves in the Boyne Valley are particularly famed.

In the gallery grave there is no distinction between the passage and the burial chamber. The wedge-shaped gallery grave has a chamber which is broader at one end than the other, enclosed within a U-shaped formation of orthostats. This type of grave is particularly common in Ireland: there is a good example at Ballyedmunduff, near Dublin.

There is also the "court cairn", a burial mound with a semicircular or oval court serving some ritual purpose in front of the tomb chamber. A tomb of this kind can be seen at Creevykeel, north of Sligo.

The stone circle of Drombeg

Characteristic monuments of the Bronze Age (*c.* 2000–500 B.C.) are the stone circles, probably used for cult ceremonies, which have left such impressive remains in Ireland. A good example is the Drombeg stone circle in Co. Cork.

   To this period, too, belong the standing stones, known in Irish as "gallain", which also had some ritual significance.

   Evidence of Bronze Age wealth is provided by the finds (e.g. in the Wicklow Mountains) of valuable gold ornaments, including "lunulae", crescent-shaped collars of hammered gold sheet.

During the Iron Age and the beginning of the Christian period (*c.* 500 B.C.–A.D. 400) ring-forts surrounded by stone or earth ramparts, known in Irish as "raths", were built to provide protection for kinship groups or clans from enemy attacks and plundering expeditions. There are said to be more than 30,000 ring-forts in Ireland, many of them preserved only in the form of fragmentary remains.

   There were also more strongly defended hill-forts, commandingly situated on elevated sites. An imposing example of a hill-fort – in Irish "lis" – is Dún Aenghus on Inishmore in the Aran Islands.

The term promontory fort (Irish "dún") is applied to a ring-fort built on a promontory or projecting tongue of land; sometimes the rampart is built across the neck of the promontory. There is a fine promontory fort at Dunbeg on the Dingle Peninsula.

   Another type of defensive structure was the "crannog", an artificial island in a lough (lake) constructed with the aid of piles. Occasionally a natural islet might be used for this purpose. As places of particular security some of the crannogs remained in occupation into the late medieval period.

   The Irish terms for the various types of fort feature in many place-names – Dungannon, Lismore, Rathdrum, etc.

Bronze Age

Iron Age

Promontory forts

51

During the Bronze Age the Celtic population of Ireland learned the technique of enamelwork, producing beautifully ornamented everyday articles as well as jewellery. They are believed to have acquired this art from the Roman provinces.

Ogham script

Towards the end of the Iron Age the ogham script, named after Ogmios, the Celtic god of writing, came into use (see Irish language, p. 21). Ogham inscriptions are usually found on the edges of erect slabs of stone or diagonally across the stone. They took the form of horizontal or sloping lines, used in various combinations to denote different letters, there being twenty such in all.

Most of those which have been preserved — some 250 out of a total of 300 — are in the counties of Kerry, Cork and Waterford. The inscriptions invariably take the form of standard formulae. The Alphabet Stone at Kilmalkedar on the Dingle Peninsula has Latin and ogham inscriptions side by side.

Ogham stone

Early Christian Period

The Early Christian period (c. 400–1170) saw a great flowering of art in Ireland, notably richly carved crosses and illuminated manuscripts.

The many monastic sites established during this period, however, produced no architecture of any significance. It is known from the chronicles of the time that the buildings were of wattle and daub, or occasionally of timber. Where these materials were not available, as on the rocky islet of Skellig Michael in the Atlantic, use was perforce made of stone. On Skellig Michael a flight of more than 600 steps was hewn from the rock to give access to a relatively sheltered terrace on which the monks built their beehive cells and oratories and buried their dead. An upright slab of stone inscribed with a cross was the forerunner of the later elaborately decorated high crosses.

The beehive hut of this period (Irish "clochán") is a small round hut of drystone masonry, corbelled to form a "false vault" and closed at the top by a flat slab of stone. This type of structure is also found in some stony and treeless Mediterranean countries, and probably originated there. On Skellig Michael the monks selected and laid their stones with such care and accuracy that the huts have remained watertight to this day.

The early churches were tiny oratories used either for individual devotions or for celebrating Mass. The corbelled walls meet at the roof-ridge, giving the building the form of an upturned boat. The interior was dark, lit only by the door or, later, by a narrow window over the altar. The Gallarus Oratory on the Dingle Peninsula is a completely preserved example of the type.

The gravestones on the monastic sites show a development from simple forms of ornament to small-scale works of art. In the later period all the arms of the cross which forms the central feature are richly decorated. The inscriptions take the form of a standard formula ("or do . . .") asking for a prayer for the dead man. Built into a wall at Clonmacnoise is a notable collection of such gravestones and fragments of gravestones. The standing stones of the pagan period were now "baptised" by the carving of a cross, often in very crude form. There are also early attempts at decorating such stones, as on the Reask Stone in Kerry, where the stylised cross resembles a flower.

High crosses

Ireland's celebrated high crosses, standing up to 16ft/5m high, are believed to have developed out of decorated standing stones of this kind. What are believed to be early forms of the high cross can be

Figure carving on the Muireadach Cross at Monasterboice

seen at Fahan and Carndonagh on the Inishowen Peninsula: stones, ascribed to the 7th c., in the form of a rough cross decorated with inter-lace ornament and crude figures in relief. The crosses at Ahenny in Co. Tipperary show a more developed form, with a slender shaft set on a base and a circle linking the arms with the upright. The whole surface of the cross is divided into panels, each filled with geometric designs: the Celts, it has been said, abhorred an empty surface. It is possible, though not certain, that such crosses were originally made of wood covered with sheet bronze, so that the crosses we have today may be merely stone copies of an earlier form. The studs at the junction of the arms, possibly representing the nails used in the construction of the earlier wooden crosses, have been cited as evidence for this theory. On the base are figural representations, not easy to interpret, which may depict scenes of monastic life. The Ahenny crosses have been dated to the 8th c., on the basis of the striking similarity between their geometric patterns and the ornament in the "Book of Kells".

From about the 9th c. the ornamental patterns on the high crosses begin to give way to figural ornament. This is the great age of the Bible crosses, set up in monastic settlements as visible signs of piety and means of instruction. The finely carved relief figures, in rectangular panels, depict Old and New Testament scenes. Groups of panels are often devoted to miraculous deliveries from difficulty or danger – Daniel in the Lion's Den, the Three Young Men in the Fiery Furnace, the Sacrifice of Isaac, David and Goliath. Figures of Paul and Anthony, the desert saints, recall the Eastern prototypes of the Irish hermits, and the fabulous creatures depicted on the sides of many crosses seem to come from the East rather than from western Europe. The central feature, however, is almost always the message of salvation – on the west face Christ crucified, on the east face Christ in glory on Judgment Day. The cross is frequently topped by a small house-like structure in the form of a shrine.

High crosses in Ireland
(a selection)

© Baedeker

1 Clonca	15 Durrow
2 Carndonagh	16 Kilcullen
3 Fahan	17 Glendalough
4 Arboe	18 Moone
5 Donaghmore	19 Castledermot
6 Drumcliffe	20 Kilfenora
7 Tynan	21 Dysert O'Dea/Ennis
8 Termonfeckin	22 Graiguenamanagh
9 Monasterboice	23 Kilree
10 Kells	24 Killamery
11 Duleek	25 St Mullins
12 Tuam	26 Ahenny
13 Bealin	27 Kilkieran
14 Clonmacnoise	

The kind of stone used depends on local conditions, but it is usually a very fine-grained sandstone. There are quarries of this stone near Kells and Monasterboice in the east of Ireland. One of the finest of such crosses is Muiredach's Cross at Monasterboice. The crosses at Clonmacnoise were hewn from erratic blocks of sandstone.

The stone used was of very variable quality: the carving on some crosses is still as clear and sharp as on the day it was done, while on others it has been worn smooth and sometimes almost effaced by wind and rain.

Where sandstone was not available and the harder granite had to be used, as at Columba's foundation of Moone in south-eastern Ireland, the carving was necessarily simplified almost to the point of abstraction. The figures on the Moone High Cross have an appearance of uniformity, but the faces are not without expression.

From about the 11th c. the representation of Biblical scenes, apart from the Crucifixion, was largely abandoned, and the crosses were again covered with ornament. Sometimes the crosses, with shorter arms and no ring, are carved with individual figures in high relief, such as the local limestone crosses of Co. Clare. The Dysert O'Dea Cross has a representation of the crucified Christ in a long draped garment and below this the dignified figure of a bishop wearing a mitre and carrying a crosier after the Roman fashion.

While there are a number of high crosses in Scotland and northern England, the round tower found in early monastic settlements is a characteristically Irish development, though there are two examples in Scotland. It is a slender and elegant structure tapering to between 60ft/18m and 100ft/30m, with a conical stone roof – the central and most prominent feature of the monastic site.

Round towers

The building of round towers is believed to have begun after the first Viking raids: thus, in addition to serving as a bell-tower, they also provided a place of safety in case of attack. The entrance was several feet above the ground, and within the tower narrow ladders gave access to the upper storeys. The various floors, of which there were usually five, were lit only by narrow windows, all facing in different directions, so that a watch could be kept for the approach of an enemy. In normal peaceful times the monks working in the open were called to services by a hand-bell. A number of these angular metal bells have survived, and examples can be seen in the National Museum in Dublin and the British Museum in London, as well as in churches in remote Scottish glens.

Some 80 Irish round towers are still standing in whole or in part. While the earliest were constructed of undressed stone, without any form of ornament, later examples have elaborately carved stone friezes and decorated doorway arches in Romanesque style. Some round towers, including the one at Monasterboice, must still be climbed on ladders. The finest example of a round tower is the one at Ardmore in Co. Waterford.

Round tower

Fine metalwork was also produced during the Early Christian period. The excellent examples of metalwork to be seen in the National Museum in Dublin show that the craftsmen of the period could practise and refine techniques inherited from the past, taking as their models articles of earlier periods in bronze, decorated with enamel or vitreous paste, or in beaten gold or silver. Among the examples of their work are such splendid ornamental brooches as the Tara Brooch and, as the monasteries became increasingly wealthy, precious vessels such as the 8th c. Ardagh Chalice. Later richly decorated cases and containers were produced for objects of particular veneration, including manuscripts and bells, bishops' crosiers and relics of the early saints. In work of this kind the artists made it a point of honour never to repeat themselves.

Metalwork

Irish crosiers have semicircular crooks, but with a straight end, and were kept in a similarly shaped bronze shrine, with a pattern of ornament which frequently ended in an animal's or bird's head. Bell shrines have the same shape as the bell. The Shrine of St Patrick's Bell is of bronze, decorated with gold filigree, silver and precious stones.

The covers of a saint's prayer-book were ornamented with bronze mountings. In one example depicting the Crucifixion the angels' garments and wings have spiral and interlace decoration.

The commonest items of this kind to have survived, however, are small house-shaped reliquaries with steeply pitched roofs like those of the Early Irish churches, made of wood with a bronze facing and

Book of Kells

In the Colonnades Gallery of the library of Trinity College, Dublin, can be seen the Book of Kells, one of the greatest artistic treasures in the world. Written by monks, it contains the four Gospels; one page is turned every day.

It has not yet been clearly established when and where the book was written, who commissioned it and who the artists were. The most widespread scientific theory of its origin and age is that it dates from the end of the 8th century and came from Iona, a barren island off the west coast of Scotland. The monastery of Iona which St Columba had founded in 563 was the place from which missionaries travelled to the mainland of Scotland, to northern England and then to the European continent. Here they influenced the founding of monasteries – for instance in Würzburg (Germany), in Luxeuil (France), in Bobbio (Italy) and in St Gallen (Switzerland). In 791 the Abbot Connachtach assembled in Iona the best artists and calligraphers of Europe. Further evidence that the Book of Kells must have originated on Iona can be found in the picture of the apostle Luke on page 201. On the upper part of the apostle's hand can be seen the word "Jonas", and Jonas was another name for Iona. In 806 the Vikings landed on the island and began to plunder and burn it. Connachtach, the abbot, and 86 of his monks were slain. According to one theory precautions to preserve the book had been made after the Vikings had attacked Iona for the first time in 795. Shortly before their second invasion the Book of Kells, still incomplete, is said to have been taken by ship across the sea to the security of the Irish Monastery of Kells (Ceananus Mor). Here it is presumed to have been completed at the beginning of the 9th century. In the 11th century it was stolen but found again three months later, although the gilded cover had been torn off. According to another theory the entire book is said to have originated in Ireland and as far as the date of origin is concerned many scholars presume this to have been at the beginning of the 8th century. Whatever may be the true explanation, it is a fact that in the 12th century the book was in the possession of the Monastery of Kells, for at this time the rules of this community of monks were written on the plain pages of the masterpiece. When Cromwell's marauding Protestant troops stormed over Ireland the book was taken for security to Trinity College Dublin.

The text of the Book of Kells is based on the Vulgate, the Latin translation of the Bible made by Hieronymus in the 4th century, but the Book of Kells does not entirely follow this version. This may be due to the fact that several sources were consulted when it was being written. Some have expressed the view that, as this work of art is larger in format than other examples of the Gospels made between the 7th and 9th centuries, it was orignally created to be used on the altar; this would account for the unusual illumination of its pages.

No costs were spared in creating the Book of Kells. The parchment for the pages was made from the hides of hundreds of calves. Pigments for the coloration were obtained from all over the world: ultramarine from the Hindu Kush mountains along the route from Persia via Constantinople, carmine from southern France and purple and gold pigment from Spain. In view of the differences in style in the artistic arrangement of the book it is thought that several artists – probably four – were engaged on the work.

In the Book of Kells each passage of the four Gospels begins with an illuminated initial. There are 2000 of these, each different from any other. At the beginning of the account of the birth of Christ in St Matthew's Gospel a whole page, measuring 13 by 10ins/33 by 25cm, is devoted to the chi-Rho monogram (a combination of the first two letters of "Christos" – "XP" in Greek). The long diagonal arms of the "X" lie obliquely across the page, while the "P" can be seen in the lower part of the right side. Among the artistically decorated ornamentation well-drawn figures and animals can be seen.

Monogram of Christ

These letters celebrate the incarnation of Christ and are reminiscent of the finest goldsmith's work. Anyone looking at the Book of Kells is inevitably reminded of the Orient, and yet this book has a fundamentally insular – that is Irish and north-British character. In the combination of its ornamentation and figurative composition it forms the highpoint of the tradition of Irish book-illumination.

decoration, which were designed to be carried on a strap round the neck.

Many works of this kind were carried off to Norway by Viking raiders and have come to light as grave-goods recovered from tombs, particularly women's tombs. Some are in Norwegian museums; others have been brought back to Ireland.

The Cross of Cong (c. 1123), brilliantly decorated in gold and blue with animals and fabulous creatures, was the last great achievement of the Irish metalworkers.

Illumination of manuscripts

The supreme intellectual and artistic contribution of the monks of the Celtic Church lay in the development of an Irish script and in the illumination of manuscripts. From the Latin script of the day they evolved a decorative half-uncial script which could be either strong and vigorous or, if the writer's artistic bent so dictated, lively and fanciful. The perfection of this script, written on thick parchment sheets, rivals the work of Islamic and Chinese calligraphers.

The urge to decorate the pages of a manuscript appears at an early stage. In the "Catach" (Helper in the Fight), St Columba's catechism, for example, the initials break out into a profusion of curls and spirals, while other letters are outlined in dots.

While in the "Catach" (c. 600) only red and blackish-brown ink is used, later illuminated manuscripts glow in many colours. Among the colours used are crimson, bright red, emerald-green, dark blue and yellow, The initials in the chapter-headings of the Gospels are formed by a pattern of interlace ornament ending in human and animal heads, or sometimes by human figures shaped like articulated puppets to form the letters. Later the initials may take up the whole of a page. Above and below the lines appear the animals familiar to men of that period – cats, mice, cocks and hens, birds, fishes. Some of these figures are true to life, but most of them belong to a fantasy world. Words and syllables are linked by curving brackets of grotesque form in the shape of human or animal bodies which can no longer be accommodated within the line and are set above or below it.

The finest achievements of Irish book illumination are the whole-page illustrations, either covered with an all-over pattern of tapestry-like ornament or depicting scriptural scenes. The whole intricate pattern is drawn with such delicacy of line that it requires a magnifying glass to appreciate all the detail. There are evident similarities between these designs and the decorative motifs on metalwork and on high crosses.

Book of Kells

The Four Evangelists with their symbols are a favourite theme. Here again the artists have largely broken away from a realistic method of representation and are seeking to give pictorial expression to their own ideas. Thus we find figures with feet turned sideways (as in Egyptian tomb-paintings), a double pair of hands, harlequin-like dress or blue hair.

Numerous examples of Irish manuscript illumination can be seen in Dublin: in the Royal Irish Academy St Columba's "Cathach" (6th c.) and the "Stowe Missal" (early 9th c.), and in the Old Library of Trinity College the "Book of Durrow" (7th c.), the "Book of Dimma" (8th c., in a silver-plated bronze case or cumdach), the "Book of Armagh" (c. 807), which contains all Four Gospels, and the undisputed masterpiece of Irish book illuminations, the "Book of Kells" (see Baedeker Special, pp. 56/57).

Recent research indicates that at some time between 790 and 820 four scribes in St Columba's Monastery on the island of Iona, off the Scottish west coast, began work on the "Book of Kells", but after Viking raids on Iona fled to Kells in Ireland, taking with them the partially completed book. In Trinity College, where the book has been preserved since the 17th c., a different page of the manuscript is shown every day.

Most of the holy men of the Celtic Church were active scribes and copyists. When they travelled they carried their manuscripts with them, and their foundations in Britain (e.g. on Lindisfarne) and on the Continent (e.g. at St Gall) also followed the insular style. In consequence a relatively large number of manuscripts have survived, most of them now in the large European libraries.

Insular style

Occasionally the Irish scribes noted down personal remarks, or sometimes verses, in the margins of their manuscripts – observations of nature, pious statements, sometimes also thoughts which are by no means pious. In some of these notes they give expression to their fear of the Vikings who brought this great flowering of art to an end.

Romanesque art came to Ireland in the 12th c. with the adoption of the Roman form of the Christian faith. Hitherto the Irish had continued to build small churches with steeply pitched stone roofs of the traditional kind; and the new style, too monumental for Irish tastes, was accepted only in part and was so considerably modified as to form a distinctive Irish Romanesque.

Romanesque art

The first church in the new style, already a masterpiece, was Cormac's Chapel on the Rock of Cashel, which was consecrated in 1134. Builders from Regensburg in Germany are believed to have worked on this church, and the Schottenkloster (Scots Monastery) in Regensburg is known to have had connections with Ireland – in the early medieval period the Irish were known as Scoti or Scotti. For the first time in an Irish church the nave is barrel-vaulted and the chancel groin-vaulted. At the junction of nave and chancel stand two square towers. The steeply pitched roof, however, follows earlier Irish models, and the carved fabulous beasts and human heads are typically Irish.

The Celtic head motif is also found in other Irish Romanesque churches, for example at Dysert O'Dea, where the principal doorway has animal masks between bearded human faces, or in Clonfert cathedral, where the richly decorated west doorway is surmounted by a high triangular pediment with geometrically arranged human heads and ornament. Zigzag mouldings on the doorway and richly sculptured chancel arches are found on other Romanesque churches in Ireland.

After a national synod in 1110 the Irish Church was gradually assimilated to the Roman Church. Diocesan government was introduced, and the power and influence of the old monasteries declined sharply.

At the same time Bishop Malachi of Armagh brought in the Cistercians, the first of the great new religious orders to come to Ireland. Mellifont Abbey, where a Burgundian architect built the fine monastic church, was the mother house of some two dozen other foundations. These new abbeys had a whole complex of buildings in addition to the church – cells for the monks, a refectory, a cloister, domestic offices, etc. The church was often called a cathedral, even though it was not one in the strict sense of a bishop's church. The monks from the older monasteries now flocked to these new foundations, bringing about the final demise of the Celtic Church.

When the Anglo-Normans conquered Ireland they built castles to provide security in a hostile country. An early form of castle was the "motte and bailey", with a timber tower built on a circular or oval mound (the motte) and an outer court (the bailey) defended by wooden palisades.

A more substantial fortification was the stone-built keep, with thick walls and a few windows. This might either stand by itself or be enclosed within an outer ward surrounded by curtain-walls. Many ruins of these almost indestructible strongholds have survived to the present day.

In the course of time still more powerful fortresses were built, on the pattern of English castles, with corner towers and massive battlemented walls.

Kilmacduagh: Romanesque and Gothic remains

Gothic art

During the Norman period, from the 13th c. onwards, the Gothic style came to Ireland. Buildings in the Gothic style were erected only by the Norman incomers, with the help of native craftsmen, and by the new religious Orders – first the Cistercians and Augustinians, later the Dominicans and Franciscans.

The churches and cathedrals which were now built, in disturbed times and with limited means, were sturdy structures with little decoration and were smaller than their counterparts on the Continent. The monasteries were built in accordance with the rules and requirements of the various Orders, but these, too, were on a smaller scale than elsewhere. Ruins such as those of Rosserilly, Co. Galway, with tower and cloister, refectory and reader's desk, bakery and fish-tank, are like a miniature edition of a Franciscan friary.

Ireland's contribution to the art of this period consists of gravestones of traditional Irish type and a few works of sculpture. Most of the artists are practically unknown. There seem to have been a number of gifted sculptors named O'Tunney in the Kilkenny area, the most notable of them being Rory O'Tunney, whose work is to be seen in the cloister of Jerpoint Abbey, near Urlingford, and in Kilkenny Cathedral. On these tombs the figure of the dead man, in full armour, lies on a stone sarcophagus under a sculptured canopy, which sometimes has Late Gothic tracery, with figures of angels, Apostles, saints and holy men around the sides; in 15th–17th c. tombs the dead man and his wife may be lying side by side. The figures are notable for the meticulous treatment of the hair and garments and for the curiously impenetrable expression on the faces.

Also typically Irish are the "sheila-na-gigs" – small carvings of obscene female figures which may be fertility symbols or intended to ward off evil spirits – which can be found in unobtrusive positions in a number of churches.

15th c. Franciscan Quin Abbey

Thereafter, given the poverty of the native Irish population, art and architecture stagnated for several centuries. It was not until the 18th c. that the Anglo-Irish ruling classes, having risen to prosperity and wealth, began to build country mansions and town houses appropriate to their status. Following the models provided by Palladio in Italy and Inigo Jones in England, they built mostly in the Classical style. A typical example is Castletown House, near Dublin, built by Alessandro Galilei and Sir Edward Lovett Pearce in 1722–32 for William Conolly, Speaker of the Irish Parliament, with plasterwork by the Francini brothers.

From the end of the Middle Ages to the present day

This flowering of architecture was followed, on a much more modest scale, by the other arts. Since the owners of the new country houses preferred an outdoor life, they were more interested in the layout of their parks and gardens than in the interior decoration of their houses. Exotic trees, immaculate lawns and terraces (as at Powerscourt in the Wicklow Mountains) meant more to them than pictures, furniture and carpets.

Nevertheless, there were some notable achievements in the minor arts, such as the elegant silver of the period. Some of the more eccentric wishes of the landowners were given expression in the "follies" they built on their estates – Greek or Egyptian temples, obelisks or artificial ruins.

From the middle of the 17th c. a period of great building activity began in Dublin, and within a bare hundred years what had been an unimportant and not particularly salubrious little town was transformed into the second city of the British Empire. Four new bridges were built over the Liffey, its banks were lined with quays, and the old town centre was surrounded by wide modern streets and squares laid out in gardens. The Royal Hospital for old and disabled soldiers, designed by Sir William Robinson on a French model, was built in 1670–87.

Georgian doorways

18th century

This building activity reached its peak in the 18th c. Dublin Castle and Trinity College were rebuilt. The short-lived Irish Parliament was housed in a new building – now the Bank of Ireland – designed by Edward Lovett Pearce. As in the rest of Europe, architects of different nationalities were at work in Dublin. Richard Castle or Cassels (1690–1751), a German, built Tyrone House and Leinster House, which is now the Parliament building. James Gandon (1743–1823), an Englishman of Huguenot origin, built the Custom House and the Four Courts, the elegant silhouette and domes of which are reflected in the waters of the Liffey, and began the King's Inns on Constitution Hill in north Dublin. Francis Johnston (1761–1829), who built both in the fashionable Classical and in the Neo-Gothic styles, was responsible for the Chapel in Dublin Castle and the General Post Office which featured so prominently in the fighting of 1916, and also St George's Church, often considered his best work.

Georgian style

In addition to such large public buildings this period also saw the building of the handsome mansions of the aristocracy and the prosperous business classes, with imposing façades behind railed front gardens. This was the heyday of the "Georgian style". The brick fronts of these Georgian houses with their tall windows are beautifully proportioned; their only form of ornament, in endless variation, lies in their painted doors with brilliantly polished knockers, flanked by columns and surmounted by an architrave and a semicircular fanlight with a light or the house number. The interior of these houses is often decorated with fine plasterwork by the Francini brothers, for example. Similar houses and terraces can be found in other towns including Limerick and Cork. Dublin's terraces of Georgian houses remained almost intact until well into this century. Since then they have fallen victim, individually or in whole streets, to the demolition man, to make room for new development. It is only in recent years and at the cost of great effort that it has been possible to save and to restore properly some of the city's finest streets and squares.

Stained glass

During the 19th c., with Catholic Emancipation, many new churches were built, and the art of stained glass enjoyed a great flowering. The first workshops soon developed into schools of stained-glass artists; new techniques were tried out and links were established with the Continent. Pioneers in this development, which was considerably influenced by the Art Nouveau movement, were Michael Healy, Harry Clarke, Sarah Purser and Evie Hone.

It is interesting to see how Irish architects and artists of the present day have taken up the forms and themes of the early period of Irish art. In church-building architects such as Liam McCormick have designed round churches of notable quality, reflecting the plan of Ireland's prehistoric stone forts. Such new churches, and churches reconstructed on the remains of older buildings, contain tabernacles, Stations of the Cross, fonts and doors of modern design by such artists as Imogen Stuart, a native of Munich.

20th century

Smaller objects of bronze, by Edward Delaney, Oisín Kelly and others, again showing the influence of the Early Celtic period, have also evolved their own characteristically Irish style. An affinity can perhaps be detected here with the brush drawings of Louis Le Broquy, who illustrated Thomas Kinsella's modern version of the "Cattle Raid of Cooley".

Literature

In the Early Celtic period poets occupied a leading position in Irish society. Seers as well as poets, they acquired their skills in special schools, usually under the direction of Druids, where, lying in the dark, they learned their texts and verses by heart.

During this period (600–1200) there came into being the great cycles of Irish/Celtic heroic sagas, which took the form of prose epics and were set against a pagan background.

Early period
Heroic sagas

In the early years of the Christian period the sagas were written down by monks; but alongside this written record an oral tradition was maintained by the "shanachies", men skilled in the art of telling tales.
A number of different cycles can be distinguished.

Shanachies

In the tales of the mythological cycle mortals still hold intercourse with divinities, who have a double aspect, now mild, now terrifying. There is no firm boundary between life and death; and the final goal for man is Tir na n'Og, the Land of the Ever Young, somewhere westward in the Atlantic.

Mythological cycle

The Red Branch cycle of tales is concerned with the Ulaid, a people who gave their name to Ulster. Their royal stronghold was Eamhain macha (Navan Fort, in Northern Ireland), their great hero CuChulainn. The subjects of the tales are cattle raids and their consequences, described in graphic, colourful and sometimes grotesque scenes. In the best known of these sagas, the "Táin Bó Cúalinge" ("Cattle Raid of Cooley"), Queen Maeve, dissatisfied with her husband's possessions, plays the role of the evil opponent of the hero, CuChulainn. The tragic love-story of Deirdre of the Sorrows is in this cycle – often likened to Tristan and Isolde, it inspired plays by Yeats and Synge.

Red Branch cycle

The third cycle, which is to be dated after the year 1000, centres on the exploits of Finn MacCool and his war band, the Fianna, which seems to anticipate some of the ideals of the later knightly culture. The theme of tragic love – the story of Diarmaid and Grainne who can also be compared with Tristan and Isolde – appears in these tales too.

Third cycle

The Folklore Commission began to record the tales of the shanachies in 1935, and they were later issued on records and tapes.

Folklore
Commission

The middle period (1200–1650) was the Age of the Bards – Celtic poets who composed and sang songs in praise of their lord or king.

Middle period
Age of the Bards

The prose literature of this period was mainly devoted to the "Fenian cycle", the fourth of the great Irish cycles; fairy-tale-like stories of adventure, often incorporating ballads.

Fenian cycle

Music

Late period
The characteristic feature of the late period (1650–1850) was the oppression of the Irish by the English conquerors, which had a detrimental influence on the development of Irish language and literature. The predominant element in literature was now folk poetry, cherished by country people and craft workers. Many of the poems gave expression to sorrow and the love of nature.

Munster poetry
Since this poetry flourished particularly in the southern Irish province of Munster it is also known as "Munster poetry".
From the 17th c. onwards the names of individual Irish authors – writing in English – begin to feature in the history of literature.

Modern period
Gaelic League
The beginning of the modern period was marked at the end of the 19th c. by the establishment of the Gaelic League (1893).

Celtic Renaissance
The object of the League, whose members included Douglas Hyde, first President of the Republic (1938–45), and the writer George Moore (1852–1933), was the revival of Irish language and literature – which came to be called the Celtic Renaissance. About the turn of the century Pádraic Pearse (1878–1916), Pádraic O Conaire (1882–1928), Peadar O Laoire (1839–1929) and others began to produce literary work in the Irish language.

Abbey Theatre
In 1899 Lady Augusta Gregory founded the Irish National Theatre in Dublin – known from 1904 as the Abbey Theatre – in which plays in both English and Irish were performed.
Some of the writers of the modern period, including William Butler Yeats, John Millington Synge and Sean O'Casey, concerned themselves with Irish traditions and the problems of Ireland; others, like Oscar Wilde and George Bernard Shaw, turned more towards Britain; but even those Irish writers who spent most of their life away from Ireland, such as James Joyce, reflect in their work the mentality and language of their native country.

Music

Irish Harp

The heyday of Irish music was in the medieval period, the favourite instrument being the harp. In the banqueting hall of the High King, at lesser courts and in the houses of the magnates of the day the "three tunes, of laughing, of weeping and of sleep" were played.
We know the names of only a few of the most celebrated harpists – many of whom were blind – and of the tunes ascribed to them. Later we hear of itinerant troubadours, who specialised in folk music. More than 200 compositions by Turlough O'Carolan (1670–1738), a blind poet and harpist, have been preserved.
Since the 17th c. the harp has appeared in the Irish coat-of-arms. It remains the symbol of the Republic today, and will also be found on official documents, coins, stamps and soldiers' buttons.
During the centuries of English rule the poverty of the people ruled out any serious musical interests, and most of the Anglo-Irish landlords, preferring an outdoor life, had little time for the arts. Dublin during its 18th c. heyday was the exception, and in 1742 Handel's "Messiah" had its first performance in the city, conducted by the composer.
Nevertheless, the musical talents of the Irish managed to find expression. The instruments used in performing light music or dance music were of the simplest – fiddles, played with great virtuosity; tin whistles, with which they produced unexpectedly strong and harmonious sounds; and goatskin drums (bodhran).

The Irish pipes (uilleann) were a softer-toned variant of the Scottish bagpipes, held under the arm and operated by movements of the elbow. These traditional instruments have been supplemented in more recent times by the concertina, the guitar and the banjo.

Folk groups all over the country use these various instruments in a rich repertoire of Irish and also Scottish, English and American tunes and songs, establishing an international reputation not only in concert halls but also in the popular "folk-clubs".

In the late 18th c. much effort was devoted to collecting the traditional Irish songs, and several volumes of old folk tunes were published. Genuine old Irish folk songs are still sung, in Gaelic and without accompaniment.

Sean O'Riada (1931–71) composed important works which opened up new avenues and pointed the way for younger colleagues after his early death.

Ireland in Quotations

Samuel Johnson (1709–84)
He had a kindness for the Irish nation, and thus graciously expressed himself to a gentleman from that country, on the subject of an UNION which artful politicians often have in view, "Do not make an union with us, Sir. We should unite with you, only to rob you. We should have robbed the Scotch, if they had had any thing of which we could have robbed them.
(quoted in Boswell's "Life of Johnson", October 12th 1779)

Sir Walter Scott (1771–1832)
There is perpetual kindness in the Irish cabin – butter-milk, potatoes – a stool is offered or a stone is rolled that your honour may sit down and be out of the smoke, and those who beg everywhere else seem desirous to exercise free hospitality in their own houses. Their natural disposition is turned to gaiety and happiness: while a Scotchman is thinking about the term-day, or if easy on that subject about hell in the next world – while an Englishman is making a little hell in the present, because his muffin is not well roasted – Pat's mind is always turned to fun and ridicule. They are terribly excitable, to be sure, and will murder you on slight suspicion, and find out the next day that it was all a mistake, and that it was not yourself they meant to kill, at all at all.
(Diary, November 21st 1825)

W. S. Landor (1775–1864)
Ireland never was contented
Say you so? You are demented
Ireland was contented when
All could use the sword and pen
And when Tara rose so high
That her turrets split the sky
And about her courts were seen
Liveried angels robed in green
Wearing, by St Patrick's bounty
Emeralds, big as half the county
("Ireland never was contented" 1853)

W. M. Thackeray (1811–63)
As there is more rain in this country than in any other, and as, therefore, naturally, the inhabitants should be inured to the weather, and made to despair an inconvenience which they can not avoid, the travelling conveyances are so arranged so that you may get as much practice in being wet as possible.

They call Belfast the Irish Liverpool. If people are for calling names, it would be better to call it the Irish London at once – the chief city of the kingdom at any rate. It looks hearty, thriving and prosperous, as if it has money in its pockets, and roast-beef for dinner: it has no pretensions to fashion, but looks mayhap better in its honest broadcloth than some people in their shabby brocade. The houses are as handsome as at Dublin, with the advantage, that the people seem to live in them.
(The Irish Sketch Book of 1842)

Friedrich Engels (1820–95)
Ireland may be regarded as the first English colony and as one which because of its proximity is still governed exactly in the old way. The people itself has got its peculiar character from this, and despite all their Irish nationalistic fanaticism, the fellows feel that they are no longer at home in their own country. Ireland for the Saxon! That is now being realised. The Irishman knows that he cannot compete with the Englishman.
(letter to Karl Marx, 1836)

O Paddy, dear, an' did ye hear the news that's going round?
The shamrock is by law forbid to grow on Irish ground!
No more St Patrick's Day we'll keep, his colour can't be seen
For there's a cruel law agin the wearin' o' the Green!
I met wid Napper Tandy, and he took me by the hand,
And he said, How's poor ould Ireland, and how does she stand?
She's the most disthressful country that iver yet was seen,
For they're hanging men an' women there for the wearin' o' the Green.
("The Wearin' o' the Green" – street ballad, later added to by
Boucicault)

*Dion Boucicault
(1822–90)*

I am in Aranmor, sitting over a turf fire, listening to a murmur of Gaelic
that is rising from a little public house under my room.

*John Millington
Synge (1871–1909)*

The steamer which comes to Aran sails according to the tide, and it
was six o'clock this morning when we left the quay of Galway in a
dense shroud of mist.

A low line of shore was visible at first on the right between the
movement of the waves and fog, but when we came further it was lost
sight of, and nothing could be seen but the mist curling in the rigging,
and a small circle of foam.

There were few passengers, a couple of men going out with young
pigs tied loosely in sacking, three or four young girls who sat in the
cabin with their heads completely twisted in their shawls, and a
builder, on his way to repair the pier at Kilronan, who walked up and
down and talked with me.

In about three hours Aran came in sight. A dreary rock appeared at
first sloping up from the sea into the fog, then, as we drew nearer, a
coastguard station and the village.

A little later I was wandering out along the one good roadway of the
island, looking over low walls on either side into small flat fields of
naked rock. I have seen nothing so desolate. Grey floods of water were
sweeping everywhere upon the limestone, making at times a wild
torrent of the road, which twined continually over low hills and cavities
in the rock or passed between a few small fields of potatoes or grass
hidden away in corners that had shelter. Whenever the cloud lifted I
could see the edge of the sea below me on the right, and the naked
ridge of the island above me on the other side. Occasionally I passed a
lonely chapel or schoolhouse, or a line of stone pillars with crosses
above them and inscriptions asking a prayer for the soul of the person
they commemorated.

I met few people; but here and there a band of tall girls passed me on
their way to Kilronan, and called out to me in curious wonder, speaking
English with a slight foreign intonation that differed a good deal from
the brogue of Galway. The rain and cold seemed to have no influence
on their vitality, and as they hurried past me with eager laughter and
great talking in Gaelic, they left the great masses of rock more desolate
than before.

Suggested Routes

In the following suggested itineraries places which have a separate entry in the A to Z section of this Guide are shown in **bold** type.
   The itineraries are designed to take in the major cities, beauty-spots and features of interest (high crosses, round towers, etc.) in the countryside. Many of the places described in the Guide, however, can be reached only on side roads off the main routes. The map at the end of the book will help in detailed planning.
   Most of the places mentioned in the Guide, whether the subject of a separate entry or not, are included in the index on p. 375.

Note

1. Dublin to Drogheda and Belfast (about 95miles/155km)

From **Dublin** the N1 leads north to Swords, an ancient little town with a ruined castle and a round tower. Continuing at some distance from the sea, it reaches the coast at Balbriggan, with its water-sports facilities, and then continues north-west to **Drogheda** on the River Boyne.

Main route

A detour can be made to the **Boyne Valley** with the famous Newgrange, Knowth and Dowth passage graves, by turning left onto the N51 immediately after crossing the Boyne.

Detour

From Drogheda the N1 runs to Dunleer. About half-way there, to the left of the road, lies the monastic site of **Monasterboice**, with fine high crosses.
   From Dunleer the N1 continues, crossing a number of rivers flowing into Dundalk Bay, to the port of **Dundalk**, only a mile or two short of the Northern Ireland border. Over the border the A1 heads north for Belfast. From Newry the A28 goes north-west to **Armagh**, from which the A3 leads north-east to Lisburn, on the main road to **Belfast**.

Main route

2. Dublin to Arklow and Wexford (about 90miles/140km)

The coast road south from **Dublin** comes in a few miles to **Dun Laoghaire**, from which there are ferry-services to Holyhead in Britain. There the N11 turns away from the coast, skirting the promontory of Dalkey, on the south side of Dublin Bay. A side road on the left leads to **Bray**, one of Ireland's leading seaside resorts. The N11 then continues along the east side of the **Wicklow Mountains**, past country of great scenic beauty and tracts of forest, to Ashford and Rathnew.
   From Rathnew the R750 follows the coast to **Wicklow**, continuing to Wicklow Head (lighthouses).
   From Rathnew it is possible either to continue on the N11 or to take the coast road (Brittas Bay, Mizen Head) to the seaside resort of **Arklow**, where the Avoca River flows into the sea. A detour can be made from here to the Vale of Avoca, to the north-west.
   From Arklow the N11 continues to Gorey and **Enniscorthy**, an attractive town on the River Slaney. The N11 then goes on to **Wexford**, where the Slaney reaches the sea. Wexford can also be reached from Gorey on the R741 and then the R742, which keeps relatively close to the coast.

◀ *The picturesque harbour of Kinsale*

From Wexford various roads continue south to the seaside resort of Rosslare and the ferry port of Rosslare Harbour.

3. Dublin to Waterford and Cork (about 160miles/260km)

Main route — From **Dublin** the N7 leads south-west to **Naas**, once the seat of the kings of Leinster. South of the town lies Punchestown Racecourse.

From Naas the N9 goes south, crossing the River Liffey at Kilcullen. Beyond this the road pases **Moone**, with its famous high cross, and Castledermot, with its round tower. It then descends into the Barrow Valley to **Carlow**, an industrial town with a ruined castle, to the east of which lies Browne's Hill dolmen, Ireland's largest megalithic tomb.

From Carlow the N9 continues south along the right bank of the River Barrow. At Leighlinbridge it crosses the river, and then continues south-west – from Whitehall onwards as the N10 – to **Kilkenny** on the River Nore, one of the most attractive towns in Ireland. From there the N10 – with possible detours to Kilree, which has a round tower and a high cross, and to the Augustinian Priory of Kells – and the N9 (beyond Knocktopher) continue to **Waterford** on the River Suir, celebrated for the production of Waterford glass.

Detour — From Waterford visits can be made to the coastal resorts of Dunmore East (R683, R684) and Tramore (R675).

Main route — The main route (N25) continues from Waterford, at some distance from the coast, to **Dungarvan**, **Youghal** – a detour, a short distance before the town, on the R673 to **Ardmore**, with a round tower – and **Cork**, the principal city in the south of Ireland and a major port.

4. Dublin to Limerick and Killarney (about 125miles/200km)

From Dublin the N7 proceeds south-west to **Naas** and **Kildare**, Ireland's great horse-breeding centre. East of the town lies the Curragh Race-course, on which race-meetings are held from spring to autumn. Crossing the River Barrow and the **Grand Canal**, the N7 continues to **Portlaoise**, an important traffic junction in the centre of Ireland. The route then takes us, with the Slieve Bloom Mountains on the right, to **Roscrea**, and from there via Nenagh to **Limerick**, on the Shannon.

Detour — From Limerick the N24 is the route south-east to **Tipperary**, from where the N74 continues east to **Cashel**, at the foot of the famous Rock of Cashel.

Main route — From Limerick the N20 and N21 (beyond Patrickswell) run via **Adare** and Newcastle West to Abbeyfeale, from where the route continues south on the N21 (to Castleisland), the N23 (to Farranfore) and the N22 to **Killarney**, in the centre of the beautiful Killarney lake district, one of the most popular holiday areas in south-western Ireland.

Killarney is a good base from which to drive round the Iveragh Peninsula on a beautiful scenic road, the **Ring of Kerry**, which hugs the coast for most of the way, with superb views.

5. Dublin to Athlone and Galway (about 135miles/220km)

From **Dublin** the N4 goes west, skirting the **Royal Canal** for part of the way, to Maynooth and Kinnegad. From there our route continues on the N6, via Kilbeggan and Moate, to **Athlone**, at the point where the River Shannon flows out of Lough Ree.

South of the town, on the east bank of the river, are the remains of the   Detour
walled-in monastic settlement of **Clonmacnoise**, with its high crosses,
which can be reached either by boat or on the Shannonbridge road.

From Athlone the main route continues on the N6 to **Ballinasloe** and   Main route
Loughrea (from which there is a possible detour to the Turoe Stone),
and then via Craughwell and Oranmore to **Galway**, on Galway Bay.

Galway, the largest town in the west of Ireland, is a good starting-
point for trips to **Lough Corrib** and around **Connemara**, a region on the
Atlantic coast where Irish is still spoken. From Galway, too, there is a
ferry service as well as an air service to the **Aran Islands**.

6. Dublin to Carrick-on-Shannon and Londonderry (about 205miles/330km)

From **Dublin** the N3 leads north-west via Dunshaughlin to Navan.   Main route

Roughly halfway between Dunshaughlin and Navan, at the village of   Detour
Tara, a road branches off on the left to the Hill of Tara, once the
stronghold of the high kings of Ireland.

Navan is an important road junction; just north of the town, at Donagh-   Main route
more, stands a round tower. From Navan the N51 and N52 (from
Delvin) continue south-west to **Mullingar**, from where the N4 leads
north-west to **Longford** and **Carrick-on-Shannon**, the starting-point for
cabin-cruiser trips on the Shannon. From here the route continues via
Boyle to **Sligo**, on Sligo Bay, to the east of which lies beautiful Lough
Gill. From Sligo the N15 goes north and north-east to **Donegal** and then
over the Barnesmore Gap and through hilly and wooded country to
Balleybofey.

From Ballbofey a detour can be made to the north-west coast of   Detour
Ireland. The N56 leads north into the N13, from which the N56 can be
followed along the coast, by way of various promontories and peninsulas – Horn Head, Rosquill Peninsula, Fanad Peninsula – and then on
the N13 to the Inishowen Peninsula, with the Grianán of Aileach, a
mighty stone fort.

The main route continues east on the N15 to Lifford where, at Strabane   Main route
Bridge, there is a border crossing into Northern Ireland. From here the
A5 runs north, parallel to the River Foyle but at some distance from it,
to **Londonderry** (Derry), a port on Lough Foyle, the old centre of which
is surrounded by its 17th c. town walls. Londonderry is a good base for
coastal trips – for example, to the Giant's Causeway or the Glens of
Antrim.

7. Sligo to Enniskillen and Belfast (about 105miles/170km)

From **Sligo** the N16 leads east and, after crossing the border into
Northern Ireland, continues as the A4 to Enniskillen. From Enniskillen
a short detour can be made to **Lough Erne**. The route then takes us
via Dungannon and past the great expanse of **Lough Neagh** to the
Northern Ireland capital, **Belfast**.

8. Londonderry to Belfast (about 60miles/100km)

From **Londonderry** the route runs inland on the A6 and B74 and then
(from Feny) on the B40 through the Sperrin Mountains, a hilly and

Connemara landscape

Lough Erne: a popular holiday area

wooded region of beautiful and varied scenery with the tourist centre of Gortin, and then via Draperstown to Magherafelt.

From Magherafelt the route (A31, A6, M22) continues to the north of **Lough Neagh** to Antrim, near which stands a well-preserved round tower. The M2 motorway then goes on to **Belfast**, a short way north of which can be found the interesting Ulster Folk and Transport Museum. From Belfast there are attractive trips along the coast north and south of the city.

Ireland from A to Z

Within each entry in this part of the Guide the various buildings and other features of interest are described in a sequence which visitors should find easy to follow whether on foot or by car.

Using this guide

Except for one or two places where the arrangement did not seem appropriate, the surroundings of the various towns are described in clockwise order commencing from the north.

It needs to be borne in mind that references to the Blackwater River are not always to the same river. Ireland has large expanses of peatbog, which give the waters of the local streams a dark tinge. Perhaps not surprisingly therefore, there are three different Irish rivers all called Blackwater. The first forms the border between Northern Ireland and the Republic to the west of Armagh, then turns north-east and flows into Lough Neagh; the second, a left-bank tributary of the Boyne, flows through Lough Ramor north-west of Kells and into the Boyne at Navan; the third and longest of the three rises a short distance north-east of Killarney and flows in an easterly direction past Fermoy and Lismore before turning south through 90° to enter the sea in Youghal Bay.

Note also that in Ireland the term "cathedral" is often applied to a church which, in the strict sense of an episcopal church, is not a cathedral at all.

Achill Island · Oiléan Acaill

B/C 1/2

Republic of Ireland
Province: Connacht
County: Mayo
Population: 3100

Achill Island (Oiléan Acaill) lies off the Republic's western coast, separated from the mainland by the narrow Achill Sound (spanned by a swing bridge). With an area of 55sq. miles/142sq.km it is the largest of Ireland's offshore islands.

Location

Hilly and L-shaped, Achill is almost entirely covered by heath and bog, the only cultivated land being in the valleys and near the coast. The hills on the northern and western sides rise to 2198ft/670m, dropping down to the sea in a series of magnificent cliffs.

Topography

Sights

The main centre on the island is the village of Achill Sound, situated close to the bridge. There are facilities for bathing and sea angling and motor-boats and sailing craft can be hired.

Achill Sound

Near the south end of the island – around which runs a road known as "Atlantic Drive" (views) – the ruins of the 15th c. Carrickkildavnet Castle (National Monument) stand on the shores of Achill Sound. Part of a vaulted stone roof and the remains of an old slipway can be seen. The castle belonged to Grace O'Malley (see Famous People).

Carrickkildavnet Castle

On the north coast, about 7 miles/11km north-west of Achill Sound, is Dugort where in the main street stands the house (with light-blue painted window frames and two chimneys) in which Heinrich Böll and his family

Dugort

◀ An Italian style garden on Garinish Island

75

Achille Island: view of Keem Bay

lived periodically from the 1950s onwards. The cottage, little used in the author's later years, was given a new lease of life in 1992. Now, for several months a year, it is available for use by writers and artists who also receive a small grant.

Among Dugort's other attractions is a good sandy beach. The surrounding area abounds with remains of cairns and chamber tombs.

Slievemore

The ascent of Slievemore (2169ft/661m), a shapely quartzite and mica cone, brings rewards in the form of extensive views to north and south. On the way up, the deserted village of Slievemore can be seen. Only ruins now remain, the village having been abandoned during the Great Famine in the middle of the 19th c.

Below the hill, accessible only from the sea and in good weather, are the Seal Caves, best seen by taking a boat with experienced boatmen from Dugort (2 miles/3km).

Keel

Some 4 miles/6km south-west of Dugort lies Keel, an attractive holiday resort with a sheltered sandy beach, 2 miles/3km long, extending south-east to the foot of Minaun Cliffs which at one point fall 800ft/240m sheer to the sea. Keel is the centre of the island's fish-processing industry.

Dooagh

With its whitewashed houses and white roofs, Dooagh, 3 miles/5km west of Keel, is the prettiest place on the island.

Keem

There is a particularly picturesque stretch of coastal scenery on the road to Keem (5 miles/8km), which has a beautiful sandy beach (Keem Beach; plentiful parking). In dry weather it is possible to walk across the at other times boggy ground to Achill Head at the western end of the island.

Croaghaun

From Keem there is another rewarding climb up Croaghaun (2068ft/630m) further to the west, culminating on the seaward side in a 4 mile/6km-long line of cliffs (magnificent views out over the Atlantic).

The cliff edge should not be approached too closely, the sea having undercut the cliffs in many places.

The pretty little resort of Dooega 5 miles/8km west of Achill Sound is a convenient point from which to climb Minaun Mountain (1840ft/560m) and Minaun Cliffs.

Dooega

Adare · Ath Dara

D 3

Republic of Ireland
Province: Munster
County: Limerick. Population: 800

Adare (Ath Dara="ford of the oak tree") lies in the south-west of Ireland on the wooded west bank of the River Maigue, some 9 miles/15km south-west of Limerick on the busy road to Killarney. In the early 18th c. refugees from the Pfalz region of Germany settled in the area between Adare and Rathkeale, which soon became known as "the Palatine" (the English name for the Pfalz). Germanic customs and traditions survived here until the late 19th c. and German names are still in evidence today.

Location

With its thatched roofs and old grey-walled church, Adare has something of the air of an English village. These picturesque cottages were built in the 19th c. by one of the Earls of Dunraven. The 14-arch stone bridge affords delightful views of the beautifully planted river banks with their backcloth of old buildings.

★Village

Sights

Adare Manor, a Neo-Gothic mansion (1832), formerly the Dunraven family seat, was converted to a luxury hotel (restaurant) some years ago.

★Adare Manor

Thatched cottages in Adare

77

It stands in a large park, the greater part of which is now a golf course. Anyone nevertheless able to gain access will find, on the banks of the river, the extensive ruins of Desmond Castle (13th c.), a truly romantic sight with its semicircular towers and lushly overgrown walls.

Also in the park are the ruins of a Franciscan friary founded in 1464, with later additions paid for by endowments. Of the friary church, the nave, choir and south transept survive (fine fonts, niches and stalls in the choir), also a beautiful cloister with an old yew tree in the centre, and conventual buildings.

Augustinian Friary

Near the bridge over the River Maigue at the eastern end of the village are the restored remains of a 14th c. Augustinian abbey which, in the 19th c., became a Protestant church and school. Since 1826 the cloister has been the mausoleum of the Earls of Dunraven.

Parish church

The Roman Catholic parish church originally belonged to a Trinitarian abbey built in the 13th c. The church took on its present size and form however only in the 19th c.

Surroundings

Croom

5 miles/8km south-east of the town on the N20 lies Croom, with a 12th c. castle restored in the 19th c. In the 18th c. the "Maigue poets" used to meet together in Croom. West of Croom are the ruins of a 15th c. church (National Monument) and a massive round tower (12th c.) the top part of which is missing.

Monasteranenagh

2½m/4km east of Croom are more monastic remains – the ruins of Monasteranenagh Abbey (National Monument), a Cistercian house dating mainly from the 12th c., with some good carving.

Rathkeale

The little market town of Rathkeale lies on the River Deel some 7 miles/11km south-west of Adare, on the main road. Near by stands Castle Matrix (1440), now restored (open: June–Sept. Mon., Wed., Thur., Sat., Sun. 2–4.30pm; period furniture and objets d'art).

Cappagh Castle

Cappagh Castle, about 5 miles/8km west of Adare, is a strongly fortified 70ft/20m-high keep (15th c.) with 16th c. turrets.

Aran Islands · Oileain Arann   C 2

Republic of Ireland
Province: Connacht
County: Galway
Population: about 1600

Location

The Aran Islands (Oileain Arann) lie in the Atlantic south-west of Galway, at distances of between 25 and 30 miles/40 and 50km offshore. There are three principal islands: Inishmore (12sq. miles/30.5sq.km in area), Inishmaan (3½sq. miles/9sq.km) and Inisheer (2¼sq. miles/6sq.km); also four other tiny uninhabited islets.

Tourism has become increasingly important to the Aran Islands in recent years. While many of the visitors are day-trippers, holiday accommodation is also available (bed and breakfast, holiday homes, small guest houses). Despite these new developments, the Aran islanders continue to preserve much of the traditional Irish culture which today has largely disappeared elsewhere; Irish remains the principal spoken tongue. Many books have been written about the islands' tough, staunchly traditional fisherfolk.

Lobster and other fishing is still carried on, providing a second source of income alongside tourism. The island fishermen still use the traditional

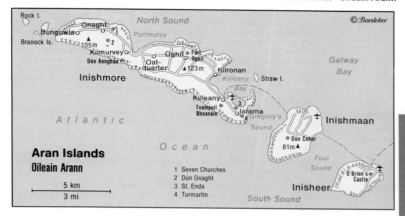

Aran Islands
Oileáin Arann

5 km
3 mi

1 Seven Churches
2 Dún Onaght
3 St. Enda
4 Turmartin

Irish curragh, a lightweight craft built from tarred canvas stretched over a wicker frame; until relatively recently these also served for transporting people and goods to and from the islands.

The Aran Islands can be reached either by sea or air. Aer Arann flies every day to all three islands from Carnmore, 4 miles/6km north-east of Galway. There are several boats a day to Inishmore from Galway and Rossaveal and, in summer, one boat a day to Inishmore from Doolin. Also in summer there is a ferry service to Inishmaan from Spiddal. Inisheer is most conveniently reached from Doolin or, in summer, from Spiddal.

Access

The islands, of karstic limestone, are rugged and infertile. By dint of unremitting toil the islanders have built up successive layers of sand and seaweed into small, irregularly-shaped fields, which they call "gardens", sheltered by drystone walls. The rocky coastline falls in terraces to the sea and there are few beaches. The island flora are of particular interest with many rare species continuing to thrive here, as they do also in the Burren (see entry).

Topography

Until quite recently the islanders still wove woollen cloth from which they made their clothing, and wore handmade shoes of hide, without heels, known as "pampooties". Still very much in evidence are the very durable hand-knitted white wool (bainin) Aran sweaters and the long, coloured, patterned woollen belts called "crios". They can be bought on the islands as well as throughout Ireland.

Hand-knitted woollens

Inishmore

Inishmore, some 7½ miles/12km long by 2 miles/3km wide, today has a population of about 900 (compared with twice that number a century ago). Life on the island is centred on the main settlement, Kilronan, to which the ferries also run.

Housed in the old coastguard station, the Aran Centre (open: daily July–Oct. 10am–7pm) informs visitors about the bleak but beautiful islands and their inhabitants.

Aran Centre

On the edge of the cliffs fringing the south-west coast of Inishmore is the islands' main attraction, the great stone fort of Dún Aenghus, one of the

★★ Dún Aenghus

79

largest prehistoric fortifications in Europe, a huge semicircle of three more or less concentric enclosures on the very brink of sheer cliffs plunging 300ft/90m to the sea. The innermost enclosure, 150ft/45m in diameter, is surrounded by a stepped drystone wall (restored at the end of the 19th c.), 20ft/6m high and 18ft/5.4m thick at the base, incorporating various passages and chambers. The middle rampart is surrounded by a defensive ring of thousands of sharp-pointed stones set close together (*chevaux-de-frise*) in the manner of a modern tank barrier. From the edge of the cliff there is a breath-taking glimpse of the surf far below, and splendid views over the sea.

Oghil Fort　　Further east is another stone fort, Oghil Fort (National Monument), with two concentric ring-walls and steps leading up to the ramparts.

Kilmurvey　　North of Dún Aenghus, at the hamlet of Kilmurvey, are the 9th c. church of St Brecan and Temple MacDuagh, an early choired church.

Dún Onaght　　On a ridge north-west of Kilmurvey stands Dún Onaght, an almost perfectly circular stone fort.

Killeany　　Around Killeany, 2 miles/3km south of Kilronan, are found remnants of numerous ecclesiastical buildings. Of particular interest is Tighlagh Eany, an early church with later features which is all that remains of the monastic settlement of St Enda (Eany). There is a very fine cross shaft with interlace ornamentation and the figure of a horseman in relief. In this same vicinity is St Benan's Church (Teampull Bheanáin), one of the smallest churches in the world, measuring only 10½×7ft/3×2m.

Inishmaan

A steep-sided hill on Inishmaan is the site of another National Monument, Dún Conor, an oval fort with, inside it, a number of stone huts (restored). From the fort there are splendid views. There is also a fine dolmen.

The cottage of the poet and dramatist J. M. Synge who, in his book "The Aran Islands" (1907), first drew attention to the unique character of this delightful little archipelago, has been carefully preserved.

Inisheer

Among the remains on Inisheer are: the medieval tower of O'Brien's Castle, prominently situated on a rocky hill; St Gobnet's Church (Cill Gobnet), a small oratory with features characteristic of Early Irish architecture; and the little St Cavan's Church which, every year on June 14th, is cleared of the sand which drifts ceaselessly over it, so that a service can be held. St Cavan's tomb is similarly swept clear of sand for the occasion.

Ardara · Arda Rath　　　　　　　　　　　　　B 3

Republic of Ireland
Province: Ulster
County: Donegal
Population: 650

Location　　Ardara (Arda Rath="earth hills") is prettily situated on the little River Owentocher in the most northerly county of Ireland, close to the east shore of Loughros More Bay, an arm of the sea penetrating deep inland.

The village is noted particularly for the manufacture of homespun tweeds, also hosiery and embroidery.

Surroundings

Glenties　　Some 7 miles/11km north-east of Ardara, on the River Owenea, lies Glenties, situated in the midst of a wooded region with good fishing in its rivers and loughs. There is a state-owned fish hatchery in the village. Glenties is also known for the manufacture of hosiery and gloves.

North-east of Glenties, Aghla Mountain (1933ft/589m; splendid viewpoint) rises above the long narrow Lough Finn, from the eastern end of which flows the River Finn. The road follows the river for several miles, running along the hillside high above it, with magnificent views.

Aghla Mountain

2 miles/3km south-west of Ardara an unclassified road branches off to the right, winding its way, with sharp bends and steep gradients, through a rugged landscape of bare hills to the Glengesh Pass and on to Glencolumb-kille (see entry).

Glengesh Pass

To the west of Ardara extends a long narrow peninsula ending in Loughros Point, with fine views.

Loughros Point

The Maghera Caves are accessible at low tide from the north shore of Loughros Beg Bay. Near by are the Essaranks Falls. Footpaths continue along the coast, with beautiful scenery; also through the Slievetooey hills (1510ft/460m) to Glencolumbkille.

**Maghera Caves
Essaranks Falls**

North of Ardara the R261 branches west off the N56. Near Kilclooney a massive, highly photogenic dolmen stands in grassy surroundings to the right of the road. (Coming from Adara turn right immediately after the church; the track leads past the bell tower and, after about five minutes, to the very prominent dolmen).

**Kilclooney
★ dolmen**

Further on lie the twin holiday villages of Narin and Portnoo, delightfully situated in the shelter of the hills on the south side of Gweebarra Bay. Narin has a fine sandy beach 1½ miles/2.5km long and an 18-hole golf course. At low tide it is possible to walk (or, more usually, paddle) to the little islet of Inishkeel, with the ruins of an old chapel on the shore.

**Narin and
Portnoo**

Dolmen, Kilclooney

Farther west, on Dunmore Head, are two ancient ring forts from which there are fine views.

Lough Doon

1½ miles/2.5km south of Portnoo, on an island in Lough Doon, stands a massive and well-preserved oval stone fort called "The Bawn" (signposted).

Rosbeg

The quiet little resort of Rosbeg, 3 miles/5km south of Portnoo, has a sandy beach and good fishing for brown trout in the loughs round it.

Ardmore · Ard mor   E 4

Republic of Ireland
Province: Munster
County: Waterford. Population: 300

Location

Ardmore (Ard mor="big hill") is an attractive little resort half-way along the south coast of Ireland. Lying some 2½ miles/4km east of the N25, it offers a good beach and fine cliffs; the village itself is a mixture of old and new.

Sights

★ Round tower

Ardmore's well-preserved round tower (12th c.; National Monument) is one of the latest such towers in Ireland, with four tapering storeys rising to a height of 95ft/29m and a round-arched doorway set high above the ground. Inside the tower are projecting stones carved with grotesque heads.

★ St Declan's Church

Adjoining the tower is the ruined St Declan's Church or "Cathedral" (13th c.; National Monument). It bears the name of a bishop who founded a monastery here in Early Christian times and who is still honoured by an annual pilgrimage (on July 24th). The blind arcading on the west gable incorporates very fine Romanesque reliefs, regrettably much weathered. In the upper tier is a figure of the Archangel Michael weighing souls, while below are seen Adam and Eve, the Judgment of Solomon and the Adoration of the Magi. In the choir of the church are two ogham stones.

Built on to the "cathedral" is St Declan's House, which is believed to contain the saint's tomb (an important station on the annual pilgrimage).

Dysert Church

About ½ mile/800m east of the main group of buildings are the ruins of Dysert Church, clearly a church of some size in its day. Near by is St Declan's Well (restored 1798), a sacred well in which pilgrims used to bathe.

St Declan's Stone

At the southern end of the beach is an erratic boulder known as St Declan's Stone. It is said that anyone crawling beneath it – an impossible feat, apparently, for those in a state of sin – will be cured of rheumatism.

Surroundings

There are many pleasant walks along the cliffs – to the sea caves at Ardmore Head and Ram Head east and south of the village; to Whiting Bay (west of Ardmore); and to the beautiful Monatray Bay (sandy beach).

Arklow · Inbhear Mor   D 5

Republic of Ireland
Province: Leinster
County: Wicklow. Population: 8650

Arklow (Inbhear Mor="broad estuary") is situated on the N11, the main road from Dublin to the south. Here the River Avoca, from which the Vale of Avoca takes its name, flows into the Irish Sea. In addition to its good sandy bays, Arklow is a lively small town with a fertiliser factory and potteries (guided tours).

Location

Arklow has had an eventful history. There is a tradition that St Patrick landed here. In later centuries the town was much fought over, changing hands several times. The last battle to take place here, during the 1798 Rising, is commemorated by a memorial in front of the Roman Catholic Church.

History

The Arklow Maritime Museum is certainly worth visiting.
   Beyond the south beach and golf course lies Arklow Rock, its Well of Our Lady still much venerated today.

Sights

Surroundings

From Arklow the R747 heads north-westwards along the River Avoca. To the right of the road, in a park with lovely rhododendrons and other beautiful shrubs, stands Shelton Abbey, now a government-run school of forestry.

Shelton Abbey

At Woodenbridge the R752 branches off northwards into the lovely Vale of Avoca, a celebrated beauty-spot. In spring the valley, fringed with green hills, is white with the blossom of wild cherry trees. In pre-Christian times, copper, lead, zinc and sulpher were all mined here; today too the Vale is becoming increasingly industrialised, as a result of which some parts are no longer as scenic as they used to be.
   The principal centre of population in the Vale is the village of Avoca, widely known for its hand-loom weaving. Avoca Handweavers welcome visitors and their hand-made goods are of course on sale.

Vale of Avoca

Some 3 miles/5km farther up the valley Castle Howard looks down from its crag upon the famous "Meeting of the Waters", where the Rivers Avonmore and Avonbeg flow into the Avoca. A good view of the confluence is obtained from the Lion's Bridge.

Meeting of the Waters

Another 2 miles/3km further on lies the Avondale Forest Park, an extensive woodland park in which stands the house where the great Irish patriot Charles Stewart Parnell (see Famous People) was born. Designed by James Wyatt and built in 1779, the mansion has a particularly lovely interior. Parnell's life is documented on video (open: daily 11am–5.30pm).

Avondale Forest Park

Armagh · Ard Macha

B 5

Northern Ireland
District: Armagh
Population: 13,000

Armagh (Ard Macha="Macha's hill") is in Northern Ireland, to the south-west of Lough Neagh. Situated at the junction of several main roads, it is the principal town of the district and, as the seat of both a Roman Catholic cardinal and Protestant archbishop, has an important place in the religious life of the province. Textiles and fish processing are the mainstays of its economy. The surrounding area is known as the "garden of Ulster" on account of its apple orchards and is particularly lovely in May when the trees are in blossom ("Apple Blossom Route, signposted, starting and finishing in Armagh).

Location

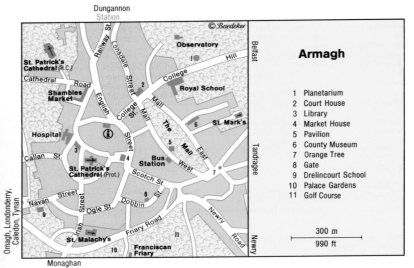

© *Baedeker*

Armagh

1 Planetarium
2 Court House
3 Library
4 Market House
5 Pavilion
6 County Museum
7 Orange Tree
8 Gate
9 Drelincourt School
10 Palace Gardens
11 Golf Course

300 m
990 ft

History	The town takes its name ("Macha's hill") from the legendary Queen Macha, who in the 3rd c. built a stronghold, now known as Navan Fort (see Surroundings, Navan Fort), on a hill 2 miles/3km to the west. Armagh gained in importance in Early Christian times, St Patrick founding a monastery and a church here in about 445. The settlement developed into a centre of missionary activity, and the "Book of Armagh" was written in the monastery. Over the centuries the town has several times been burned down and rebuilt.
The town	Armagh is a friendly little town, many of its buildings being constructed of the pink, yellow or reddish sandstone known as "Armagh marble", a favourite building material of the 18th c. architect Francis Johnston (1761–1829), himself a native of Armagh. Johnston designed many public buildings and Georgian town houses along the town's principal thoroughfare, the elongated green known as The Mall.

Sights

County Museum	The County Museum (open: Mon.–Sat. 10am–1pm and 2–5pm) occupies a former school house in The Mall dating from the first half of the 19th c. In addition to interesting sections devoted to archaeology and natural and local history, the museum possesses a sizeable library. Also on display are paintings by George Russell (1867–1935) and James Sleator (1889–1950), the latter having painted the portraits of many local dignatories.
Court House	At the north-west end of The Mall stands the Court House, designed by Francis Johnston and built 1805–09.
Observatory	From the Court House, College Hill runs north-east, past, on the right, the Royal School founded in 1608 by James I, to the Armagh Astronomy Centre, where the Observatory, established in 1791, is open to the public. The Centre also incorporates a Planetarium, opened in 1968 (presentations

every afternoon except Sunday), and a Hall of Astronomy in which are displayed assorted pieces of astronomical apparatus and a model of a spacecraft.

Proceeding south-west from The Mall, and past the fine 18th c. Market House, St Patrick's Protestant Cathedral is reached. It stands on the site of the church founded by St Patrick in the 5th c. The cathedral acquired its present aspect in the course of a 19th c. restoration by Lewis Cottingham. Notable features of the interior are a 10th c. crypt, several monuments (including that of Sir Thomas Molyneux) and a bust of Archbishop Richard Robinson who, in the 18th c., was responsible for so much of what makes Armagh the attractive place it is today. On the cathedral's outside wall can be seen a tablet supposedly marking the grave of the Irish king Brian Boru, killed at the Battle of Clontarf in 1014 and buried here by his own wish.

St Patrick's Protestant Cathedral

Likewise commandingly situated on a hill, in the north-west of the town, is the Roman Catholic St Patrick's Cathedral, a Neo-Gothic building (1840–73) the interior decoration of which includes mosaic work by Italian artists.

St Patrick's Roman Catholic Cathedral

To the south of the town, on land once belonging to the old Archbishops' Palace, are the remnants of a Franciscan friary founded in 1266.

Franciscan friary

The former stables of the old Archbishops' Palace now house craft workshops and a café. Horse-drawn carriages can also be hired here.

Palace stables

Surroundings

Navan Fort (Eamhain Macha), 2 miles/3km west of Armagh on the A28, was for centuries the seat of the kings of Ulster. There are graves and earthworks and, from the hill, a fine panorama of the surrounding country; also a Visitor Centre with information on the fort and its history.

Navan Fort

9 miles/14km west of Armagh lies the village of Caledon, 2 miles/3km south-west of which stands Caledon House, a part-Georgian, part-Regency mansion (1779) set in beautiful gardens.

Caledon

At Tynan, south of Caledon, are a number of 12th c. high crosses carved with biblical scenes.

Tynan

Athlone · Ath Luain

C 4

Republic of Ireland
Province: Leinster
County: Westmeath
Population: 9450

Athlone (Ath Luain="ford of Luan") is situated almost exactly at the geographical centre of Ireland. It lies on the River Shannon which, to the north of the town, flows through Lough Ree and forms the provincial boundary between Leinster and Connacht. Athlone is a busy road and rail junction and also a haven (marina) for pleasurecraft on the Shannon (see entry) and Lough Ree. It has developed a number of light industries and is the main shopping and commercial centre for the region. Not far to the east of the town is the powerful Athlone long-wave radio transmitter.

Location

This has been an important crossing-point of the Shannon since time immemorial. By the end of the first millennium A.D. the river was already spanned by a wattle bridge. In the 13th c. a bridgehead was constructed comprising a castle and riverside defences; again and again in later centuries these were the scene of fierce fighting, being several times razed and rebuilt.

History

Sights

Athlone Castle
Known also as King John's Castle, Athlone Castle was built in 1210 on the instructions of England's King John. It acquired its present appearance mainly at the beginning of the 19th c. Designated a National Monument in 1970, the castle now houses a Visitor Centre with several exhibition rooms highlighting the history of the town and the flora and fauna of the Shannon region. A small section celebrates the life and work of the distinguished Irish tenor John McCormack (1884–1945), born in Athlone (open: Apr.–Sept. daily 10am–4.30pm).

Church of
St Peter and
St Paul
The Neo-Renaissance Church of St Peter and St Paul, close by the bridge, dates from 1937. The tenor John McCormack is one of several well-known figures depicted in the stained glass.

Surroundings

Poets' Country
From Athlone the N55 runs north-eastwards through the so-called Poets' Country of Oliver Goldsmith and John Keegan Casey. Goldsmith went to school in Lissoy (described in his "Deserted Village").

Bealin
4½ miles/7km east of Athlone, on a by-road near the Athlone radio transmitter, lies the village of Bealin where, on a nearby hill in the grounds of Twyford House, stands a 9th c. high cross (National Monument) carved with hunting scenes, entwined animal figures and other ornamental patterns.

Athy · Baile Atha h-I   D 5

Republic of Ireland
Province: Leinster
County: Kildare. Population: 4300

Location
Athy (Baile Atha h-I="ford of I"), the largest town in Co. Kildare, lies south-west of Dublin on the River Barrow, at a point which was an important fording-place. A branch of the Grand Canal (see entry) joins the Barrow at this same point.

Sights

White's Castle
White's Castle, built by the Earl of Kildare in the 16th c. to protect the bridge across the Barrow, is a massive rectangular structure with corner turrets. The bridge has the unusual name of "Crom-a-boo", from the war-cry of the Desmonds (an Earl of Desmond was appointed governor by the English in 1420).

Woodstock Castle
½ mile/800m north, on the L18, is the 13th c. Woodstock Castle, likewise built to guard the river crossing. It was severely damaged in 1649.

Dominican church
Downstream from White's Castle stands the Dominican church (1963–65; by John Thompson), built on a pentagonal plan with an ingenious, spherically-vaulted roof. Inside are several notable works of art including fine stained glass and Stations of the Cross by George Campbell.

Court and Market
House
The old Court and Market House, a fine Georgian building (18th c.), is now the fire station.

Surroundings

4½ miles/7km north-east of Athy, on the N78, is the Motte of Ardskull, a 30ft/9m-high circular earthwork dating from the 12th c.

Motte of Ardskull

Ballitore, 5 miles/8km east of the Motte of Ardskull, was once a Quaker settlement with a famous school. The former Meeting House is now a bookshop and small museum. Another attraction is the Crookstown Historical and Heritage Centre in a restored mid-19th c. mill; the mill-wheel still operates. The numerous exhibits illustrate the techniques of corn-milling and bread-making over the centuries (open: Apr.–Sept. daily 10am–7pm; Oct.–Mar. Sun. 10am–4pm).

Ballitore

Just off the N9 at Moone, south of Ballitore, by a ruined 13th c. church (to the right of the road when coming from Dublin), stands a slender high cross, 17½ft/5m high, decorated with a series of superb bas reliefs in a naïve style: on the east side Daniel with seven lions, Abraham's sacrifice, Adam and Eve, and the Crucifixion; on the west side the Twelve Apostles, the Crucifixion, the Virgin Mary and St John; on the north side the Miracle of the Loaves and Fishes, the Flight into Egypt, the Three Men in the Fiery Furnace and assorted animals; on the south side further human figures and animals.

Moone
★high cross

At Baltinglass, on the N81 east of Moone, can be seen remains of a 12th c. Cistercian monastery, Valle Salutis (National Monument), the nave and chancel being decorated with stone carvings in a mixture of styles (Irish Romanesque, Cistercian). A section of the transept has been restored; the tower and east window date from the 19th c. Rising above the village, to the north-east, is Baltinglass Hill (1237ft/377m) with, on its summit, a large megalithic tomb (New Stone Age; National Monument). Around this a hill fort was evidently constructed at a later date (sometime between 500 B.C. and A.D. 500 ?). Stone ramparts are still visible. From the top of the hill there is a superb panoramic view.

Baltinglass

Further interesting ruins are found at Castledermot, 5 miles/8km south of Moone on the N9. They include the remains of a very ancient monastery (National Monument) with a Romanesque doorway, a round tower, the upper part of which is medieval, and two granite high crosses embellished with biblical scenes. The relief of David with his harp on the more northerly of the two crosses is of particular interest as one of the few early representations of an Irish harp. On the south side of Castledermot are the ruins of a Franciscan friary (National Monument) founded in the 14th c. and dissolved in the 16th c.

Castledermot

3 miles/5km along the road leading north-west from Castledermot back in the direction of Athy, lies Kilkea Castle, dating from 1180. Considerably altered in the 19th c., it is now a luxury hotel and health farm.

Kilkea Castle

Ballina · Béal an Aithe

B 2

Republic of Ireland
Province: Connacht
County: Mayo
Population: 6900

Ballina · Béal an Aithe

Location

Ballina (Béal an Aithe="mouth of the ford") lies in the far north-west of Ireland, in bog country on the banks of the River Moy, at the point where it widens out before entering Killala Bay on the Atlantic coast.

As the largest town in Co. Mayo, Ballina is the marketing centre for an extensive hinterland. For anglers it makes a good base from which to fish the River Moy and two well-stocked loughs, Conn and Cullin.

Sights

The Roman Catholic cathedral (20th c.) has fine stained glass. Close by are the remains of a 15th c. Augustinian friary. Near the railway station there is a dolmen (National Monument) marking the grave of four brothers said to have murdered their foster-father, a bishop, in the 6th c.

Surroundings

Inishcrone

Inishcrone (also spelled Enniscrone), a good 9 miles/15km north of Ballina, is a popular holiday resort at the wide mouth of the River Moy in Killala Bay. It has two well-appointed spas offering sulphur and other medicinal baths as well as sea-water baths and saunas.

The remains of Castle Firbis, about 2½ miles/4km north of Inishcrone on the R297, are of interest because the MacFirbis family produced several notable scholars. It was a MacFirbis who compiled the "Great Book of Lecan", an important early 15th c. genealogy (c. 1416; now in the Royal Irish Academy, Dublin); two other codices were also compiled here.

Foxford

At Foxford, a quick 10 miles/16km south of Ballina on the N57, the Foxford Woollen Mills Visitor Centre has recently been opened. The River Moy, winding its way through the little town, once provided the water-power which drove the spinning mills. Set up in one of the old mill buildings, the Visitor Centre explains the process of wool production in the 19th c. and today (open: Mon.–Sat. 10am–6pm, Sun. 2–6pm).

Lough Conn,
Lough Cullin,
Pontoon

From Ballina the R310 runs south before crossing the narrow isthmus separating Lough Conn, famous for its pike, from Lough Cullin (fine views from the bridge). Fishing in both loughs is free. Pontoon is a popular fishing resort where boats can be hired.

Nephin Mor

Heading north again from Pontoon, the R315 skirts round the southern and western sides of Lough Conn. Over to the left, rising from the low-lying countryside, is the impressive silhouette of Nephin Mor (2626ft/800m). Seen from a distance from the north-east, it has the all the majesty of a sacred mountain.

Crossmolina

At the north-west end of Lough Conn, on the N59, lies Crossmolina. As well as a peat-fired power-station, numerous remains of ring forts and other ancient structures are found in the surrounding area. 6 miles/10km south-east, on a peninsula reaching out into the lough, are the ruins of Errew Abbey (13th c.; National Monument).

Ballycastle

From Crossmolina the R315 continues north to Ballycastle, in an area of outstanding Atlantic coastal scenery. On Downpatrick Head, 4 miles/6km north, the forces of nature have sculpted fantastic shapes in the sandstone cliffs along the shore and the isolated stacks in the sea.

★★Céide Fields

Céide Fields, located 5 miles/8km west of Ballycastle on the R314, is a Neolithic archaeological site extending over 3¼sq. miles/10sq.km. It illustrates how this area would have appeared c. 5000 years ago when incomers cleared the forests and laid out pasture. The new arrivals lived in individual farmsteads, each with a long narrow piece of ground separated from its neighbours by walls. Intriguingly, if one of these walls has had to be diverted round an obstacle such as a rock, all the adjacent walls follow suit. To the uninitiated the remains of these walls, exposed from beneath a thick layer of peat, appear less than impressive. However a Visitor Centre, opened in spring 1993, puts this remarkable discovery into perspective (open: mid Mar.–May, Oct. daily 10am–5pm; Jun.–Sept. daily 9.30am–6.30pm; Nov. daily 10am–4.30pm; the excavation site itself is accessible at all times). More excavations, this time dating from 1500 B.C., can be seen near Belderg, 5 miles/8km west.

Returning eastwards from Ballycastle, it is worth taking the minor road along the coast via Rathlackan to Carrowmore, there branching left to the sea at Lackan Bay. The road comes to an end at Kilcummin where the picturesque ruins of a little 7th c. church, with a sacred well and old gravestones, stand in lonely isolation by the shore. Further south the road passes by the remains of Rathfran Friary (13th c.; National Monument); surviving from the church are the nave, choir and a 15th c. chapel.

Kilcummin, Rathfran Friary

4 miles/6km further south, at Killala, stands a well-preserved round tower 84ft/26m high, adjoining which is a small 17th c. "cathedral". In 1798 a French expeditionary force, having landed in Kilcummin Bay to support the rebellion, held out in Killala for some time against British troops.

Killala

Not far beyond Killala a side road branching off left runs south-eastwards to Moyne Abbey, a 15th c. Franciscan house close to the sea. Considerable remains survive, albeit in state of ruin, including the nave, choir (with side chapel) and tower of the church, the cloister with its vaulting, the chapter-house, refectory, kitchen and dorters.

★Moyne Abbey

2½ miles/4km south, and well worth a visit, is Rosserk Friary (National Monument), another 15th c. Franciscan house preserving extensive remains (to reach it, continue past Moyne Abbey on the same small road in the direction of Ballina, eventually turning left at the signpost). A richly carved doorway leads into the aisleless church with a chapel in the south

Rosserk Friary

Moyne Abbey

transept. There are lovely windows, a double font (with a carving of a round tower on one of the supports) and a square tower. The conventual buildings are two-storeyed.

Ballinasloe · Béal Átha an Sluagh   C 3

Republic of Ireland
Province: Connacht
County: Galway
Population: 6400

Location

Ballinasloe (Béal Átha an Sluagh="mouth of the ford of the hosts") lies in the centre of Ireland on the N6 south-west of Lough Ree.

A place of some military importance in earlier times, Ballinasloe is now a busy market town, famous for its horse, cattle and sheep fairs. The great October Fair is the biggest in Ireland. Before the days of motor traction, when cavalry were still a major force in warfare, this particular horse fair could claim to be the largest in Europe.

Ballinasloe is the western terminus of the Grand Canal (see entry) although today the final section is no longer navigable.

Sights

The town has a number of handsome 18th c. houses. Above the River Suck rises Ivy Castle (19th c.), erected on the foundations of an earlier stronghold. In a park on the south-west edge of the town stands Garbally Court, a fine Late Georgian mansion built of the local limestone (now a school).

Surroundings

Clontuskert Abbey

5 miles/8km south of Ballinasloe on the R355 are the ruins of an Augustinian house, Clontuskert Abbey (National Monument). The west doorway of the church (1471) is notable for its carvings – Michael weighing souls, saints, a pelican, a mermaid with a mirror, etc.

★Clonfert

From Clontuskert the R355 continues to Laurencetown, beyond which a side road on the left leads to Clonfert, 13 miles/21km south-east of Ballinasloe and site of an ancient monastic settlement. The doorway of the "cathedral" (National Monument), below the massive west tower, is a supreme example of Irish Romanesque sculpture. Above six recessed orders of round-headed arches, richly decorated with stylised patterns and borne on inward-sloping columns, rises a tall triangular pediment embellished with a row of five narrow blind arches and, above them, a panel decorated with a diamond pattern; the lower half of each diamond is recessed and carved with a human head, while the upper half has carved ornamentation. More heads, alternately bearded and clean-shaven, adorn the arches and other available spaces. The east windows in the choir are among the finest examples of Late Romanesque art. The (later) decoration of the interior is also notably fine, especially that of the arches supporting the tower (with figures of angels and a mermaid), the chancel arch, and the 15th c. windows.

Kilconnell Abbey

7 miles/11km west of Ballinasloe, on the R348, stands Kilconnell Abbey (National Monument), a Franciscan friary founded in 1353. The church, with its slender, graceful tower rising above the crossing, and beautifully carved west doorway, is a splendid example of Gothic architecture. In the north wall are two remarkable canopy tombs, the first, to the left of the entrance, embellished with figures of saints displaying foreign, probably French, influence, the other in the choir. Around the church are conventual buildings with many masons' marks.

Aughrim

At Aughrim, 2½ miles/4km south-east of Kilconnell, there is an interesting local museum with material from the Stone Age onwards. The Aughrim

Interpretative Centre (open: May–Sept. daily 10am–6pm) commemorates
a 1691 battle referred to in Irish history as "Aughrim's great disaster".

Ballinrobe · Baile an Rodbha   C 2

Republic of Ireland
Province: Connacht
County: Mayo
Population: 1450

Ballinrobe (Baile an Rodbha="town of the River Robe") is situated in the   Location
west of Ireland at the point where the N84 crosses the River Robe. To the
west of the town is Lough Mask (good fishing) and beyond it the range of
hills known as the Partry Mountains, of which the highest is Benwee
(2206ft/672m). Ballinrobe is popular both as an angling centre and as a base
from which to explore the surrounding area.

Surroundings

The road from Ballinrobe to Ballintubber (N84) crosses the narrow isthmus   Lough Mask,
between Loughs Mask and Carra. The shores of both are heavily indented,   Lough Carra
and the two are linked by an underground stream. A cairn on an islet in the
green waters of Lough Carra marks the grave of the writer George Moore
(1852–1933).

9 miles/15km north of Ballinrobe, on a by-road off to the right of the N84,   ★Ballintubber
lies Ballintubber, or Ballintober, Abbey (National Monument), an Augusti-   Abbey
nian house founded in 1216. Despite the devastation wrought by Cromwell's troops in 1653, it has remained a place of active worship ever since.
The cruciform church and cloister were sensitively restored in 1963–66. A
not usually accessible chapel in the choir contains an elaborate altar-tomb
with finely carved figures on the pediment.
   The abbey lay on the pilgrim route to Ireland's holiest mountain, Croagh
Patrick (see Louisburgh), glimpsed in the distance through the arches of the
cloister.

About 6 miles/10km south of Ballinrobe a side-road branching off towards   Lough Mask
the east shore of Lough Mask leads to Lough Mask House and park. In the   House
last quarter of the 19th c. this was the residence of Captain Charles Boycott
(1832–97), agent of an English landlord, who treated the tenants so badly
that, one day in 1880, they resolved to have nothing further to do with him.
Eschewing violence, they simply refused to work for him or sell him their
produce. Labourers had thereupon to be brought in from the northern
counties to gather in the potato harvest under military protection, render-
ing the crop totally unprofitable. This form of passive resistance eventually
compelled Boycott to retreat to England, at the same time enriching the
English language with a new word.

On Inishmaine, a small island in Lough Mask, separated from the park by a   Inishmaine
narrow strip of water, are the ruins of a small 13th c. Augustinian friary   Island
(National Monument). The cruciform church boasts some good carving
(animals, foliage).

Ballybunion · Baile an Bhuinne-aneigh   D 2

Republic of Ireland
Province: Munster
County: Kerry
Population: 1350

Location	Ballybunion (Baile an Bhuinne-aneigh="town of the sapling") is a popular family resort in south-west Ireland. It lies on a more or less west-facing stretch of coast where the Shannon emerges from between the headlands flanking its estuary ("Mouth of the Shannon") to disgorge at last into the Atlantic. With its sea-caves, rugged cliffs, coves and seemingly endless fine sandy beaches, Ballybunion offers a wide variety of attractions for seaside holidays in a thoroughly delightful area.

Sights

Caves, footpath	In the cliffs to the north of the town are many caves, some accessible only by boat, others reachable on foot at low water. A 3 mile/5km-long footpath runs along the top of the cliffs between Doon Cove and Doon Point – both with remains of headland forts – and past the old stronghold of Lick Castle.
Knockanore Mountain	To the east of Ballybunion, rising out of the flat surrounding countryside, is Knockanore Mountain (866ft/264m), from which there are superb views.

Surroundings

Ballylongford	From Ballybunion the R551 leads north-east to Ballylongford, at the head of a narrow inlet. On the west side of the inlet stands Carrigafoyle Castle (15th c.; National Monument), with a 85ft/26m-high keep (lovely views).
	To the east of the little town are the ruins of a beautiful Franciscan house, Lisloughtin Abbey (15th c.; National Monument). The church has a fine west window and there are remains of conventual buildings.
Tarbert	5 miles/8km beyond Ballylongford on the R551 lies Tarbert, from where a car ferry crosses the Shannon to Killimer (Co. Clare; see Kilkee).
	The Tarbert Bridewell (open: Apr.–Oct. daily 10am–6pm) gives an insight into crime and punishment in the 19th c. (wax figures are used to reconstruct scenes in the former courthouse and adjoining prison, telling the story of Thomas Dillon's conviction and punishment).
	1¼ miles/2km north, on Tarbert Island (connected to the mainland by a causeway), are a lighthouse and old battery.
Listowel	Listowel, a busy little town about 9 miles/14km south-east of Ballybunion, is said to have more pubs than houses. It is famous for its Writers' Week, held every year in June. Harvest Festival is another major event in the local calendar, being still combined with a marriage fair (end of September).
Cashen Bay	South of Ballybunion the River Feale flows through a fjord-like estuary, Cashen Bay, to the sea. Here there is a well-known salmon-hatchery, Cashen Fishery, which visitors can inspect.
★Rattoo Round Tower	1¼ miles/2km south, on the site of an old monastic settlement (Rattoo), are a 15th c. church and the excellently preserved 92ft/28m-high Rattoo Round Tower (National Monument).

Bantry · Beanntraighe   E 2

Republic of Ireland
Province: Munster
County: Cork
Population: 2900

Location	Bantry (Beanntraighe="descendants of Beann") lies sheltered by surrounding hills in the extreme south-west of Ireland, at the head of the famous and beautiful bay which bears its name. The influence of the Gulf

View of Bantry Bay from Bantry House ▶

Bantry House

Stream is evident in the climate and vegetation of the area, with tall fuchsia hedges and palms frequent features of the landscape.

History

Bantry Bay has twice been entered by French fleets – once in 1689, in support of James II, and again in 1796, bringing aid to the Irish rebels. Neither expedition was successful. In 1796 the ships could not even put in to land on account of fog and violent storms.

The town

Though lively enough, Bantry is not a particularly attractive town, an impression reinforced by the presence of the deep water oil terminal on nearby Whiddy Island, capable of handling supertankers.

★ Bantry House

Opening times
House and park:
daily 9am–6pm
(8pm in spring and
summer)

In lovely grounds on the outskirts of the town stands Bantry House, a Georgian mansion begun in 1740. In 1771 alterations were carried out by the first Earl of Bantry, and in 1840 the house was substantially enlarged by the addition of two side wings, creating a long, finely proportioned building of fourteen bays. It boasts a valuable collection of works of art from all over Europe (icons, Gobelins, French furniture) while mosaics from Pompeii embellish the hall.

There is a pretty tea-room, comfortably furnished; in summer teas are also served out of doors.

Park

The park, with Italian-style terraces and statuary, is laid out on the slopes of a hill. From the terraces there are extensive views over Bantry Bay, with its islands and inlets.

Armada Museum

Situated opposite Bantry House is the Bantry French Armada Exhibition Centre (open: Easter–Sept. daily 10am–6pm). In the winter of 1796 a French fleet of 43 vessels carrying 16,000 men was dispatched to support the "United Irishmen" in their resistance to the British. Bad weather prevented all but sixteen ships from reaching Bantry Bay, and after only a minor skirmish or two the French were forced to withdraw. In 1985 the wreck of the French frigate "La Surveillante" was discovered lying in 100ft/30m of water. There is a model of the ship in the Armada Museum.

Surroundings

Two roads run through particularly lovely scenery near Bantry, the first north-east over Cousane Gap to Macroom (see entry), the second the coast road to Glengarriff (see entry), with magnificent views of the sea and the hills

Scenic drive

To the north of the town on the Glengarriff road are the Donemare Falls on the River Mealagh. There is good fishing in the river and in Drombrow Lough above it, also in Lough Bofinna.

Donemare Falls

Extending south-west of Bantry is the long and scenically magnificent Sheep's Head peninsula, with good beaches at Kilcrohane and Ahakista on the peninsula's south coast.

Sheep's Head Peninsula

There is a splendid drive round the peninsula to its westerly tip, the Sheep's Head. Between Kilcrohane and Gouladoo the road skirts the foot of Seefin (1116ft/340m), from which there are splendid views to the north over Bantry Bay and the hills of the Beara peninsula beyond.

Belfast · Béal Feirste   B 5/6

Northern Ireland
Province: Ulster
District: Belfast
Population: 300,000 (conurbation 550,000)

Belfast (Béal Feirste="sandy ford") is situated in the north-east corner of Ireland at the outflow of the River Lagan into Belfast Lough. The "capital" of Northern Ireland since 1920, it is an important industrial city and port. On Queen's Island is the famous Harland and Wolff shipyard, established in 1859. One of the largest shipyards in the world, employing 10,000 men, it made its name at the beginning of the century when it built mainly passenger ships, among them the "Titanic", launched in 1912. Today oil tankers and freighters have replaced the liners.

Location

Belfast already possessed a fort in the early Middle Ages but this was destroyed in 1177. Subsequently a castle was built, control of which was often disputed between the native Irish and their English conquerors. In 1613 the town which had grown up around the castle was granted a charter by James I. The manufacture of linen had long been an important industry in Belfast, and it received a further boost in the latter part of the 17th c. when Huguenots fleeing from France introduced improved industrial methods. The newcomers also contributed to the development of the town's intellectual life. Following the union with Britain (1800), Belfast became the industrial capital of Ireland. Its splendid 19th c. buildings earned it the soubriquet "Athens of the North". In addition to linen manufacture, rope-making, shipbuilding and tobacco all contributed to its economic success. The city however never really recovered from the period of depression between the two World Wars, and unemployment remains extremely high (in some areas 50% of the male working population are without jobs).

History

Belfast city centre lies on the west bank of the River Lagan, which is spanned by several bridges within the city boundary. Donegall Square and the adjoining streets, Royal Avenue in particular, are the main shopping area, with several large department stores. The university district, with its narrow, quiet, tree-lined streets of small shops, galleries and Victorian houses is especially attractive.

City centre

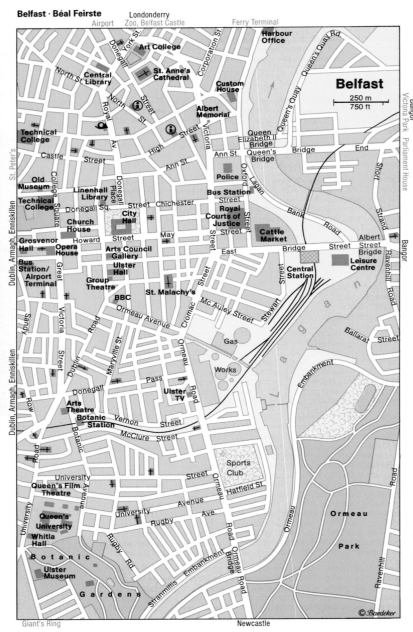

Belfast · Béal Feirste

Londonderry
Airport Zoo, Belfast Castle   Ferry Terminal

York St.

Harbour
Office

Corporation St.

Belfast

250 m
750 ft

Queen's Quay Rd.

Queen's Quay

Victoria Park · Parliament House

Bangor

Donegall

Art College

**Central
Library**

North St.

St. Anne's
Cathedral

**Custom
House**

**Albert
Memorial**

Queen
Elizabeth II
Bridge

Queen's
Bridge

Bridge

End

Short

Strand

Royal
Av.

North
St.

Street

High
Street

Victoria

Ann St.

Castle   Street

**Technical
College**

College Square

Ann St.

**Old
Museum**

**Linenhall
Library**

Donegall
Place

Street   Chichester

Police

Bus Station
Street

Oxford Street

Lagan

Bank   Road

**Technical
College**

Donegall Sq.

**City
Hall**

**Royal
Courts of
Justice**
Street

Albert
Street
Brigde

**Church
House**

Howard   Street

May   Street

**Cattle
Market**

Ravenhill   Road

**Grosvenor
Hall**

**Opera
House**

**Arts Council
Gallery**

**Ulster
Hall**

East   Street

Bridge   Street

**Central
Station**

**Leisure
Centre**

St. Peter's

Dublin, Armagh, Enniskillen

**Bus
Station/
Airport
Terminal**

Great

Victoria

Street

Dublin

Road

Sandy

Row

**Group
Theatre**

BBC

St. Malachy's

Ormeau   Avenue

Cromac   Street

Mc Auley Street

Stewart   Street

Gas

Works

Ballarat   Street

Embankment

L a g a n

Maryville St.

Donegall

Pass

Ormeau   Road

**Ulster
TV**

**Arts
Theatre**

**Botanic
Station**

Vernon   Street

McClure   Street

Sports
Club

Street

Hatfield St.

O r m e a u

P a r k

Ormeau   Avenue

Ave.

University   Avenue

**Queen's Film
Theatre**

University

Road

University   Rugby   Road

**Queen's
University**

Whitla Hall

Rugby   Rd.

B o t a n i c

**Ulster
Museum**

G a r d e n s

Stranmillis   Embankment

Ormeau
Bridge

Ormeau   Road

Ravenhill   Road

Giant's Ring   Newcastle

© Baedeker

For many years now Belfast has suffered repeatedly from terrorist violence associated with the Northern Ireland conflict. The "troubles", as the bloody sectarian dispute over Ulster's continued union with Britain is euphemistically known, exercise a profound influence on the everyday life and economic fortunes of the city. The boundaries between Catholic and Protestant districts away from the city centre are not always as clearly defined as they are in mainly Catholic West Belfast, where barbed-wire and walls separate the two communities. Segregation extends to schools, pubs and other areas of social life.

Northern Ireland conflict

Following the IRA ceasefire on September 1st 1994, security in Belfast was gradually relaxed. Though armoured vehicles still patrol the streets, the police and military presence is considerably reduced. In September 1994 the European Union allocated a budget of 2.4 million ecus for projects intended to bring the Catholic and Protestant communities closer together.

Central Belfast

Focal point of the city centre is Belfast's City Hall (Donegall Square), a huge Renaissance-style palazzo (1898–1906) designed by Sir Brumwell Thomas, with four corner towers and a massive dome. The magnificently-appointed Banqueting Hall, 165ft/50m long, can be visited (Free guided tours: July–Sept. Mon.–Fri. 10.30am and 2.30pm; Oct.–Jun. Wed. 10.30am; other tours by arrangement, tel. (01232) 320202, ext. 2618). In front of the building are statues of Queen Victoria and prominent citizens of Belfast, and on the west side a War Memorial in a Garden of Remembrance. There is also a sculptural group commemorating the loss in 1912 of the "Titanic", the ill-fated liner built at Belfast's Harland & Wolff shipyard.

City Hall

On the north side of Donegall Square stands the Linen Hall Library (1788), with an exhibition on the history of linen manufacture.

Linen Hall Library

Opened in 1895, the Grand Opera House, west of City Hall in Great Victoria Street, was altered and enlarged in 1980. Lacking a permanent company of its own, it stages touring company productions during the winter season (opera, drama, musicals, ballet, etc.; about 1000 seats). The Opera House also hosts the annual Belfast Festival.

Grand Opera House

The Crown Liquor Saloon, now a National Trust listed building, has a quite unique atmosphere with gas lamps, marble-topped bar and abundance of mahogany.

Crown Liquor Saloon

On the northern edge of the city centre is St Anne's Cathedral, principal church of the Anglican Church of Ireland, begun in 1898 (the original architect being Sir Thomas Drew). On the west front of the Neo-Romanesque basilica are three arched portals with fine sculptural decoration. The baptismal chapel boasts an unusual mosaic ceiling made of hundreds of thousands of tiny pieces of glass. In the same chapel is the tomb of Sir Edward Carson (died 1935), leader of the Ulster Unionists.

St Anne's Cathedral

South-east of the cathedral, close to the River Lagan, stands the Custom House (1854–57), its gable adorned with figures of Britannia, Neptune and Mercury.

Custom House

A short distance round the corner in the High Street can be seen the Albert Memorial Clock Tower, popularly known as Belfast's Big Ben on account of its likeness to that other famous clock. Erected in 1869, it commemorates Prince Albert, Queen Victoria's Consort.

Albert Memorial Clock Tower

South Belfast

¾ mile/1.2km south of Donegall Square, reached by way of Bedford Street, Dublin Road and University Road, are the Tudor-style buildings of the

Queen's University

97

Belfast Opera House

Queen's University (1845–94), an independent institution since 1909. Inside one of the red brick buildings there is a history museum.

Botanic Gardens

Immediately south of the university campus lie Belfast's very pleasant Botanic Gardens. The elegant Palm House was erected between 1839 and 1852 (gardens open all day; Palm House, Mon.–Fri. 10am–5pm, Sat. and Sun. 2–5pm; to 4pm daily Oct.–Mar.; closed lunchtime).

Ulster Museum

Also located in the Botanic Gardens is the Ulster Museum (open: Mon.–Fri. 10am–5pm, Sat. 1–5pm, Sun. 2–5pm). It has a substantial number of exhibits from Celtic and Early Christian times (swords, harps, jewellery, etc.), as well as a collection of gold and silver items recovered in 1968 from the wreck of the "Girona", a 16th c. Spanish galleon which foundered off the north Irish coast. The museum art gallery is particularly strong in 17th and 18th c. European painting and Irish art of various periods; it also has collections of Irish glass and silver. Evidence of the scale of Irish emigration over many years, especially to the United States, is provided by the portraits of prominent people of Northern Irish descent, including ten American presidents.

North Belfast

Zoological Gardens

The Zoological Gardens (open: daily 10am–5pm, in winter until 3.30pm except Fri. until 2.30pm; admission free) are attractively laid out on Cave Hill.

Belfast Castle

Half-way up the hill stands Belfast Castle (1870), for a time the home of the 7th Earl of Shaftesbury, it is now a heritage centre (open: daily 9am–6pm).

Cave Hill

From the castle it is simple matter to reach the top of Cave Hill (1182ft/360m), volcanic in origin, with a profile said to resemble Napoleon's. In clear weather there are splendid views of the city, Lough Neagh to

The Northern Ireland Parliament Building

the west and the Irish Sea coast to the east, with the Isle of Man in the far distance.

Stormont

3 miles/5km east of the city, at Stormont, stands the imposing Classical-style building erected in 1929–32 to house the Northern Ireland Parliament. Today occupied by departments of the Northern Ireland Office, the building was badly damaged by fire in January 1995. The attractive grounds are open to the public though the buildings themselves are not. In front stands a monument to Sir Edward Carson.

Parliament Building

Situated in delightful surroundings some 3 miles/5km further north, at Cultra, is the Ulster Folk & Transport Museum (open: Apr.–Jun. and Sept. Mon.–Fri. 9.30am–5pm, Sat. 10.30am–6pm, Sun. noon–6pm; July and Aug. Mon.–Sat. 10.30am–6pm, Sun noon–6pm; Oct.–Mar. Mon.–Fri. 9.30am–4pm, Sat. and Sun. 12.30–4.30pm; admission fee). It takes the form of a traditional Irish village complete with village shop, trade premises, school and church, all removed from their original sites and re-erected stone by stone. The transport collection ranges from donkey creels to aircraft.

★ Ulster Folk & Transport Museum

Surroundings

Along the northern and southern shores of Belfast Lough, the wide inlet on which the city lies, are a series of popular seaside resorts. The coast immediately northwards of the lough is particularly beautiful.

Belfast Lough

Half-way along the north side of the lough, 7 miles/11km from Belfast, is Carrickfergus which, before being displaced by Belfast, was a considerable port. It is noted for its splendidly preserved Norman castle, one of the finest in Northern Ireland. Known in medieval times as Kragfargys Castle, it

★ Carrickfergus Castle

stands on a spur of black basalt which was originally completely surrounded by water except on the north side. For some 750 years it was a place of great military importance, strategically sited to control the harbour and Belfast Lough.

Begun by the Norman John de Courcy between 1180 and 1204, the castle was taken by King John in 1210 after a year-long siege. In 1316 it fell to the Scots. In the 16th c. it was renovated and the fortifications strengthened but thereafter was allowed to decay. In 1760 it was captured by the French – the last time it fell into enemy hands. In the 18th c. it was used as a prison. Later, after the defences were further strengthened, it became a military depot and arsenal, continuing to serve as such until 1928.

The most notable features are the massive keep (small military museum; magnificent Norman Great Hall on the third floor; superb views from the top), the gatehouse with twin towers (in the east tower a chamber known as "the Chapel" on account of its unusual window), and cannon dating from the 16th to the 19th c. (open: Mon.–Sat. 10am–6pm, Sun. 2–6pm; in winter until 4pm; admission fee).

Carrickfergus Castle

20 m
66 ft

Gate-house
Chapel
Outer Ward
Middle Ward
Keep
N.E. Angle Tower
Inner Ward
Postern Gate

© Baedeker

Island Magee	From Carrickfergus a particularly lovely section of coast road runs by way of Whitehead, a popular seaside resort, to Island Magee, not in fact an island but a peninsula, 7 miles/11km long and 2 miles/3km wide. A striking feature on the peninsula's east side is a stretch of basalt cliffs, 253ft77m high, known as the Gobbins, containing several caves. There are numerous legends associated with the cliffs and the caves. At the end of the peninsula there is a dolmen.
Larne	Quarries and cement works disfigure the coast road from Whitehead to Larne, a busy industrial town and seaside resort on Larne Lough. Of interest here are the remains of Olderfleet Castle (three-storeyed keep). There are ferry services from Larne to the Scottish mainland (Cairnryan) and across the lough to Island Magee.

From Larne a romantically beautiful stretch of road follows the coast to Cushendun. After passing through the Black Cave Tunnel the road rounds Ballygalley Head with its great basalt crags. Ballygalley is a popular seaside resort with an old castle now a hotel. From here to Glenarm, a little harbour at the mouth of the River Glenarm, the road is flanked by white limestone cliffs. The next seaside resort is Carnlough, with a small harbour and good sandy beach.

Waterfoot	Waterfoot is delightfully situated in a magical spot at the near end of Red Bay on the Antrim coast, lying encircled amphitheatre-like by sandstone

cliffs at the mouth of Glenariff, one of the loveliest of the Glens of Antrim extending away to the south-west. A few miles beyond Waterfoot are the little resort of Cushendall and its better known neighbour Cushendun.

The road along the south side of Belfast Lough and down the coast also has beautiful scenery and no shortage of attractive little places. Holywood, a suburb of Belfast, has remains of the 12th c. Franciscan friary of Sanctus Boscus (= "holy wood", hence the name).

Holywood

From here the road continues via Crawfordsburn to Bangor, the most popular of Northern Ireland's seaside resorts, with wide sandy beaches, lovely promenades and plenty of entertainment and sports facilities (and on the debit side an increasing number of unattractive tower blocks). Features of interest include the Castle and Castle Park, and the Abbey Church, on the site of a monastery founded in 555.

Bangor

Round the coast from Bangor, Copeland Island (bird sanctuary) can be seen out to sea.

Farther south, at Donaghadee, is the start of the 20 mile/32km-long Ards Peninsula. From Donaghadee a road runs along the Irish Sea coast to Ballywater (lovely beach), Ballyhalbert and Cloghy, where it turns inland to Portaferry on the peninsula's southern tip.

Ards Peninsula

There is a ferry service between Portaferry and Strangford on the mainland. There is also a road round to Strangford, the first section of which, on the A20, skirts the west side of the peninsula along the shores of Strangford Lough. After passing through Ardkeen (ruined castle) and Kircubbin, the road comes to Grey Abbey, with remains of a Cistercian abbey founded in 1193, one of the best preserved in Ireland. Notable features include the fine Perpendicular windows and magnificent west doorway.

The road continues, passing Mount Stewart House and Gardens (beautiful park with many dwarf trees), to Newtownards, famous for its linen and a good base from which to explore the coastal scenery and the Mourne Mountains to the south. It has a town hall of 1770 and a ruined Dominican church (1244). The Old Cross in the High Street has been several times restored.

Newtownards

From here there is a fast route back to Belfast (6 miles/10km); alternatively, turn south, heading first for the whiskey-distilling town of Comber, and then on down the west side of Strangford Lough to Downpatrick (21 miles/34km).

Gardening enthusiasts may prefer instead to make a detour inland to the little town of Saintfield, to visit the lovely Rowallane Gardens with their many rare flowers and plants.

★Gardens of Rowallane

Killyleagh, on the west side of Strangford Lough, was the birthplace of Sir Hans Sloane, founder of the British Museum. Hilltop Castle overlooks the little lakeside resort. The scenery here is particularly beautiful, with the Mourne Mountains shimmering blue in the distance.

Killyleagh

Downpatrick is the county town of Co. Down. Here in 432 St Patrick (see Famous People) began the conversion of Ireland. 2 miles/3km further north is Saul where he landed, built his first church and is said to have died. Downpatrick Cathedral, the seat of a bishop, was built in 1790 on the remains of an earlier church from which a 17th c. font and a number of capitals survive. A granite stone in the churchyard, said to mark St Patrick's grave, dates only from 1900.

Downpatrick

From Saul a road follows the shore eastwards to Strangford, an old Viking settlement beautifully situated at the southern end of Strangford Lough. The strategic importance of this particular area is shown by the fact that there are four 16th c. Anglo-Norman castles in the immediate vicinity. Audley Castle is open to the public.

Strangford

Ardglass	No fewer than seven castles protected Ardglass, south of Strangford, once an important harbour but now just a fishing village. One of them, Jordan's Castle, has considerable remains, including a square keep. West of the village of Killough on the other side of the bay there is a very fine beach.
St John's Point	At St John's Point begins a magnificent scenic road along probably the most beautiful stretch of coast in Northern Ireland, to Newry (39 miles/62km). It skirts the wide Dundrum Bay, large areas of which are exposed at low tide, until the bay ends at Newcastle.
Dundrum	Dundrum is a picturesque fishing village with good sandy bathing beaches and an interesting tower surrounded by a moat, all that remains of an old castle.
Newcastle	Newcastle offers all the amenities of a seaside resort, including a golf course. It lies at the western end of Dundrum Bay at the foot of Slieve Donard (2796ft/852m), the highest of the Mourne Mountains. The climb to the summit takes about two hours and is rewarded with magnificent views extending as far as the Scottish coast. Beyond Newcastle the road begins to ascend, with the sea on the left and the ever-changing backdrop of the Mourne Mountains (the home of many rare plants) on the right. It passes through some quiet little fishing and farming villages, including Glassdrummond and Annalong from which a number of summits between 1700 and 2450ft/518 and 747m – Rocky Mountain, Slieve Bignian, etc. – can be climbed.
Kilkeel	Kilkeel is a favourite resort with fishermen, since there are good catches to be had both from the sea and from the River Kilkeel and nearby Carlingford Lough. Around Kilkeel are a number of prehistoric tombs and dolmens.
Carlingford Lough	Beyond Kilkeel, between Greencastle (north) and Greenore (south), Carlingford Lough cuts deep inland, with a road along either shore. From Kilkeel another road winds through the Mourne Mountains (steep gradients) to Hilltown.
Hilltown	Hilltown, at the foot of the Mourne Mountains on their north-west side, is a good base from which to climb and walk in the hills, coloured by the ever-shifting hues of their granites and schists.
Rostrevor	On the north side of Carlingford Lough, surrounded by woodland (mainly oaks), is Rostrevor, a charming and peaceful little holiday resort ideal for boating, pony-trekking, fishing or walking.
Newry	The port and industrial town of Newry lies on the River Newry and a canal, with the Mourne Mountains to the south-east and the Camlough Mountains to the west. The tower of St Patrick's Church, the first Protestant church in Ireland, dates from 1578. Near by stands the Neo-Gothic Roman Catholic cathedral. Worth visiting in the surroundings are the pretty village of Bessbrook (north-west) and Derrymore House, a thatched 18th c. Georgian-style manor-house.
Hillsborough	The E01 leads north-east from Newry back to Belfast. 9 miles/16km short of the capital the road passes by the trim little town of Hillsborough. Here, in 1650, Colonel Arthur Hill erected a fort (open: Tues.–Sat. 10am–7pm, Sun. 2–7pm; in winter until 4pm) to secure the road between Dublin and Carrickfergus. It was converted to a splendid mansion in the 18th c.

Belmullet · Béal an Mhuirthead   B 2

Republic of Ireland
Province: Connacht
County: Mayo. Population: 1000

Belmullet (Béal an Mhuirthead="ford on the sea") is situated in the north-west of Ireland on the narrow isthmus linking the Mullet Peninsula to the mainland. This isolated little spot is a good base from which to explore the 15 mile/25km-long peninsula and the country to the north.

Location

Surroundings

The west coast of the Mullet Peninsula, exposed to Atlantic storms, is totally devoid of vegetation; the east side, with numerous little coves, almost completely encloses Blacksod Bay. There are lovely beaches on both sides of the peninsula, particularly at the narrowest point around Elly Bay (east side).

Mullet Peninsula

The peninsula boasts many ancient remains. On Doonamo Point, 5 miles/7km north-west of Belmullet (no signpost), are the remnants of a clifftop fortress with a great rampart 200ft/60m long and 18ft/5.5m high in places, stretching across the neck of the headland and enclosing three beehive-shaped huts and the ruins of a ring fort.

Doonamo Point

At Fallmore, near the south end of the peninsula, are the ruins of St Dairbhile's Church (National Monument).

Fallmore

From Blacksod Point, at the southern tip of the peninsula, there is a fine view across to Achill Island (see entry) and the tall peak of Slievemore. From the west side, where there used to be a signal station, there are views of the small islands offshore, which were inhabited in early times and preserve many Early Christian remains.

Blacksod Point

3 miles/5km south of Belmullet the R314 branches off the R313 in a north-easterly direction to Glenamoy from where a delightful detour can be made to Benwee Head (10 miles/16km; road ends at Portacloy, final ¾ mile/1km on foot), rising in sheer and rugged cliffs 843ft/257m above the sea (magnificent views).

Benwee Head

North of Portacloy, a group of seven precipitous rock stacks known as the Stags of Broadhaven rise 328ft/100m from the sea.

Stags of Broadhaven

From Glenamoy the R314 crosses the moors to Belderg, no more than 1¼ miles/2km from the coast with its rugged cliff scenery. Also near by is the Céide Fields archaeological site (see Ballina) where extensive remains of early (1500 b.c.) settlement and cultivation have been uncovered.

Belderg

Splendid panoramic views of the entire area can be enjoyed from the Hill of Glinsk (1017ft/310m), 4 miles/6km to the west. 1¼ miles/2km further west again is Moista Sound, an inlet enclosed on all sides by cliffs.

Glinsk

Birr · Biorra   C 4

Republic of Ireland
Province: Leinster
County: Offaly
Population: 3700

Birr (Biorra="well springs"), a thriving little market town, is situated in the heart of Ireland at the intersection of two main roads (N52, N62) on the western edge of Co. Offaly. Immediately west of the town is the confluence of two good fishing rivers, the Little Brosna and the Camcor.

Location

The town is laid out on a regular plan, with four principal streets meeting in Emmet Square. There are many handsome 17th and 18th c. houses,

The town

especially in Oxmantown Mall and St John's Mall. In St John's Mall there is a monument to the 3rd Earl of Rosse, a famous astronomer.

★Birr Castle Demesne

Opening times
Park only,
daily 9am–6pm

Built in the early 17th c. by Sir Lawrence Parsons, Birr Castle was besieged on a number of occasions. In the 18th and 19th c. it was several times altered and enlarged. The magnificent park, laid out along the River Camcor in the mid 18th c., is open to visitors, though the castle itself is not. More than 1000 tree and plant species thrive here, a particular source of pride being the box hedges, over 200 years old and standing 30ft/9m high. Though well worth a visit whatever the time of year, the park is at its loveliest in spring when the magnolias are in bloom and again in the autumn when the trees take on a myriad autumnal hues.

In about 1840 the 3rd Earl of Rosse, to whose descendants the castle still belongs, designed and built a giant telescope – for some 80 years the largest in the world – which he set up in the castle grounds. With this telescope he made the first discovery of a spiral galaxy. The objective lens from the telescope is now in the Science Museum in London, but the tube and walls on which the telescope was mounted can still be seen in the park. There is a model of the telescope and a small display of optical apparatus. Temporary exhibitions are mounted in an Exhibition Gallery.

Surroundings

Banagher

Banagher lies on high ground on the east bank of the Shannon 8 miles/13km north-west of Birr. The gun positions constructed by English forces in the 17th c. can still be seen.

Clonony Castle

5 miles/8km north-east of Banagher stand the imposing ruins of the Clonony Castle (16th c.). En route to the castle the road passes Shannon Harbour, at the junction of the Shannon with the Grand Canal (see entries). Old warehouses and an old-established hotel (1806) testify to the importance of this little haven.

Kinnitty

Kinnitty is a pretty village at the foot of the Slieve Bloom Mountains east of Birr. From the village an excursion can be made into the delightful little Forlacka Glen.

St Ciaran's Bush

Beyond the Clareen crossroads on the road running south-west from Kinnitty, a hawthorn known as St Ciaran's Bush grows in the middle of the roadway. Ciaran, a 5th c. saint, founded a monastery here.

Leap Castle

A mile or two south stands Leap Castle, a stronghold of the O'Carrolls burned down in 1923 but still impressive even in its ruined state.

Blarney · An Bhlarna   E 3

Republic of Ireland
Province: Munster
County: Cork
Population: 2000

Location

Blarney (An Bhlarna="the plain") lies near the south coast of Ireland, 5 miles/8km north-west of the county town, Cork. Numerous souvenir shops and an endless stream of coaches reveal the trim village to be an obligatory stop on the itinerary of every round-Ireland tour operator.

Blarney has a long tradition of woollen manufacture which has recently been revived. An old mill complex has been restored and converted into a craft centre (Blarney Woollen Mills).

★Blarney Castle

With walls 18ft/5.5m thick and an 82ft/25m-high tower, the 15th c. Blarney Castle was once the most impregnable in Munster. Now a picturesque ruin set in a large park, the chief attraction for tourists is the famous Blarney Stone, believed to bestow the gift of eloquence on anyone who kisses it. The origin of this tradition is unknown.

How the castle came to enrich the English language with a new word is, on the other hand, well documented. Queen Elizabeth I had instructed her Lord Deputy in Ireland to bid Cormac MacCarthy of Blarney abandon the traditional system under which the clans elected their own chieftains and accept instead the grant of his lands from the Crown. MacCarthy, while seeming to agree to the proposal, repeatedly put forward plausible excuses for failing to carry it out, causing the Queen to declare in exasperation: "This is all Blarney; what he says he never means". Hence the use of "blarney" to mean fair words intended to deceive without giving offence.

Anyone who wants to kiss the Blarney Stone – or observe the contortions of those who do – must first climb up to the battlemented parapet around the top of the tower. There, to succeed in the quest, it is necessary to lean backwards head first over the abyss (holding onto a steel frame and gripped firmly by an attendant) in an attempt to kiss the underside of the stone. Many people will find far more to interest them in the magnificent views from the battlements.

Opening times
Mon.–Sat.
9am–7pm, May–Sept. until 6pm,
Sun.
9.30am–5.30pm
(in winter
until 5pm or dusk)

Blarney House (completed 1874), in the castle grounds, overlooking the lake, has been carefully restored and has a fine interior (open: June–mid Sept. Mon.–Sat. noon–6pm).

Blarney House

In the park is a pretty dell known as Rock Close with an assortment of boulders and pieces of stone of interesting shape, also a stone circle – not a prehistoric monument but another example of 18th c. landscaping.

Rock Close

Blarney Castle

Blarney House

Bloody Foreland · Cnoc Fola   A 3

Republic of Ireland
Province: Ulster
County: Donegal

Location and
scenery

Bloody Foreland (Cnoc Fola) is a broad headland in the far north-west corner of Ireland, between Ballyness Bay to the north and Gweedore to the south. It gets its name from the reddish tinge which the rocky coast takes on at sunset. The sea is then bathed in the same reddish hue, and Tory Island, a few miles offshore, assumes a dream-like quality, glowing softly in the dusk.

There is a good road encircling the area. This being a part of Ireland where Irish is still commonly spoken, two always well-attended summer schools in the language are put on here, at Bunbeg and Cloghaneely.

Sights

Dunlewy

To the south-east lies the long, narrow Lough Dunlewy, with good salmon and trout fishing. At the Lakeside Centre (Dunlewy village; open: May–Sept. Mon.–Sat. 11.30am–6.30pm, Sun. noon–7pm), the process of woollen manufacture is illustrated and explained – this sheep-rearing area is famous for its tweeds and other woollen goods.

Errigal Mountain

North of the lough rises Errigal Mountain (2429ft/740m), the highest in the region, a gleaming white quartzite cone, visible from afar. It has a double summit, with two high points only 30ft/9m apart linked by a ridge known as One Man Path. The best route up (no mountaineering experience necessary) is from the east via a marked path starting out from the parking place

Mount Errigal

on the R251; allow 1½ to 2 hours. From the top there are magnificent views – northward towards the wild and lonely Lough Altan with Aglamore (1313ft/400m) rising sheer from its waters; eastward towards the glaciated Derryveagh Mountains; southward towards the rocky Poisoned Glen, so called on account of the spurge which grows there; and westward over the great expanse of Gweedore and the Atlantic coast beyond.

From Bunbeg a boat can be taken to the islands in Gweedore Bay (Innishinny, Gola and others), all with superb rock and cliff scenery. There are beautiful beaches on the mainland coast, including the large Magheraclogher Strand.

Gweedore Bay

To the north, in Ballyness Bay, are Gortahork and Falcarragh, from which Muckish Mountain (2166ft/660m) can be climbed. The ascent is stiff but the views from the top are stupendous.

Muckish Mountain

Near Falcarragh, in Myrath churchyard, is a large ancient cross hewn from a single block of stone.

Myrath

Tory Island

Tory Island, lying some distance off the north side of Bloody Foreland, is the largest of the islands in this area. Although inhospitable, it has been inhabited for over 4000 years. Having begun to decline in Elizabethan times, the population today fluctuates around the 200 mark, higher in summer, lower in winter. Highpoint of the islanders' week is the Saturday night *ceili*, a get-together with music and dancing in the island's two villages.

Tory Island's only "sights" are a few scant remains of buildings, the most interesting being an unusual, 55ft/17m-high round tower of undressed stone (National Monument).

There is no scheduled ferry service to the island (enquire in Bunbeg or Maheraroarty about any sailings). Access depends very much on the weather and rough seas can and often do make crossings to this far-flung outpost of Europe impossible for days on end.

Boyle · Mainistir na Buille

C 3

Republic of Ireland
Province: Connacht
County: Roscommon. Population: 1750

Boyle (Mainistir na Buille="monastery of the pasture river") is situated on the north bank of the River Boyle in the north-west of Ireland, at the foot of the Curlew Hills. The river, which links Lough Gara and Lough Key, is spanned by an old bridge. A market centre, Boyle is one of the principal towns of Co. Roscommon.

Location

On the north side of the town stand the ruins of Boyle Abbey (National Monument), a Cistercian house founded from Mellifont in 1161. Of the cruciform church, now roofless, there survive in a good state of preservation the nave, choir and transepts (lovely capitals carved with human figures, animals and foliage); of the conventual buildings only the guest house and kitchen remain (open: mid June–mid Sept. daily 9.30am–6.30pm).

★Boyle Abbey

Surroundings

North-east of the town lies forest-fringed Lough Key, with many bays, promontories and islets and, extending along its southern shore, the

★Lough Key
Forest Park

Boyne Valley

Lough Key Forest Park (open: daily 10am–7pm) with a very well-equipped camping site, a restaurant, a childrens' paddling pool, picnic sites, etc. as well as facilities for rowing, motorboat hire, fishing and walking. There is also an interesting bog garden. On an island in the lough are the picturesque, green-mantled ruins of an old abbey. An observation tower provides good views over the park.

Strokestown

Strokestown, about 17 miles/28km south-east of Boyle, is a charming little town laid out in 1800 on an axial plan. One of its attractions is a craft centre where traditional Irish crafts continue to be practised (displays and craftshop). Another is the handsome country house belonging to Lord Hartland, situated in a spacious park on the outskirts of the town (Strokestown Park House; open: June–Aug. Tues.–Sun 10am–5pm). The house, which took on its present appearance around 1730, has recently been restored. In 1994 the Famine Museum opened in the old stables; documents, photographs and other exhibits help recount the story of the Great Famine of 1845–49.

Drumanone

Just off the R294 at Drumanone (not far from Boyle) is a large chambered tomb with a massive capstone measuring 15×11ft/4.5×3.3m.

Monasteraden

West of Lough Gara, at Monasteraden in Co. Sligo, is one of the most celebrated of the many holy wells found in this area, dedicated to St Attracta. It has walls on three sides, on one of which is a relief of the Crucifixion.

Boyne Valley   C 5

Republic of Ireland
Province: Leinster
County: Meath

Location

At Slane, near the town of Drogheda on the east coast of Ireland, between Dublin and Belfast, the River Boyne begins a broad sweep southward and then north again. Here in the Boyne valley there is a large pre-Christian burial ground with three great tumuli (south-east of Slane at Knowth, Newgrange and Dowth, in that order; all National Monuments) dating from around 5000 B.C.

★★Newgrange

Opening times
In summer, daily
10am–6 or 7pm.
In winter, daily
10am–4.30pm
(visitors are
shown round by
the custodian)

Until 1962 Newgrange lay beneath an earth mound, barely distinguishable from its surroundings; excavation was only completed in the late 1970s. Largest of the three great tumuli, it comprises a more or less heart-shaped mound of turf and stones some 295ft/90m in diameter and 36ft/11m high, surrounded by a kerb of horizontal slabs stabilising the whole. The vertical drystone retaining wall is a reconstruction of the original, based on the results of archaeological research. Around the kerb, at a few yards distance, there was originally a ring of 38 pillar stones, of which twelve survive.

The entrance to the tumulus, on the south-east side, is marked by a threshold stone carved with spiral decoration. It leads into a narrow passageway, 66ft/20m long, formed from 43 uprights between 5 and 8ft/1.5 and 2.4m high and roofed over with massive lintels. At the end of the passage is the main burial chamber with a 20ft/6m-high vault. Built about 3200 B.C., this corbelled dome is so perfect in its construction that it has not only survived for over 5000 years but remains completely watertight even after long spells of wet weather. The structure is so designed that, for a period of about 15 minutes at the winter solstice, the rays of the sun shine directly

Entrance to the Newgrange tomb

into the otherwise completely dark chamber through an opening above the entrance. During the tour of the site this effect is reproduced using a source of artificial light. Three side chambers, each containing a shallow basin hollowed out of a stone, open off the main one, making the structure as a whole cruciform in plan. When excavated the stone basins were found to contain remnants of ash and bones. Many of the stones are carved with spirals, lozenges, wave patterns, serpentine designs or zigzag ornamentation. This decoration from distant prehistory powerfully enhances the effect inside the tomb.

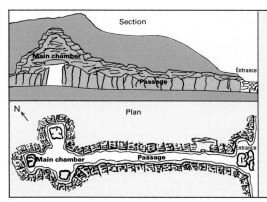

Section

Main chamber

Entrance

Passage

N

Plan

Main chamber   Passage

Entrance

Newgrange

Passage grave in the Boyne Valley

The chambered mound of Newgrange with its cruciform tomb chamber is one of the most remarkable monuments of the kind in western Europe. The roof over the entrance is so constructed that the sun shines directly into the chamber at the winter solstice.

5 m
16 ft

© *Baedeker*

Other sights in the Boyne Valley

Knowth
The tumulus at Knowth is still in process of excavation. Visitors are admitted to the site (open: May–mid June and mid Sept.–Oct. daily 10am–5pm, mid June–mid Sept. daily 9.30am–6.30pm) but not to the tumulus itself. The mound, 33ft/10m high and roughly 280ft/85m across, conceals two passage graves. As at Newgrange, this main mound would have been the burial place of a chieftain or king and his kin, lesser persons being buried in the eighteen smaller tumuli grouped around it. Knowth appears to have been in use as a burial and cult site at various different times from the pre-Christian era onwards.

Dowth
In the burial mound at Dowth (not open to the public), a 27ft/8m-long passage leads into one of two principal chambers. Branching off this circular chamber are several side-chambers.

Slane Hill
To the north of Slane rises Slane Hill (492ft/150m), where in 433 St Patrick is said to have signalled the triumph of Christianity in Ireland by lighting the Paschal fire in defiance of a kingly ban.
On the hill are the ruins of a Franciscan friary (National Monument) with a 16th c. church and conventual buildings laid out around a cloister (individual rooms with fireplaces, alcoves and ambry).

Slane Castle
In the grounds of Slane Castle (1¼ miles/2km west of Slane) are the ruins of a Gothic church. The castle itself was extensively damaged in a fire.

Beauparc House
Further up the valley stands Beauparc House (1750) with, opposite it, the picturesque ruins of Castle Dexter.

Bray · Bri Cualann   C 5

Republic of Ireland
Province: Leinster
County: Wicklow
Population: 23,000

Location
Bray (Bri Cualann="hill of Cuala") lies a little way south of Dublin in a beautiful, sheltered bay on the Irish Sea, between the Dalkey promontory to the north and Bray Head to the south. It is one of Ireland's largest and oldest seaside resorts favoured mainly by Dubliners. Bray has excellent sports facilities – tennis, golf courses (9 hole and 18 hole), swimming, sailing and motor-boating.

The town
Bray's centrepiece is the Esplanade, a spacious promenade extending for almost 1¼ miles/2km along the bay (shingle beach), with a bandstand, putting green and other amusements. At the north end is a yacht harbour, to the south Bray Head, rising steeply from the sea to a height of 800ft/240m. A footpath known as the Great White Way runs from the south end of the Esplanade, past a small ruined 13th c. church, to the summit of the headland (1½ hours there and back). Half-way up, at Eagle's Nest, there is a café. From the top there are fine views over the sea and inland.

Surroundings

Rathmichael
2½ miles/4km north-west of Bray stand the ruined 16th c. Rathmichael church and the stump of a round tower (National Monument). On the south wall of the church are a number of unusual early gravestones and a cross.

River Dargle
2½ miles/4km west of Bray the River Dargle, which flows through the town to the sea, enters the romantic Glen of the Dargle, a thickly wooded, rocky

gorge with a massive, projecting crag known as Lover's Leap. A narrow path runs alongside the river, and a winding road leads into the upper part of the glen.

To the right of the R761 as it heads south from Bray lies Kilruddery, a fine country mansion (1820) with lovely gardens (open: May, June and Sept. daily 1–5pm). The park, with its twin canals, laid out in the late 17th c., still retains much of its original character. In the 19th c. a winter garden was added.

Kilruddery

Also to be seen south of Bray are the distinctive outlines of the Sugar Loaf Mountains – the Little Sugar Loaf (1106ft/337m) and Great Sugar Loaf (1628ft/496m), both affording extensive views.

Sugar Loaf Mountains

Greystones, 5 miles/8km south of Bray on the R761, is a pleasant resort in wooded countryside, with tennis courts, a golf course (18 holes) and good bathing in the bay; sailing boats and motor boats can be hired.
   The Bray Harriers hunt over the surrounding district.

Greystones

1½ miles/2.5km south-west of Greystones, a little way in from the coast, lies Dalgany, a delightful small village in a wooded setting with an 18-hole golf course. From here an excursion can be made to the Glen of the Downs, a national forest with a well-laid out nature trail.

Delgany

Bundoran · Bun Dobhrain   B 3

Republic of Ireland
Province: Ulster
County: Donegal
Population: 1600

Bundoran (Bun Dobhrain="mouth of the Dobhran") is situated on the Atlantic coast in the far north of Ireland, on the N15 from Donegal to Sligo. This popular seaside resort, with excellent facilities for sport and recreation, lies on the south side of Donegal Bay, with Benbulben to the south of the town.

Location

Bundoran's main thoroughfare is lined with hotels and restaurants. The town's principal attraction is its beach of fine sand, with cliffs at either end carved into fantastic shapes by the sea. From here there are any number of delightful walks, one of them north to the cliffs and caves on Aughrus Head, with the Puffing Hole, a funnel-like cavity through which water is ejected with considerable force. Beyond this is Tullan Strand with a cairn, a dolmen and a stone circle.

The town

Surroundings

North-east of Bundoran, on the River Erne, which flows out of Lough Erne, is the busy little town of Ballyshannon. On the north-west side of the town is the restored Abbey Mill and close by the ruins of a Cistercian abbey, Assaroe. Also worth visiting is the Donegal Parian China Pottery (on the Bundoran Road; open: Mon.–Fri. 9am–6pm, Sat. and Sun. 10am–8pm). The pottery's wares can be observed in the making as well as purchased.

Ballyshannon

3 miles/5km north-west, on the coast, are the ruins of Kilbarron Castle, seat of Michael O'Clery, foremost of the Four Masters (see Donegal) who jointly compiled the famous "Annals" recording the history of Ireland and its leading families from the earliest origins in legend up to their own time in the 17th c.

Kilbarron Castle

South of Bundoran lies Lough Melvin (coarse fishing) with a very pleasant drive along its south side from the nearby village of Kinlough.

Lough Melvin

Burren · Boirinn   C/D 2/3

Republic of Ireland
Province: Munster
County: Clare

Location
The Burren (Boirinn="stony place"), half-way up the west of Ireland on the south side of Galway Bay, is an extraordinary tract of karst country, a flat plateau formed from unfolded carboniferous limestone strata rising in terrace-like stages from the coast. When Cromwell's soldiers arrived here they are said to have complained of "too few trees to hang anyone, too little water to drown anyone and too little earth to bury anyone".

⋆ Topography
The Burren is a unique place well worth taking time off to explore, a landscape of rounded hills of porous grey rock and barren limestone pavements, little streams which seep away into the scarred surface of the land, underground rivers, caves and swallow holes, loughs which are full one day and dry the next, and an exotic mixture of arctic, alpine and Mediterranean flora vying for a foothold in any crack or cranny capable of holding the slightest bit of soil.

Burren Way
A marked footpath known as the Burren Way runs from Ballyvaughan to Ballynalacken, 2 miles/3km north of Doolin, taking in many of the more important sights in the Burren.

Through the Burren

For those with cars there is a choice of three routes through the Burren – the N67 direct from Ballyvaughan in the north-east to Lisdoonvarna in the

Landscape of the Burren

south-west; the R480/R476 running more or less eastward through the interior of the area; and the R477, mostly following the coast and offering an alternative route back to Ballyvaughan from Lisdoonvarna.

Ballyvaughan, a small fishing village, makes an excellent base from which to explore the area.

Ballyvaughan

6½ miles/10km north-east, in a valley just off the N67, are the ruins of Corcomroe Abbey (National Monument), a Cistercian house founded in 1180. The church is well preserved (choir, nave, south aisle, transepts with chapels). The choir has figural carving, fine masonry, lovely vaulting and simple but pleasing tombs. Very little remains of the rest of the abbey, dissolved in 1564.

★ Corcomroe Abbey

A few miles from Ballyvaughan, on the right of the N67, stands the unusually-shaped keep of Newtown Castle (circular on a pyramidal base).
    After a steep climb the N67, known locally as "the Corkscrew Road", reaches its highest point (720ft/220m).

Newton Castle

To the west rises Slieve Elva (1109ft/340m), in the vicinity of which are several streams which disappear beneath the ground. Here also is found Polinagollum Cave, the most extensive in Ireland, of which some 7½ miles/12km of passages have so far been explored.

Slieve Elva

A few miles before Lisdoonvarna, on the left of the road, stands Cahermacnaghten (National Monument), a stone fort with a ring-wall 100ft/31m in diameter and the remains of a castle where the O'Davoren family kept alive the study of traditional Irish law until late in the 17th c.

Cahermacnaghten

1¼ miles/2km south of Ballyvaughan the R480 branches off southward from the Corkscrew Road. A short distance along lies the Ailwee Cave, with many miles of underground passages of which a small, well-laid out and lit section is open to the public (open: mid Mar.–Nov. daily 10am–5.30pm, July and Aug. until 6.30pm). At the entrance is a Visitor Centre, restaurant and shop, in buildings of local stone successfully blending in with the landscape. Highlights of the guided tour of the cave include impressive stalactitic and stalagmitic formations, an underground river which becomes a raging torrent during periods of heavy rain, and traces left on the cave floor by bears prior to the last Ice Age (the temperature inside the cave, a steady 42°F/10°C, would have made it an ideal place for them to spend the winter).

★ Ailwee Cave

The R480 continues south through a remote area dotted with ancient remains. On the left of the road (signposted but anyway impossible to miss) stands the Poulnabrone Dolmen, a huge megalithic tomb dating from about 3000 B.C.

★ Poulnabrone Dolmen

A little way off to the right of the R480, at Caherconnell, there is a fine ring fort.

Caherconnell

The area around Carran, 3 miles/5km east, is particularly rich in remains. A signpost in the village points the way to Temple Cronan (National Monument; 1¼ miles/2km north-east), a small Early Christian church with Romanesque grotesque heads on the exterior.

Carran

Above a steep-sided valley beyond Carran, in the direction of Killinaboy, stands Cahercommaun (unsignposted; access through private property), a particulary impressive ring fort with three circuits of stone ramparts.

Cahercommaun

At the junction of the R480 with the R476 are the imposing ruins of Leamaneh Castle (National Monument), a tower house of 1480 enlarged in 1640 by the addition of a residential wing.

Leamaneh Castle

Poulnabrone dolmen

Killinaboy	2½ miles/4km east, in Killinaboy, are the ruins of an interesting church (16th c.?) with a well-preserved sheila-na-gig over the south doorway, and the stump of a round tower.
Corofin	The R476 continues south-east through wooded hills, past the lovely Lough Inchiquin and the ruins of Inchiquin Castle (1459), to Corofin, itself beautifully situated and with excellent trout and coarse fishing in the River Fergus and numerous local loughs.
Kilfenora	In the other direction, the R476 leads west from Leamaneh Castle to Kilfenora, which until the 18th c. was the see of a bishop. The west end of the modest "cathedral" (12th c.; National Monument) is roofed and still used for worship; the roofless choir contains fine 13th and 14th c. gravestones. There are a number of high crosses including, in a field 110yd/100m to the west, one carved with a Crucifixion and other rich ornamentation. Finest of all is the Doorty Cross, on the east side of which are carved the figures of three bishops and a double-headed bird.
Burren Display Centre	Situated in Kilfenora is the Burren Display Centre (open: Mar.–Oct. daily 10am–5pm, in summer until 6 or 7pm). An audio-visual presentation and small exhibition provide an insight into the geography, flora and fauna, etc. of the Burren. Adjoining are a tea-room and information centre.
Ballykinvarga	2 miles/3km north-east of Kilfenora at Ballykinvarga is a ring fort with remains of huts and *chevaux-de-frise* within a double ring-wall.
Lisdoonvarna	Lisdoonvarna, 4½ miles/7km north-west of Kilfenora, is Ireland's leading spa, a resort very popular with Irish holidaymakers (tennis, pitch and putt course, amusement park). The radioactive springs contain sulphur, magnesium, iron and iodine. The town's Spa Wells Health Centre is open from June to October.

Kilfenora: Cathedral . . .

. . . with beautiful tracery

About 5 miles/8km west of Lisdoonvarna lies the fishing village of Doolin, with good bathing and fishing. In settled weather several boats a day cross from Doolin Pier to the Aran Islands (see entry).

Doolin

What principally brings tourists flocking to Doolin from far and wide however are its pubs where Irish folk music can be heard every evening throughout the summer months.

Starting from Lisdoonvarna there is a delightful coastal drive along the western edge of the Burren. At first the R477 winds its way north-west-wards past Ballynalackan Castle (the Burren Way, see above, starts at Ballynalackan) before dropping down to the coast and turning northwards. To seaward lie the Aran Islands and on the landward side the sloping flanks of Slieve Elva with the occasional ruined church and stone fort.

From the bare and wind-swept Black Head, at the most northerly point on the coast road, there are extensive views over Galway Bay. Here the road swings south-east along the shores of Ballyvaughan Bay. To the left is seen Gleninagh Castle (16th c.; National Monument), a four-storeyed tower house with circular corner turrets. Shortly afterwards the road enters Ballyvaughan.

Black Head

Cahir · Cathair Dhuin Iascaigh

D 4

Republic of Ireland
Province: Munster
County: Tipperary
Population: 2100

Cahir · Cathair Dhuin Iascaigh

Location

Cahir (Cathair Dhuin Iascaigh="stone fort of the dun abounding in fish") lies on the River Suir in southern Ireland, at the junction of the N8 and N24. To the west of the town the Galtee Mountains rise to a height of 2954ft/900m.

There is evidence that the small rocky islet in the Suir was occupied by a fort as early as the 3rd c.

Sights

★Cahir Castle

Cahir Castle (National Monument), one of the largest in Ireland and frequently used as a setting for films, was constructed in the middle of the 12th c., though the building seen today dates mainly from the 15th and 16th c. After an eventful history of destruction and rebuilding, in recent decades the castle has been extensively restored. It consists of a massive three-storeyed keep and great hall, with two spacious wards or courts, all enclosed within strong high outer walls reinforced by round and rectangular towers. In the living quarters the furnishings of 500 years ago have been re-created (open: mid June–mid Sept. daily 9am–7.30pm; mid Sept.–mid Oct. and Apr.–mid June daily 10am–6.30pm; mid Oct–Mar. daily 10am–1pm and 2–4.30pm).

Swiss Cottage

In Cahir Park, which runs down to the water's edge, stands the Swiss Cottage, so-called because of its resemblance to a Swiss chalet. This little country house was designed in 1810 by the British architect John Nash. The interior was recently restored and the building can now be visited (open: May–Sept. daily 10am–6pm; mid Mar.–Apr. and Oct.–Nov. Tues–Sun. 10am–1pm and 2–4.30pm).

St Paul's Church

Nash also built the Protestant St Paul's Church (1817–20), an essay in the Neo-Gothic style.

Cahir Castle

Surroundings

4 miles/6km north of Cahir is an interesting group of medieval structures (National Monuments): the Motte of Knockgraffon, a 12th c. Anglo-Norman stronghold built to protect a ford over the Suir; the ruins of a 13th c. church and tower; and remains of a 16th c. castle. Near by is a churchyard with another ruined church.

Motte of Knockgraffon

5 miles/8km south of Cahir lies the picturesquely-situated village of Ard-finnan, with a 15-arched bridge across the Suir. On the banks of the river are two towers belonging to a castle which was believed impregnable until Cromwell's troops bombarded it with artillery and took it by storm.

Ardfinnan

The R665 runs south-west from Ardfinnan, passing Castle Grace, a fine ruined castle (13th c.?) just beyond Clogheen, from where the R668 (the "Vee") winds its way south, with many hairpin bends, through the Knock-mealdown Mountains. There are far-ranging views from Knockmealdown (2658ft/810m), highest of the hills.

Knockmealdown Mountains

South-west of Cahir, on a minor road branching left off the N8 some 5 miles/8km from the town, is Burncourt Castle (National Monument), the empty shell of a many-gabled Elizabethan mansion built in 1641–45 and burned down by Cromwell only five years later in 1650.

Burncourt Castle

North-west of Cahir, between the Galtee Mountains and a parallel wooded ridge of hills to the north, extends the wide Glen of Aherlow, once an important pass between the lowlands of Co. Tipperary and Co. Limerick. Scene of many a battle in olden times, the glen later became a refuge for outlaws and the dispossessed. Attractive and fertile, it is good walking country.

Glen of Aherlow

Carlow · Ceatharlach

D 5

Republic of Ireland
Province: Leinster
County: Carlow
Population: 12,000

Carlow (Ceatharlach = "fourfold lake"), county town of Co. Carlow, lies south-west of Dublin on the River Barrow, at the intersection of the N9 and N80. It has a variety of industry, including a sugar-beet factory, flour-mills and maltings, but little to interest tourists.

Location

Strategically situated on the border of the English Pale, Carlow was a stronghold of the Anglo-Normans. Fortified with a rampart in 1361, it was afterwards frequently beseiged, taken and burned down. In the last battle to be fought here, in 1798, 640 Irish rebels were killed. The battle and the fallen are commemorated by a modern Celtic-style high cross in Church Street, where the dead were buried.

History

Sights

Access to Carlow Castle (National Monument) is from Castle Hill Street. Of the main structure, originally square, there survives only the east side, with two massive round towers at the corners (13th c.). The inner precinct remains closed.

Carlow Castle

At the junction of Athy Road and Dublin Road is the handsome Neo-Classical Court House (1830).

Court House

St Patrick's College (1793) was one of the first Irish seminaries sanctioned by the British.

St Patrick's College

Surroundings

Oak Park	2 miles/3km north-east of Carlow on the Dublin Road (N9) is the beautifully wooded Oak Park, with an 18-hole golf course.
Browne's Hill ★Dolmen	2 miles/3km east of the town, on land belonging to Browne's Hill, a country house built in 1763, is a huge dolmen (National Monument), 4000 years old and the largest in Ireland. The front end of the capstone, which weighs 100 tonnes, is carried on three uprights; the collapsed rear end rests on the ground.
Tullow	Continuing east the R725 comes in 7½ miles/12km to the small town of Tullow, a centre for fishing the River Slaney and its tributaries.
Rathgall	About 3 miles/5km east of Tullow, in Co. Wicklow, is the ring fort of Rathgall (National Monument), a hill-top stronghold with three concentric ramparts and ditches, probably built in the early centuries A.D. as the seat of the kings of South Leinster. Inside the fort a Bronze Age forge was discovered containing over 400 fragments of clay moulds used to make bronze swords and spear-heads. To the north of the fort can be seen the well-preserved Haroldstown Dolmen (National Monument), with a double capstone borne on ten uprights.
Aghowle Church	From the R725 a small road (signposted) leads to the ruined Aghowle Church (12th c.). Noteworthy features include the doorway, a slender granite cross and various old tombs.
Leighlinbridge	South of Carlow the N9 passes through Leighlinbridge, with the ruins of the Black Castle (16th c.; National Monument) on the site of an earlier fortress built in 1180 to protect the crossing of the River Barrow.
Old Leighlin	2 miles/3km west is an older village, Old Leighlin, where there was already a monastic community in the 7th c. Still to be seen is a ruined 13th c. church, much altered in the 16th c., with interesting Gothic doorway to the choir, font, stalls and tombs (16th c.).
Muine Bheag	From Leighlinbridge the R705 runs south-east to Muine Bheag (or Bagenalstown), an attractive small town which makes an ideal base for anyone keen on fishing or hunting. In the vicinity are two 13th c. castles, both National Monuments – Ballymoon Castle, an empty shell with walls 8ft/2.5m thick and 20ft/6m high and rectangular towers, and Ballyloughlan Castle, the remains of which are notable for the number of fireplaces.
Borris	Continuing its way towards the southern tip of Co. Carlow, the R705 comes to Borris, which has a 9-hole golf course. Between the town and the river is Borris House.
Blackstairs Mountains	Borris is a convenient point from which to explore the Blackstairs Mountains east of the town. Mount Leinster (2576ft/785m) is the highest of the hills, crowned by a television tower.
St Mullin's	9 miles/15km beyond Borris, in the extreme south of the county, lies St Mullin's, in the churchyard of which there are both Early Christian and medieval remains (National Monuments) – a church with a spiral staircase, an oratory (St James's Chapel), an assortment of other buildings, the stump of a round tower, and a granite high cross. Outside the monastic precinct can be seen a Norman fortress.
Clonmore	A little to the west of Carlow is the village of Clonmore with an early 13th c. castle of the same name. With its corner towers the castle is typical of its period. The churchyard, which is cut in two by the road, also contains interesting remains. North of the road stands a beautiful and well preserved high

cross; south of the road there is a fragment of another fine cross (both National Monuments).

Just over a mile/2km further west, in the churchyard at Killeshin (Co. Laois), there is a 12th c. Romanesque church with a doorway notable for its carving and high-pitched pediment.

   From the churchyard there is a lovely view over the low-lying country-side, with the Wicklow Mountains in the distance.

Killeshin

Carrick-on-Shannon · Cara Droma Ruisg

C 3

Republic of Ireland
Province: Connacht
County: Leotrim. Population: 2000

Carrick-on-Shannon (Cara Droma Ruisg="weir of the marshy tract"), county town of Co. Leitrim, lies in north central Ireland. It is the starting-point for inland cruising on the Shannon (Lough Allen) and the Shannon–Erne Waterway (see below) re-opened in 1994.

Location

Carrick-on-Shannon has preserved few buildings from earlier centuries apart from the Court House (1825) and Protestant Church (1827).

The town

Surroundings

A few miles north of Carrick, the Shannon–Erne Waterway branches off the River Shannon. Closed for more than a century, it was re-opened in May 1994 linking two of the most popular recreational inland waterways in Europe, the Shannon and Upper and Lower Lough Erne in Northern Ireland. Opened originally in 1860, the canal was never an economic success; in its first five years only eight boats passed through, and in 1869 it was closed. Following extensive restoration work it now has a least depth of 5ft/1.5m and is a mecca for boating enthusiasts. The 48 miles/78km from Carrick to Belturbet (see Cavan) can be negotiated by an ordinary cruiser in about 16 hours.

Shannon–Erne Waterway

The R280 runs north via the prettily situated village of Leitrim (from which the county takes its name) to Drumshanbo, an anglers' paradise at the southern end of Lough Allen. Continuing north along the west side of the lough, the road passes through what was once mining country around Arigna.

Lough Allen

About 8 miles/13km north-east of Carrick-on-Shannon is Fenagh, with two churches, both National Monuments, on the site of a former monastery. The more southerly of the two has a fine west doorway and east window (14th/15th c.), the other (15th c.) dressed stones from a pre-Norman building; both have barrel-vaulting at the west end.

Fenagh

A good 9 miles/15km south-east of Carrick lies Lough Rinn, on the north-east side of which stands Lough Rinn House set in a delightful park. The 19th c. house built by the 3rd Earl of Leitrim has an interesting interior (open: May–Sept. daily 10am–7pm).

Lough Rinn Estate

Carrick-on-Suir · Carraig na Suire

D 4

Republic of Ireland
Province: Munster
Counties: Tipperary and Waterford. Population: 5600

Location	Carrick-on-Suir (Carraig na Suire="rock of the Suir") lies near the south coast of Ireland on the River Suir. Since the river here forms the boundary between Co. Tipperary and Co. Waterford, the town is in both.
History	In 1541 Henry VIII of England assumed the title King of Ireland. From then on, particularly in the reign of Elizabeth I, the English sought to consolidate their hold on the country by introducing English landowners. During the 16th and 17th c. these newcomers built numerous fortified Tudor mansions, the finest of which is Ormonde Castle in Carrick-on-Suir.

Sights

Ormonde Castle	Ormonde Castle (National Monument), once the seat of the Earls Butler of Ormonde, consists of a fortified tower (1450) and a manor house built on to it in 1568. It was actually built for Elizabeth I, but the Queen seems never to have stayed there. It is a typical Elizabethan mansion with a long gabled front and, inside, a long hall and gallery extending almost the whole length of the building, decorated with stucco likenesses of the Queen and members of the Ormonde family. From the tower there is a magnificent view of the river and the surrounding countryside (open: mid June–mid Sept. daily 9.30am–6.30pm).
Tholsel	In the centre of the town, near the medieval bridge, stands the old Tholsel (Town Hall), originally a town gate, topped by a clock tower.

Surroundings

Kilkeeran	North of Carrick-on-Suir, on the boundary between Co. Kilkenny and Co. Tipperary, are two villages with notable high crosses, Kilkeeran (5 miles/8km) and Ahenny (6 miles/10km).
	Of the three crosses in the churchyard at Kilkeeran, the west cross (9th c.) is especially fine. On the east side of the base are eight horsemen, on the other three sides interlace work and geometric patterns. The lower part of the shaft is divided into panels with various patterns, among them intertwined geese-like creatures.
★ Ahenny	In the churchyard at Ahenny stand two particularly fine crosses (both National Monuments), with figural decoration only on the bases. The more northerly of the two has figures of monks carrying crosses, a headless man on a pony, horsemen and horses, a procession of seven ecclesiastics carrying crosiers, and assorted animals. The base of the other cross is very badly weathered. The crosses themselves are covered with finely carved geometric designs (spirals, interlace work, rosettes). Because the patterns so resemble those in "The Book of Kells", they are assumed to date from the 8th c.
Comeragh Mountains, Monavullagh Mountains	South-west of Carrick-on-Suir the Comeragh and Monavullagh Mountains extend towards the sea. This is good climbing country, particularly the area around Lough Coumshingaun, a small tarn in a horseshoe-shaped corrie ringed by cliffs below the highest of the summits (2560ft/780m).

Cashel · Caiseal Mumhan   D 4

Republic of Ireland
Province: Munster
County: Tipperary
Population: 2400

Cashel (Caisel Mumhan="stone fort of Munster") lies inland in southern Ireland on the N8. Approached through flat countryside along any of the roads converging on the town, the famous Rock of Cashel is a prominent landmark, a steep-sided crag to the north of the town, crowned by a magnificent cluster of ruins.

Location

The rock was fortified by the kings of Munster as early as the 4th c. In 450 St Patrick, having baptised King Aengus here, made Cashel the see of a bishop; a number of later kings were also bishops. The legendary Brian Boru was crowned here, and in 977 made Cashel his principal seat. An O'Brien later presented the Rock to the Church and soon afterwards, in 1127, Bishop Cormac MacCarthy began the construction of Cormac's Chapel. In 1152 the bishopric became an archbishopric. After the Reformation, Elizabeth I appointed Protestant archbishops. The cathedral, built in the 13th c., was damaged by fire in 1495 and again in 1647. After being restored in 1686 it was abandoned in 1749 and fell into decay. Finally, in 1874, the state assumed responsibility for it and it was declared a National Monument.

History

★★ Rock of Cashel

The Rock of Cashel (National Monument) rises 200ft/60m above its surroundings. The walled precinct is entered through the Hall of the Vicars Choral (15th c.), formerly for the use of laymen and minor canons. Today it has been turned into a little museum (upper floor with furniture of the period). St Patrick's Cross is also preserved here, having been removed from its site in front of the cathedral where a replica now stands.

Opening times
Daily 9am–7pm (from mid Sept.– mid June from 9.30am until 4.30 or 5.30pm)

On one side of St Patrick's Cross is a relief of the Crucifixion, on the other a relief of the saint himself. The base, richly ornamented with geometric

St Patrick's Cross

Cashel Cathedral

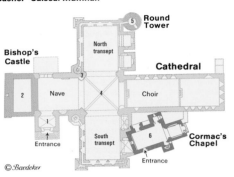

Cashel
Caiseal Mumhan

1 Porch
2 Archbishop's Palace
3 Staircases
4 Central tower
5 Round tower
6 Cormac's Chapel

© Baedeker

10m
33 ft

designs, may have been the coronation stone of the kings of Munster and stood on the spot where St Patrick baptised King Aengus. Tradition has it that, during the ceremony, the saint accidentally struck the king's foot with his crosier; Aengus made no comment, believing this to be part of the ritual.

Cormac's Chapel

Cormac's Chapel (1127–32; now being restored), which is enclosed by the choir and south transept of the cathedral, is the most interesting Romanesque church in Ireland. The architecture and sculpture show the influence of German (probably Regensburg) and English masters, while preserving a distinctively Irish character (expressed, for example, in the steeply pitched stone roof and the corbelling of the barrel-vaulting).

The transepts are like towers. The walls, both external and internal, are relieved by blind arcading and a variety of sculptural decoration. The old main doorway (now facing the angle between the choir and south transept) is richly articulated and has a fine tympanum depicting a centaur hunting a lion with a bow and arrow. The chapel contains a 12th c. stone sarcophagus finely carved with Scandinavian-style ornament.

Cathedral

The cathedral itself, now roofless, still retains something of the grandeur of a medieval episcopal church. The choir and transepts are longer than the (unfinished) nave. The transepts have preserved their three-bayed gable-ends and their corner turrets. In the angles between nave and transepts, spiral staircases of 27 steps ascend inside small circular towers to the massive central tower, with access to roof walks around the nave and the transept. Each is connected to the other, as well as to the round tower (see below), by a series of passageways and flights of steps within the thickness of the walls – a shrewdly contrived arrangement from the point of view of defence. In the north transept are a number of fine tombs, one of them with figures of Apostles and saints, including St Thomas Becket.

In the choir is the tomb of Archbishop Myler MacGrath, who died in 1622 at the age of 100. Having converted to Protestantism, he was for several years both a Protestant Archbishop appointed by Elizabeth I and a Roman Catholic one, since it was some time before he was dismissed from office by the Vatican!

Round Tower

The north transept of the cathedral is built on to a well-preserved round tower dating from the same period as Cormac's Chapel. It is 92ft/28m high with a doorway 12ft/3.6m above the ground.

Bishop's Castle

At the west end of the cathedral stands the Archbishop's Palace, more a fortified castle than a palace, comprising a massive square tower (15th c.) the west wall of which is thick enough to contain a staircase within (no access).

Other sights

Near the Rock car park, Comhaltas Ceoltéori Eireann, an organisation dedicated to the promotion of Irish folk music and art, has opened the Brú Ború Cultural Centre. Each season three plays are produced daily (except Sun. and Mon.) in the adjoining theatre; other events are also arranged. A restaurant, exhibition room and shop selling art and craftwork complete the complex (open: Oct.–Mar. Mon.–Fri. 9am–5pm; Apr.–Sept. daily 9am–11pm).

Brú Ború

The Dominican Abbey (National Monument) near the base of the Rock preserves a number of handsome old windows.

Dominican Abbey

The Folk Village, a few yards further along, re-creates the urban and rural life of the area (open: Mar. and Apr. daily 10am–6pm; May–Oct. daily 9.30am–7.30pm).

Folk Village

When no longer needing the protection of their castle on the Rock, the Protestant Archbishops built a palace in the town. This handsome brick building of 1730 is now the Cashel Palace Hotel, tastefully furnished in 18th c. style (entrance on the north side of Main Street).

Cashel Palace

Quirke's Castle (in Main Street), a 15th c. tower house, is today also a hotel.

Quirke's Castle

St John's Cathedral (in John Street), is a pleasing Neo-Classical building (1750–83; tower 1812) erected to replace the cathedral on the Rock, by then falling into disrepair. Set into a wall in the churchyard are a series of fine tomb effigies preserved from Cashel's medieval churches.

St John's Cathedral

Near by is the Diocesan Library, endowed by Archbishop Bolton in 1741, with a collection of rare prints and maps.

Bolton Library

Hore Abbey with the Rock of Cashel in the background

Surroundings

Hore Abbey

West of Cashel lies Hore Abbey (National Monument), a Cistercian House founded in 1266, with the ruins of the church and conventual buildings; the chapter-house is well preserved. The central tower of the church was a 15th c. addition.

Castlebar · Caislean an Barraigh   C 2

Republic of Ireland
Province: Connacht
County: Mayo
Population: 6400

Location

Castlebar (Caislean an Barraigh="Barry's castle"), county town of Co. Mayo, lies in the north-west of Ireland, at the junction of the N5 and N60. It has a small local airport.

Castlebar is always full of anglers, attracted to the town by the excellent fishing in the loughs to the south – Lough Mallard, Castlebar Lough and Islanddeady Lough.

History

In 1798 a French and Irish force, having landed near Castlebar, routed a superior British force in an engagement known as "Castlebar Races".

The town

The main feature of this little market town, which also has some light industry, is a green called The Mall, lined with lime trees.

Surroundings

Turlough

On the N5 3 miles/5km north-east lies Turlough, with an unusually short and squat round tower (well-preserved; National Monument) in the churchyard. Adjoining it is a ruined 17th c. church.

★Straid

Beyond Turlough, on the Foxford road at Straid, is a ruined abbey church containing fine sculptures and tombstones. One tomb in particular, dating from about 1475, is considered the best example of the Flamboyant style in Ireland. The saints depicted on it appear to be having a good chuckle – no one knows why.

Mayo

From Castlebar the N60 runs south-east through the Plain of Mayo, passing by the village of Mayo, with remains of a once-famous abbey founded by St Colman in the 7th c.

Knock

The N60 continues to Claremorris from which the N17 leads north-east to Knock, a place of pilgrimage which attracts more than a million visitors every year. To guarantee them a comfortable journey, an airport suitable for jumbo-jets was opened here in 1986. The new church (1984), dominating the village, can accommodate 6000 people.

Knock's fame goes back to 1879 when fifteen local people claimed to have seen the Madonna, accompanied by St Joseph and St John the Evangelist, behind the old parish church. This miraculous appearance, said to have lasted two hours, is commemorated by larger than life-size figures set up on the site. In 1979 the Pope considered Knock important enough to make a personal visit.

Near the church a folk museum was opened in 1987, documenting 19th c. rural life (open: May–Oct. daily 10am–6pm; July and Aug. until 7pm). The principal attraction is the "museum in a museum" – a thatched cottage complete in every detail.

Ballyhaunis

The R323 runs east from Knock to Ballyhaunis, with remains of an Augustinian priory; the church has been restored.

Cavan · An Cabhan

Republic of Ireland
Province: Ulster
County: Cavan
Population: 3200

Cavan (An Cabhan="hollow place"), county town of Co. Cavan, is situated in a pleasant area of lakes and hills close to the border with Northern Ireland. Here the N3 coming from the south-east intersects with the N54/N55 which run north–south.

Location

The town was completely destroyed by British forces in 1690. An old tower marks the site of an abbey, founded in about 1300, around which the original settlement developed.

The town

Cavan is noted for its crystal, which can be seen being made at a local factory (open: Mon.–Fri. 9am–5.30pm, Sun. 2–5pm).

Cavan Crystal

Surroundings

5 miles/8km north is Ballyhaise, with a pretty 18th c. Market House and Ballyhaise Castle (1731; by Richard Cassels), now occupied by an agricultural college.

Ballyhaise

The R188 runs north-east from Cavan to the little town of Cootehill, to the north of which lies Bellamont Forest. Here, on the shores of Dromore Lough is a fine Palladian mansion, Bellamont House (1729; not open to the public).

Cootehill,
Bellamont Forest

At Cohaw, 3 miles/5km south-east of Cootehill on the R192, there is a megalithic grave mound (National Monument). Excavated in 1949 it has a double entrance court and five chambers.

Cohaw

The road continues to Shercock, near Lough Sillan (campsite), renowned for its large pike.

Lough Sillan

8 miles/13km farther south, in the extreme east of the province, lies Kingscourt, where rich deposits of gypsum have brought the growth of modern industries. The main street has attractive 17th and 18th c. houses. St Mary's Parish Church boasts lovely stained glass windows (1947–48) by Evie Hone.

Kingscourt

The R165 makes its way west through the hills to the little market town of Bailieborough, which has a Court House of 1817 and Market House of 1818.

Bailieborough

Virginia, 9 miles/15km south of Bailieborough, was named after the Virgin Queen, Elizabeth I. Prettily situated on the wooded shores of Lough Ramor, it offers a wide range of sports and recreational facilities (9-hole golf course, fishing in Lough Ramor, bathing beach, boat hire).

Virginia

Jonathan Swift wrote "Gulliver's Travels" while staying at Cuilcagh House, a mansion belonging to the Sheridan family 1¼ miles/2km north of Virginia.

Cuilcagh House

To the south of Ballyjamesduff (west of Virginia), on the R194, lies the village of Mount Nugent, with good fishing in Lough Sheelin.

Lough Sheelin

There is good coarse fishing also in the irregularly-shaped Lough Gowna, some 12 miles/20km south of Cavan. It can be reached via Gowna, or direct from Lough Sheelin by driving west.

Lough Gowna

Farnham House	To the north-west of Cavan, beyond the golf course, Farnham House stands in lovely grounds.
Lough Oughter	Farther west is Lough Oughter, an intricate maze of inlets and channels through which the River Erne flows. The wooded tracts around the lough have become the Killykeen Forest Park (lovely walks). The ruined Clough Oughter Castle is typical of a 13th c. Irish circular tower house.
Cornafean	Not far south of the lough at Cornafean there is a privately-run local museum.
Kilmore	Kilmore, a mile or two south of Farnham House and the seat of a bishop, boasts a 19th c. Protestant cathedral incorporating a fine late Romanesque doorway. In the churchyard can be seen the richly-decorated tomb of Bishop William Bedell who, in the 17th c., made the first translation of the Bible into Irish. Also in the town is a well-preserved motte and bailey.
Killeshandra	Reached from Cavan by way of Kilmore, Killeshandra lies surrounded by small loughs on the west side of Lough Oughter. It has a church of 1688.
Drumlane	Proceeding west from this mini lake district, the R201 comes after 3 miles/5km or so to Drumlane. Here, in a lovely setting between two loughs, stand a round tower and a church (National Monument), both belonging to a former monastery. The church dates from the 13th to 15th c., the tower, still standing 45ft/14m high, and with carvings of birds (badly weathered), from the 12th c.
Belturbet	The road continues north to Belturbet, near the Northern Ireland border. It is a centre for cruising on the River Erne (good fishing), linked to the Shannon by the Shannon–Erne Waterway (see Carrick-on-Shannon).
Ballyconnell	The hilly countryside with its many loughs extends for another 10 or 12 miles/15 or 20km west of Belturbet. Ballyconnell is a popular coarse fishing centre with a 17th c. church.
Iron Mountains	From Ballyconnell, the R200 climbs steeply up into the Iron Mountains, crossing the Bellavally Gap before descending to Glengevlin at the foot of Cuilcagh Mountain (2070ft/630m, the highest of the range). Hereabouts are the headwaters of the Shannon which has its source in the Shannon Pot. Good climbing country.

Cliffs of Moher · Aillte an Mhothair   D 2

Republic of Ireland
Province: Munster
County: Clare

Location	The Cliffs of Moher (Aillte an Mhothair="cliffs of ruin") rise vertically from the sea on the west coast of Ireland, just south of Galway Bay.
★★Coastal scenery	Sheer cliffs stretch in an unbroken line for some 5 miles/8km from Hag's Head in the south, where they are 400ft/120m high, to O'Brien's Tower in the north, where they reach 656ft/200m. Between these two points the coast immediately back from the cliffs forms a more or less level plateau. From the top of the cliffs narrow bands of vegetation can be seen clinging to the cliff face while, far below, the surf surges and thunders, ceaselessly pounding the foot of the cliffs and the isolated stacks.
O'Brien's Tower	From the car park at the information centre (café) a path leads to a nearby sandstone platform on the cliff edge and to O'Brien's Tower which, particu-

Cliffs of Moher

larly on a clear day, affords splendid views seawards and across to the Aran Islands. The viewing tower was built by Sir Cornelius O'Brien in 1835 along with a little tea-room (tower and information centre open: Mar.–Oct. daily 10am–6pm).

While the magnificent view from O'Brien's Tower usually has to be shared with a host of fellow tourists, it is rare to encounter another soul on the walk to Hag's Head, 3 miles/5km from O'Brien's Tower, at the southern end of the cliffs. The narrow path hugs the cliff edge and care is required in strong winds. The watch tower on Hag's Head dates from the beginning of the 19th c.

Walk to Hag's Head

Surroundings

From the Cliffs of Moher the road leads east to the fishing village of Liscannor, then past the ruins of Kilmacreehy Church (15th c.) and along Liscannor Bay with its lovely sandy beach, to Lahinch. Square white houses and a promenade skirting the shore above the breakers give this popular resort an almost Mediterranean air. It has two 18-hole golf courses and a variety of sports and recreational facilities.

Lahinch

2½ miles/4km east of Lahinch is another resort, Ennistymon, situated in a wooded valley where the River Cullenagh cascades down through a rocky gorge. There is good fishing for brown trout (also a horse fair).

Ennistymon

7½ miles/12km south of Lahinch on the N67 a side road branches off to Spanish Point, a rugged promontory on which one of the ships of the Spanish Armada was wrecked in 1588 with the loss of hundreds of lives. Near the point are a 9-hole golf course and a good sandy beach.

Spanish Point

Clonakilty · Clanna Chaoilte   E 3

Republic of Ireland
Province: Munster
County: Cork
Population: 2700

Location	Clonakilty (Clanna Chaoilte="O'Keelty's clan") lies on the south coast of Ireland in Clonakilty Bay. The head of the bay is almost totally enclosed by the Inchadoney Peninsula. There are good sandy beaches and facilities for water sports and sea-angling.
The town	Clonakilty was established in 1614 by the 1st Earl of Cork, for occupation by English immigrants. Today it is a small market town in a fertile agricultural area, with an interesting local museum and beautiful park, Kennedy Gardens. The town post office is housed in an old Presbyterian church (1861).

Surroundings

Timoleague	6 miles/10km east, on the T71 and R600, lies Timoleague, with an abbey founded in 1240 which in its day was an important religious centre. The present ruins (church with south aisle and transepts, tower, remains of conventual buildings) date from later centuries. Also well worth a visit are the Castle Gardens with their huge rhododendron bushes and several varieties of palm.
Courtmacsherry	2½ miles/4km from Timoleague, on the R601, is Courtmacsherry, a fishing village on the south side of a narrow inlet. At the entrance to the village is a plaque commemorating the various tragedies that have occurred in these coastal waters.

Timoleague: ruins of the Abbey . . .   *. . . and Castle Gardens*

On the peninsula to the south-west of Clonakilty, near Castle Freke, are the ruins of Benduff Castle and the remains of a Templars' commandery.

Benduff Castle

Picturesquely situated on a hill by the sea, on the north-west side of Rosscarberry Bay, the little town of Rosscarberry once boasted a 6th c. monastery with a famous school. One or two fragments of it survive near the ancient cathedral (restored in the 17th and 19th c.).

Rosscarberry

About 2 miles/3km west of Clonakilty stands Coppinger's Court (National Monument), a ruined 17th c. manor-house with picturesque turrets, gables and chimneys.

Coppinger's Court

On a hill just off the road to Glandore (R597) is the Dromberg Stone Circle (National Monument), dating from about the beginning of the Christian era. During excavation, a cremated body was found in the centre of the ring of seventeen upright stones, and a short distance west, the remains of two circular huts. These have been dated to the 2nd–4th c. A.D.; they were probably used by hunters rather than as dwellings.

★ Dromberg Stone Circle

Glandore is a prettily-situated resort with a mild climate and good fishing and bathing.

Glandore

Clonmacnoise · Cluain Mic Nois

C 4

Republic of Ireland
Province: Leinster
County: Offaly

The ancient monastic settlement of Clonmacnoise or Clonmacnois (Cluain Mic Nois="meadow of the son of Nos") is situated in the very heart of Ireland, on high ground above a broad bend of the Shannon.

Location

With its many graves scattered about among the ruined buildings and high crosses from the Early Christian and medieval periods, the walled monastic precinct resembles a large and lonely churchyard.

A pilgrimage to Clonmacnoise takes place every year on St Ciaran's Day (September 9th), climaxing in an outdoor service conducted before a canopied altar.

Much the pleasantest – if slowest – way of reaching Clonmacnoise is by boat from Athlone (see entry).

According to tradition, the monastery was founded in January 545 by St Ciaran, who died in the same year. It developed into the most celebrated religious centre in Ireland and soon acquired the status of a university. As well as the monks working in its scriptoria, who produced valuable manuscripts including the "Book of the Dun Cow" (11th c.) and the "Annals of Tighernach" (12th c.), it also had craftsmen making crosiers, reliquaries and other articles.

History

The treasures it contained no doubt attracted the raiders who plundered and burned the monastery several times between 834 and 1204 – first the Vikings, then in the 12th c. the Normans, who in 1179 reduced more than 100 buildings to ashes. However, it was only after English troops had carried off whatever they could lay hands on in 1522, and Cromwell's forces had devastated the site again a century later, that the monastery fell into final ruin. Clonmacnoise has enjoyed the protected status of a National Monument since 1955.

Clonmacnoise
Cluain Mic Nois

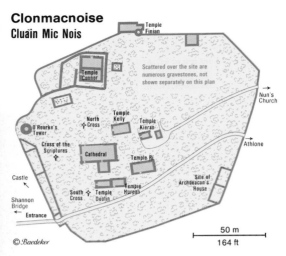

Temple Finian

Temple Connor

Scattered over the site are numerous gravestones, not shown separately on this plan

Nun's Church

North Cross

Temple Kelly

Temple Kieran

O'Rourke's Tower

Cross of the Scriptures

Cathedral

Temple Ri

Athlone

Castle

Shannon Bridge

Entrance

South Cross

Temple Doolin

Temple Hureen

Site of Archdeacon's House

50 m
164 ft

© Baedeker

★★ Monastic Site

The walled enclosure (open: in summer, daily 9am–7pm; in winter, daily 10am–5 or 6.30pm) is entered from the car park on the west side. At the entrance is a Visitor Centre in which some gravestones are kept (to avoid further damage being caused by weathering).

The precinct itself is a typical Irish monastic site laid out in a manner very different from monasteries elsewhere in Europe. Several small churches (11th–13th c.) are dotted about the enclosure, between which would have stood numerous wattle and daub huts for the members of the community.

Gravestones

To the left of the entrance are some 200 Early Christian gravestones, including some with ogham inscriptions. They are set into the enclosure wall grouped together by age, giving an excellent overview of the different styles from the 8th to the 12th c. Many grave inscriptions incorporating the phrase "OR DO . . ." (=a prayer for . . .) followed by an Irish name. Many of the slabs are extremely beautiful and very finely worked.

Cathedral

In the centre of the main group of buildings stands the cathedral, incorporating work dating from the 10th to the 15th c. Note especially the figures of St Patrick and two other saints above the north doorway, dating from the Middle Ages. The sacristy is 16th c.

Temple Kieran

To the east of the cathedral is the cell-like St Ciaran's Oratory (Temple Kieran), a tiny 9th c. church probably containing the tomb of the founder.

Other buildings

At the north end of the precinct are the 11th c. Temple Connor, now a Protestant church (closed), and the 12th c. Temple Finian (Temple Finghin) with a 56ft/17m-high round tower built on to the chancel.

O'Rourke's Tower

A second round tower, known as O'Rourke's Tower, stands alone on the bank of the Shannon (with a gateway).

Cross of the Scriptures

In front of the cathedral is one of the finest high crosses in Ireland, the Cross of the Scriptures, also known as Flann's Cross after King Flann (877–915) to whom it is dedicated (though the inscription is almost completely illegible). Standing more than 13ft/4m high, the cross, of soft sandstone, was carved early in the 10th c. On the west face are the Vigil at the Tomb, the Arrest, the Betrayal and, higher up, the Crucifixion. On the east face, King Dermot is depicted helping St Ciaran erect the corner post of the church; above are a number of unidentified figures, and above these, the Last Judgment. On the south face are a bishop and David with his harp, and on the north face another bishop, a man with pan pipes and a falconer. The base of the cross has a hunting scene with horsemen, chariots and various animals.

More high crosses

On the north side of the cathedral is the shaft of another high cross (North Cross) with figures and patterned decoration. A third high cross (South Cross; 9th c.) stands south of the cathedral, with a Crucifixion on the west face and panels decorated with intertwined animals and plants.

The ruins of Clonmacnoise beside the Shannon

Cross of the Scriptures

Nun's Church   To the east of the monastic enclosure, reached by a pathway from Temple Kieran, lies the ruined Nun's Church, of which the entrance doorway and chancel arch are both well-preserved. They are richly ornamented, with a particularly elaborate pattern on the capitals of the chancel arch.

Clonmacnoise and West Offaly Railway

Operates
End of Apr.–Oct.
daily 10am–5pm

A small scenic railway, originally built for transporting peat, operates in the summer months from the Bord na Mona Blackwater Works near Shannonbridge, not far from Clonmacnoise. The 40 minute trip to Banagher (4 miles/7km), takes in many places of geological, historical and botanical interest around the Blackwater bog (demonstration of peat-cutting).

Clonmel · Clua in Meala   D 4

Republic of Ireland
Province: Munster
County: Tipperary. Population: 12,400

Location

Clonmel (Clua in Meala="honey meadow"), county town of Co. Tipperary, lies near Ireland's south coast, in an attractive setting on the north bank of the River Suir. To the south of the town are the Comeragh Mountains. Clonmel is a market town with some industry (principally cider-making), in an area with a reputation for horse- and dog-breeding. Laurence Sterne, author of "Tristram Shandy", was born in Clonmel in 1713.

In 1815 the first regular passenger service between two Irish towns was instituted here by an Italian immigrant, Charles Bianconi, a picture-framer by trade, who, having prospered and become mayor of the town, introduced a horse-drawn vehicle service between Clonmel and Cahir. "Bianconi Cars" later became established throughout southern Ireland.

Sights

St Mary's Church

Next to the Protestant St Mary's Church (National Monument) can be seen parts of the old rampart walls and three towers. The church, with an octagonal tower, was most recently reconstructed in 1857. Notable features include the tracery of the east window and a number of 16th and 17th c. monuments.

West Gate

Near by, West Gate, a former town gate, closes off O'Connell Street; next to it stands the Roman Catholic Church, with a Neo-Classical façade and good plasterwork ceiling.

Main Guard

The Main Guard, at the other end of the street, is said to have been designed by Wren. It bears the arms of Clonmel and the Earls of Ormonde (whose seat this was).

Other sights

In Parnell Street stands the Town Hall where the civic insignia are kept. Beyond it are the Court House (1800) and, diagonally opposite, the municipal library housing an art gallery and local museum.

Surroundings

Donaghmore

5 miles/8km north, on a side road off the R688, Donaghmore boasts a ruined Romanesque church (National Monument) with a fine doorway and chancel arch.

Fethard

4½ miles/7km further on lies the little town of Fethard, still with an old-world atmosphere. The Protestant church incorporates part of an earlier 15th c. building, while the Roman Catholic church, at the east end of the town, preserves enough from an old Augustinian church to give some impression of the original. Part of the old town walls also survive.

Slievenamon (2330ft/710m), north-east of Clonmel, and the Comeragh Mountains to the south (highest peak Knockamaffrin, 2439ft/743m), provide plenty of scope for climbing and hill walking.

Slievenamon, Comeragh Mountains

The Falconry at Anner House, on the north bank of the Suir 2½ miles/4km east of Clonmel, has a collection of birds of prey (demonstrations of falconry).

The Falconry

Further east, on a hill on the river's heavily-wooded south bank, are the lovely grounds of Gurteen Le Poer (18th c.).

Gurteen Le Poer

Cong · Cunga Feichin

C 2

Republic of Ireland
Province: Connacht
County: Mayo
Population: 200

The village of Cong (Cunga Feichin="isthmus of Feichin") lies in the far west of Ireland, on the isthmus between Lough Mask to the north and Lough Corrib to the south (good fishing in both loughs), to the north of Galway Bay and close to the county boundary between Mayo and Galway.

Location

The last high king of Ireland, Roderick O'Conor, died in Cong in 1198, having spent the last fifteen years of his life here in monastic seclusion.

Cong is a charming little village. In the main street stands a 14th c. stone market cross, with inscriptions.

Village

Sights

At the entrance to the village are the ruins of Cong Abbey (12th c.; National Monument), an Augustinian house. A finely sculptured doorway and a number of early 13th c. capitals in the cloister (restored), represent striking examples of Irish Romanesque art. Equally interesting is the so-called Anglers' Hut (also restored) on the river bank, from which the monks were able to fish through a hole in the floor.

★ Cong Abbey

Cong's processional cross ("Cong Cross"), made for King Turlough O'Conor in about 1123, is now in the National Museum in Dublin (see entry).

Near the abbey, in a park on the shores of Lough Corrib (see entry), stands Ashford Castle, which took on its present 19th c. aspect when in the ownership of the Guinness family. In 1939 it became a hotel which today is one of the finest in Ireland.

Ashford Castle

Surroundings

Lough Mask and Lough Corrib are linked by underground streams which flow beneath the isthmus separating them. The limestone of the area is pitted with caves.

Lough Mask

The most interesting of the caves are Kelly's Cave (National Monument), thought to have been a Bronze Age burial site, and the Pigeon Hole. Both are easy of access (the key to Kelly's Cave is kept in Cong).

Kelly's Cave, Pigeon Hole

To the west, beyond the isthmus, lies Joyce's Country, a hilly region traversed by green valleys and lonely roads. It takes its names from a Welsh family who settled here in the 13th c.

Joyce's Country

Ashford Castle (hotel)

Lough Nafooey   A delightful round tour can be made from Cong, through a charming blend of hill, valley and river scenery. From Cong head first for Clonbur and then for Lough Nafooey, with views of the Paltry Mountains; after crossing the saddle into the valley of the River Joyce, turn south to follow the L101 along the western tip of Lough Corrib and so back to Cong.

Connemara   C 1/2

Republic of Ireland
Province: Connacht
County: Galway

Location   Connemara is the area extending along the heavily indented west coast of Ireland to the north of Galway Bay. Its inhabitants remain steeped in tradition and in large parts of Connemara Irish is still spoken. Roads signs are in Gaelic only.

★★Topography   With its ranges of hills, bare isolated peaks, valleys with peat-blackened loughs and coastline of sheer cliffs and sandy bays, Connemara is one of the most attractive places in Ireland, appealing alike to tourists, sportsmen and those in search of a quieter, more relaxed kind of holiday.

Clifden

The main centre of population in Connemara is Clifden, a little market town in the extreme west. It lies at the head of Clifden Bay, one of the many narrow, fjord-like inlets which here reach inland in the direction of the Twelve Bens, Connemara's great landmarks further east. The famous Connemara Pony Show with its associated traditional contests and competi-

Clifden, chief town of Connemara

tions, attracts many visitors every August. Below the town the River Owenglin makes its way to the sea in a series of picturesque waterfalls.

Heading west from the town along Sky Road there are some superb views. The road leads to the abandoned Clifden Castle (1815).

Sights

At the right time of year an interesting spectacle can be witnessed at Weir Bridge, to the south of the town. Here during the spawning season vast numbers of salmon can be seen struggling upstream against the fast-flowing current.

Further south still are the remains of the very first transatlantic wireless station, set up here by Guglielmo Marconi (1874–1937), the Italian radio pioneer who, in 1896, came to live in England. Also in the area is a monument to Sir William Alcock (1892–1919) and Sir Arthur Whitten Brown (1886–1948) who, on June 14/15th 1919 made the first non-stop flight across the Atlantic, taking off from St John's, Newfoundland, and crash-landing here.

Tours in Connemara

The contrasts so typical of the Connemara scenery – whether in the landscape itself or in the play of light and colour – are best appreciated by making several separate excursions.

From Clifden the N59 runs northwards, skirting the coast past little white cottages scattered among stony fields, drystone walls and rocky coves.

At Streamstown, a few miles north of Clifden, the light-coloured Connemara marble is worked. The quarries can be visited.

Streamstown

A side road branches left to the fishing village of Cleggan (lobsters). On Cleggan Hill (fine views) are the ruins of a 19th c. watch-tower.

Cleggan

135

Connemara

Inishbofin

From Cleggan a boat can be taken to Inishbofin. The island, today with a population of about 200, was occupied by monks in the 7th c. On it can be seen ancient promontory forts, stone houses, and the remains of a barracks built by Cromwell's troops (1652–57) who turned it into a sort of internment camp for monks and priests. But the island is also worth visiting for its lovely sandy beaches and rugged cliffs and the scope it offers for sailing and sea-angling.

Letterfrack

The N59 proceeds via Moyard to Letterfrack, a community founded in the 19th c. by the Quakers. The mild climate here allows tall fuchsia hedges to flourish.

★Connemara National Park

Letterfrack is the main gateway into the Connemara National Park, with a Visitor Centre in the village (open: park, all the year round; Visitor Centre, May–Sept. daily 10am–6pm). The Visitor Centre has information on the flora, fauna and history of settlement of the 49,400acre/2000ha park, which can be explored on foot on shortish waymarked paths or a longer full day's tour.

Tully Cross, Renvyle

From Letterfrack a side road on the left leads to Tully Cross and Renvyle. At the end of the Renvyle Peninsula – lovely coastal scenery of sandy beaches alternating with cliffs – are the remains of a 14th c. castle, a church and a small dolmen.

Kylemore Abbey

The N59, continuing east from Letterfrack, follows the valley of the River Dawros to the loughs at Kylemore, nestling amid hills. This particular area is at its loveliest when the rhododendrons and fuchsias are in bloom. To the left, above the first lough, stands the palatial Kylemore Abbey, built in the 19th c. by a wealthy merchant as a country-house but now occupied by Benedictine nuns. Part of the abbey is a girls school and closed to the

Landscape near Kylemore Abbey

public; otherwise visitors are welcomed (open: Apr.–Nov. daily 10.30am–6.30pm; restaurant; craft centre).

Passing Kylemore Lough and Lough Fee, the road winds its way down to Killary Harbour, a 10 mile/16km-long fjord-like inlet, somewhat gloomy in shadow but delightful when the sun shines. There was once a British naval base here.

Killary Harbour

Northwards across the water the beautiful Vale of Delphi can be glimpsed between the bulk of Mweelrea (2688ft/819m) and Ben Gorm (2297ft/700m). This lovely valley, classical in aspect, got its name when the then Marquess of Sligo called his fishing lodge there Delphi.

Vale of Delphi

The road follows the south side of the inlet to Leenane, a good centre for fishermen and climbers. The Leenane Cultural Centre (open: Mar.–Oct. daily 10am–6pm) celebrates the tradition of woollen manufacture for which the area is known. The Centre has its own land on which are kept several breeds of sheep.

Leenane

The River Erriff, flowing through Co. Mayo to its outflow in Killary Harbour, here cascades down the lovely Ashleag Waterfall.

Ashleag Waterfall

From Leenane the R336 cuts directly through the hills southward to Maam Cross, following the river as it skirts the edge of the delightful Joyce's Country (see Cong).

Maam Cross

Beyond Maam Cross, the R336 continues south through a maze of little loughs to arrive after 6 miles/9km in Screeb, situated on a narrow and much-indented arm of the sea which, were it not for the tide-marks along the shore, could easily be mistaken for an inland lough. The tiny fields which are a feature of this area have been painstakingly built up from layer after layer of seaweed alternating with sand and protected by drystone walls.

Screeb

From Screeb the R340 hugs the shores of Kilkieran Bay to Carna (fishing for sea-trout in the bay and for brown trout in nearby loughs).

Carna

On two islets in Lough Skannive are crannogs (lake pile-dwellings).

Lough Skannive

8 miles/13km further along the coast road (R340, R342), a by-road on the left drops down to Cashel Bay. Cashel is much favoured by anglers.

Cashel

The coast road, regained a little further west, goes on to Roundstone, a community established in the early 19th c. for migrant Scottish fishermen. It is now a holiday resort popular with artists and nature-lovers (beautiful shell beaches).

Roundstone

Beyond Roundstone the R341 continues round Ballyconneely Bay to Bally-conneely; on the coast 2¼ miles/4km south is an 18-hole golf course.

Ballyconneely

The hinterland of Connemara, with the Twelve Bens (east of Clifden) and the Maamturk Mountains, is lonely and sparsely populated – very different from the coastal strip. Dominating this central part are the Twelve Bens, of which Benbaun (2389ft/718m) is the highest and the others not much lower. Mosses and lichens colour the steep rock faces, with splashes of purple heather and the glistening white of quartz from which the mountains are formed.

The Twelve Bens, Maamturk Mountains

Below the Bens on the south side lies Ballynahinch Lough with, on its southern shore, Ballynahinch Castle (now a hotel), an 18th c. mansion built by the Martin family who, during the Great Famine of 1845–49, sold off much their property to help the poor. On a wooded islet in the lough can be seen a ruined castle.

Ballynahinch Lough

Cork · Corcaigh   E 3

Republic of Ireland
Province: Munster
County: Cork
Population: 136,000

Location

Cork (Corcaigh="marshy place") is the largest city in Ireland apart from Dublin and Belfast; it has an international airport. Cork lies near the south coast, at first sight well inland but in fact on an arm of the sea, access to open waters being through a narrow strait called Passage West.

Along with Limerick, Cork is one of the Irish Republic's biggest industrial centres after Dublin. Industries include brewing and distilling, food processing, textiles, footwear and chemicals. Several multinational corporations including Ford and Dunlop are represented here. Cork's magnificent harbour has contributed significantly to the economic standing of the town, particularly the deep-water port at Cobh on the outer harbour from where the produce of the surrounding region, primarily agricultural, is exported.

Cork is also the intellectual capital of southern Ireland, with many cultural institutions including the Cork Literary and Scientific Society founded in 1820. It has a college of the National University of Ireland and two cathedrals, Roman Catholic and Protestant.

History

Cork's history began with the founding of a monastery by St Finbarr (7th c.) on a small alluvial island in the River Lee, where St Finbarr's Cathedral now stands. The monastery and the settlement which grew up around it flourished in spite of several Danish raids, and were later incorporated into the fortified base which the Danes established there. After the arrival in Ireland in 1172 of the English King Henry II, the town was several times captured, recovered and retaken, being now in English, now in Irish hands. In 1248 it was surrounded by a new circuit of walls; in 1378 it was burned down by the Irish; in 1495 it was taken by Perkin Warbeck, the Yorkist Pretender to the English throne; and in 1642 it was captured by Irish insurgents who were driven from the city in 1644 and again in 1649. In 1690 the city walls were finally pulled down.

During the Civil War in 1920 two mayors of Cork were killed and large areas of the city damaged by fire.

The town

The centre of Cork is to all intents and purposes an island, sandwiched between two arms of the River Lee, the North and South Channels. The river spanned by several bridges within the city, flows into Lough Mahon (as Cork Harbour is also known).

The quays along the river, with their limestone walls, are lined with trees. The cityscape as whole, however, is not particularly attractive. Cork's war-torn history has ensured that few really ancient buildings survive. There are, though, some fine 18th c. buildings, and the central area of the city between the North and South Channels is given architectural character by the churches and other buildings dating from the early 19th c. The main shopping district is the area around St Patrick's Street.

City centre

St Patrick's Bridge, spanning the North Channel, is a convenient starting point for a circuit of Cork city centre. First proceed east along Merchant's Quay to the Custom House on the furthest tip of the island, there doubling back along Lapp's Quay bordering the South Channel to Parnell Bridge, continuing west along South Mall to its junction with the spacious Grand Parade. Where Grand Parade narrows into Corn Market Street, turn right into St Patrick's Street and so back in a wide sweep to St Patrick's Bridge. With some minor detours this walk takes in most of the principal city centre sights.

City centre walk

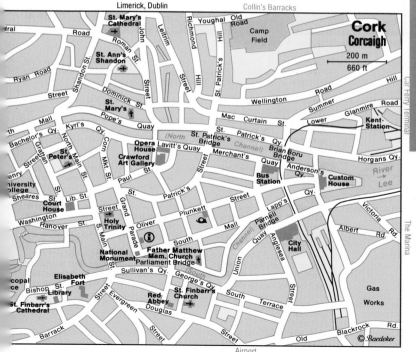

139

View of Cork from St Anne's Church, Shandon

City Hall	From Lapp's Quay there is a good view across the South Channel to the City Hall, reflected in the waters of the slow-flowing river. Built in the mid 1930s, it boasts an assembly hall with seating for 2000.
Father Matthew Memorial Church	Off to the left of South Mall, on the banks of the South Channel which here enters a sharp bend, stands the Father Matthew Memorial Church (Holy Trinity; 1825), a Neo-Gothic building designed by G. R. Pain. It commemorates the "Apostle of Temperance", Father Matthew (1790–1861), who preached the unpopular doctrine of abstinence and "made an idea into a crusade".
St Finbarr's Church	On the far side of the South Channel can be seen St Finbarr's Church, also known as the South Chapel. Built in 1766, it has late 18th c. furnishings; in the interior is a figure of the dead Christ by Hogan.
Red Abbey Tower	A short distance west, almost completely surrounded by later buildings in Abbey Street, is the Red Abbey Tower, one of the few relics of Cork's medieval monastic houses. During the siege in 1690, John Churchill, later Duke of Marlborough, is said to have made his headquarters here.
St Finbarr's Cathedral	Farther west still rise the prominent spires of St Finbarr's Cathedral (1865–80), in French Early Gothic style, with a richly furnished and decorated interior including fine mosaics in the choir. The cathedral's eight bells, cast by Abel Rudhall, are from an earlier church of 1750 on the same site.
Grand Parade	Adorning Grand Parade are the Berwick Fountain and a monument to Irish patriots.
Church of the Holy Trinity	Just to the left, in Washington Street, stands Holy Trinity Church, also known as Christ Church (1720; by Coltsman). Among relics from an earlier building is the tomb of Mayor Ronan and his wife (mid 16th c.).

City Hall

St Mary's Church

Two blocks further along on the north side of Washington Street is the Court House (1832), with a handsome portico.

Court House

From Liberty Street continue east to Corn Market Street, with the old market at its southern end. The carefully restored Victorian covered market hall with its arches, fountains and galleries is always a hive of activity with a brisk trade in fruit vegetables, meat and fish.

Corn Market Street

The Crawford Municipal Art Gallery on Emmet Place, a few hundred yards further east, has a collection of sculpture and modern Irish art (open: Mon.–Sat. 10.30am–5pm).

Crawford Art Gallery

From Emmet Place, a side street leads south to St Patrick's Street, the city's main shopping thoroughfare. Built over an old arm of the River Lee, it runs in a broad arc to St Patrick's Bridge.

St Patrick's Street

Northern District

Across the river to the north stands the Dominican Church of St Mary's (1832–39) with, on the high altar, a reputedly miraculous image of the Virgin (14th c. Flemish work in ivory).

St Mary's

Just a little to the north of St Mary's is one of the city's landmarks, St Ann's Church, Shandon (1722). Its handsome tower – looking rather like a telescope drawn out in three stages and popularly known as "the pepperpot" – is of parti-coloured stone, red sandstone on the north and east sides, grey limestone on the south and west. In the tower hang eight bells cast by Abel Rudhall in 1750, with a celebrated carillon (for a small charge visitors can ring the bells themselves). Although only 120ft/36m high, because of the church's elevated situation, the tower (very narrow stairway) affords a wide panorama of the city.

★St Ann's Shandon

St Mary's
Cathedral

A couple of streets further up the hill can be seen the Neo-Classical St Mary's Cathedral (1808), the interior of which was renewed in Neo-Gothic style in 1820 following a fire.

Collins Barracks

To the east, in Old Youghal Road, lie the Collins Barracks with, in the chapel, a three-light stained glass window by Evie Hone (1939; viewing by appointment).

St Patrick's

South of the Barracks, near Lower Glanmire Road, stands the Corinthian-style St Patrick's Church (1836; by G. R. Pain), unfortunately disfigured by an extension of 1894.

Custom House

From St Patrick's Church cross the Brian Boru Bridge to regain the island. On the right is the large bus station, to the left the Custom House (1814), now the Harbour Master's Office.

Western District

Cork Public
Museum

West of the city centre between the river and Mardyke Walk are sports grounds and Fitzgerald Park with a range of recreational facilities. A handsome Georgian house in the park is home to the Cork Public Museum (open: Mon.–Fri. 11am–1pm and 2–5pm, Sun. 3–5pm). The museum provides comprehensive coverage of the history of the region from prehistoric times to the present day. There are also collections of silver, glass and the crochet- and lace-work for which Cork was famous.

University
College

South of the museum, beyond Western Road and across the South Channel, lies University College (founded 1845), part of the National University of Ireland, with some 4000 students. Many of the Neo-Classical buildings are well preserved, the Goal Gate (1818) being particularly fine. The Honan

Grounds of Fota House

Cobh with its Neo-Gothic church

Chapel has lovely stained glass by Sarah Purser and Harry Clarke. The college possesses interesting collections of e.g. ogham stones and early prints of Cork, which can be viewed by appointment.

Surroundings

Near the N8 about 4½ miles/7km north-east of the city stands Riverstown House, which acquired its present aspect in the mid 18th c. when it was the residence of the Bishop of Cork. The interior is well worth seeing (open: May–Sept. daily 10am–4pm).

Riverstown House

Fota Island, east of Cork and linked to the city by a bridge, has several attractions, the first being the Fota Wildlife Park (open: Apr.–Sept. daily from 10am except Sun. 11am; Oct. Sun. only from 11am; last admission 5pm; admission fee) with a variety of waterfowl and many species of animal including giraffes, zebras, antelopes and monkeys; a visit always proves a hit with children. Separate from the wildlife park are Fota House and the adjoining grounds (Fota Arboretum included in fee for Wildlife Park). The house with its notable art collection is to be opened to the public after restoration. New varieties of tree are constantly being added to the already extensive collection in the arboretum.

★Fota Island

Situated south-east of Cork is Great Island, surrounded by arms of the sea and joined to the mainland by bridges. On its south side, 15 miles/24km from Cork, lies Cobh, a relatively modern town and busy deep-water port. Around the harbour, above which Cobh's fine and richly decorated Neo-Gothic church stands sentinel, the townscape is particularly picturesque. An additional attraction for tourists is Cobh the Queenstown Story, opened in 1993. Housed in an old railway building (1862), it documents the eventful history of the town (open: daily 10am–6pm; admission fee).

Cobh

Because of it prime strategic location, the area around Cork Harbour abounds with fortifications from many different periods. There are also many small resorts to which holidaymakers are drawn by the mildness of the climate.

Cork Harbour

At the outer end of Passage West stands Monkstown Castle (17th c.; National Monument), now the clubhouse of a golf course.

Monkstown Castle

The R609 and R612 run south to Carrigaline (8 miles/13km) and then east to Crosshaven, a popular holiday resort with good sandy beaches at the outflow of the River Owenboy into an arm of Cork Harbour.

Crosshaven

Derry

See Londonderry

Dingle Peninsula

D 1/2

Republic of Ireland
Province: Munster
County: Kerry

The Dingle Peninsula is the most northerly of the hilly promontories which reach out into the Atlantic from the far south-west corner of Ireland. It extends westward for more than 30 miles/50km, from the low-lying country around Killorglin and Tralee.
This is a predominantly Irish-speaking area (Gaeltacht) where old customs, traditions and crafts are still very much alive.

Location

Inch Beach on Dingle Peninsula

★Topography   The highest point of the peninsula, Brandon Mountain (3085ft/940m), crowns a chain of hills which at Brandon Head plunge almost straight into the sea from a height of 2462ft/750m. To the west of this range is a rolling coastal plain studded with typical Irish farmsteads and hamlets. Here there are few stone walls; corn is grown in small square fields, and purply-red fuchsia hedges, pale green ferns and black moss add their distinctive colourings to the landscape.

Scenic drive

Caherconree   From Tralee (see entry) the road runs west along Tralee Bay to Camp. South-east of the village rises Caherconree (2668ft/813m). Beneath the peak stands a massive promontory fort. A path goes up to the fort from a car park on the road from Camp to Aughills (board).

Inch   At Camp the R559 bears south-west and winds its way up through hilly country. In 5 miles/8km a side road branches off on the left and runs south to Inch, a sheltered seaside resort from which a 3 mile/5km-long ridge of dunes extends into the sea (lovely sandy beach).

Doonsheane   The R559 continues on its way to Dingle, sea on one side, hills on the other. Just before Dingle turn left and then sharp left again to reach, at Doonsheane, the ancient circular burial ground of Ballytaggart, containing a number of ogham stones (National Monument), some with crosses.

★Dingle   Dingle itself, the chief place on the peninsula and the most westerly town in Europe, lies in a sheltered bay with good beaches surrounded on three sides by hills. It is an excellent centre for sea-angling and boating, with other facilities including mini-golf; but above all the pretty little port with its brightly painted houses is a good base from which to visit the many antiquities at the western end of the peninsula.

House fronts in Dingle

West of Dingle, at Milltown, is a large standing stone known as the Mile-stone; near by are two others, "the Gates of Glory".

Milltown

Continuing west the road comes to Ventry, 2 miles/3km north-west of which, on the Ballyferriter road, are the ruins of Rahinnane Castle (15th c.; National Monument), in a circular enclosure surrounded by a 30ft/9m-deep moat.

Rahinnane Castle

From Ventry the route follows the peninsula's rocky south coast. About 220yd/200m off to the south on the left hand side of the road at Fahan, Dunbeg, a fine promontory fort (National Monument) with four earthen ramparts and a substantial stone wall, stands directly overlooking the sea. Within the fort are the remains of a house, square in plan within its circular exterior wall. An underground passage leads from the innermost part of the fort to the outer defences.

Dunbeg

A few miles further west at Glanfahan can be seen clusters of beehive huts, each cluster enclosed by a wall, making a total of 417 structures, every one built without the use of mortar; also 19 souterrains and 18 standing stones (all National Monuments).

Glanfahan

At the south-western tip of the peninsula is Slea Head. From the narrow road below Mount Eagle there are extensive views.

Slea Head

The Blasket Islands can be reached by boat, weather permitting, from the little fishing harbour of Dunquin. Information about the islands is available from the Blasket Centre, also in Dunquin (open: Easter–Sept. daily 10am–6 or 7pm).

Blasket Islands

The main island, Great Blasket, was inhabited until 1953 when the islanders – said to have been, in the enjoyment of their settled way of life, "the happiest people on earth" – were moved to the mainland. The abandoned village street can be seen on the hillside; in the centre of the island are the ruins of a church (National Monument) of uncertain age. From the island's highest point (937ft/285m) there is a view over Blasket Sound to the rugged coast of Kerry. In 1588 one of the ships of the Spanish Armada, the "Santa Maria de la Rosa", ran aground in Blasket Sound.

4 miles/6km north-west of Great Blasket lies the small island of Inishtooskert, with the ruins of a little church, a well-preserved beehive hut, and three crosses (National Monuments).

Dún an Oir

From Dunquin the drive continues northwards. After about 2 miles/3km, a side road leads left past a beach and a hotel, beyond which turn left again and then first right to arrive at the site of an ancient castle, Dún an Oir (= "fort of gold"), today marked only by a monument. Here in 1580, 600 Spanish and Irish soldiers who had surrendered to the English, were massacred.

Reask

Returning to the main road proceed through Ballyferriter and on to Reask where, amidst the remains of a hermitage, stands a notable Early Christian cross-pillar decorated with tendril patterns.

★Gallarus Oratory

The next call is at Gallarus Oratory (National Monument). Shaped like an upturned boat (gallarus="curious house"), it has walls more than 3ft/1m thick and so carefully constructed that, even without the use of mortar, the little chapel (measuring only 15×10ft/4.5×3m) is still completely weatherproof after 1200 years.

From the chapel's slightly elevated site, the ruins of Gallarus Castle (16th c.; National Monument), a four-storeyed keep with vaulted rooms, can be seen 1¼ miles/1km further west.

Kilmalkedar

At the crossroads above Gallarus turn sharp left for Kilmalkedar Church, one of the most important ecclesiastical sites on the peninsula, where a monastery (National Monument) was founded in the 7th c. It preserves a Romanesque church (12th c.) with fine sculpture in the tympanum of the doorway and on the chancel arch. The blind arcading of the interior shows, as indeed does the rest of the church, the influence of Cormac's Chapel at Cashel (see entry). In the church is the Alphabet Stone, with ogham and Latin characters side by side. In the churchyard stand an old sundial, a large monolithic cross, and another ogham stone. 150yd/140m away is St Brendan's House (medieval) with, nearby, an oratory (St Brendan's Oratory).

Brandon Mountain

On Brandon Mountain are the remains of another St Brendan's Oratory and a number of stone huts (National Monuments). The ascent, best tackled from Cloghane or Faha, or alternatively from the west (clearly marked paths), is well worth the effort not only for its own sake but also the magnificent views from the top.

Connor Pass

More superb views can be enjoyed on the exceptionally scenic road from Dingle over the Connor Pass.

Rough Point

With Beenoskee rising high to the right of the road, to the left a long promontory extends northwards, reaching a good way out to sea. At its landward end is Castlegregory, a quiet little resort situated between Lough Gill and Tralee Bay. From here it is a further 4½ miles/7km to Rough Point at the tip of the promontory, off which lies a group of small islands.

Donegal · Dún na nGall   B 3

Republic of Ireland
Province: Ulster
County: Donegal
Population: 2200

Donegal Abbey

Donegal (Dún na nGall="fortress of the foreigners"), county town of Co. Donegal, is situated well north on Ireland's west coast, at a point where the River Eske flows into Donegal Bay and where the N56 meets up with the N15.

Location

Originally a Celtic settlement, the town owes its present aspect to the English who, in the 17th c., laid it out on a regular plan around a market square, appropriately called the Diamond, around which the life of this busy little town revolves. The obelisk in the market square was erected as a memorial to the Four Masters (see below, Donegal Abbey).

The town

Sights

On the rocky bank of the River Eske only a short distance from the market place stands the imposing ruin of Donegal Castle (National Monument), principal seat of the O'Donnells, princes of Tir Chonaill. Falling into English hands in 1607, the large square keep (1505) was altered by the insertion of windows. At the same time a splendid carved fireplace embellished with coats of arms was added to the main floor, and in 1610 a fortified manor-house (now in process of restoration) was built on to the tower.

Donegal Castle

Picturesquely situated at the mouth of the River Eske are the remains of Donegal Abbey (National Monument), a 15th c. Franciscan house where the Four Masters, Michael O'Clery and his three assistants, compiled their celebrated annals ("Annals of the Four Masters"), a monumental work of Irish history. (Coming from Ballyshannon, take the side road branching left at the entrance to the town.)

Donegal Abbey

Also well worth a visit is the Donegal Craft Village, a collection of arts and crafts workshops grouped around a courtyard on the outskirts of the town on the Ballyshannon road.

Donegal Craft Village

Surroundings

Lough Eske

5 miles/8km north-east of the town lies Lough Eske, offering good fishing. A road runs round the lough, from the north end of which a detour can be made to a waterfall 2 miles/3km further north, up a valley.

Blue Stack Mountains

The valley climbs higher into the Blue Stack Mountains and to a beautiful little tarn, Lough Belshade, in a corrie with steep rock sides.

Lough Derg

3 miles/5km south of Donegal, the R232 branches left off the N15 to Pettigo, from where the R233 leads north through desolate countryside to Lough Derg. In the lough lies Station Island, known in the Middle Ages as St Patrick's Purgatory and the destination every year of large numbers of pilgrims. The churches and pilgrim hospices on the island can be seen from the shores of the lough. During the pilgrimage season (June to August), only pilgrims are allowed onto the island.

In pagan times a cave on Station Island was believed to be the entrance to the underworld; the island became known as St Patrick's Purgatory when a journeying medieval knight claimed to have seen the fires of Purgatory in the cave.

The pilgrims who make what has been called "the hardest pilgrimage in Christendom" are today almost exclusively Irish. They spend three days on the island performing the various penances prescribed, mainly vigils and fasting.

Rossnowlagh

12 miles/20km south of Donegal at Rossnowlagh, a holiday resort on the Atlantic coast with a lovely sandy beach, is a modern Franciscan friary which also houses the Donegal Historical Society Museum (open: daily 9am–6.30pm). Its collection of Stone Age and Bronze Age material includes a finely wrought sword found in the course of building work in the neighbouring town of Ballyshannon.

Mountcharles

Mountcharles, a village on a steep hillside 4½ miles/7km west of Donegal (N56), enjoys splendid views; there is good fishing in Eany Water.

Drogheda · Droichead Atha   C 5

Republic of Ireland
Province: Leinster
County: Louth
Population: 24,000

Location

Drogheda (Droichead Atha="bridge over the ford") is situated on the east coast of Ireland on the River Boyne, at the point where it is crossed by the N1 and shortly before its outflow into the Irish Sea. With its port and various industries – cement works, steel works, breweries – it is a considerable industrial centre.

History

In 911 the Danes captured the little town standing on the site of an earlier settlement at a ford over the Boyne. They developed it into a well-defended stronghold. Later the Anglo-Normans built a bridge and fortified the settlements on both sides of the river. In the 14th and 15th c. Drogheda was one of the four principal towns of Ireland, with the right of coining and, from 1465, a university. Parliament met there several times up until the 17th c. In 1649 the town was taken by Cromwell's forces, and in 1690, following the Battle of the Boyne, it surrendered to William of Orange's army.

Sights

St Lawrence's Gate

Drogheda had originally ten gates of which only St Lawrence's Gate (National Monument) survives. It has two massive round towers with a

St Lawrence's Gate, Drogheda

loopholed connecting wall, a vaulted arch on the upper level, and barrel-vaulting at street level, all crenellated, enclosing a low entrance passage.

At the other end of St Lawrence's Street, on the left, is the old Tholsel (Town Hall), a domed building now occupied by a bank.

Tholsel

To the right, on the corner of St Peter's Street and William Street, stands the handsome St Peter's Church (1748; Church of Ireland; by Francis Johnston), the interior of which has fine Rococo stucco work.

St Peter's
Protestant Church

The Roman Catholic St Peter's Church, on the right hand side of West Street, the continuation of St Peter's Street, was erected as a memorial to Oliver Plunkett, Archbishop of Armagh, executed at Tyburn in London in 1681. His embalmed head is kept in a reliquary in the Neo-Gothic church.

St Peter's
Catholic Church

Millmount Fort (National Monument), on the south side of the river, beyond the bridge at the end of Shop Street, was built on top of a passage grave similar to the one at Newgrange in the Boyne Valley (see entry). Fortified in the 12th c. it continued in use as a fort until 1800. Some of the rooms now house a museum documenting the town's history. A fine view of Drogheda is obtained from the fort.

Millmount Fort

Downstream, the river is spanned by the Boyne Viaduct, a splendid example of mid 19th c. railway engineering.

Railway Viaduct

Surroundings

4 miles/6km north-east of Drogheda, at Baltray, there is a championship golf course; also good bathing from a sandy beach 3 miles/5km long.

Baltray

2 miles/3km further north, Termonfeckin boasts a three-storey tower house (15th c.; National Monument) which has a fine spiral staircase and an

Termonfeckin

unusual vaulted roof, this latter constructed in exactly the same fashion as the vault at Newgrange, some 4000 years older. Beside St Feckin's Church stands a richly decorated high cross (10th c.; National Monument) with, on the east side, a Crucifixion, on the west side Christ in Glory, and on the other two sides geometric designs and interlace.

Clogherhead
2½ miles/4km beyond Termonfeckin lies the village of Clogherhead and, on the north side of Clogher Head itself, the little harbour of Port Oriel, with lovely sandy beaches.

Dunleer
At Dunleer, 9 miles/13km north-west of Clogherhead, is the Rathgory Transport Museum (open: Sat. and Sun. 2–6pm; fine collection of veteran and vintage cars).

Maiden Tower
To the east of Drogheda, at Mornington, on the Boyne estuary, stands a lighthouse from the Elizabethan period, called the Maiden Tower (a reference to the Virgin Queen).

Bettystown, Laytown
South-east of Drogheda, in Co. Meath, are the seaside resorts of Bettystown (18-hole golf course) and Laytown. Both have 6 mile/10km-long beaches.

Gormanston
Farther south, on the N1, Gormanston, a mansion of 1786, is now occupied by the Franciscans. The park on the east side is well laid out with walks and has a "tea-house" of clipped yew hedges.

Fourknocks
Inland, between the R108 and R152, can be seen the important prehistoric site of Fourknocks (1800–1500 B.C.; National Monument), consisting of a large passage grave and two smaller burial mounds. The large grave has a number of scribed stones, including one which depicts a face, drawn with a few simple strokes – the clearest representation of a human face surviving from Irish prehistory.

Duleek
5 miles/8km south-west of Drogheda, on the River Nanny (good fishing), lies Duleek where, on land belonging to the priory (National Monument), are the ruins of a church and a high cross. The church contains a number of fine monuments and a tumba carved with figures of saints, a Crucifixion, angels and coats of arms. The rather squat cross (probably 10th c.) has a Crucifixion, various figures, ornament and symbols of the Evangelists. The Dowdall Cross (1601; National Monument), standing by the roadside, shows continental influence; it is decorated with figures of saints and a coat of arms.

Athcarne Castle
3 miles/5km south of Duleek stands Athcarne Castle, a fortified Elizabethan manor-house (1587).

★ Mellifont Abbey
At Tullyallen, 2½ miles/4km north-west of Drogheda on the R168 (signposted to Collon), a side road leads left to Mellifont. Here, on the River Mattock, are the ruins of Mellifont Abbey (National Monument), once an important Cistercian house, founded in 1142 and built with the help of monks from France. By 1272 it had become the mother house of 24 other monasteries. After the Dissolution of the Monasteries (1539) it was converted into a fortified manor-house. Only a few remains of the original building have been preserved – a castle-like gatehouse with a massive tower, the fine crypt of the church, part of the two-storey well-house or lavabo in the cloister (arches reconstructed) and the finely vaulted chapterhouse (14th c.) in which a variety of architectural fragments are now displayed. Part of the floor of the chapter-house has been laid with attractively-patterned glazed tiles from the church. Stumps of walls and marks on the ground indicate that the abbey was laid out in the manner of Clairvaux (open: May–mid June and mid Sept. to Oct. daily 10am–5pm; mid June–mid Sept. daily 9.30am–6.30pm).

Drumcliffe · Droim Chliabh   B 3

Republic of Ireland
Province: Connacht
County: Sligo

The village of Drumcliffe (Droim Chliabh="back of the baskets") lies on the   Location
deep bay of the same name in north-west Ireland, just to the north of Sligo.
St Columba founded a monastery here in 574, the last abbot of which died
in 1503.

Sights

The grandfather of W. B. Yeats (see Famous People) was for many years the   Yeats' Grave
parish priest here, and the great Irish poet is buried in the churchyard. His
gravestone bears the inscription which he himself composed:

Cast a cold eye
On life, on death.
Horseman, pass by!

On the path leading up to the church is a high cross (c. 1000; National   ★ High cross
Monument) with, on its east side, Adam and Eve, Cain and Abel, Daniel in
the Lions' Den and Christ in Glory, and on the west side the Presentation in
the Temple, two figures and the Crucifixion; the cross is further decorated
with fabulous beasts and interlace ornament.

Surroundings

To the north of the village, Benbulben (1697ft/517m), a flat-topped hill with   Benbulben
steeply scarped sides furrowed by gullies, rises abruptly out of the plain.
This extraordinary table mountain features prominently in Irish legend.
Here Queen Maeve and the Ulster hero CuChulainn fought for possession
of a herd of giant cattle, and here Diarmaid bled to death after his struggle
with the great mountain boar of Benbulben. The slopes of the hill were also
the scene of a historical event, the "Battle of the Books" at Cuildrevne in
561, which led to St Columba's departure from Ireland. The hill, which
forms part of the Dartry Mountains, is of interest to geologists and botanists. Those not deterred by the lack of a path will be rewarded by extensive
views from the top over the surrounding low ground and westward to the
Atlantic.

From Drumcliffe a delightful excursion can be made to Glencar Lough, a   Glencar Lough
few miles east of the village. At the east end of the lough is a lovely waterfall
in a setting of dense greenery.

4 miles/6km north-west of Drumcliffe, in a park, is Lissadell House (open: Lissadell House
June–mid Sept. Mon.–Sat. 10.30am–noon and 2–4.30pm), built in 1834 for
the grandfather of the sisters Constance and Eva Gore-Booth. Constance
(1884–1927), later Countess Markiewicz, afterwards became involved in
nationalist politics in Dublin and took part in the 1916 Rising. Her sister Eva
was a writer. Yeats, who wrote a poem about Constance, stayed in the
house on several occasions.

South-west of Lissadell a small peninsula reaches out into Drumcliffe Bay.   Pigeon Holes
On it, at the fishing village of Raghly, are the Pigeon Holes – two holes in the
rock into which the sea is driven with tremendous force by way of subterranean channels.
    Also in this area are the picturesque ruins of Ardtermon Castle (17th c.).

5 miles/8km north of Drumcliffe, on the N15, lies Grange, from where a side   Inishmurray
road runs west to Streedagh. There a boat can be hired to cross to the island

151

of Inishmurray (which can also be reached from Mullaghmore, see below). The island, 4½ miles/7km west of Streedagh, was still inhabited in the earlier part of this century. On it is an excellently preserved Early Christian monastic settlement (National Monument) founded by St Molaise in the early 6th c. and abandoned 300 years later after being raided and plundered. The monastery buildings were used by the island's later inhabitants and were thus preserved. The remains give an excellent impression of what such a settlement was like. A ring-wall between 10 and 15ft/3 and 4m high and of similar thickness at the base, with five entrances, surrounds an oval precinct measuring 60×45yd/53×41m, divided into four enclosures of differing sizes. Within the precinct are the Men's Church, the little Oratory of Teach Molaise, the Church of the Fire, a beehive hut and altar-like structures of masonry. On one of these are the famous Curse Stones, round speckled stones which are believed to be effective in putting a curse on an enemy. All round the island are various memorial stones and station chapels, which were visited by pilgrims in a prescribed sequence. From St Patrick's memorial, at the eastern tip of the island, there is a fine view of the mainland.

★Creevykeel   5 miles/8km north of Grange, near the village of Cliffoney, is the Creevykeel Court Cairn (National Monument), one of the finest in Ireland. A wedge-shaped stone wall encloses an open court, beyond which are a double-chambered gallery, two further chambers and the remains of yet another. The site is thought to be about 4500 years old.

Mullaghmore   From Cliffoney a minor road leads on to the Mullaghmore Peninsula, with a
Peninsula   sheltered sandy beach, a small-craft harbour and good sea-angling. The hotel arranges trips to the island of Inishmurray (see above).

Dublin · Baile Atha Cliath/Dubhlinn   C 5

Republic of Ireland
Province: Leinster
County: Dublin
Population: 1.1 million (including suburbs)

Location   Dublin (Baile Atha Cliath="town of the hurdle ford", or Dubhlinn="dark pool") lies in the broad sweep of Dublin Bay, between the rocky promontory of Howth to the north and the headland of Dalkey to the south.

Capital of the Irish Republic, Dublin is the undisputed economic and cultural centre of the country as well as its political centre. Almost a third of the population of the Republic live here.

Dublin is a city of startling social contrasts. Strolling through the fashionable residential districts on the south bank of the Liffey, or through the elegant shopping quarter, it seems almost inconceivable that large areas, especially north of the Liffey, should be so dreary and run down (but not so surprising perhaps given that the unemployment rate exceeds 20%). The proportion of young people on drugs is relatively high, and beggars are a not uncommon sight on Dublin's streets. Despite this, most Dubliners and most visitors to the city are bewitched by Dublin's charm; it is a warm-hearted place, with something of a southern feel to it, a place where individuality is almost a passion.

History   The oldest Irish name for the city, and the one still generally used, Baile Atha Cliath, refers to the ancient ford across the Liffey at this point. St Patrick is believed to have visited Dublin in 448 and converted many of the inhabitants. Subsequently a Christian community grew up around the ford; then in 840 the first Danes appeared, occupying the town and establishing a fortified base from which to conduct both their raids and their

Christ Church Cathedral, Dublin ▶

trade. In 988 the Irish king Mael Sechnaill II captured the town, and in 1014 the High King of Ireland, Brian Boru, broke the power of the Danes by his victory at nearby Clontarf (now a suburb of the city). It was not until 1170 however, that the Danes were finally driven out by the Anglo-Normans. Two years later Henry II came to Dublin to receive the homage of the Irish chieftains. The town now became the capital of the area over which the English held sway, known as the Pale (from "palisade"), the security of which relied upon the castles of the Anglo-Norman knights. During the conflicts of the 15th and 16th c., the Dubliners generally aligned themselves with forces opposed to the English Crown. But in the 17th c. they sided with the Royalists against Cromwell (who captured the town in 1649) and later with James II against William of Orange.

In the 18th c. Dublin prospered and the population rose from 65,000 to 200,000. A Wide Street Commission and Paving Board were set up and there was a great boom in building both by the public authorities and the more affluent among Dublin's citizenry.

At the beginning of the 19th c. a brief interlude of independence was brought to an end by political union with Great Britain. There followed a period of repression and resistance: in 1844 the Lord Mayor of Dublin, Daniel O'Connell, was imprisoned for "incitement to discontent", and a few years later the leaders of the Land League movement, among them Charles Stewart Parnell, were thrown into Kilmainham Gaol. Political assassinations took place, carried out by a secret society, and separatist agitation grew.

In 1916 the Easter Rising occurred in Dublin, the General Post Office and other public buildings being occupied by the rebels. In 1919, on the initiative of Sinn Fein ("We Ourselves"), an independent parliament met in the Mansion House, presided over by Eamon de Valera. On May 25th 1921, during the Civil War, the Custom House was set on fire. In spite of the ratification of the treaty of January 1922 establishing the Irish Free State, domestic conflict persisted in Dublin until 1927. It was not until 1931 that most of the public buildings were finally restored. Throughout the Second World War the Irish Republic remained neutral, though in 1941 a number of German bombs were dropped on Dublin as the result of an error.

In the decades immediately following the Second World War, Dublin was largely allowed to stagnate. Only in very recent times has a programme of regeneration been put in place, with entire districts of the city ear-marked for redevelopment, a process that is still continuing (the most recent example being Temple Bar). Tax and other incentives are used to encourage people back into the centre, and a lavish public relations exercise has been launched in an attempt to improve the city's image – 1988 was chosen (somewhat arbitrarily it has to be said) for celebration of the thousandth anniversary of Dublin's foundation, and in 1991 Dublin was named European City of Culture.

★The city

The River Liffey splits the city into a northern and a southern half before reaching its outflow into the harbour. Much of the inner city lies on the right bank, bounded to the south by a number of fine parks, with a smaller but nevertheless significant nucleus on the north bank. The two are linked by several bridges, of which the most important is O'Connell Bridge. Further upstream, the Father Matthew Bridge crosses the Liffey at the same point as the original ford.

As well as the domes and Neo-Classical facades of its numerous 18th and early 19th c. public buildings, fitting tribute to the skill of men such as Sir Edward Lovett Pearce, Richard Cassels, Thomas Cooley, James Gandon and Francis Johnston, the architectural face of Dublin owes much to the numerous private houses of the same period, their plain but elegant style bestowing a pleasing unity on street after street. Unfortunately many have already disappeared, demolished in a wave of uncontrolled property speculation to make way for offices. This destruction has largely been halted in recent years, not least as a result of opposition by citizens' action groups.

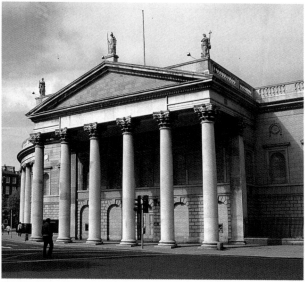

Bank of Ireland

A number of tourist trails are signposted in the city centre (brochure available from Tourist Information Offices). | Tourist trails

Street names in Dublin are in English and Irish. In many older streets the houses are still numbered consecutively, up one side and down the other. Note also that the appellation "Place" or "Square" is not confined to squares as such but may refer to a street. | **N.B.**

Although apart from the two cathedrals few Dublin buildings are older than the 18th c., the city's handsome Georgian streets and squares, its public buildings, museums and libraries, offer a wealth of interesting sights. They can best be appreciated by following a number of separate walks. | City walks

City Centre – South-East

O'Connell Bridge, which spans the Liffey (here 138ft/42m wide) in the centre of the city, makes a good starting point for a sightseeing walk. Built in 1792–94, it was widened in 1880. It is one of ten bridges crossing the river in the inner city area. | O'Connell Bridge

From the south end of Connell Bridge Westmoreland Street leads south to College Green and the substantial building of the Bank of Ireland. Originally designed (1729; by Sir Edward Lovett Pearce) to house the Irish Parliament, in 1802, following the Act of Union, it was sold to the bank. The elegant curved façade with its different orders and sculptural groups – the result of alterations carried out at different times – ranks as one of Dublin's finest. | ★Bank of Ireland
 The noble banking hall, converted from the old Commons' Chamber, can be seen during banking hours. Groups of visitors may also make arrangements to view the former Lords' Chamber, which has a coffered ceiling and fine chandelier.

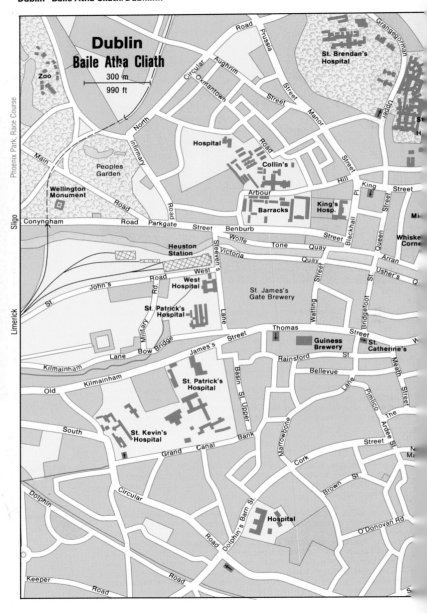

Dublin
Baile Atha Cliath
300 m
990 ft

Zoo

Phoenix Park, Race Course

Peoples Garden

Wellington Monument

Sligo

Conyngham

Limerick

Road
Prussia
Aughrim
Circular
Oxmantown
North
Infirmary
Main
Road

St. Brendan's Hospital

Grangegorman

Upper

Street
Manor
Street

Hospital
Collin's
Arbour
Barracks
Hill
Blackhall

King's Hosp.
King Pl.
Queen
Street
Street

Road
Parkgate
Street
Benburb
Wolfe
Tone
Quay
Street

Heuston Station
Steeven's
Victoria
West
West Hospital
St. Patrick's Hospital
John's
Road
St.
Military
Lane
Bow Bridge
Lane
Kilmainham
Old
Kilmainham
South
St. Kevin's Hospital
St. Patrick's Hospital
James's
Street
Basin
St. Upper
Bank
Grand
Canal
Circular
Road

Dolphin

Keeper
Road
Road

Dolphin's Barn St.
Hospital

Quay
St. James's Gate Brewery
Watling
Bridgefoot
Usher's
Arran
Whiskey Corner
Mi

Thomas
Street
Guiness Brewery
St. Catherine's
Rainsford
St.
Bellevue
Lane
Pimlico
Ardee St.
The
Marrowbone
Cork
Brown St.
Street
Meath Street
Street
O'Donovan Rd.

156

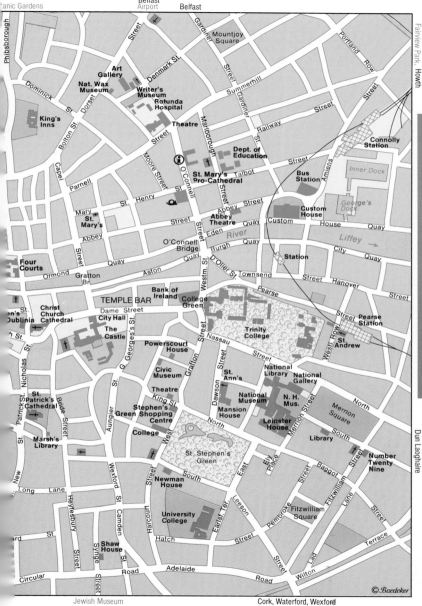

Dublin · Baile Atha Cliath/Dubhlinn

★Trinity College

Situated opposite the Bank of Ireland is the main entrance to Trinity College, in spacious park-like grounds which are open to the public.

Until 1793 membership of the university, founded by Elizabeth I in 1592 (1591 is often cited, the date of foundation, March 3rd 1591, becoming March 13th 1592 on adoption of the Georgian calendar in 1751), was confined to Protestants. Even after that Roman Catholics were still excluded from holding fellowships and scholarships until 1873. In 1903 women were admitted to degrees for the first time. Alumni of Trinity College have included Samuel Beckett, Edmund Burke, Robert Emmett, Oliver Goldsmith, Jonathan Swift, J. M. Synge and Oscar Wilde. It now has about 6000 students.

Until well into the 17th c. the university was housed in makeshift wooden buildings. The oldest surviving range, the red brick "Rubrics", now in use as student accommodation, was erected in 1690. In front of the college's 300ft/90m-long main façade stand statues of Oliver Goldsmith and Edmund Burke by Henry Foley (1863 and 1865 respectively).

After the noisy traffic of College Green the entrance court of Trinity College is a haven of peace. To the left is the Chapel (open, since 1973, to any Christian denomination having a chaplain to the University), and on the right the Examinations Hall (1779–91; originally a theatre), both designed by Sir William Chambers. Beyond the Chapel is the Dining Hall (1743; by Richard Cassels), hung with portraits of notable members of the university. Ahead, in the centre of Library Square, can be seen the Campanile (1853) with, near by, a sculpture by Henry Moore.

★★Old Library

For tourists the most interesting building on the campus is the Old Library (1712–32; open: Mon.–Fri. 9.30am–4.45pm, Sat. 9.30am–12.45pm; admission fee). As a copyright library (since 1801) it is entitled to receive, as of right, a copy of every book published in Ireland and Great Britain. It now has a collection of some 5000 manuscripts and two million printed books. Among its treasures are manuscripts, incunabula and early printed books, the most famous of which, the 8th c. "Book of Kells", is displayed on the ground floor in the so-called Colonnades. This superbly illuminated manuscript of the four Gospels consists of 680 richly decorated pages, one of which is open to view each day. The illumination on the opening page of each Gospel and of each individual chapter is particularly elaborate (see Baedeker Special).

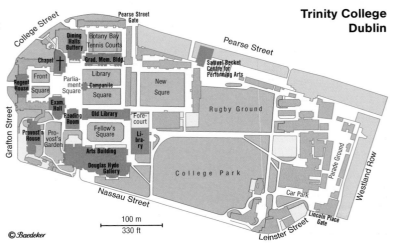

Trinity College Dublin

© Baedeker

Other especially valuable treasures include "The Book of Durrow" (7th c.), the "Book of Dimma" (8th c.) and the "Book of Armagh" (9th c.).

From the ground floor a handsome staircase by Cassels leads up to the Long Room, 200ft/60m in length, with a timber barrel-vaulted roof. As well as marble busts of famous members of the university, it contains an Irish harp, one of the oldest instruments of its kind.

Accommodated in the Arts Building on the campus is a special tourist attraction called the "Dublin Experience", a multi-media presentation on the history of the city (showings: May–early Oct. daily 10am–5pm, starting on the hour; admission fee). | "Dublin Experience"

In the same building is the Douglas Hyde Gallery which mounts periodic exhibitions of Irish Contemporary Art. | Douglas Hyde Gallery

On the north side of the campus stands the recently completed Samuel Beckett Theatre for Performing Arts, chiefly used by drama students at the university. | Samuel Beckett Theatre

East of Trinity College, in Westland Row, is St Andrew's Church, a handsome Neo-Classical building (1832–37). | St Andrew's Church

Leaving the campus via the gate at the south end of College Park, proceed south down Kildare Street where a gateway on the left gives access to an important group of buildings. The National Library (1890), to the left of the entrance, has collections of early printed books (notably 17th c. Irish literature), old maps and topographical works, also a newspaper archive. | National Library

To the right of the entrance stands the National Museum (open: Tues.–Sat. 10am–5pm, from 10.30am Fri., Sun. 2–5pm; admission fee for special exhibitions) housing a rich collection of Irish antiquities from prehistoric times to the end of the medieval period. | ★★ National Museum

The entrance rotunda (bookshop; special exhibitions) leads into the Great Hall with a display of Irish gold-work. Items of especial value are displayed in the Treasury and include in particular: 11th and 12th c. crosiers; the Ardagh Chalice (early 8th c.), silver with gilt ornament, gold filigree handles; among the processional crosses, the Cross of Cong (1123), of oak with silver and gilt bronze animal ornament; among a number of shrines, that of St Patrick's Bell (12th c.), decorated with silver gilt, gold filigree and ornamental stones; and various reliquaries, among them the Breac Maod hóg Reliquary (11th c.) with an exact depiction of the dress of the period.

Also in the Great Hall is an exhibition under the title "Dublin 1000", with finds from the Viking period uncovered during excavation of a building site on Wood Quay (since filled in and over-built with office blocks). Elsewhere on the ground floor is a room devoted to "The Road to Independence", an exhibition and video-presentation illustrating Irish history between 1900 and 1921. In the gallery of the Great Hall are antiquities spanning a period of more than 7000 years (c. 6000 B.C. to 1800 A.D.) among which two in particular stand out: the Tara Brooch (700–750), of gilded bronze inlaid with silver, copper and enamelwork; and the Moylough Belt Shrine (8th c.), a reliquary of silvered bronze with enamel ornament, designed to be attached to a belt. Other rooms on the upper floor contain metal-, glass- and ceramicware, porcelain and textiles. The cabinets of Irish silver and the collection of musical instruments are of special note.

To the rear of the Library and Museum, set back from the street (entrance in Merrion Street), stands Leinster House, home of the Republic of Ireland Parliament and seat of the Dáil Eireann (House of Representatives) and Seanad Eireann (Senate). This sober and dignified building (1745; by Richard Cassels) was originally the town house of the Dukes of Leinster. There is a Visitors' Gallery but to enter you need an introduction from a Member of Parliament. | Leinster House

Dublin · Baile Atha Cliath/Dubhlinn

Trinity College: Campanile

National Gallery

Natural History Museum

Adjoining Leinster House to the north is the Natural History Museum (open: Tues.–Sat. 10am–5pm, from 10.30am Fri., Sun. 2–5pm), which has a large collection displaying the fauna of Ireland (including skeletons of prehistoric animals). It also houses the Blashka Collection (glass models of marine creatures).

★National Gallery

Also with its entrance on Merrion Street is the National Gallery (open: Mon.–Sat. 10am–5.30pm, Thur. to 8.30pm, Sun. 2–5pm). First opened in 1864, it has since been extended, most recently in 1968.

There are several rooms devoted to representative works by Irish painters including George Barrett, James Barry, Francis Danby, Nathaniel Hone the Elder, Nathaniel Hone the Younger, Robert Hunter, James Latham, James Arthur O'Connor, Walter Osborne, Thomas Roberts, Patrick Tuohy, Jack Butler Yeats (brother of the poet W. B. Yeats) and John Butler Yeats (the poet's father). In addition there is a wide-ranging collection of works by non-Irish artists: American (John Singer Sargent, Gilbert Stuart, Benjamin West, James MacNeill Whistler); English (John Constable, Thomas Gainsborough, William Hogarth, Thomas Lawrence, William Turner); Flemish (Gerard David, Anthony Van Dyke, Jacob Jordaens, Peter-Paul Rubens, Jan van Scorel, David Teniers the Younger); French (Camille Corot, Edgar Degas, Eugène Delacroix, Claude Monet, Alfred Sisley); Italian (Fra Angelico, Giovanni Bellini, Michelangelo, Tintoretto, Titian, Paolo Veronese); and Dutch (Peter Claesz, Jan van Goyen, Pieter de Hooch, Jan Steen, Rembrandt van Rijn, Salomon and Jacob van Ruisdael, Emanuel de Witte). While the collection of Spanish paintings is relatively small, it includes works by such major artists as Francisco de Goya, El Greco, Bartolomé Esteban Murillo and Francisco de Zurburán. German painting is represented by Lucas Cranach the Elder and Wolf Huber.

Today, the large number of portraits belonging to the National Gallery (of, among others, Brendan Behan, Sir Roger Casement, Eamon de Valera and James Joyce) are mostly on display in Malahide Castle (see below). A

National Gallery of Ireland
Gailearaí Náisiúnta na hÉireann

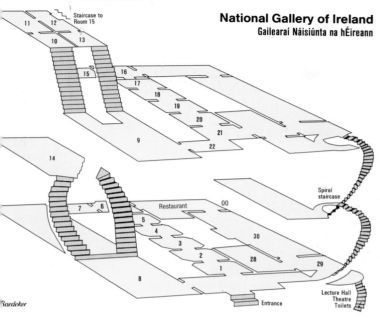

Irish and	9–13 Italian school	18 Rembrandt and his circle
British schools	14 Temporary exhibitions	19 French school
Jack B. Yeats	15 German and	20–21 Spanish school
Bookstall	Flemish schools	22 Vestibule
Shaw Room	16 British school	28 In process of rearrangement
(Portraits)	17 Dutch school	30 French school

few however can be seen in the Gallery's Shaw Room, so named in honour of George Bernard Shaw (1856–1950) who bequeathed a third of his estate to the Gallery in recognition of its contribution to his own early development. The Gallery also possesses a collection of 31 water-colours by Turner which, under the terms of the bequest, can only be put on public display during the month of January, to protect them from over-exposure to light. At other times of the year they can be seen by arrangement. Distributed throughout the rooms are sculptures from the 16th c. to the present day, among them works by Auguste Rodin and Aristide Maillol.

On the ground floor are a bookstall and restaurant, and in the basement a library and lecture theatre.

To the south-west of the National Gallery lies Merrion Square, surrounded on three sides by handsome Georgian houses. Among previous residents have been Oscar Wilde's parents, Daniel O'Connell and W. B. Yeats. On the west side of the square is the Rutland Fountain (1791).

★Merrion Square

No. 29, one of the fine Georgian houses in Lower Fitzwilliam Street, at the south-east corner of Merrion Square, has been turned into a museum (open: Tues.–Sat. 10am–5pm, Sun. 2–5pm, closed two weeks before Christmas; admission fee). The house is furnished exactly as it was at the end of the 18th c. when Olive Beatty, a widow, moved in with her three children.

No. 29

National Gallery: "Apple Gathering" (Osborne) and "A Connemara Girl" (Burke)

Fitzwilliam Square	Fitzwilliam Street runs south to Fitzwilliam Square (c. 1825), the best preserved Georgian square in Dublin. Fitzwilliam Street itself, also Georgian, is another good example of the style, with the additional attraction of a view of the Wicklow Mountains in the distance to the south-west.
Ely Place	Return northward up Pembroke Street and left into Baggot Street, where turn left again into Ely Place, a cul-de-sac of elegant Georgian houses of about 1770. The finest is Ely House (No. 8), with a handsome staircase and good quality stucco ceilings; it is now the headquarters of a charity, the Knights of St Colombanus.
St Stephen's Green	Opposite Ely House, Hume Street leads into the east side of St Stephen's Green, a 20acre/9ha park laid out in 1880 at Arthur Guinness's expense. It has flower beds, ponds and a variety of monuments, including a fountain ("The Three Fates") by Joseph Wackerle, a gift from the German people in gratitude for Irish help in relieving distress following the Second World War. The park is a popular place of recreation; in July and August there are concerts of Irish music.
	Concealed behind a highly ornate Victorian façade is the ultra-modern St Stephen's Green Shopping Centre opened in 1989. On the west side of the park can be seen the Royal College of Surgeons (1806), and on the south side the Department of Foreign Affairs (No. 80), formerly the residence of Lord Iveagh, with a large garden. Also on the south side is the Neo-Byzantine University Church (1854).
Newman House	Another pair of buildings on the south side of St Stephen's Green (Nos. 85 and 86) are known as Newman House. They are owned by University College and have recently been thoroughly restored. These houses (open: June–Sept. Tues.–Fri. 10am–4.30pm, Sat 2–4.30pm, Sun. 11am–4.30pm; admission fee) are especially renowned for their stucco work. No. 85 was

St Stephen's Green Shopping Centre: exterior and interior

built in 1738 for Captain Hugh Montgomery; No. 86 was designed by Robert West. The buildings commemorate John Henry Newman, the first rector of the Catholic University, precursor of Dublin's University College.

A short distance south of St Stephen's Green are the former buildings of University College itself. This, like the colleges at Cork and Galway, is part of the National University of Ireland, an institution which makes a speciality of the study and preservation of the Irish language. Following rapid expansion in the mid 1960s the college moved to a spacious new campus at Belfield, 3 miles/5km south-east on the N11, now with some interesting modern buildings. Only the Faculties of Medicine and Architecture remain in the original buildings here in Earlsfort Terrace.

University College

From Earlsfort Terrace a detour can be made to Synge Street, two or three blocks further west. No. 33 Synge Street was the birthplace in 1856 of George Bernard Shaw. Following extensive restoration the house once again appears at it would have done in the latter half of the 19th c. when it was the home of the Shaw family (open: May–Sept. Mon.–Sat. 10am–5pm, Sun. 2–6pm).

Shaw House

In 1990 a small Jewish museum was opened in conjunction with a newly restored synagogue, in Walworth Road, at the south end of Synge Street (open: May–Sept. Tues., Thur., Sun. 11am–3.30pm; Oct.–Apr. Sun. 10.30am–2.30pm).

Jewish Museum

In Dawson Street, to the north of St Stephen's Green, is the Mansion House (1705), official residence, since 1715, of Dublin's Lord Mayor (with the Round Room, 1821, by John Semple); also the Royal Irish Academy, the library of which (open: Mon.–Fri. 9.30am–5.30pm; closed during the 2nd half of August) contains a priceless collection of manuscripts of the 6th to the 17th c., including the "Cathach", a psalter written by St Columba.

Mansion House, Royal Irish Academy

Ulysses – a literary Baedeker

Bronze plaque in road surface

June 16th is a kind of holiday in Dublin – it is "Bloomsday". Hundreds of people, alone or in small groups, can be seen walking through the city centre. They pause in front of many a crossing and building and search thoughtfully in their books as they look around them. The 800 page tome they are referring to is a travel guide. Not the usual kind of travel guide – this one is a novel! A literary masterpiece of the 20th c. It is the novel "Ulysses" by the Irish author James Joyce (1882–1941), one of the most important writers of this century. "Ulysses" describes the events of a particular day – June 16th 1904 from eight in the morning to about three the next morning – in the lives of three of Dublin's inhabitants, the advertising agent Leopold Bloom, his wife Molly and the teacher and writer Stephen Dedalus. In his novel (first edition Paris, 1922; it did not appear in England and the USA until 1933 and 1936 respectively owing to its "treatment of sexual matters in the everyday language of the lower classes"). Joyce describes in so much detail the route taken that day through the Irish capital by Bloom and Dedalus that it can still be followed today. "Ulysses" is, if you like, "a literary Baedeker" (Frank Delaney). While writing his major work Joyce remarked to a friend "I want to paint such a complete picture of Dublin that if this town were to disappear in an earthquake it could be rebuilt according to this book".

Since June 16th 1954, when four Dubliners first celebrated this day upon which Leopold Bloom walked around Dublin, "Bloomsday" has become a hit with visitors. Joyce's followers focus mainly on the eighth chapter of the novel; it begins in Middle Abbey Street and ends in Kildare Street. Bronze plaques set into the pavement mark the route and refer to the corresponding page numbers of the English standard edition. (Further information can be found on the "Ulysses Map of Dublin" published by the tourist office.)

"Ulysses" consists of 18 episodes. The first three centre around the writer and teacher Stephen Dedalus. He has breakfast with friends in Martello Tower, an old tower in Dublin Bay, then teaches in the school where he has a talk with the headmaster and goes for a walk along the beach alone, deep in conversation with himself. Leopold Bloom, a modern Everyman, advertising agent by profession, first appears in the fourth episode. First breakfast with his wife Molly, followed by his daily odyssey through Dublin: the post office, a church service, the public baths, the cemetery (to a funeral), the newpaper offices, a pub, a restaurant and the library. In the library Bloom and Dedalus catch a brief glimpse of each other. Then the Ormond restaurant, Barney Kiernan's pub, the Dublin Strand. In the women's hospital Bloom visits a relative who is in labour. Then he goes to Bella Cohen's brothel with some companions. He and Dedalus leave the brothel together slowly developing a liking for each other. They stop off in a coaching inn before going to Bloom's flat at 7 Eccles Street. When Dedalus goes home Bloom lies down to sleep beside Molly. The 18 episodes have their parallel in the 24 verses of Homer's "Odyssey": Bloom wandering the streets of Dublin compares with Odysseus travels around the Greek islands.

Traditional narrative techniques are brilliantly laid open to question in this novel. It is an epic, a chronicle, a drama, a report, an essay and a character novel all in one. The action in its traditional sense is the backcloth. "Ulysses" is one of the first novels to be influenced by Freud's deep psychological observations. The 20 or so hours from the everyday life of these three Dubliners – their actions, encounters with other Dubliners, their thoughts, wishes and dreams – are not so much descriptions as reflections (stream of consciousness). The chief formal devices include inner monologues, chains of association, changing narrative perspective, interrupted chronology and occasional ungrammatical syntax; all of which do not make the novel easy to read. With this new form of linguistic expression, in particular the stream of consciousness style of narrative technique which he developed, James Joyce had a decisive influence on the 20th c. novel.

In the past decades Dublin, which has been untouched by wars and natural catastrophes, has undergone radical topographical changes. Many streets and alleys have lost their original form, houses have been demolished or are ready for demolition. Only the larger streets have survived but not as Joyce described them. Even Leopold Bloom's house, 7 Eccles Street, one of the most famous streets in English Literature no longer exists. Other properties have been completely altered. In this regard "Ulysses" dramatically highlights the changes that have taken place to a city in the 20th c.

As with so many other settings in the novel the pubs have disappeared: "Barney Kiernan's", where the "cyclops banquet" took place, "Burke's", where the pair got drunk before going on to the brothel, and the coaching inn of the Eumaeus episode which Bloom and Dedalus visit after the brothel. But a hint of the Dublin of James Joyce is still there. In the dark alleys by the quay; in the streets which lead down to the river; behind Trinity College; in the houses with the canopies in Grafton Street; in the National Library.

The site where the first chapter of the novel, "Telemachus", begins, Martello Tower in Sandycove (suburb of Dun Laoghaire), has been preserved. Joyce himself lived in this tower once, today it is the Joyce Museum. A visit to Glasnevin cemetery ("Hades") is interesting – Joyce's parents are buried here as are the Irish heroes Daniel O'Connell and Charles Stewart Parnell. In Duke Street the "Bailey", which used to be frequented by Bloom, is one of the smartest pubs in Dublin today; to Joyce fans it is the "Burton" of the "Laestrigonian episode". For fear of court proceedings because of the unappetising scenes of gluttony Joyce did not use the pub's real name. In the hallway of the "Bailey" is the original door of 7, Eccles Street. The house itself had to give way to new building a few years ago. Opposite the "Bailey" is the pub "Davy Byrne's" where Bloom, hungry but sickened by "Bailey's", came for a gorgonzola sandwich. This snack is only available on the menu on Bloomsday. A small cheap souvenir of the official or personal Bloomsday can be purchased at the over 100 year-old chemists "Sweny" (Lincoln Place). Here Joyce fans, like Leopold Bloom on June 16th 1904, always buy a piece of lemon soap.

Visitors normally only see facsimiles; the originals can be viewed by special arrangement.

St Ann's Church — Also in Dawson Street stands St Ann's Church (1720; by Isaac Wills), with a mid 19th c. Neo-Romanesque façade and good woodwork in the interior.

Grafton Street, Bewley's Café — From Dawson Street, Anne Street runs west to Grafton Street, one of the city's principal shopping thoroughfares (pedestrianised). Not to be missed is a visit to Browne & Thomas, a superior traditional department store. A respite from shopping can be enjoyed at Bewley's Café (78 Grafton Street), a favourite rendezvous for Dubliners. With its dark wooden furniture, marble-topped tables and sublime windows by Irish artist Harry Clarke, it preserves an authentic coffee-house atmosphere. The part of the café on the ground floor known as "Bewley's Museum" is usually somewhat less noisy.

Powerscourt Town House — An alleyway near Bewley's Café leads to Powerscourt Town House, an imposing mansion (1771–74) built by Robert Mack for Viscount Powerscourt, now converted into an elegant department store and offices (Powerscourt Town House Centre, open: Mon.–Sat. 9am–6pm). Around the attractive covered courtyard are cafés, classy shops and galleries. Note the fine stucco work adorning the staircase, hall and individual shops.

Civic Museum — A few doors along is the Civic Museum (open: Tues.–Sat. 10am–6pm, Sun. 11am–2pm) in a building of 1765–71 originally occupied by the Society of Artists. Among the numerous exhibits on display are old street plans and models of Dublin.

Inner City – South-West

Temple Bar — A short distance west from O'Connell Bridge lies the district known as Temple Bar, between the south bank of the Liffey and Dame Street. Originally earmarked for redevelopment as the site of a new central railway station, this Old City area with its 200 year-old houses and cobbled streets, once populated by craftsmen, tradespeople, artists and writers, was thankfully reprieved and the decision taken to renovate it while preserving its historic character. Many of the houses in its narrow lanes and alleyways (some of which are now pedestrianised), have already been restored. Others have been converted into small shops, studios, pubs and restaurants. Street art thrives and Temple Bar is gradually rediscovering itself as an artists' quarter.

Halfpenny Bridge — Of iron construction, the elegant Halfpenny Bridge spanning the Liffey to the north of Temple Bar was built in 1816 and paid for by tolls – hence the name (officially it is called Liffey Bridge).

City Hall — The City Hall stands on the south side of Dame Street at the south-west corner of Temple Bar. Formerly the Royal Exchange (1769–79; by Thomas Cooley), the imposing domed building is now the headquarters of Dublin Corporation. The entrance hall is adorned with statues of local notabilities. Among documents in the archives are several royal charters, the earliest of which, dated 1172, grants the territory of Dublin to the city of Bristol (open: Mon.–Fri. 9am–1pm, 2.15–5pm).

★ Dublin Castle — Beyond the City Hall stands Dublin Castle, the main entrance of which is on Cork Hill. The hill now occupied by the Upper Yard was probably the site of a Celtic and later a Danish fort (foundations dating from the Viking and Norman periods have been preserved). In 1204 King John began the construction of a castle (completed in 1226) of which little survives, and then much altered, in the present building, the greater part of which dates from the 18th and 19th c. From the reign of Elizabeth I to the establishment of the

Dublin Castle
State Apartments

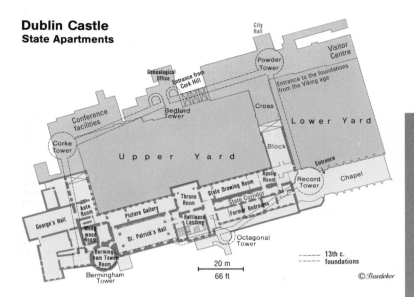

Irish Free State in 1921, Dublin Castle was the official residence of the Viceroy and seat of British administration.

At the east end of the Upper Yard a passage leads through into the Lower Yard. To the right is the Record Tower, one of the four old corner towers, well preserved with almost 16ft/5m thick walls, which gives some impression of what the medieval castle was like. The Neo-Romaneque Chapel (1807–14) is notable for its unusual external decoration of over a hundred limestone heads of famous Irishmen.

When not in use for official purposes the State Apartments (open: Mon.–Fri. 10am–12.15pm and 2–5pm, Sat. and Sun. 2–5pm; admission fee) are shown to visitors in the course of a conducted tour lasting about half an hour (entrance across Upper Yard from the Castle's main entrance in Cork Street). Notable features are the colourful Donegal and Killybegs carpets, the chandeliers of Waterford glass and the pavement of green Connemara marble in the entrance hall. The conducted tour takes in the following rooms: St Patrick's Hall, with a painted ceiling (1778) and the banners of the Knights of St Patrick; the blue Wedgwood Room with pictures by Angelica Kauffmann (?); the picture gallery with portraits of Viceroys; the Throne Room, richly decorated in gold (1740), with an 18th c. throne; the long State Drawing Room with its original furniture; and the Apollo Room or Music Room, with a ceiling of 1746. After viewing the State Apartments visitors are shown the remains of the medieval fort (entrance by the Powder Tower).

State Apartments

From the Castle a narrow street, Castle Street, runs west. By Nos. 7 and 8 is the entrance to the little St Werburgh's Church (1759), with a beautiful interior which can be seen by appointment (tel. 72 06 73).

St Werburgh's Church

Castle Street leads into Christchurch Place, in which stands one of Dublin's two principal churches, Christ Church Cathedral (open: daily 10am–5pm),

Christ Church Cathedral

Dublin Castle: Throne Room

the cathedral of the Anglican dioceses of Dublin and Glendalough. In its present form it is the result of a major reconstruction in 1871–78; of the original 13th c. church there remain the crypt, which extends under the whole length of the nave, a doorway in the south transept and perhaps parts of the transepts. Enough remains, however, including some sculpture, to give an impression of the magnificence of the old church. The crypt contains numerous architectural fragments of different periods and 17th c. statues of Charles II and James II. In the nave is a fine recumbent tomb effigy of a knight, identified as Strongbow, with, to the side, a small half-length figure incorrectly described as "Strongbow's Son". Other monuments in the choir include the tomb of a 13th c. bishop.

Dublinia

The former Synod Hall, linked to the cathedral by a bridge, now houses a multi-media presentation called "Dublinia" (open: May–Oct. Mon.–Sat. 9am–5pm, Sun. 10am–4pm). Here the history of Dublin is portrayed, from the coming of the Normans (1170) up to the dissolution of the monasteries (1540). About an hour should be allowed for viewing the exhibition, which by means of a succession of scenes, an informative video presentation and

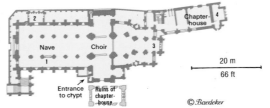

Christ Church Cathedral

1 Tomb of Strongbow
2 Baptistery
3 Lady Chapel
4 Library

© Baedeker

numerous exhibits including a scale model of the city, tools and art work, illustrates this phase of Dublin's history.

Christ Church Cathedral continued to exercise a leading role through all the vicissitudes of Irish history down the centuries. This was despite the fact that, in the 13th c., another church, only ¼ mile/400m away to the south, was also elevated to cathedral status, which status it has retained, in defiance of all subsequent changes, to this day. St Patrick' Cathedral, 305ft/93m long, is the largest church in Ireland, and like Christ Church, Anglican by denomination (open: Mon.–Fri. 9am–6pm, Sat. to 5pm to 4pm in winter, Sun. to 4.30pm; admission fee).

★St Patrick's Cathedral

At the time of its foundation in the 11th c., the church stood on a marshy site outside the town walls. Like Christ Church Cathedral it too has suffered from over-restoration (1864–69). The massive tower at the north-west corner dates from the end of the 14th c., the steeple from 1739.

The church is entered from the south side. The tall interior in severe Early English style, is of impressive effect. It contains numerous monuments and tombs. At the second pier to the right of the entrance are the tombs of Jonathan Swift (1667–1745) and his "Stella" (Hester Johnston, 1681–1728). To the left of the nearby door is a bust of Swift, with an epitaph which he himself composed: "He lies where furious indignation can no longer rend his heart." Swift was Dean of St Patrick's for 35 years.

Other notable monuments include: to the right of the baptismal chapel (old font) the Boyle Monument (1631) commemorating the Earl of Cork, with a number of coloured figures, including a child who is believed to be Richard Boyle, in adulthood the celebrated physicist; on the north wall, opposite the entrance, the monument of Turlough O'Carolan (1670–1738), last of the Irish bards; on the north wall of the choir, a marble effigy of Archbishop Fulk de Saundfort (d. 1271); on the south wall of the Lady Chapel an effigy of Archbishop Tregury (d. 1471); on the south wall of the choir, four brasses, the finest of which are those of Dean Sutton (d. 1528)

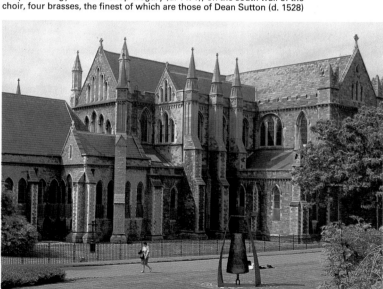

St Patrick's Cathedral

St. Patrick's Cathedral

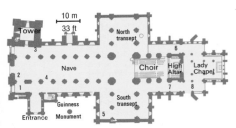

© Baedeker

1 Baptistery
2 Boyle Monument
3 Monument of Turlough O'Carolan
4 Tombs of Swift and Hester Johnson ("Stella")
5 Monument of Lady Doneraile
6 Effigy of Archbishop Fulk de Saundfort
7 Brasses of Dean Sutton, Dean Fyche, etc.
8 Effigy of Archbishop Tregury

and Dean Fyche (d. 1539); and at the south-west corner of the south transept, the typically 18th c. monument of Lady Doneraile (1780).

The choir was, from 1783 to 1869, the Chapel of the Order of the Knights of St Patrick, whose banners, swords and helmets can be seen above the stalls.

In the little park near the cathedral, twelve tablets let into the wall commemorate Irish writers.

Marsh's Library

To the right of St Patrick's an alley runs in a curve to Marsh's Library (open: Mon.and Wed.–Fri. 10am–12.45pm and 2–5pm, Sat. 10.30am–12.45pm), the city's oldest public library, founded by Archbishop Marsh and built in 1701 by Sir William Robinson. The façades were renewed in 1863–69, but the attractive interior has been preserved practically unchanged, including the "cages" in which readers of rare books were obliged to work under the eye of the custodian.

St Audoen's Church

Returning along Patrick Street and Nicholas Street to Christ Church, and turning left into High Street, St Audoen's, Dublin's only surviving medieval church (Protestant; National Monument) can be seen on the right. Of the original structure there remain the 13th c. nave in which services are still held, the choir and the south aisle (both roofless) and two chapels. In the porch are the Portlester Monument (1496) and a number of gravestones.

St Catherine's Church

High Street continues by way of Cornmarket into Thomas Street West. On the left is the massive façade of St Catherine's Church (1769; by John Smyth) in front of which Robert Emmet, who had led a rising against the British, was hanged in 1803.

Guinness's Brewery

Some 550yd/500m farther west lies the expansive site of the St James's Gate Brewery, better known as Guinness's, where 60% of the beer drunk in Ireland is brewed (see Baedeker Special, pp. 318/19).

The brewery, founded by Arthur Guinness in 1759 and located here since 1761, prospered in spite of subsidised competition from imported English beers. In the early 19th c. Napoleon's Continental system brought economic problems, as did the catastrophic famine of the 1840s; but in spite of this Guinness's grew to become Ireland's largest brewery, and by 1870 the largest in the world. Exports likewise continued to grow. The first Guinness brewery outside Ireland was established in London in 1936, and there are now breweries as far afield as Nigeria, Ghana, the Cameroons and Malaysia. The Dublin brewery exports 40% of its total production.

In the brewery's Visitor Centre (Guinness Hop Store, Crane Street), the individual stages in the brewing process can be followed; the Transport Museum shows how beer was transported in past centuries. After an informative film about the company and the brewing business, visitors are invited to sample the famous beer (open: Mon.–Fri. 9.30am–5pm; Sat. and public holidays 10.30am–4.30pm; admission fee).

Inner City – North

Downstream of O'Connell Bridge, east of Eden Quay and the unsightly railway bridge (1889), stands the Custom House (not open to the public), a magnificent building designed by James Gandon (1743–1823), an English architect of Huguenot descent who was responsible for many buildings in Dublin. After the building had been completely burned out in 1921 during the Civil War, the exterior was restored from the original plans. The long façade with its Doric portico, and the 125ft/38m-high domed tower surmounting it, are best seen from the opposite side of the river. Most of the fine statues and sculpture are by the Dubliner Edward Smyth. Though less magnificent than the main façade, the north front is also of notable quality.

★ Custom House

To the west of the Custom House is the new Abbey Theatre (1966; by Michael Scott); the main theatre has 638 seats, the small Peacock Theatre 157 seats. It is built on the site of the old Abbey Theatre, burned down in 1951, the first directors of which were W. B. Yeats and Lady Gregory. Plays are staged in Irish as well as in English.

Abbey Theatre

Proceeding north along Marlborough Street, Tyrone House (1741; by Richard Cassels) is seen on the right. Now occupied by the Department of Education, it has a handsome staircase and good stucco work by Francini.

Tyrone House

Facing stands St Mary's Pro-Cathedral, Dublin's principal Roman Catholic church, built in 1816–25 on the model of the Temple of Theseus in Athens. The high altar was the work of Peter Turnerelli. Masses are also said here in Italian and Spanish.

St Mary's
Pro-Cathedral

Parallel to Marlborough Street, two streets farther west, is O'Connell Street, Dublin's main north–south artery. Originally a good residential street, it lost many of its fine old buildings during the fighting of 1916–22 and is now a shopping and commercial thoroughfare, with cinemas and restaurants.

O'Connell Street

Along the middle of the street are a series of statues of Irish patriots, including Daniel O'Connell (near O'Connell Bridge) and Charles Stewart Parnell (see Famous People, in both cases), as well as the "Apostle of Temperance", Father Matthew. Not long ago a sculpture of the river-goddess Anna Livia was set up near the main post office – and immediately dubbed "the floozie in the jacuzzi" by Irish wits.

On the west side of the street stands the imposing General Post Office (1815–17; by Francis Johnston), which in 1916 became the headquarters of the rebels under the leadership of Patrick Pearse and James Connolly. The Irish patriots are commemorated in the main hall ("Death of CuChulainn").

General Post
Office

Immediately past the Post Office, Henry Street leads west off O'Connell Street. A little way along it is Moore Street, where fruit and vegetable stalls create a colourful picture.

Moore Street

From Upper O'Connell Street, turn right into Parnell Street, then left along Gardiner Street to reach Mountjoy Square (1792–1808), an example of a once-fashionable and elegant square which had come down in the world and is now gradually being rehabilitated.

Mountjoy Square

From the north-west corner Gardiner's Place leads into Denmark Street, on the right-hand side of which is Belvedere House (1785; by Michael Stapleton), a dignified building with a fine interior. Since 1841 it has been a Jesuit school, James Joyce being its most celebrated pupil.

Belvedere House

Denmark Street opens onto Parnell Square, part of which is occupied by a Garden of Remembrance, laid out in 1966, with a sculpture by Oisin Kelly – "Lir's Children" (1970). The garden is dedicated to all who gave their lives for Irish independence. The most interesting of the buildings around Parnell Square are the Gate Theatre (founded in 1928 in part of the old

Parnell Square

Custom House by the River Liffey

View of O'Connell Street from O'Connell Bridge

Fruit and Vegetable market in Moore Street

Assembly Rooms), and Richard Cassel's Rotunda Hospital, the main building of which, linked to the wings by colonnades, is topped by a domed
tower. A lovely staircase leads up to the chapel which has a fine stucco
ceiling with numerous figures in strong relief.

On Parnell Square North stands Charlemont House (1762; by the English
architect Sir William Chambers; porch added in 1930), today occupied by
the Hugh Lane Municipal Gallery of Modern Art, founded in 1908 (open:
Tues.–Fri. 9.30am–6pm, Sat. 9.30–5pm, Sun. 11am–5pm). Hugh Lane, after
whom the gallery is named, was a prominent member of Irish artistic and
literary circles early this century. He was also an art collector who quickly
developed an interest in Impressionism and later artistic movements. He
accumulated an outstanding collection (including works by Camille Corot,
Edgar Degas, Juan Gris, Edouard Manet, Claude Monet, Pablo Picasso,
Camille Pissaro and Auguste Renoir). At the time of his death Lane had
loaned the collection to the Tate Gallery in London, but in his will he left it to
the City of Dublin. After protracted argument the collection was divided,
the two halves being rotated on a five-yearly basis between Dublin and
London.

Municipal
Gallery of
Modern Art

In 1991 the Dublin Writers' Museum was opened in two 18th c. houses
(Nos. 18 and 19) situated next to the art gallery. No. 18 honours the great
Irish writers, including Jonathan Swift, Oscar Wilde, W. B. Yeats, George
Bernard Shaw and James Joyce – manuscripts, first editions, letters,
photographs and writing implements are on display; the adjacent building
serves as a meeting-place for contemporary writers and for exhibiting and
conducting readings from their work. There are also temporary exhibitions, a bookshop and a café (open: Mon.–Sat. 10am–5pm, Sun. and public
holidays 11.30am–5pm; admission fee).

Dublin Writers'
Museum

To the west of Parnell Square, in Granby Row, can be found the National
Wax Museum (open: Mon.–Sat. 10am–5.30pm, Sun. noon–5.30pm), with

National Wax
Museum

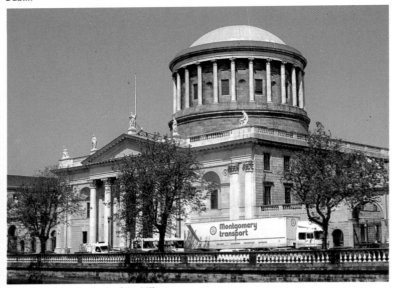

Four Courts, on the bank of the Liffey

wax figures of Irish politicians (Charles Stewart Parnell, Douglas Hyde, Eamon de Valera), actors and writers (James Joyce), and prominent international personalities (Ronald Reagan, Pope John Paul II).

King's Inns

From Granby Row turn left into Upper Dorset Street (which as the N1 is the main road to the airport), then along its continuation Bolton Street to Henrietta Street, a cul-de-sac on the right. Away at the far end, raised on a tall base, are Dublin's Inns of Court, the King's Inns (1795; by James Gandon; the two wings on the west front are later additions), home to the ruling body of the Irish legal profession, with a fine Dining Hall (sculpture by Edward Smyth) and large library.

St Mary's Church

Continuing down Bolton Street, branch left into Capel Street, off to the left of which in Mary Street stands St Mary's Church (1702), Dublin's oldest unaltered Protestant church, with rich carving on the organ-loft and galleries. In 1966 the Church authorities made a present of the churchyard to the city of Dublin for a memorial garden dedicated to Wolfe Tone, leader of the United Irishmen.

★Four Courts

Capel Street descends to the Liffey at Gratton Bridge. About ¼ mile/400m upstream, on Inns Quay, is an architectural masterpiece by James Gandon, the Four Courts, seat of the Irish High Court. Built between 1786 and 1802, it incorporated an older building (1776–84; by Thomas Cooley). After being badly damaged by gunfire during the Civil War in 1922, it was restored in 1931 with only minor alterations. The 456ft/139m-long façade overlooking the river, embellished with a fine Corinthian portico, is capped by a great domed rotunda, a prominent Dublin landmark. The central hall beneath the dome gave access to the four courts from which the building takes its name – the Exchequer, Common Pleas, King's Bench and Chancery Courts.

St Michan's Church

West of the Four Courts in Church Street is St Michan's Church (1095; much restored) in the crypt of which can be seen a number of mummified bodies which, because of the tannic acid in the air, do not decay. Of rather greater interest is the carving on the gallery depicting seventeen musical instruments. Handel is reputed to have played the church organ, built in 1724 (open: Mon.–Fri. 10am–12.45pm and 2–4.45pm, Sat. 10am–12.45pm).

In Bow Street, parallel to Church Street, the Irish Whiskey Corner Visitor Centre occupies a former storehouse of the Jameson Distillery, which closed in 1972. A film illustrates the 1000-year history of Irish whiskey; afterwards visitors have an opportunity to sample the product (open: May–Oct. Mon.–Fri. 11am–3.30pm).

Irish Whiskey Corner

½ mile/800m farther west, in Blackhall Place, can be seen the King's Hospital, also known as the Bluecoat School. The school was founded in 1669, but the present handsome building (by Thomas Ivory) dates only from the last quarter of the 18th c.; the dome was added in 1894. The interior has fine stucco work and carving.

King's Hospital

Immediately west of the school are the extensive Collins Barracks (18th c.).

Collins Barracks

Outer Districts – North

From Collins Barracks Parkgate Street leads west to Phoenix Park. This vast public park (1996 acres/808ha) owes its name, not to the phoenix on a column set up in 1747 by the Viceroy, Lord Chesterfield, who established the park, but to the Irish name of a nearby spring, Fionn Uisage ("clear water"). In that part of the park north of Main Road are the People's Garden, the Zoological Gardens (open: daily 9.30am–6pm; admission fee), noted for their success in breeding lions, a polo ground, the former viceregal lodge and now official residence of the President of the Irish Republic (1751–54; by Nathaniel Clements), and the Apostolic Nunciature. South of the road stands the Wellington Monument (1817; by Sir Robert Smirke), a huge obelisk 200ft/60m high which makes an eye-catching landmark for visitors coming from the city, with beyond it various sports grounds, the US Ambassador's residence and, at the far end, the Ordnance Survey Office. At the north end of the park is the Phoenix Park Race Course.

★Phoenix Park

Leaving the park by either of the two northern exits – Cabra Gate or Ashtown Gate – proceed east along Navan Road and Cabra Road before turning north up Phibsborough Road to the Glasnevin or Prospect Cemetery, an extensive burial ground in which are situated the graves of Daniel O'Connell, Charles Stewart Parnell, Sir Roger Casement and many other Irish patriots.

Glasnevin Cemetery

North-east of the cemetery, bounded by the River Tolka, are the 50 acre/20ha Botanic Gardens (open: in summer Mon.–Sat. 9am–6pm., Sun. 11am–6pm; in winter Mon.–Sat. 10am–4.30pm, Sun. 11am–4.30pm). The wrought-iron Palm House was built in 1842–50 by Richard Turner.

Botanic Gardens

From the Botanic Gardens, follow the River Tolka south-east to Fairview Park, laid out on land reclaimed from the sea adjoining the harbour.

Fairview Park

North of the park, in the Marino district, reached via Malahide Road, stands the Marino Casino (1765–71; National Monument), a summer residence built by William Chambers for the first Earl of Charlemont, with sumptuously appointed rooms and a handsome staircase. In the basement are extensive domestic offices beneath a terrace flanked by four lions (open: June–Sept. daily 10am–6.30pm; admission fee).

Casino Marino

From Fairview Park Clontarf Road and its continuations skirt the north side of Dublin Bay to Howth, picturesquely spread over the slopes of a rocky promontory of quartzite and schist. The older part of the town lies on the

★Howth

Landscape on the Howth Peninsula

Howth: Fishing . . .   *. . . and Yacht Harbour*

north-east side of the peninsula. Here there is a large fishing and leisure-craft harbour, from which a boat can be taken to Ireland' Eye, a rocky islet 1¼ mile/2km offshore, with a little church and a Martello tower.

Above Howth harbour are the ruins of St Mary's Collegiate Church (14th–15th c.; National Monument), with two aisles of differing length. In the south aisle can be seen the handsome tomb of the Lawrence family (c. 1470).

West of the church is the 15th c. Howth Castle, a battlemented stronghold of irregular plan, much restored. The lovely park is open to the public (daily 8am–sunset) though the castle itself is not. Part of the park belongs to a golf club; elsewhere there is a French-style garden (18th c.) with 30ft/9m-high beech hedges and a profusion of rhododendrons, and a Transport Museum where old vehicles (tractors, double-decker buses, trams, etc.) are displayed (open: Sat. and Sun. 2–6pm; admission fee).

The highest point on the peninsula (best reached from "The Summit", a district at the eastern end) is Ben of Howth (568ft/173m), on which can be seen a burial mound; from the top there are panoramic views.

There is an attractive cliff walk along the east and south sides of Howth Peninsula, passing the Baily Lighthouse (1814), a short distance off the path at the south-eastern tip of the peninsula, and St Fintan's Chapel (9th c.?). The view over the expanse of Dublin Bay to Dún Laoghaire (see entry) is magnificent.

Outer Districts – South

Either side of the River Dodder in south-east Dublin lies the residential district of Ballsbridge, with dignified early 19th c. houses, parks and sports grounds. At the junction of Shelbourne Road and Pembroke Road are the United States Embassy, a circular building of 1964, and a number of new hotels.

Ballsbridge

East of the bridge (1791) over the Dodder, to the right of Merrion Road, can be seen the Royal Dublin Society Showgrounds. This extensive open site with its carefully tended turf, low white fences and handsome buildings, is the venue for the Kerrygold Dublin Horse Show, which takes place every year in August. The huge show, with more than 2000 horses and a full programme of races, displays, trials, prize-giving ceremonies and auctions, attracts visitors and buyers from far and wide. The show is a major event in the city's social calendar, with dances in large hotels.

Royal Dublin Society

A Spring Show is also held, in conjunction with a trade fair, at the beginning of May, devoted to stock-breeding, agricultural produce and machinery. While nowadays mainly concerned with agricultural science and stock-breeding, the Royal Dublin Society also has a cultural programme of concerts and lectures on subjects of more general interest, as well as a library of over 150,000 volumes for use by its members.

550yd/500m further south, Shrewsbury Road branches rightwards off Merrion Road. Here, at No. 20, is the Chester Beatty Library and Gallery of Oriental Art (open: Tues.–Fri. 10am–5pm, Sat. 2–5pm; conducted visits Wed. and Sat. 2.30pm), founded by an American who settled in Dublin in 1953. Among the principal treasures in this valuable collection are: in the Garden Library, French Books of Hours of the 14th and 15th c. and a prayer-book which belonged to Philip II of Spain; in the New Gallery, works of Far Eastern art including Chinese cups of rhinoceros horn (11th c.) and Japanese coloured woodcuts, Islamic prints, Sanskrit manuscripts (12th–13th c.), Indian miniatures, Babylonian clay tablets (2500–2300 B.C.) and numerous texts in all the Near Eastern languages. The items on show in the New Gallery are changed from time to time, there being insufficient space to display the whole collection.

Chester Beatty Library and Gallery of Oriental Art

Merrion Road continues south-eastwards to Merrion Strand and along the shores of Dublin Bay to Dún Laoghaire (see entry).

Merrion Strand

Dublin

Donnybrook — Situated in the Donnybrook district beyond the River Dodder is the national radio and television station, with a tall transmission tower. This was the site of the famous Donnybrook Fair, established by King John in 1204 and suppressed in 1855.

Museum of Childhood — A mile/1.5km farther south, at 20 Palmerston Park, is the Museum of Childhood, with a collection of dolls from 1730 to 1940, rocking horses and other toys (open: July and Aug. Wed.–Sun. 2–5.30pm; Sept.–June Sun. 2–5.30pm; admission fee).

Rathfarnham — South-west lies the Rathfarnham district, with a castle of the same name (National Monument). This stately mansion dating from 1593 is currently being restored (guided tours only; open: June–Oct. daily 10am–5 or 6pm). The restored former stables have been turned into workshops for traditional crafts.

Drimnagh — In the Drimnagh district north-west of Rathfarnham stands Drimnagh Castle (15th c.), with a well-preserved moat and outer ward. The castle itself is incorporated into a later building occupied by the Christian Brothers (open: Apr.–Sept. Wed; Sat. and Sun. noon–5pm; Oct.–Mar. Sun. noon–5pm; last tour 4.30pm; admission fee). Formerly lying outside the town, the castle was built to deter cattle-thieves.

Kilmainham Jail — Further along Nass Road in the direction of the city, north of the Grand Canal, extends the Kilmainham district. Here, between Emmet Road and Inchicore Road, is Kilmainham Gaol (1792) in which up until 1924 numerous Irish patriots were imprisoned and many were executed. In the entrance archway is a carving of intertwined serpents and chains, a sinister foretaste of the atmosphere within. Since 1960 the prison has been restored and is now a museum commemorating the patriots who were confined here (open: June–Sept. daily 10am–6pm; Oct.–May Wed. and Sun. 2–6pm). The cells in which the executed died can be visited and numerous exhibits give a grim insight into the darker side of Irish history.

★Irish Museum of Modern Art (Royal Hospital) — Continue towards the city along Kilmainham Lane then turn left into Military Road to arrive at the main entrance to the Royal Hospital, which today houses the Irish Museum of Modern Art. The building was erected between 1680 and 1687 by order of Charles II as a hospital "for maimed and infirm soldiers". In the 1980s no expense was spared in restoring Sir William Robinson's Neo-Classical building in the Franco-Dutch style (the tower dates from 1701), those who worked on the interior winning international acclaim. The Great Hall, with many portraits of kings and viceroys, is now used for concerts, banquets and conferences. Of particular interest in the chapel are the wood-carving and the Baroque stucco ceiling (a copy of the original destroyed in 1902). Some rooms have been furnished in their original style while others have been enlarged to provide exhibition space for the Irish Museum of Modern Art, which moved into its fine new premises in 1991. It would be hard to imagine a grander setting for its collection of 20th c. Irish and international art (open: Hospital – July and Aug. Tues.–Sun noon–5pm, rest of year Tues.–Sat. 2–5pm, guided tours Sun. 2–4.30pm, weekdays by appointment; Museum – Tues.–Sat 10am–5.30pm, Sun. noon–5.30pm).

Surroundings of Dublin – North

Santry — Heading north from Dublin the N1 passes through Santry where St Papan's Church (1709) boasts a 14th c. font, a reredos of 1709 and a fine pulpit.

Swords — Swords, 4 miles/6km farther on, is an ancient small town with the ruins of Swords Castle (13th–15th c.; National Monument). The castle, pentagonal in plan, was the seat of the archbishops of Dublin. It preserves a chapel, the gatehouse and towers. Adjacent to the village church stand a 74ft/22.5m-high round tower (entrance and roof modern) and the tower (14th c.) of a former monastic church.

Continuing north on the N1, turn off after 2 miles/3km onto the R126 for Donabate where, in 1992, Newbridge House together with its surrounding park and farm, were transformed into a museum portraying rural life in Ireland as it was in the 18th c. Open to the public are Newbridge House itself, built in the mid 18th c., various workshops and estate workers' cottages, and the adjoining farm complete with livestock and 18th c. implements, etc. (open: Apr.–Sept. Tues.–Fri. 10am–1pm and 2–5pm, Sat. 11am–1pm and 2–6pm, Sun. 2–6pm; Oct.–Mar. Sat. and Sun. 2–5pm; admission fee).

Newbridge House

Rejoin the N1, soon forking rightwards on the R127 to Lusk. It too boasts a round tower (National Monument), all that remains of a 9th c. monastery suppressed by the Anglo-Normans. The square tower seen near by belongs to a later structure. The church (1847) contains a number of good medieval tombs.

Lusk

On the coast to the east of Lusk lies the village of Rush, a bulb-growing centre from where a boat can be taken to Lambay Island. In the 8th c. the island was the scene of one of the first Viking incursions; fortifications dating from about 1550 can still be seen. The rocky islet (of porphyry; highest point 427ft/130m) is now a bird sanctuary; it can be visited only with the permission of the owner, Lord Revelstoke.

Lambay Island

From Lusk the R127 runs north-east past the ruined church (15th c.; National Monument) and castle of Baldongan, to Skerries (good sandy beach, 18-hole golf course). Just offshore are three little islets – St Patrick's Island, with a ruined church; Colt Island; and Shenick's Island (reached by foot at low water) with a Martello tower.

Skerries

North of Skerries on the Balbriggan road (R127) lies the Ardgillan Demesne, a restored country house standing in a large park (open: garden – daily 10am–5pm; house – Apr.–Sept. Tues.–Sun. 11am–6pm; Oct.–Mar. Wed.–Sun. 11am–4.30pm except late Dec.–end Jan. Sun. only 2–6pm; conducted tours Jun.–Aug. Thur. 3.30pm; admission fee).

Ardgillan
Demesne

Balbriggan itself is a quiet seaside resort on the River Delvin, with lovely beaches and a 9-hole golf course.

Balbriggan

Surroundings of Dublin – North-East

From the city's north-eastern suburbs, or alternatively from Howth, the R106 can be followed to the little resort of Portmarnock, with its beautiful 2 mile/3km-long Velvet Strand and well-known championship golf course.

Portmarnock

Situated about 1¼ mile/2km west of Portmarnock is St Doulagh's Church (13th c.), with its original stone roof, a chapel and a battlemented tower (15th c.). Cells in the tower, above the chapel and in the crypt suggest that this may have been a hermitage.

In a field 110yd/100m north-east there is a well, in a octagonal well-house with a stone roof.

★St Doulagh's
Church

From Portmarnock the R106 skirts the coast to Malahide, a popular little seaside resort. South-west of the town, in lovely gardens, stands Malahide Castle, which from the 13th c. to 1975 was owned and occupied by the Talbot family and now belongs to the city of Dublin. Much rebuilt and altered in the course of its history, it shows a variety of architectural styles – medieval, Georgian and modern. The Great Hall with its oak roof is the only

★Malahide Castle

Dublin

Beach at Portmarnock

Malahide Castle

one in Ireland to have preserved its medieval aspect and to have continued (until 1975) to serve its original purpose. The castle now houses the National Portrait Gallery (open: Mon.–Fri. 10am–12.45pm, 2–5pm, Sat. 11am–6pm, Sun. 11.30am–6pm; Nov.–Mar. Sat. and Sun. 2–5pm; admission fee), a branch of the National Gallery in Dublin. The pictures in the collection are of interest both on account of the artists represented (among them William Hogarth and Sir Joshua Reynolds) and also their subjects (Anne Boleyn, Robert Dudley, James Gandon, Jonathan Swift, Daniel O'Connell, etc.).

Another attraction, in the park of Malahide Castle, is the Fry Model Railway (open: Mon.–Fri. 10am–5pm, Sat. 11am–6pm, Sun. 2–6pm). It is the work of an Irishman, Cyril Fry, who spent many years creating the railway to a scale of 1:43; in its originality and detail it surpasses most others.

Surroundings of Dublin – South

See Dún Laoghaire

Surroundings of Dublin – West

2½ miles/4km north-west of Tallaght on the R113 lies Clondalkin, a monastic settlement founded by St Mochua in the 7th c., of which nothing remains but an 84ft/25.5m-high round tower (National Monument), with its original roof and an external staircase (18th c.), and, in the churchyard, two granite crosses and a font (all National Monuments).

Clondalkin

The N4 follows the course of the Liffey through the suburb of Chapelizod to Lucan, once a much-frequented spa. To the west stands Lucan House (1776), with beautiful interiors by James Wyatt, Michael Stapleton and Angelica Kauffmann.

Lucan

Finglas, on the north-west outskirts of Dublin on the N2, has a ruined medieval church and a 12th c. high cross in the churchyard. On a hill 2 miles/3km west can be seen Dunsink Observatory which, from 1782 to 1921, was the observatory of Trinity College Dublin.

Finglas

3 miles/5km north of Finglas, to the right of the N2, stands Dunsoghly Castle (15th c.; National Monument) which, unusually among Irish castles, still preserves its original oak roof beams. It is a square tower with rectangular corner turrets; far-ranging views can be enjoyed from the parapet walks. The roof structure provided the model for the reconstruction of Bunratty Castle (see Ennis). To the south of the castle are the remains of a small chapel (1573).

★Dunsoghly Castle

Dundalk · Dún Dealgan

B 3

Republic of Ireland
Province: Leinster
County: Louth
Population: 29,000

Dundalk (Dún Dealgan="Delga's fort") lies on the east coast of Ireland near the Northern Ireland border, where Dundalk Bay forms a sheltered harbour. With a variety of industry (engineering, printing, tobacco, footwear) the town has a busy and prosperous air.

Location

In the 10th c. the Irish inhabitants of the area were attacked by Viking raiders, and a naval battle was fought in the bay. The town was fortified in

History

1185. In 1253, and again in 1315, it was burned down. Thereafter for 300 years it was a cornerstone in the defence of the English Pale (the territory in the east of Ireland under English control). In 1690 it was taken by William of Orange, and in 1724 its fortifications were pulled down.

Sights

In the centre of the town, in Crowe Street (near the bus station), are two handsome 19th c. buildings, the Court House and Town Hall. Farther east, in Seatown Place, can be seen an old windmill, a massive seven-storey structure. On the main street leading north stands St Nicholas's Church (18th c.; with an older tower). St Patrick's Cathedral, built in 1848, is modelled on King's College Chapel, Cambridge. A short distance east is a newly opened museum which documents Dundalk and its history.

Surroundings

Cooley Peninsula

2 miles/3km north-east of the town a side road (R173) branches off the N1 and runs east into the Cooley Peninsula, an attractive hilly promontory between Dundalk Bay and Carlingford Lough, an arm of the sea.

★ Proleek Dolmen

A little way along the R173, at Ballymascanlon, stands the Proleek Dolmen (National Monument; in the grounds of the Ballymascanlon Hotel). It has a capstone weighing some 40 tonnes carried on only three uprights. Tradition has it that anyone who can throw a pebble onto the capstone without it rolling off will have their wish fulfilled.

Carlingford

On the north-east side of the peninsula lies the ancient small town of Carlingford, dominated by the massive King John's Castle (13th c.; National Monument) on a crag above the harbour. Near by can be seen the Tholsel, an old gate-tower in which the elders of the town used to meet. In a little street off the Square is the old Mint (National Monument), a 15th c. fortified tower house with curious window carvings. Taaffe's Castle opposite the railway station has a large square keep (16th c.) with a fine spiral staircase. Carlingford Forest, west of the town, is excellent walking country; one road leads up to an observation point from which there is a fine panorama of Carlingford and the coastal scenery.

Blackrock

On the coast south of Dundalk is the little resort of Blackrock with an 18-hole golf course, tennis courts and facilities for water-sports. Trout and salmon fishing in the River Fane.

Dromiskin

3 miles/5km farther south, in the graveyard at Dromiskin, just off the N1, are a 56ft/17m round tower and a high cross, both dating from the earliest years of a monastery established here in the 6th c. Adjoining is a 13th c. church. All are National Monuments. There are a number of well-preserved castles within a few miles' radius.

Castlebellingham

At Castlebellingham, 1¼ miles/2km south of Dromiskin, Bellingham Castle stands in a beautiful setting on the River Glyde. It has been renovated and is now a hotel (handsome yew hedges).

Ardee

15 miles/24km south-west of Dundalk on the N52 the little town of Ardee lies on the River Dee, with a 9-hole golf course and good fishing. It has two castles – Hatch's Castle and Ardee Castle, a square keep which now houses a small museum. St Mary's Protestant Church, which incorporates parts of an older building, has a carved font.

Louth

Louth, now just a village, to the north of Ardee, was at one time a place of such importance that it gave its name to the county. St Mochta's House (National Monument) is a vaulted two-storey oratory (12th c.) with a stone roof. Near by are the ruins of a 14th c. church.

Inniskeen

At Inniskeen, 5 miles/8km north of Louth, a redundant church has been turned into a museum of local history, one section of which is devoted to the former Great Northern Railway which passed through the town. On the site of an old monastery is the stump of a round tower (National Monument).

To the east on the N53, almost within the Dundalk built-up area, rises a 60ft/18m-high earthwork said to be the birthplace of the legendary hero CuChulainn. The site is now occupied by a building of 1870; fine views.
    A short distance away is Castletown Castle (15th c.), a four-storey structure with flanking towers.

Castletown Castle

4½ miles/7km north-west of Dundalk are the ruins of Castleroche (13th c.; National Monument), a triangular structure with bastions; it is particularly impressive when seen from the plain.

Castleroche

Dungarvan · Dún Garbhain

D 4

Republic of Ireland
Province: Munster
County: Waterford
Population: 6600

Dungarvan (Dún Garbhain="Garvan's fort") lies half-way along the south coast of Ireland in a sheltered bay at the mouth of the River Colligan. North of the town are the Comeragh and Monavullagh Mountains, rising to a height of 2560ft/780m. The town is the administrative centre of Co. Waterford (with the exception of the city of Waterford itself), and is also a busy marketing centre, with leather-processing works.

Location

The town extends on both sides of the River Colligan which is spanned by a bridge of 1815 with a 74ft/23m arch. On the right bank of the river are the ruins of Dungarvan Castle (built in 1185 and subsequently much altered), a massive circular keep surrounded by fortified walls. Near by in the 17th c. Old Market House, a small municipal museum has been established. In the churchyard of the parish church, can be seen the Holed Gable, a peculiar structure with a number of circular openings, the function of which is unknown.
    In Abbeyside, on the left bank of the river, is a tower which belonged to a 13th c. Augustinian abbey and now serves as the belfry of the adjoining church. Near by stands a curious shell house.

Sights

Surroundings

Off the R675 to the east of Dungarvan, on the far side of the bay, lies Clonea, a popular little seaside resort with a good sandy beach, a 9-hole golf course and two camp-sites.

Clonea

South of the town (ferry service) the Cunnigar Peninsula also has good beaches. There is a pleasant walk by way of Ring – with an Irish-language school – and the little, old-world fishing village of Ballynagaul, to Helvick Head (which can be reached also on the R674), with fine views of Dungarvan Harbour and the hills to the north.
    The region south of Dungarvan Harbour, between the N25 and the sea, is the only area apart from the west coast where Irish is still predominantly spoken.

Cunnigar Peninsula

2½ miles/4km north-west of Dungarvan, on the N72, is a monument to the celebrated greyhound Master McGrath, three-times winner of the Waterloo Cup and defeated only once in 37 races.

Greyhound Monument

The Touraneena Heritage Centre (open: daily 10am–8pm), about 9 miles/ 15km north of Dungarvan on the R672, comprises a farmhouse furnished as it would have been at the close of the 19th c. together with an old smithy.

Touraneena Heritage Centre

Dún Laoghaire
C 5

Republic of Ireland
Province: Leinster
County: Dublin. Population: 54,000

Location

Dún Laoghaire (pronounced Dunleary; = "Leary's fort") lies at the south end of the wide sweep of Dublin Bay, below the north-easterly foothills of the Wicklow Mountains. At the beginning of the 19th c. it was still a small fishing village, called at that time Kingstown following a visit by King George IV in 1821. A century later it acquired its present name. Today Dún Laoghaire is an attractive suburb of Dublin (see entry), a seaside resort and residential town much favoured by prosperous Dubliners, and an important port, terminus of the car ferry services to and from Britain (Holyhead). It is also Ireland's premier yachting centre, with the headquarters of almost all the country's major yacht clubs.

The town

Dún Laoghaire's elegant residential suburbs extend eastwards into the hills. The town's commercial life, on the other hand, is concentrated in the streets around the harbour.

Sights

Harbour

At the time of its construction (1817–21) the large harbour was a masterpiece of contemporary civil engineering. Its east pier is a popular promenade, with concerts in summer. The somewhat quieter west pier attracts mainly anglers.

National
Maritime Museum

A redundant seafarers' church a little to the south of the harbour now houses the National Maritime Museum (open: May–Sept. Tues.–Sun.

House fronts in Dun Laoghaire

2.30–5.30pm). A comprehensive collection of model ships, paintings, photographs, documents, etc. provide a fitting tribute to Ireland's seafaring tradition.

A minor road leads from the harbour, skirting the bathing beach, to Joyce's Tower, situated on a rocky promontory with an extensive view over Dublin Bay. It was one of the Martello towers built during the Napoleonic Wars to keep a watch for possible invasion. In 1904 James Joyce lived for some time in the tower, and he describes it in "Ulysses". It now houses a museum (open: Apr.–Oct. Mon.–Sat. 10am–1pm and 2–5pm, Sun. 2.30–6pm; at other times by arrangement with the tourist office) containing original manuscripts and rare editions of Joyce's work as well as personal mementoes.

Joyce's Tower

Surroundings

Along the coast to the north of the town, extending into the suburbs of Dublin, are the residential districts of Monkstown and Blackrock. Monkstown has a 19th c. church with towers like chess pawns. Blackrock has very popular seawater swimming-baths.

Monkstown, Blackrock

To the south, now continuous with Dún Laoghaire, is the ancient little town of Dalkey, another residential area favoured by better-off people from the capital. In Main Street stand two relics of the town's medieval defences, Archbold's Castle (16th c.; National Monument) and another castle which is now the town hall.

Dalkey

Just off the coast lies a small islet, Dalkey Island, with the remains of an old church (National Monument) and a Martello tower. From Sorrento Terrace and Sorrento Park, on the town's south beach, there are magnificent views. The old granite quarries are a good practice ground for rock-climbers.

Dalkey Island

To the south of Sorrento Point stretches Killiney Bay, with the seaside resort of Killiney. The slopes of the hills are studded, almost Mediterranean-like, with villas of different periods set in well-groomed gardens, while beyond the railway line, which here follows the coast, the beach is rocky. The mid 19th c. Ayesha Castle and grounds in Victoria Road can be visited by arrangement (tel. 852323). There are some lovely walks in Killiney Hill Park. The highest point, marked by an obelisk dating from 1741, affords superb views of the surrounding hills and the sea.

Killiney

To the west of Killiney, just off the R117, is the village of Kilternan. On a nearby hill can be seen the impressive Kilternan Dolmen (c. 2000 B.C.; National Monument), with a capstone 6ft/1.8m thick borne on ten orthostats.

Kilternan Dolmen

On the R117 a short distance north of Kilternan are Fernhill Gardens with old trees, a rock-garden and a water-garden. The park is privately owned.

Fernhill Gardens

Ennis · Inis   D 3

Republic of Ireland
Province: Munster
County: Clare
Population: 6200

Ennis (Inis="river meadow"), county town of Co. Clare and an important road and rail junction (N18, N68), is situated in the west of Ireland, on the River Fergus.
    Shannon International Airport is only 15 miles/25km distant. With its extensive hinterland and its light industries, Ennis is a considerable market and commercial centre.

Location

The River Fergus flows in broad curves through the town which, with its narrow winding streets has preserved something of its medieval aspect.

The town

Sights

At the end of Abbey Street stands Ennis Friary (National Monument; open: June–Sept. daily 9.30am–6.30pm), a Franciscan house founded in 1241 which in the mid 14th c. was a flourishing community with 375 friars and 600 students. The church dates from the original foundation but has been much altered. It has some very fine sculpture, including a figure of St Francis with the stigmata (on the south-west side of the tower), the Mac-Mahon monument of about 1475 (on the south wall), a royal tomb with scenes from the Passion and a small representation of the Scourging, with the "cock-in-the-pot" (for an explanation of the legend, see Kilkenny, St Canice's Cathedral).

Ennis Friary

Near the abbey, in Harmony Row, is the De Valera Museum and Library (open: Mon.–Wed., Fri. 11am–1pm, 2.15–5.30pm and 7–9pm, Thur. 11am–1pm and 2.15–5.30pm), with material on Ennis and the surrounding area and the history of Ireland. Among the exhibits is the fountain pen with which Eamon de Valera and Neville Chamberlain signed the 1938 treaty under which Britain gave up its naval bases in Ireland.

De Valera Museum and Library

Surroundings

6 miles/10km east of Ennis on the R469 is Quin, with Quin Abbey (1402; National Monument), the well-preserved ruins of a Franciscan friary built on the foundations of an earlier castle, the bastions of which can still be seen. The church has tombstones of the 15th to 19th c.; well-preserved cloister.
  On the other side of the little river stands the 13th c. St Finghin's Church (National Monument), the tower being a later addition.

★ Quin Abbey

2½ miles/4km farther south-east on the R469 lies Knappogue Castle, a tower house dating from 1467, restored in 15th c. style, with furniture of the period (open: May–Oct. daily 9.30am–5.30pm). In summer medieval-style banquets are held in the 19th c. annexe.

Knappogue Castle

A further 1¼ mile/2km along the R469, a small road to the left leads to an estate signposted "Craggaunowen Project". In the mid 1960s this land was acquired by John Hunt, an art collector, who restored the 16th c. Craggaunowen Castle and around it created an impressive open-air museum (open: mid Mar.–Oct. daily 10am–6pm).
  The castle itself contains a small collection of medieval religious art from the Hunt Collection (see Limerick, National Institute for Higher Education), mostly continental in origin. The gatekeeper's lodge, to the left of the castle entrance, has been turned into a chapel (notable 15th c. bronze cross).
  In the grounds are reconstructions of some of the earliest types of man-made structure in Ireland, including a crannog (Bronze Age pile dwelling) in a small lough and a stone ring fort, both with huts and implements of the period. Displayed in a specially built glass shed is the leather boat in which Tim Severin and his crew re-enacted the medieval voyages of St Brendan (see Famous People).

★ Craggaunowen Project

The R462 continues south to Six milebridge, a pretty little village with a delightful 18th c. mansion, Mount Ievers (1736) which has been described as "a Georgian doll's house". From here a minor road runs south-west to the village of Bunratty.

Six milebridge

◀ *The high cross of Dysert O'Dea, near Ennis*

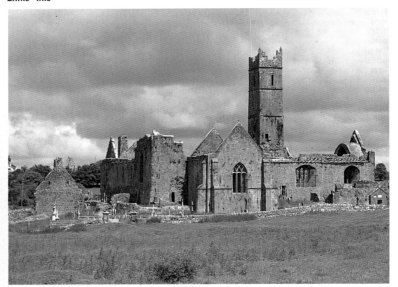

Quin Abbey

Craggaunowen Project: a stone ring-fort

Bunratty Castle and Folk Park are one of Ireland's principal tourist attractions. Following an eventful history of destruction and rebuilding, the 15th c. castle was acquired in 1954 by Viscount Gort and magnificently restored; it is now managed by Shannon Free Airport Development Ltd. The great hall and banqueting hall, chapel and residential apartments are furnished with an outstanding collection of pieces from the late Middle Ages and early Renaissance (open: daily 9.30am–5pm; June–Aug. park open until 7pm). Medieval-style banquets are laid on for holidaymakers in the banqueting hall. Basement shop.

★★ Bunratty Castle and Folk Park

Bunratty Folk Park, to the rear of the castle, is an interesting open-air museum with numerous cottages, shops and workshops such as were found all over Ireland in the late 19th c. In the centre of the park a whole village street has been reconstructed.

At Cratloe, a short distance east of Bunratty, is a 17th c. mansion, Cratloe Woods House (open: June–mid Sept. Mon.–Sat. 2–6pm).

Cratloe

Leather goods, jewellery, woollens, pottery, etc. can be seen in the making as well as purchased at the Ballycasey Workshops (open: Mon.–Fri. 10am–6pm), about 4 miles/7km west of Bunratty on the approach road to Shannon Airport.

Ballycasey Workshops

Being only 7 miles/11km from Shannon International Airport, Bunratty naturally attracts large numbers of tourists. The airport, the most westerly in Europe, opened in 1945 and boasted the world's first duty-free shop. Shannon having long since lost its importance as a touch-down point for trans-atlantic flights, a development company, Shannon Free Airport Development Ltd., has instead succeeded in attracting a range of industries here (precision tools, electronic equipment, industrial diamonds, etc.). The town of Shannon has a population of 7000.

Shannon International Airport

On the way north from Shannon Airport to Ennis, the N18 passes through Newmarket on Fergus, a small market town and commercial centre. A little to the north, Dromoland Castle, built in about 1830, stands resplendent in extensive grounds. The castle is now a luxury hotel and golf course but the lovely park remains open to the public.

Newmarket on Fergus

Nearer to Ennis the road crosses the River Fergus at Clarecastle, with the ruined castle from which the village, and possibly the county of Clare also, takes its name.

Clarecastle

A good ¾ mile/1km farther north on the N18 are the ruins of Clare Abbey (National Monument), founded in the 12th c. and extended at various times down to the 15th c.

Clare Abbey

3 miles/5km south-west of Ennis on the N68, in a beautiful setting on a lough, are the remains of Killone Abbey (12th c.; National Monument), one of Ireland's few nunneries.

Killone Abbey

Having followed the N85 north-westwards from Ennis to Fountain Cross, turn north onto the R476, arriving after 4 miles/6km at Dysert O'Dea (National Monument). Dysert O'Dea Castle (1480) has been extensively restored and now houses a small archaeological museum (open: May–Sept. daily 10am–7pm).

★ Dysert O'Dea

The castle is the start of a history trail (accessible at all times) taking in a series of historical and archaeological remains in the near vicinity, the most interesting of which are a church, a round tower and a high cross. The church seen today dates from the late 17th c., when it was reconstructed more or less in its original form (12th/13th c.). It has a fine Romanesque doorway carved with beautiful geometric designs, foliage and rather Mongoloid masks. At the north-west corner of the church stands the stump of a round tower, still 40ft/12m high; and in a field to the east is a high cross, with an unusual figure of the Crucified Christ, fully clothed, on the east side; the other sides are divided into panels with a variety of geometric patterns, human figures and interlace designs with animals.

Dysert O'Dea Castle . . .   *. . . and a Romanesque church doorway*

Enniscorthy · Inis Coirthe   D 5

Republic of Ireland
Province: Leinster
County: Wexford
Population: 5000

Location

Enniscorthy (Inis Coirthe="rock island") lies in the south-east corner of Ireland on the main road from Dublin to Wexford. The town is built on the west side of the River Slaney, both banks of which rise sharply above the river. The Slaney is navigable up to this point and carries a considerable traffic between Enniscorthy and Wexford (about 15 miles/25km south).

Sights

Enniscorthy Castle

The town developed as a market and distribution centre around Enniscorthy Castle (1586; National Monument), a rectangular keep with corner towers. Now restored it houses the Wexford County Museum with finds from the Stone Age onwards and documents relating to local crafts (open: June–Sept. Mon.–Sat. 10am–1pm and 2–6pm, Sun. 2–5.30pm; Oct.–May daily 2–5.30pm).

St Aidan's Cathedral

St Aidan's Cathedral, commandingly situated above the river, is a Neo-Gothic church by Pugin (1840).

Vinegar Hill

Fine views can be enjoyed from Vinegar Hill (east of the town), where there are also remains of a windmill (National Monument).

Surroundings

Ferns, about 8 miles/13km north of Enniscorthy on the N11, was once the county's episcopal see. The road crosses the site of an old abbey (National Monument), with three churches and other buildings. The present Protestant church incorporates some work from an earlier building; in the churchyard are three high crosses. Ferns Castle (National Monument) is a large rectangular keep with circular towers at the corners; in one of the towers there is a beautifully vaulted 13th c. chapel.

Ferns

Further north-east, still on the N11, lies Gorey, once with an important cattle market. Courtown, on the coast near by (R742), is a popular family seaside resort with lovely sandy beaches and an 18-hole golf course.

Gorey, Courtown

The Blackstairs Mountains to the west of Enniscorthy offer plenty of scope for hill walking and climbing.

Blackstairs Mountains

Enniskerry · Ath na Scairbhe

C 5

Republic of Ireland
Province: Leinster
County: Wicklow. Population: 1200

Enniskerry (Ath na Scairbhe="rugged ford"), one of the prettiest villages in Ireland, lies south-east of Dublin to the west of Bray, in a wooded hollow in the foothills of the Wicklow Mountains.
    Enniskerry is a good base for walking in the hills and for a visit to nearby Powerscourt.

Location

★★Powerscourt Gardens

About ½ mile/800m south of the village is the entrance to the demesne of Powerscourt, with gardens and a landscaped park which are among the most beautiful in Ireland. The gardens were completed in 1875, the culmination of 30 years work.

Opening times
Mid May–Oct.
daily
9.30am–5.30pm

The house, the centrepiece of the grounds, was once an imposing granite mansion (1731; by Richard Cassels), approached along a mile-long avenue. Today only the façade still stands, the building having been gutted by fire in 1974. From the house, situated on a rise, the gardens extend down the slope, with terraces, statuary, tessellated pavements, an ornamental lake and fine wrought iron work. In the grounds are plantations of exotic trees, beds of rhododendrons and other flowering shrubs, also an Italian and a Japanese garden and a deer-park. From various viewpoints there are magnificent prospects of the surrounding hills – Great Sugar Loaf, 1631ft/497m; Kippure, 2430ft/740m.

An hour's walk away lies the celebrated Powerscourt Waterfall, the highest in Ireland, formed by the River Dargle tumbling over a 400ft/120m-high cliff into the valley below. At its most impressive after a rainy spell, the waterfall can be visited all year round (open: in summer daily 9.30am–7pm; in winter 10.30am until dusk; marked footpath from Powerscourt Gardens).

Powerscourt Waterfall

About 2 miles/3km upstream the Glencree River joins the Dargle, flowing down from Glendoo Mountain through a lovely valley. A delightful road ascends the valley to a group of 18th c. buildings known today as St Kevin's, originally a barracks erected by the British for the protection of the Military Road.

Glencree River

In a dip near by there is a German military cemetery, seldom totally deserted, more usually with one or two people praying, Irish fashion, in

German Military Cemetery

191

Powerscourt Gardens: only the façade of the mansion remains

front of the crosses, or reading the inscriptions in English, Irish and German on the triangular headstones: ''. . . but the war sent me to sleep in Glencree''.

Surroundings

The Scalp   About 2 miles/3km north of Enniskerry the Dublin road (R117) passes through the Scalp, a rock gorge littered with granite boulders hewn from the hills by glaciers during the last Ice Age.

Fanad Peninsula   A 4

Republic of Ireland
Province: Ulster
County: Donegal

Location   Situated in the far north of Ireland and of Co. Donegal, the Fanad Peninsula extends northward for some 12 miles/20km between the narrow fjord-like inlet of Mulroy Bay to the west and Lough Swilly, the broad estuary of the River Swilly, to the east. An area of spectacular cliff and coastal scenery, the peninsula terminates in Fanad Head.

Circuit of the Peninsula

Milford   From Letterkenny (see entry) the N56 runs north to Milford, a fishing centre at the head of Mulroy Bay. The village has a modern church. Near by is a waterfall known as the Grey Mare's Tail. There is good fishing in Lough Fern and other small loughs in the neighbourhood.

From Milford the R246 makes its way north along the east side of Mulroy
Bay. Just before Kerrykeel (also spelt Carrowkeel) is a dolmen with a
massive capstone measuring 6 by 12ft/2 by 4m. Kerrykeel lies at the foot of
the Knockalla Mountains, known hereabouts as the "Devil's Backbone".

Kerrykeel

The R246 and its continuation lead to Fanad Head at the northern tip of the
peninsula (fine views). The return is down the west side of Lough Swilly.

Fanad Head

Beyond Portsalon, which has a picturesque little harbour and an 18-hole
golf course, are a group of spectacular tunnels in the cliffs, known as the
Seven Arches, up to 300ft/90m long, 20ft/6m wide and 30ft/9m high; also
the Great Arch of Doagh Beg.

Portsalon

The Knockalla Mountains, which can be seen ahead, falls steeply to the
loughside. On the slopes is a 19th c. gun position directed against a
possible French invasion.

Knockalla
Mountains

The R247 leads past Otway golf course (9 holes) to Rathmullan, an attractive seaside resort with a sandy beach. At Rathmullan are the ruins of a
Carmelite friary (15th c.; National Monument), with a church which a 17th c.
bishop converted into his residence. Near the harbour a gun emplacement
known as the Battery, built at the beginning of the 19th c. in anticipation of a
French invasion, has been turned into a Visitor Centre (open: May–Sept.
Mon.–Sat. 10am–6pm, Sun. 12.30–6pm) devoted in particular to the "Flight
of the Earls" – it was from Rathmullan in 1607 that the Earls of Tyrone and
Tyrconnell fled to France accompanied by a band of friends and supporters. Afterwards their vast estates in Ireland were confiscated and
re-settled by English and Scots.

Rathmullan

Fermoy · Mainistir Fhear Muighe

D 3

Republic of Ireland
Province: Munster
County: Cork
Population: 3100

The little market town of Fermoy (Mainistir Fhear Muighe="abbey of the
plainsmen") lies inland from the south coast of Ireland between spurs of
the Knockmealdown and Nagles Mountains. A major cattle auction is held
in the town.
    This is excellent salmon and trout fishing country and angling competi-
tions take place regularly in the area. There is also good coarse fishing; the
Blackwater is the only river in Ireland where roach are found.

Location

Castle Hyde, a Late Georgian house on the banks of the Blackwater in the
west of the town, was the ancestral home of Douglas Hyde, President of the
Irish Republic from 1938 to 1945.

Sights

Surroundings

10 miles/16km north on the N8 lies Mitchelstown, a small country town
with a creamery producing butter and cheese. An 18th c. planned town, it
grew further in the 19th c. Buildings of interest include an attractive group
of almshouses (1780) known as Kingston College.

Mitchelstown

Located 7 miles/11km north-east in Co. Tipperary is the extensive limestone cave system known as the Mitchelstown Caves (open: summer only,
daily 9am–6pm). Desmond's Cave was the refuge of a 16th c. Earl of
Desmond who had a large price put on his head. The New Cave, discovered
in 1833, contains fine stalactitic and stalagmitic formations; 390ft/120m

Mitchelstown
Caves

long and 40ft/12m high it is believed to be the largest cave in the British Isles.

Labbamolaga Church	Labbamolaga, in hilly country 5½ miles/9km north-west of Mitchelstown on the R665, has ruins of a modest Early English church (National Monument).
Castlelyons	4½ miles/7km south-east of Fermoy lies Castlelyons where are found the remains of a 15th c. priory (National Monument) comprising a church with a beautiful west doorway and a tower and other buildings. A few miles east, on a crag above the River Bride, stands a 14th c. tower house, Conna Castle (National Monument).
Anne's Grove Gardens	Driving west from Fermoy on the N72, branch off northwards in Castle-townroche to arrive after another 2 miles/3km at Anne's Grove Gardens, a delightful park with many exotic trees and flowers on the banks of the River Awbeg (open: Apr.–Sept. Mon.–Sat. 10am–5pm, Sun. 1–6pm).
Killavullen	Continue in the direction of Mallow, passing the village of Killavullen. Not far to the west on a cliff above the Blackwater stands the ancestral home of the Hennessy family, whose cognac distilled in France is renowned the world over.
Mallow	Mallow, an important sugar-refining centre, lies 30 miles/50km west of Fermoy in the wooded valley of the Blackwater, a river well stocked with fish. In the 18th and 19th c. the town was a much-frequented spa, but preserves only a little of the atmosphere of those days. It has a number of notable buildings: the Court House, the Market House, a picturesque half-timbered clock tower and some good 18th c. dwelling-houses; also one or two relics of its fashionable heyday – the old Spa House, the racecourse and three gushing springs in Fermoy Road. At the south-east end of the town are the ruins of Mallow Castle (16th c.; National Monument), with a small museum.
Ballybeg Abbey, Buttevant	In close proximity to one another on the N20 north of Mallow are Ballybeg Abbey (13th c.; National Monument), possessed of a very fine dovecot, and, in the little town of Buttevant, the ruined church of a Franciscan friary (13th c.; National Monument) with a handsome choir and crypt (under-building on a steep river-bank).
Kilcolman Castle	A short distance north-east are the ruins of Kilcolman Castle, in which the poet Edmund Spenser (1552–99) lived for thirteen years.
Kanturk	The small market town of Kanturk, 12 miles/20km west of Mallow, boasts a massive early 17th c. fortified house (National Monument) which belonged to the MacCarthys. When news of the scale of the project reached England alarm bells started to ring, and an order to suspend work was issued; the castle was never finished.
Liscarroll Castle	9 miles/15km north-east of Kanturk are the ruins of Liscarroll Castle (National Monument), a handsome tower house built in the 13th c. but later much altered; it is surrounded by a walled outer ward with defensive towers.
Tullylease	North of Kanturk on the R579 at Tullylease are the ruins of a 13th–15th c. monastery (National Monument). It has a number of Early Christian grave-stones built into the walls, including one in particular on the east end of the church embellished with fine ornament in the style of the 8th c. "Book of Lindisfarne" and a Latin inscription.
Labbacallee Cairn	North-west of Fermoy on the R512 can be seen the Labbacallee Cairn (National Monument), an unusually large Neolithic wedge-shaped gallery with a rectangular main chamber and a smaller chamber to the rear.

A short distance further on, at Glanworth, the River Funshion is spanned by an ancient thirteen-arched bridge (view). In the surrounding area are a number of ruined castles along the river.

Galway · Gaillimh

Republic of Ireland
Province: Connacht
County: Galway. Population: 47,000

Galway (Gaillimh) is picturesquely situated at the north-east end of Galway Bay, at the point where the short tidal River Corrib, coming from Lough Corrib, disgorges its abundant flow of water into the Atlantic.

Galway is the see of the diocese of Co. Galway, and has a university (part of the National University of Ireland), in which much of the teaching is in Irish (summer courses for visitors in July and August). Irish culture and language are also promoted by Taebhdhearc na Gaillimh, an Irish-language theatre.

In the last two decades Galway has experienced a 40% increase in population with a corresponding economic and cultural upsurge and an increase in tourism. Although Galway itself has no really outstanding features, it is an excellent centre for exploring the west of Ireland.

There is a regular ferry service from the harbour to the Aran Islands (see entry), the terminal being at the end of Lough Atalia Road. There are likewise regular air services to the islands from Carnmore Airport, some 5½ miles/9km to the east.

Location

There was a settlement on this site from the earliest times. After the building of a castle in 1124 and its capture by Richard de Burgo in 1232, Galway rapidly developed into a flourishing Anglo-Norman town. The "fourteen tribes of Galway" – aristocratic merchant families – transformed the town into a kind of city state, maintaining the English connection in defiance of all Irish assaults (the Irish in fact were barred from entering the town). Galway was destroyed by a great fire in 1473 but was soon rebuilt. Trade with the countries of western Europe, particularly Spain, brought

History

Galway
Gaillimh

1 Salmon Weir Bridge
2 O'Brien's Bridge
3 Claddagh Bridge
4 Court House
5 Town Hall
6 Franciscan Friary
7 Lynch's Castle
8 St. Nicholas Church
9 Lynch's Window
10 Nora Barnacle House
11 Taebhdhearc Theatre
12 Eyre Square Shopping Centre
13 Aran Passenger Terminal
14 Bus Terminal

300 m
990 ft

© Baedeker

195

wealth and prosperity. During the 16th and 17th c. there was a celebrated grammar school here which is said at one time to have had 1200 pupils. In the 17th c. the town supported the Irish cause and suffered widespread destruction at the hands of Cromwell's forces; in 1691 it was further damaged when it fell to William of Orange's army.

The town

The central area of Galway lies on the east bank of the River Corrib; and although few old buildings have survived, the narrow winding streets still have a certain atmosphere. The walls of a number of houses have stones with coats of arms carved on them, relics of Galway's heyday.

For centuries Galway had active trading relations with Spain and has preserved something of this Spanish influence – manifested architecturally, for instance, by houses built around an open courtyard.

Sights

Eyre Square, Kennedy Park

The centre of Eyre Square has been landscaped as a memorial to US President John F. Kennedy, who was of Irish descent. On its north-west side stands Browne's Gateway, the doorway of an old patrician mansion which has been re-erected here. Also in the square is a striking monument to the Irish-language poet Pádraic O'Conaire (1882–1923), seen seated on a rock.

Eyre Square Shopping Centre

Situated west of Eyre Square is the eponymous modern shopping centre which, with its cafés, has become a popular meeting place. Part of the old town wall has been restored and incorporated into the complex.

★Lynch's Castle

Eyre Square leads to Williamsgate Street, one of the town's main shopping thoroughfares, and to Lynch's Castle (16th c.; National Monument). Today occupied by a bank, the tall grey building with coats of arms on the façade was considerably altered during restoration in the 1960s. The castle was formerly the residence of the Lynches, an aristocratic family several of whom became mayors of Galway. It was while holding that office that one of the Lynches condemned his own son to death for the murder of a young visiting Spaniard. When no one else proved willing, he carried out the sentence with his own hands – so giving rise to the expression "lynch law".

Lynch's Window

A black marble tablet on the wall of the old prison in Market Street marks the spot (Lynch's Window) where the execution is said to have taken place.

★St Nicholas's Church

St Nicholas's Church (National Monument), also in Market Street, was built in the 14th c. and, although much altered later, has preserved the aspect of a medieval parish church. Notable features are the triple gables of the west front, the gargoyles (rare in Ireland) and, in the interior, a number of tombs and a reader's desk.

Nora Barnacle House

A short distance from the church (in Bowling Green) stands the house of James Joyce's wife Nora Barnacle, where the writer often stayed. On Wednesdays in summer, literary evenings are held here (open: Mon.–Sat. 10am–5pm).

Salmon Weir Bridge

Further upstream the River Corrib is spanned by the Salmon Weir Bridge (1818). In spring (mid May) countless salmon can be seen making their way up river to the huge expanse of Lough Corrib (see entry), a journey of only 4 miles/6km from the sea.

Strong tidal currents are experienced in the river here, with a powerful flow downstream on the ebb and an equally powerful flow upstream when the tide turns.

Cathedral

The Cathedral (St Nicholas and the Assumption), on the right bank, was consecrated in 1965. One of the largest churches in Ireland (300ft/100m long by 155ft/47m wide), it occupies the site of a prison in which many Irish

Eyre Square Shopping Centre

Lynch's Castle

patriots were confined. Building costs were met almost entirely by public subscription. There are good mosaics in the side chapels.

Of the town's three bridges the middle one, O'Brien's Bridge, is the oldest, its existence being first recorded in 1342.

O'Brien's Bridge, Claddagh Bridge

The Claddagh Bridge (a swing bridge) at the south end of the town, takes its name from an old fishermen's quarter on the right bank of the Corrib, occupied for centuries by a fishermen's guild but now replaced by modern buildings. Today the only reminder of the old guild is the traditional "Claddagh ring", in the form of two hands clasping a heart. Worn as an amulet it is handed down from mother to daughter.

On the east side of the Corrib, below Claddagh Bridge, is the old town gate known as the Spanish Arch (1594), leading to Spanish Parade, once the favourite promenade of Spanish merchants. The arch now houses the Galway City Museum, with material on the history of Galway, and old weapons found in Galway Bay (open: summer daily 10am–5pm).

Spanish Arch, City Museum

Surroundings

North-east of Galway on the N17, Claregalway has the ruins of a Franciscan friary (National Monument) founded in 1290 and enlarged in the 15th c. On a tombstone in the church there is a representation of a primitive plough.

Claregalway

From Carnmore proceed to Oranmore and from there south on the N18 to Clarinbridge, a pretty little village where the excellent local oysters and shellfish can be sampled.

Clarinbridge

1¼ mile/2km south of Clarinbridge, at Kilcolgan, the N67 branches off to the right, leading after ¾ mile/1km to the ruined Drumacoo Church (National Monument), with finely carved windows and doorway; also notable is St Surney's Well.

Kilcolgan

Dunguaire Castle

Dunguaire Castle	10 miles/6km further south-west on the N67 stands Dunguaire Castle, a 16th c. fortified tower house complete with furnishings and open to visitors. In the evenings "medieval banquets" are held in the hall.
Salthill	Situated immediately west of Galway, and today continuous with it, is Salthill (Irish name Bothar na Tra="shore road"), a leading seaside resort on the north side of Galway Bay. Though its not so luxurious hotels, bingo halls and amusement arcades will not appeal to everyone, it does have a lovely seafront promenade above a broad sandy beach from where there are extensive views of the hills of Clare, the Burren and the Aran Islands.
Spiddal	The R336 follows the coast to Barna and Spiddal, a pretty little resort with good fishing. Irish crafts flourish in the Spiddal Craft Centre (open: May–Oct. Mon.–Sat. 9am–5.30pm, Sun. 1–6pm) with a range of goods on sale.

Glencolumbkille · Gleann Cholaim Cille   B 3

	Republic of Ireland Province: Ulster County: Donegal Population: 250
Location	Glencolumbkille (Gleann Cholaim Cille="St Columba's glen") is a picturesque holiday resort in the far north of Ireland, at the most westerly point of Co. Donegal. It lies in a valley opening into Glen Bay on the Atlantic, with a sandy bay and magnificent cliff scenery in the surrounding area.
Glencolumbkille area	The area around Glencolumbkille is one of the Irish-speaking parts of Donegal. Here St Columcille (Columba) lived in solitude and meditated.

Folk Museum in Glencolumbkille

Surroundings of Glencolumbkille: beautiful scenery and a lovely beach

Another tradition has it that Bonnie Prince Charlie, last in the line of Stuart Pretenders, spent some time here when fleeing from the British.

In the middle of the present century, when Glencolumbkille was in danger of dying through lack of employment, Father James McDyer set up a co-operative to maximise agricultural potential and market local hand-made art and craftwork. The undertaking proved successful. Thatched cottages were built for holiday letting and a Folk Museum established to attract day-trippers.

Pilgrimage

Every year on June 9th (St Columba's Day) a pilgrimage takes place here, the route – a circuit of some 3 miles/5km on the hillsides around the village – being marked by a series of stone slabs and pillars inscribed with crosses and geometric designs; the largest of these stones can be seen beside the church (National Monument). Pilgrims complete either three or seven full circles, from time to time adding a stone to the heaps accumulating around the stations. The pilgrimage must be completed before sunrise.

Sights

Folk Museum

The open-air museum (open: Apr.–Sept. Mon.–Sat. 10am–6pm, Sun. noon–6pm) at the west end of the village consists of four thatched cottages furnished with items dating from 1700 to 1900, together with a 19th c. schoolhouse. There is also a shop selling local products and a tea-room serving home-made cakes. This entire project too was the brainchild of Father James McDyer.

Surroundings

Malinmore

South-west of Glencolumbkille lies Malinmore, a pretty little resort with a bay and picturesque cliffs. Nearby, at Cloghanmore, is a court cairn (National Monument) some 3500 years old.

Rathlin O'Birne

There is good fishing in the coastal waters extending out to the island of Rathlin O'Birne, which has a number of antiquities (6th c) and a lighthouse.

Glendalough · Gleann da Locha   C/D 5

Republic of Ireland
Province: Leinster
County: Wicklow

Location

The celebrated monastic settlement of Glendalough (Gleann da Locha ="glen of the two lakes") lies a little way inland from the Irish Sea coast some 25 miles/40km south of Dublin. On summer weekends it tends to be crowded with day-trippers; weekdays are generally quieter.

Turn off the R755 – running south from Bray through the hills to Arklow – at Laragh, into a wooded valley opening out to the west. After about a mile Glendalough comes into view, famous both for its monastic remains and for its scenic beauty. Grouped around the two lakes from which the village takes its name, are the impressive, and for the most part well-preserved, remains of a religious centre which was once among the most influential in Ireland.

Topography

Enclosed by hills of varying heights between 2130 and 2460ft/650 and 750m, the valley of the River Glenealo, which narrows sharply further upstream, offers plenty of scope for walking, scrambling and climbing. The valley cuts through the Glendalough Forest Park in the Wicklow Mountains (see entry).

History

St Kevin first took up his abode in this remote valley as a hermit seeking solitude. His piety and learning attracted so many disciples however, that

200

he founded a monastery. When in 618 he died at an advanced age, Glenda-lough's period of greatness was only just beginning; after his time the Glendalough school is said to have had more than a thousand students. The annals tell of Viking raids and, in the 12th c., a number of damaging fires. In 1163 an abbot of Glendalough, Laurence O'Toole, was appointed Archbishop of Dublin. The Anglo-Normans made the monastery subject to the see of Dublin; then, after a fire in 1398, it steadily declined. In 1875–80 the buildings were restored and have been meticulously maintained ever since.

★★Monastic Settlement

The opening times given refer to the Visitor Centre, the monastic site itself being open at all times. Car parks are provided at the Visitor Centre and between the Upper and Lower Lakes. By far the best plan is to see the highly informative video film at the Centre first, then start the tour of the site at the Upper Lake, the real heart of the complex. A delightful path known as the Green Road then leads from the Upper Lake to the remains of the monastic settlement near the Visitor Centre.

Opening times
Daily
9.30am–5pm
(6.30pm in summer)

Exhibits in the Visitor Centre include a model of the site as well as various gravestones, capitals and other masonry. Of special interest is a 12th c. high cross (Market Cross) with a Crucifixion, the figure of an abbot, and interlace ornament; this may once have stood on the pilgrim route to Glendalough.

Visitor Centre

Accessible only by boat, the little rectangular Teampull na Skellig ("Church of the Rock") stands on a quarried-out platform by the lakeside. The oldest fragment of the partly restored church dates from the 7th c.

Teampull na Skellig

About 220yd/200m further east is a cavity in the cliff known as St Kevin's Bed (or hermitage), in all probability a Bronze Age burial-place.

St Kevin's Bed

Easier to reach is St Kevin's Cell, the beehive hut in which the saint is said to have lived.

St Kevin's Cell

By a small bridge are remains (nave, chancel) of the 11th c. Reefert Church; the projecting stones at the corners supported the rafters.

Reefert Church

Between the Upper and Lower Lake, to the right of the car park, stand an ancient stone fort (the Caher) and three stone crosses (probably boundary stones originally but afterwards stations on the pilgrimage circuit).

The Caher

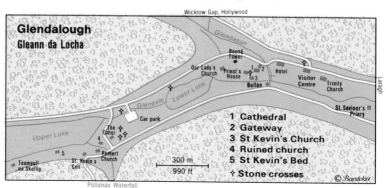

Wicklow Gap, Hollywood

Glendalough
Gleann da Locha

Glendasan

Round Tower

Our Lady's Church

Priest's House

Hotel

Visitor Centre

Trinity Church

Laragh

Bullan

Lower Lake

Glenealo

St. Saviour's Priory

Car park

The Caher

Upper Lake

Reefert Church

Teampull na Skellig

St. Kevin's Cell

300 m
990 ft

1 **Cathedral**
2 **Gateway**
3 **St Kevin's Church**
4 **Ruined church**
5 **St Kevin's Bed**
✝ **Stone crosses**

© Baedeker

Pollanas Waterfall

Glendalough · Gleann da Locha

Gateway   The main group of monastic buildings lie further downstream near the Visitor Centre. Access to the precinct dating from the heyday of the monastery was through an entrance gateway.

Round Tower   Near the gate stands the exceptionally well preserved round tower, 102ft/31m high and 16ft/5m in diameter at the base. It is still very much as it was when first built apart from the roof which was reconstructed using the old stones. The doorway is more than 10ft/3m from the ground.

St Mary's Church   West of the round tower is the granite-built St Mary's Church or Church of Our Lady (10th c.), venerated up until the 18th c. as St Kevin's burial place.

Priest's House   Beyond this is the Priest's House, a 12th c. building in Irish Romanesque style with an interesting carving of much earlier date on the lintel of the doorway.

Cathedral   The largest building on the Glendalough site is the cathedral, with nave, chancel and sacristy (11th and 12th c.). It acquired cathedral status at the beginning of the 13th c.

St Kevin's Church   Perhaps the most remarkable of all the buildings at Glendalough however is St Kevin's Church, traditionally – though mistakenly – known as St Kevin's Kitchen on account of its chimney-like belfry. This barrel-vaulted oratory of hard mica schist with steeply pitched roof dates from the 11th/12th c. It houses a small number of old stone carvings discovered on the site.

Trinity Church   Trinity Church (11th–12th c.), on the right of the Laragh road, still has its original granite chancel arch.

St Saviour's Priory   Further to the east, on the far side of the river, stands the most recent complex of buildings, St Saviour's Priory (12th c.; reconstructed about

Glendalough Round Tower   *St Kevin's Church*

1875). Some fine Romanesque carvings on the chancel arch and windows and some conventual buildings are the only original work to survive.

Glengarriff · Gleann Garb

E 2

Republic of Ireland
Province: Munster
County: Cork. Population: 150

Glengarriff (Gleann Garb="rugged glen") lies in the far south-west of Ireland at the mouth of a 6 mile/10km-long valley where the River Glengarriff flows into Bantry Bay. The village is wholly given over to the holiday and tourist trade, with a large amount of holiday accommodation in private houses. Day-trippers come mainly to visit Garinish Island offshore or to do a circuit of the Ring of Beara.

Location

Glengarriff's location makes it particularly attractive as a destination. In the favourable climate of the region, bathed in the warm moist air of the Gulf Stream, a mantle of vegetation of almost tropical luxuriance – fuchsias, yews, hollies and arbutus – garbs the rocky hillsides reaching down to the sea.

Village

★★Garinish Island · Ilnacullin

Of the many little islands in the bay the one most worth visiting is Garinish, which lies offshore to the east of the R572. Small boats run regularly to the island from Glengarriff, a 15 minute crossing during which seals are often to be seen basking on the rocks. The gardens, with their magnolias, rhododendrons, camellias and many exotic trees, were only laid out between 1910 and 1920. The oldest building on the island is the Martello tower,

Opening times
Mon.–Sat.
10am–4.30pm,
Sun. 1–5pm

View of Glengarriff and some of its islands

dating from Napoleonic times; the others, blending beautifully with the landscaping, were erected only when the gardens were first established.

Among the best known personalities to visit Garinish was George Bernard Shaw (see Famous People). In 1923 he spent several months in a house on the island writing the greater part of "Saint Joan".

★Ring of Beara

Glengarriff is a good base from which to explore the peninsula jutting out westwards into the Atlantic. Though not nearly so well known as the Ring of Kerry (see entry), this 84 mile/135km drive offers no less spectacular scenery. Strung across the interior of the peninsula are the Caha and Slieve Miskish Mountains which reach heights of between 1313ft/400m and 2297ft/700m.

Castletownbere

The R572, skirting the shores of Bantry Bay with the Caha Mountains on one side and the sea on the other, loops around Adrigole Harbour before resuming its westward course to Castletownbere.

About 2 miles/3km south-west of Castletownbere stand the ruins of Dunboy Castle, a turn of the 20th c. building in a mixture of styles, erected over the remnants of a castle destroyed in 1602. The view is magnificent.

Bere Island

Offshore can be seen the striking silhouette of Bere Island where today there is a sailing school.

Dursey Island

Off the western tip of the peninsula lies Dursey Island, separated from the mainland by Dursey Sound. Only a dozen people live on the island (access by cablecar for those of strong nerve).

Eyeries

North of Castletownbere the R571 crosses a saddle in the Slieve Miskish Mountains to the trim little village of Eyeries.

At Ballycrovane, a little to the east, a huge ogham stone (National Monument) can be seen from the road. Situated on private land it stands 17ft/5.2m high and looks for all the world like a piece of modern sculpture.

Derreen Garden

Beyond Eyeries the road continues north-east to Lauragh in Co. Kerry where the beautiful Derreen Gardens can be visited (open: Apr.–Sept. daily 11am–6pm). Mossy paths lead through woods, past lush rhododendrons, eucalyptus and bamboo groves with view after superb view of the sea.

From Lauragh a road crosses the Healy Pass (1066ft/325m) to Adrigole and thence back to Glengarriff.

Gort · Gort lase Guaire   C 3

Republic of Ireland
Province: Connacht
County: Galway. Population: 1100

Location

Gort (Gort lase Guaire="Guaire's field by the shore") lies in the far west of Ireland to the south of Galway Bay. It attracts visitors mainly on account of the many features of interest in the surrounding area.

The town

The little town is neatly laid out around a large central market place, with two early 19th c. churches.

Surroundings

Coole Park

On the north side of the town, to the west of the N18, lies Coole Park, former home of the authoress Lady Gregory (1852–1932) where once the cream of

204

Irish writers and poets were entertained. Destroyed in 1941, nothing now remains except a magnificent avenue of cedars and a copper beech bearing the initials of many Irish literati (George Bernard Shaw, Yeats, O'Casey and others). The estate is now a national forest and deer-park.

Coole Park Interpretative Centre has information on the flora and fauna of the region as well as a collection of portraits of Lady Gregory and her literary associates (open: Apr.–Sept. daily 9.30am–6.30pm; park open at all times).

On the banks of a stream about 4½ miles/7km north-east of Gort stands Thoor Ballylee, a four-storeyed 16th c. keep purchased and restored by W. B. Yeats (see Famous People) who lived in it from 1921 to 1929. His period of residence is commemorated by a stone tablet with some lines of verse by him. The tower has been carefully restored and now appears as it did during Yeats' lifetime. It contains a museum of Yeats memorabilia including first editions of his works (open: Apr.–Sept. daily 10am–6pm).

★Thoor Ballylee

South-east of Gort lies Lough Cutra. The River Beagh flows out of the lough, whereupon – like other rivers in this limestone region – it several times disappears below ground only to reappear again. The lough itself is highly picturesque, with a number of small wooded islets on which there are the ruins of churches and a castle. Commandingly situated on the shore of the lough is Lough Cutra Castle (1810; by John Nash), complete with tower and battlements. The castle is not open to the public.

Lough Cutra

South-west of Gort on the R460 are the ruins of Kilmacduagh (National Monument), a monastic site with several churches and a round tower. The round tower, 112ft/34m high, is excellently preserved, but leans about 2ft/60cm from the perpendicular; the entrance is 25ft/7.8m above the ground. Beside it is the cathedral (12th/15th c.) with nave, chancel and transepts; in the north transept are fine popular-style representations of

★Kilmacduagh

Yeats' Thoor Ballylee

Kilmacduagh Round tower

the Crucifixion. To the right of the cathedral stands St John's Church (12th c.), and adjoining it a fortress-like 13th c. building, probably the abbot's lodging. At the north-west corner of the precinct is O'Heyne's Church (13th c.), with a fine chancel arch; close by are the remains of another small church. On the other side of the road, opposite the cathedral, is St Mary's Church (12th c.). The entire site, set in green meadowland on the shores of a lough with the Burren Hills in the background, is exceedingly picturesque.

Grand Canal   C 3–4

Republic of Ireland
Length: 80 miles/130km

Course
The Grand Canal links Dublin Bay to the Shannon (see entry), following a fairly direct westerly course from Dublin (see entry), by way of Naas and Tullamore (see entries) to Shannon Harbour. Differences of height are overcome by a total of 52 locks.

History
Construction of the canal began in 1756. Soon afterwards the project was taken over by a Dublin company and by 1777 had been carried forward as far as the River Morrell, one of the purposes of this section being to improve the city's water supply. Two years later the completed section was opened to navigation. In 1785 the Barrow Line, a branch canal from Robertstown to Athy, was brought into use. In 1804 the whole canal was completed and the first barges began to ply between Dublin and Shannon Harbour. Thereafter, until the middle of the 19th c., various other branch canals were constructed to towns lying near the main canal. With the coming of the railways the economic importance of the canal declined, which process continued in the 20th c. until, by about 1960, commercial traffic on the branch canals had ceased.

Pleasure-craft
The Grand Canal is now used mainly by pleasure-craft, subject to the following maximum dimensions: length overall 60ft/18.5m, beam 13ft/3.9m, draught 4ft/1.2m, air draught 9ft/2.75m. Every craft must bear a name or a number. The maximum permitted speed is 3mph/5kmph. Vessels keep to the right, with overtaking on the left. Locks can only be worked during daylight hours. Hire-craft are available at various places along the canal.

Hill of Tara

See Tara

Horn Head · Corran Binne   A 4

Republic of Ireland
Province: Ulster
County: Donegal

Location
Horn Head (Corran Binne="hollow in the hills") is the northernmost extremity of a peninsula jutting into the Atlantic in the far north of Ireland. It is reached by way of the N56.
The best starting point for excursions to Horn Head and the surrounding area is Dunfanaghy, with an 18-hole golf course and the little harbour of Port-na-Blagh near by. 1¼ mile/2km further east, on a sheltered bay, lies Marble Hill. All these places have beautiful sandy beaches.

Landscape on Horn Head

From Dunfanaghy there is a delightful walk along the west coast of the peninsula to Horn Head. The headland rises straight from the sea to a height of about 600ft/180m, with views northward over the boundless ocean, broken only by numerous islands and promontories, and inland to splendid ranges of hills, with Muckish Mountain and Errigal Mountain as backdrops. Horn Head is well-known for its seabird colonies

It is also possible to drive to the tip of the peninsula. The best view of the cliffs is obtained from Traghlisk Point on the east side.

Topography

Surroundings

South-east of the village of Marble Hill, on the Ards Peninsula which sticks out into the bay of Sheep Haven, is a Capuchin friary. The grounds and parkland can be visited on application to the fathers.

Ards

To the south of the friary, beautifully situated on a promontory, are the ruins of Doe Castle (16th c.; National Monument), a four-storeyed keep surrounded by defensive walls and towers. Chieftains from many leading Donegal families are interred in the burial ground.

Doe Castle

6 miles/10km south of Dunfanaghy lies Creeslough, with a picturesque bridge over the Duntally River, a waterfall and St Michael's Church, a fine modern building (1971; by Liam McCormick and partners).

Creeslough

Inishowen Peninsula · Inis Eoghain

A 4/5

Republic of Ireland
Province: Ulster
County: Donegal

Location

The Inishowen Peninsula (Inis Eoghain="Eoghain's island") is the northernmost part of Ireland; its most northerly point is Malin Head.

To the west of the peninsula Lough Swilly, a broad arm of the sea, cuts deep inland; to the east lies the great and virtually land-locked expanse of Lough Foyle with Northern Ireland beyond. Malin Head, at the extreme north-western tip, looks out across open ocean. A 100 mile/160km-long signposted route, the "Inis Eoghain 100", makes a circuit of the peninsula.

Buncrana

The principal centre of habitation on the peninsula is Buncrana (population 4000), a popular seaside resort on the east side of Lough Swilly, with a 3 mile/5km-long beach, Lisfannon Strand. In recent years a greater range of entertainment and leisure facilities have become available to holiday makers, the majority of whom come from Northern Ireland. Buncrana and the surrounding area have a tradition of textile manufacture; today 2000 jobs are provided by the American textile firm "Fruit of the Loom" (factory shop).

O'Doherty's Keep

Beautifully situated on the lough is O'Doherty's Keep, a well-preserved but architecturally undistinguished stronghold (14th/17th c.; National Monument).

Buncrana Castle

Beyond the bridge stands Buncrana Castle (1716; by Vaughan), a handsome mansion with a beautiful interior, unfortunately falling into a state of disrepair.

Vintage Car & Carriage Museum

The nearby Vintage Car and Carriage Musuem has a collection of vintage cars, carriages and Victorian bicycles (open: in summer, daily 10am–8pm).

Tullyarvan Mill

Tullyarvan Mill, erected in the 19th c., stands at the edge of Buncrana on the road to Dunree Head. It has been carefully restored and now houses a small textile museum and museum shop (open: Apr.–Sept. Mon.–Sat. 10am–6pm, Sun. noon–6pm).

Circuit of the Peninsula

Dunree Head

Setting out from Buncrana, start by taking the by-road going north-west to Dunree Head. At Fort Dunree (4 miles/6km) there is a military museum with a video presentation covering the history of the fort and area (open: Apr.–Sept. Tues.–Sat. 10am–6pm, Sun. noon–6pm).

Gap of Mamore

Continue over the Gap of Mamore, a breathtakingly steep pass with gradients of up to 30%. The magnificence of the scenery is best appreciated when, as in this case, crossing from the south.

Dunaff Head

At the most northerly point on this stretch of road lies Dunaff Head (superb cliffs, much-frequented by rock-climbers, and exceptional views).

Ballyliffin

Rejoining the R238 at Clonmany continue to Ballyliffin with its 2 mile/3km-long beach, Pollan Strand. Picturesquely situated on the northern tip of the Doagh Peninsula are the ruins of Carrickabrahey Castle.

Carndonagh

Next stop is Carndonagh, a little town with shirtmaking factories and a distillery. Opposite the church stand three Early Christian monoliths (all National Monuments), of which the most noteworthy is the 7th c. St Patrick's Cross, one of the earliest in Ireland. The cruciform motif is only hinted at in the arrangement of the Celtic interlace decoration; in the lower half is the figure of a man with extended arms, flanked by smaller figures; the reverse has more interlace work and a human figure. On either side of the cross are smaller stones with reliefs of David with his harp, a bird, a man with two bells and other devices. More monuments can be seen in the churchyard at the rear.

3 miles/5km north of Carndonagh the road reaches Malin. Here the R242 branches off leftwards past the handsome Malin Hall (1758), to Malin Head (magnificent cliff scenery).

    1¼ mile/1km west of the point is Hell's Hole, a narrow cleft through which the incoming tide surges with awesome force.

Malin Head

From Malin Head a long succession of cliffs up to 790ft/240m high stretch south-east to Glengad Head.

Glengad Head

Continue south to Culdaff, a fishing centre (sea trout), and then a further 2 miles/3km south again to Clonca where there is a ruined church, a fine but badly weathered high cross with a representation of the Miracle of the Loaves and Fishes as well as two male figures and geometric designs, and a finely carved tombstone (all National Monuments).

Culdaff, Clonca

At Carrowmore there is a group of high crosses (National Monuments).

Carrowmore

The R238 proceeds next to Moville, a popular resort on Lough Foyle and once a departure point for ships crossing the Atlantic.

Moville

2½ miles/4km to the north-east lies Greencastle, with the ruins of a large castle (1305; National Monument). Nearby is a Martello tower (1810), now a hotel.

Greencastle

From Greencastle continue north-east on the R241 for 2½ miles/4km to Inishowen Head from which another range of superb cliffs (with views across to the Northern Ireland coast) extends north-westward. The cliff scenery and the delightful valley of Glenagiveny attract many visitors.

Inishowen Head

To complete the circuit of the peninsula, follow the R238 along the shores of Lough Foyle to Muff (border crossing to Londonderry, see entry, in Northern Ireland). There head west on the R239 to rejoin the R238 (to Buncrana) south of Burnfoot.

Muff

Further south of Burnfoot, at the intersection of the R238 with the N13, can be seen a notable modern church by McCormick and Madden. Dedicated to St Aengus, the circular building with its band of windows and curving roof canopy surmounted by a pyramidal glass spire, may well have been influenced by the Grianán of Aileach (see below), only 2½ miles/4km away to the south.

St Aengus Church

Grianán of Aileach (Grianán="sun palace") is an Early Christian circular stone fort surrounded by three concentric earth ramparts, commandingly situated on a 790ft/240m-high hill. The windowless outer wall, constructed without mortar, stands 17ft/5m high and is 13ft/4m thick at the base; it encloses a grass-covered area 79ft/24m in diameter, entered via a low doorway. The wall is terraced on the inside, with steps leading up to each level; within the thickness of the wall are a series of small chambers and passages. The period of construction of the fort, which from the 5th to the 12th c. was the seat of the kings of Ulster, is unknown. It was extensively restored in 1874–78. From the walls of the fort there are breathtaking views over the the surrounding countryside and loughs.

★Grianán of Aileach

4½ miles/7km north-west, at Fahan on the shores of Lough Swilly, a very ancient cross-slab (8th c.) can be seen in a former monastic churchyard adjoining the modern church. Two crudely carved figures flank the cross which itself is of elaborate interlace work; on one of the edges is a Greek inscription, something of a rarity in Ireland.

Fahan

Kells · Ceanannus Mor   C 5

Republic of Ireland
Province: Leinster
County: Meath. Population: 2600

Location

Kells (Ceanannus Mor="great residence") lies in the wooded valley of the Blackwater 25 miles/40km inland from the Irish Sea coast, at the intersection of the N3 and N52.

Book of Kells

The name of Kells is primarily associated with the very famous "Book of Kells", a magnificently illuminated manuscript of the four Gospels now in the library of Trinity College Dublin (see Dublin; see also Baedeker Special). A facsimile can be seen in St Columba's Church, a modern building in the centre of town.

History

A monastic settlement was established at Kells by St Columba in the 6th c.; in the 9th c. monks from Iona sought refuge here having been driven from the Scottish island by Viking raids. In later centuries the settlement was several times plundered and subsequently restored. The town was fortified by the Anglo-Normans and maintained its importance until the Dissolution of the Monasteries in 1551.

Sights

Round Tower

Beside the church stands a 100ft/30m-high round tower (10th c.; National Monument) with five windows at the top; the original roof is missing.

★South Cross

Near by is the South Cross or Cross of St Patrick and St Columba (National Monument), probably erected in the 9th c. It has a wealth of sculptured

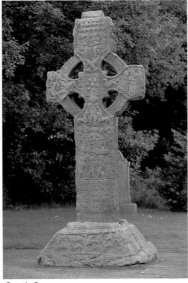

South Cross   St Columba's House

ornament: on the base a train of chariots, animals and interlace; on the south face in ascending order the Fall, Cain and Abel and the Three Men in the Fiery Furnace, then Daniel in the Lions' Den, the Sacrifice of Isaac (left), Paul and Anthony in the Wilderness (right) and higher up David with his harp and the Miracle of the Loaves and Fishes; on the west face the Crucifixion and Christ as Judge. Other details include a representation of David killing the lion and the bear and a number of panels with interlace ornament and fabulous beasts.

Some 33yd/30m away can be seen the stump of a very large cross (National Monument) on the east side of which are unusual representations of the Baptism of Christ in the River Jordan (two rivers flowing together), the Marriage in Cana (?), the Presentation in the Temple (?), David with his harp and the Entry into Jerusalem (?), and on the west side Adam and Eve, Noah's Ark, etc. An unfinished cross beside the church gives an insight into the sculptor's method of working. | More high crosses

North-westward, beyond the churchyard walls, stands St Columba's House (National Monument; bear left on leaving the churchyard), an oratory with a steeply pitched stone roof (probably 10th c.). The interior measures 24×21ft/7.2×6.3m, the walls, more than 4ft/1.2m thick, inclining inwards to meet at the ridge. There is an upper chamber (entered via a steep ladder) the wall of which supports the roof. The original entrance was 6½ft/2m above the ground. | ★St Columba's House

The Market Cross (National Monument) in Cross Street (National Monument), in the centre of the town, is of considerably later date than the high crosses referred to above. An inscription states that it was erected in 1688 though modelled on a much earlier 9th c. one. | Market Cross

Surroundings

The estate of Headford, on the north-east side of the town, has a handsome Georgian manor house (1770), now occupied by a school. | Headford

12½ miles/20km west of Kells (R168 and R154) lie the Loughcrew hills, of which Slieve na Calliagh ("Witch's Hill") is the highest. Scattered over two adjacent summits (access from a car park on the road between Drumore and Millbrook) are 30 or so Neolithic chambered cairns, only a few having their chambers intact. Cairn T, in the eastern group, is perhaps the most interesting; 120ft/36m in diameter, it has a large main chamber with side chambers and many stones with scribed ornament. | Slieve na Calliagh

A walk in the hills is rewarded with superb views of the fertile countryside of Meath laid out some 985ft/300m below.

From Kells the N3 runs north-west towards Virginia (see Cavan, Surroundings). To the left just outside the town, on the Hill of Loyd, can be seen a memorial tower of 1791 (delightful views). | Hill of Loyd

2½ miles/4km farther along, on the banks of the Blackwater, are the ruins of St Ciarán's Church, with three simple high crosses (National Monuments), an Early Christian gravestone and a holy well. | St Ciarán's Church

Republic of Ireland
Province: Munster
County: Kerry
Population: 1200

Colourful houses in Kenmare

Location	Kenmare (An Neidin="little nest"), a friendly little seaside resort at the south-western tip of Ireland, lies at the outflow of the River Roughty into the long inlet known as the Kenmare River.
	The town is noted for its high-quality lace, and also for its excellent woollen goods. The principal source of income, however, is tourism.
The town	Despite the obvious influence of tourism, Kenmare, a planned town founded in 1775, still retains considerable charm. Its two main streets form an "X", the upper arms of which enclose a pleasant green. Not far to the west on the banks of the River Finnihy is a Druids' Circle, a ring of fifteen standing stones, 49ft/15m in diameter, with a dolmen in the centre.

Surroundings

Ring of Kerry	Kenmare makes a good base from which to set out round the Ring of Kerry (see entry), the exceptionally scenic circuit of the Iveragh peninsula.
Ring of Beara	Not quite so well-known, and perhaps a little less spectacular – though highly rewarding all the same – is the drive round the Ring of Beara, circling the peninsula of that name south of Kenmare (see Glengarriff).

Kerry

See Ring of Kerry

Kildare · Cill Dara   C 5

Republic of Ireland
Province: Leinster
County: Kildare. Population: 4000

Kildare (Cill Dara="church of the oak") lies in a slightly elevated situation in | Location
the east of Ireland, on the Dublin to Limerick road (N7). St Brigid of Kildare
(453–521), who like St Patrick is Patron Saint of Ireland, founded a famous
double monastery here. It had both monks and nuns and was headed
jointly by a bishop abbot and an abbess. The nuns tended St Brigid's "fire",
a perpetual flame which was finally extinguished only at the dissolution of
the monastery.

Today Kildare is the centre of Ireland's bloodstock and horse-racing
industry.

Sights

The town's past glories are recalled by St Brigid's Cathedral (1223), which | St Brigid's
has undergone numerous restorations, most recently in 1875–96. It con- | Cathedral
tains a number of medieval monuments, notably the tomb of one of the
Fitzgeralds of Lackagh (d. 1575).

In the churchyard stands a fine round tower, 105ft/32m high, probably one | Round tower
of the last to be erected in Ireland; it can be climbed without difficulty. The
roof is modern.

Tully, on the south-eastern outskirts of Kildare, is the home of Ireland's | ★★Irish National
National Stud, which can be visited along with the notable Japanese | Stud/Japanese
Gardens (open: mid Feb.–mid Nov. daily 9.30am–6pm). The Visitor Centre, | Gardens
opened in 1993, leads first to the Gardens, established using plants specially imported for the purpose at the beginning of the present century. The
Gardens take the form of a "Path of Life", each of the 20 "stations" representing a stage in man's journey from the cradle to the grave. The final
station is the "Gate to Eternity" – through which visitors pass only to find
themselves still unmistakably earthbound in the National Stud, which has
produced many famous racehorses.

The stud was established in about 1900 by a Scot, William Hall-Walker,
whose breeding methods were eccentric to say the least. Stallions and
mares were paired according to their zodiacal signs, and a horoscope was
drawn up for every foal. If the omens were not good, the foal was sold. For
all this, Hall-Walker became a successful breeder. In 1915 he presented his
stud to the British government; in 1943 it was handed over to the Irish
government.

Walking round the grounds visitors see some valuable breeding stallions
and in spring and summer the mares and their foals at pasture. The saddler
and smith can also be watched at work. Another attraction here is the Irish
Horse Museum, covering the history of the horse from the Bronze Age to
the present day. Among the many exhibits on display is the skeleton of
Arkle, one of the most celebrated of Irish racehorses.

East of the National Stud lies the world-famous racecourse known as "The | "The Curragh"
Curragh", surrounded by a vast stretch of fine grassland from which it
takes its name. The Irish Derby (so called after the 12th Earl of Derby) is run
here every year at the end of June/beginning of July.

Surroundings

On the Hill of Allen, 5 miles/8km north of the town on the R415, there once | Hill of Allen
stood a castle belonging to the kings of Leinster. The site is now occupied
by a tower (1859) with Latin inscriptions; extensive views.

The famous race-course "The Curragh"

Old Kilcullen   At the eastern edge of the Curragh, on the River Liffey (bridge of 1319), is the little town of Kilcullen, 2 miles/3km south of which lies Old Kilcullen. Once a walled town with seven gates, Old Kilcullen preserves the remains of a monastery (National Monument) founded by St Patrick, with a very interesting fragment of a 9th c. high cross on which are representations of David and the lion (north side), Samson with the lion (west side), bishops, other unidentified figures, and interlace ornament. A second cross-shaft is badly weathered. Nearby are remains of a round tower and of a Romanesque church (12th c.).

Dún Ailinne   Between Kilcullen and Old Kilcullen, on the west side of the N78, stands the hill-fort of Dún Ailinne, once a stronghold of the kings of Leinster. Its 15ft/4.5m-high walls enclose an area 150yd/135m in diameter. Most unusually, the circular ditch is inside rather than outside the walls. The site remained occupied from the Bronze Age until about 1800.

Monasterevin   Monasterevin, 7 miles/11km west of Kildare, is an ancient little market town with handsome late 19th c. houses.
Moore Abbey, an elegant 18th c. house on the site of a monastery, is now a home for the mentally handicapped. North of Monasterevin the Grand Canal (see entry) crosses over the River Barrow by means of an aqueduct.

Kilkee · Cill Chaoidhe   D 2

Republic of Ireland
Province: Munster
County: Clare
Population: 1400

The attractive family holiday resort of Kilkee (Cill Chaoidhe="church of St   Location
Caoidhe"), is situated on a crescent-shaped bay on the west coast of
Ireland, its long sandy beach protected from the Atlantic by the Duggerna
Rocks. Along the beach to the west, past some impressive rock formations,
stands Lookout Hill, from which vantage point, 200ft/60m above the sea,
beautiful far-reaching views are obtained in clear weather (care required on
the edge of the cliffs).

Surroundings

South-east of Kilkee (N67) lies the little market town of Kilrush, with a   Kilrush
harbour (Kilrush Creek Marina) 2 miles/3km further south on the estuary of
the Shannon. Recently enlarged and modernised the haven offers good
berthing and other facilities for pleasure-craft (boats available for charter).
    The Heritage Centre in the Town Hall takes as its theme "Kilrush in
Landlord Times" (open: Mon.–Sat. 11am–6pm, Sun. 2–6pm).

From Kilrush it is possible once again to go by foot ferry to Scattery Island   Scattery Island
(information from the Scattery Island Centre, Merchants Quay, Kilrush)
with the ruins of a 6th c. monastery (National Monument) founded by St
Senan. Barely ½sq. mile/1sq.km in area but assured of its place in ecclesiastical history, the island remained inhabited until 1978, since when the
village has fallen into decay. The round tower, one of the tallest in Ireland
(115ft/35m), can be seen from some way off; it is unusual in having the
entrance at ground level. To the east is the "cathedral", to the north a 12th c.
Romanesque church and to the south-east an early church with medieval
additions. The monastery, a place of great importance in the 14th and
15th c., was destroyed in the reign of Elizabeth I.
    The island is the focus of several seafaring superstitions: for their
maiden voyage, newly-built craft would be sailed around the island
"with the sun"; and pebbles from Scattery carried in a ship were believed
to protect it from shipwreck.

The N67 comes to an abrupt end at Killimer, 5 miles/8km south-east of   Killimer
Kilrush. Here a car ferry crosses the Shannon estuary to Tarbert (see
Ballybunion), thus saving, on a north/south journey, a detour of some
55 miles/89km around the estuaries of the Fergus and the Shannon (hourly
departures).

Another very pleasant drive from Kilkee follows a minor road south-west   Fooagh Point
along the coast to Fooagh – once a small spa with a chalybeate spring – and
Fooagh Point, with a holy well and magnificent rock scenery (tunnels,
caves, cliffs).

Above the harbour at Carrigaholt, across on the other (south) side of the   Carrigaholt
peninsula, are the fine ruins of a tall, slender tower house (15th c.; National
Monument) in a well-preserved outer ward; the turret facing towards the
pier is modern. There is an Irish-language college in the village.

A delightful road then runs south-west from Carrigaholt to Kilbaha, 2½   Loop Head
miles/4km beyond which lies Loop Head (lighthouse). Just off the point
stands an isolated stack known as Diarmaid and Grainne's Rock. The views
are breathtaking.

Kilkenny · Cill Chainnigh   D 4

Republic of Ireland
Province: Leinster
County: Kilkenny
Population: 10,000

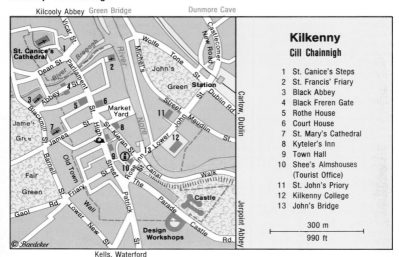

Kilcooly Abbey   Green Bridge   Dunmore Cave

Kilkenny

Cill Chainnigh

1   St. Canice's Steps
2   St. Francis' Friary
3   Black Abbey
4   Black Freren Gate
5   Rothe House
6   Court House
7   St. Mary's Cathedral
8   Kyteler's Inn
9   Town Hall
10 Shee's Almshouses
    (Tourist Office)
11 St. John's Priory
12 Kilkenny College
13 John's Bridge

300 m
990 ft

Kells, Waterford

Location

Kilkenny (Cill Chainnigh="Canice's church") is situated in the south-east of Ireland on the banks of the peat-brown River Nore. The town enjoys a degree of prosperity, reflecting not only the presence of several small industrial firms, but also its role as a market for local agricultural produce and as a focus for tourism. The Kilkenny Design Centre, dedicated to improving the quality of design and packaging of Irish products, has built up an excellent reputation throughout Ireland, as a consequence of which it attracts craftsmen and artists who settle in the town.

History

A church was built here in the 6th c. by St Canice. In pre-Norman times it was the seat of the kings of Ossory, later passing into the hands of the Ormondes. During the 14th c. a number of parliaments met in Kilkenny, including the one in 1366 which approved the infamous Statute of Kilkenny. This made it high treason for an Anglo-Norman (i.e. an Englishman settled in Ireland) to marry an Irishwoman, adopt Irish customs, speak Irish or wear Irish dress, while at the same time prohibiting Irish people from living in a walled town. Although rigorously enforced, the statute failed in its object of preventing the assimilation of Anglo-Normans and Irish. From 1642 to 1648 the town was the seat of the Confederation of Kilkenny, an independent Irish parliament which brought together both the Old Irish and the Anglo-Irish Catholics; later, however, the Confederation split into two camps and the Anglo-Irish allied themselves with the English. In 1650 Cromwell took the town, the Irish garrison being permitted to march out with full honours.

★★ The town

Kilkenny is considered by many to be second only to Dublin in its attraction for visitors. Its narrow winding streets lend it an atmosphere of old-world charm; its terraces of handsome Georgian houses give it elegance. Recent decades have seen a comprehensive programme of restoration of the historic architectural fabric, as a result of which today the whole of Kilkenny once again presents a medieval aspect.

From time immemorial the town has been divided into three districts or wards – Irishtown, with the cathedral as its central landmark; High Town to the south, dominated by Kilkenny Castle; and on the other bank of the River Nore, the eastern district, with St John's Priory.

St Canice's Cathedral

Irishtown

At the north end of the town, just off Vicar Street, stands St Canice's Cathedral, one of the finest in Ireland. Built on the site of an earlier church, it was begun about 1251 and completed in 1280. The massive squat tower (14th c.) and exterior walls of the aisles, transepts and clerestory are all topped by crennellations. In spite of much restoration (most recently in 1863–64) the interior has preserved its spacious character.

⋆ St Canice's
Cathedral

It contains many fine monuments, including the tombs of Henry de Ponto (1285; the oldest of the tombs) and of Edmund Purcell (1549), both in the north aisle. The Purcell tomb has a carving of a theme frequently found in Irish sculpture – a cock crowing on the edge of a cooking-pot. This is a representation of the old Irish legend that, following Christ's Resurrection, a servant carried the news to the High Priest's kitchen. The cook scoffed at the story – as unlikely, he said, as that the cock cooking in the pot would come to life again: whereupon the cock jumped out of the pot and crowed.

In the choir can be seen the tombs of Bishop de Ledrede (d. 1360) and Bishop Rothe; in the south transept the tomb of the 8th Earl of Ormonde and his wife (1539); and in the south aisle the tombs of Viscount Mountgarrett (in armour), Bishop Walsh (1585) and a lady in old Irish dress. In the north transept is St Ciarán's Chair, of black marble, and in the nave a 12th c. font.

By the south transept stands a 100ft/30m-high round tower with numerous windows; the roof is not original. From the top (very steep and narrow staircase) there are fine views of the city and the surrounding area.

Round tower

From the cathedral St Canice's Steps (1614) lead down to Dean Street.

St Canice's Steps

High Town

St Francis' Friary
Parliament Street, running south, crosses the little River Bregagh, the boundary between Irishtown and High Town. Just to the left, on ground belonging to Smithwick's Brewery (guided tours and beer tasting: summer only, Mon.–Fri. 3pm), are the ruins of St Francis' Friary (National Monument), founded in about 1232 and extended in 1321 when the lovely seven-light east window was inserted. The slender tower has fine sculpture.

Black Freren Gate
Continue southwards down Parliament Street to Abbey Street where, to the right, can be seen one of the gates of the old town defences, Black Freren Gate.

Black Abbey Church
A little further to the west stands Black Abbey Church, once the church of a Dominican friary founded in 1225. The church has been completely restored in the present century; the south transept is essentially 14th c. and the tower 15th c. Notable features of the interior include a medieval alabaster carving of the Trinity and a crudely carved oak figure of St Dominic.

★Rothe House
On returning to Parliament Street, the next building to catch the eye is Rothe House, a merchant's house built between 1594 and 1610 in the Elizabethan style with two adjacent inner courtyards (restored 1966). It is now occupied by the City and County Museum (open: Apr.–Oct. Mon.–Sat. 10.30am–5pm, Sun. 3–5pm; Nov.–Mar. Sat, Sun. 3–5pm).

Courthouse
The Court House on the opposite side of the street dates from the 19th c. It was built on the remains of the 13th c. Graces's Castle.

St Mary's Cathedral
Higher up to the right can be seen St Mary's Cathedral (1843), with a 200ft/60m-high tower.

Kyteler's Inn
The oldest building in the town is Kyteler's Inn (in St Kieran Street), today restored with an old-style interior. It is still an inn. It is said that in the 14th c. a woman called Alice Kyteler lived here. Surviving four different husbands, suspicion fell on her and she was condemned as a witch. She herself fled to safety; but a culprit was needed so her elderly servant perished at the stake instead.

Town Hall
In High Street, the southward continuation of Parliament Street, stands the Tholsel (1761), now the Town Hall, in which the civic insignia and muniments (dating back to 1230) are preserved. The building was completely restored in 1987 following a fire.

St Mary's Hall
South-east of the Town Hall, in a lane between High Street and St Kieran Street, is St Mary's Hall, originally a parish church (13th c.?) but now a community centre. It contains a number of monuments from the old church, notably the tomb of Richard Rothe (d. 1637) and, in the churchyard, a monument with figures of Faith, Hope and Charity and the Twelve Apostles.

Shee's Almshouses
Not far from St Mary's Hall, in Rose Inn Street, are Shee's Almshouses; founded in 1582 by Sir Richard Shee, they remained in use as almhouses until 1895. Following comprehensive restoration the building now accommodates the Tourist Information Office and Cityscope Exhibition, the latter illustrating in miniature Kilkenny in the 17th c. (open: May–Sept. Mon.–Sat. 9am–6pm, Sun 11am–5pm; Oct.–Apr. Tues.–Sat. 9am–12.45pm and 2–5pm).

★Kilkenny Castle
On the east side of the Parade stands Kilkenny Castle, begun by William de Marshal in the 13th c. and over the years much altered and enlarged, especially in the 17th c. by the 1st Duke of Ormonde, and in the 19th c. (picture galley wing). From 1391 to 1931 the castle was the principal seat of

the Butler family. Finely situated on a bank above the river, and surrounded by gardens, the castle is open to the public.

Some of the former state rooms have been restored, the Victorian Great Hall being particularly charming (open: June–Sept. daily 10am–7pm; Apr., May daily 10.30am–5pm; Oct.–Mar. Tues.–Sun. 10.30am–12.45pm and 2–5pm, Sun. from 11am).

Across on the other side of the Parade are the Butler family's old stables, now occupied by the Kilkenny Design Centre (open: daily except Sun. Jan.–Mar. 9am–6pm). A wide range of good quality Irish products (textiles, jewellery, glass, ceramics, etc.) are on sale and craftsmen can be seen at work. Their designs are used throughout Ireland, a striking feature being the employment by many artists of Celtic motifs as seen, for instance, in illuminated manuscripts such as the Book of Kells.

★Kilkenny Design Centre

Eastern District

From the busy junction by Shee's Almhouses, John's Bridge crosses the river to the eastern district. In Lower John Street is Kilkenny College, a handsome Georgian building of 1782 and successor to St John's College (founded 1666) which counted Jonathan Swift and George Berkeley among its pupils. It is at present being converted for use as the County Hall.

Kilkenny College

Across the street stands St John's Priory (13th c.; National Monument). Of the church there survives only the chancel, with beautiful windows and capitals; the Lady Chapel is still used for worship.

St John's Priory

Surroundings

Dunmore Cave (National Monument), 6 miles/10km north of Kilkenny, is reached by taking a side-road branching off the N78 (N.B. on many maps the cave is incorrectly shown further south near the N77).

★Dunmore Cave

A little above the entrance to the cave a Visitor Centre has been constructed (open: mid Mar.–mid June Tues.–Sat. 10am–5pm, Sun. 2–5pm; mid June–mid Sept. daily 10am–5pm; mid Sept.–mid Mar. Sat., Sun. 10am–5pm). On display are items excavated from the cave (bones, coins, primitive tools), many of which date from the 10th c. In 928, 40 people fleeing from raiding Vikings took refuge in the cave but were discovered and cruelly slaughtered. Among the most impressive formations in the cave is a stalagmite over 19ft/6m high known as the "Market Cross".

The N77 leads north to Ballyragget where the ruins of Ormonde Castle (15th–16th c.) can be seen, a keep surrounded by walls and four round towers. One particular Countess of Ormonde was renowned for her courage in leading her soldiers into battle.

Ballyragget

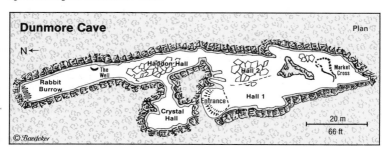

219

Clara Castle	4½ miles/7km east of Kilkenny, reached on a minor road branching left off the N10, stands the privately owned Clara Castle (15th c.), an unusually well preserved six-storey tower house which still has its original oak beams, giving an excellent impression of the character of a fortified dwelling of the period. Among the features of particular interest are the forecourt, a passage with a "murder hole" (a hole in the roof through which intruders could be pelted with missiles), a fine fireplace, and a secret room (privately owned, key available locally).
Gowran	A mile/1.5km further on, the R702 branches rightwards to Gowran, with a fine old parish church (c. 1275; National Monument) the tower of which (14th or 15th c.) has been incorporated into the present 19th c. building standing on the site of the original choir. The interior has fine pointed arches and columns of black marble; good sculpture and monuments (14th–17th c.).
Thomastown	11 miles/18km south of Kilkenny, reached on the N9 from Gowran or the R700 direct from Kilkenny, lies Thomastown, with a ruined 13th c. church (National Monument) and, in the Roman Catholic parish church, a high altar from Jerpoint Abbey (see below).
Kilfane	The village church at Kilfane, on the N9 north of Thomastown, is noteworthy for its larger than lifesize effigy of Sir Thomas de Cantwell on his tomb (13th c.; National Monument).
Graiguenamanagh	From Kilfane a minor road runs east to join the R703 leading to Graiguenamanagh, a small town on the River Barrow (good fishing), with the ruins of a Cistercian house, Duiske Abbey (National Monument). In the churchyard, on the south side of the chancel, are two small granite high crosses with carvings of Biblical scenes and abstract ornament.
Inistioge	5 miles/8km south-east of Thomastown on the wooded banks of the River Nore, here spanned by a graceful 18th c. bridge, lies Inistioge, with the remains of an Augustinian abbey founded in 1210. The nave, Lady Chapel and tower of the church still survive. The tower, of which the lower part is square and the upper part octagonal, is now a mausoleum.
	From Inistioge, Brandon Hill (1677ft/511m) can be easily climbed. On the summit are a cairn and a stone circle; fine views of the Barrow and Nore valleys.
★★Jerpoint Abbey	About 2 miles/3km south-west of Thomastown stands Jerpoint Abbey (National Monument), one of the finest ruined monasteries in Ireland (open: mid June–Sept. daily 9.30am–6.30pm; Apr.–mid June and the first half of Oct. Tues.–Sun. 10am–1pm and 2–5pm). The abbey, founded in 1158, was occupied by the Cistercians from 1180 until its dissolution in 1540.
	The layout shows Cistercian influence. The church, with nave and side aisles, transepts and an altar niche at the east end, is flanked to the south by the (restored) cloister round which are grouped the conventual buildings. Of these only the sacristy, chapter-house and day-rooms on the east side have been preserved. Above the crossing, as the rule of the Order required, rises a handsome 15th c. tower (closed for fear of collapse). The nave is divided in roughly equal proportion into the monks' choir and lay brothers' choir. The church has many fine monuments, including the tombs of Bishop O'Dulany of Ossory (d. 1202), Katerine Poher and Robert Walsh (d. 1501; by Rory O'Tunney) and two 13th c. knights. Note the rows of figures known as "weepers" on the tombs.
	The double columns of the arcading in the cloister are embellished with a fine set of carved figures forming what has been described as "a Late Gothic picture-book". They were the work of Rory O'Tunney, of whom nothing is known except that he came from a renowned family of sculptors and is believed to have been active between 1501 and 1552.

Jerpoint Abbey

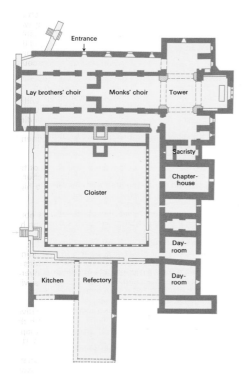

Jerpoint Abbey is one of the most impressive monastic ruins in Ireland. It was founded in the 12th c., probably by Donal, Lord of Ossory.

Originally a Benedictine house, the abbey passed into the hands of the Cistercians in 1180. It was much influenced by the French Abbey of Clairvaux, the most famous monastic house in the West.

The most notable features of the architecture are the cloister and the tower (both 15th c.). There is an abundance, unusual in a Cistercian house, of fine sculpture.

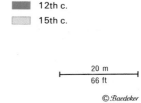

■ 12th c.

□ 15th c.

20 m
66 ft

© Baedeker

6 miles/10km west of Thomastown, at Kells – not to be confused with the better-known town of that name (see entry) in the north of the Republic – are extensive remnants of a fortified Augustinian priory (National Monument) founded in 1193. The surviving buildings, dating from the 14th and 15th c., constitute an exceedingly impressive group of medieval remains. The church, with nave, transepts, chancel and Lady Chapel, has a tower above the crossing and two further towers, one of which was probably the prior's lodging. On the south side of the church are remains of conventual buildings, laid out around a courtyard and protected by a wall with two towers; further south again is a spacious outer court enclosed by a wall with five towers.

Kells

2 miles/3km south of Kells, on a narrow by-road, lies Kilree, with the remains of yet another monastery (National Monument): a roofless round tower 95ft/29m high; a ruined church (good 17th c. monument in the choir); and a badly weathered high cross (9th c.?) with representations of Biblical scenes and geometric designs.

Kilree

6 miles/10km south-west of Kilkenny on the N76 is Callan, a busy little market town which was strongly fortified in medieval times and has preserved a number of old buildings. Of the 15th c. Augustinian priory (National Monument) only the church, a long rectangular building with a central tower, survives; fine carved choir-stalls. In the town centre are the ruins of St Mary's Church (16th c.; National Monument), with fine detailing.

Callan

The choir (restored), which is still used for worship, contains an old font. In the nave are a number of good monuments (16th and 17th c.), including that of John Tobyn, by Rory O'Tunney. Elsewhere Rice House has been carefully restored to convey an impression of a typical farmhouse of the late 18th c.

Killamery

At Killamery, 5 miles/8km south of Callan, on the border of Co. Tipperary, there is a 9th c. high cross (National Monument). The decoration, unfortunately badly weathered, includes a chariot procession, a hunting scene, David with his harp and other biblical themes, and much geometric and animal ornamentation.

Freshford

Freshford, north-west of Kilkenny on the R693, has a church of 1730 (National Monument) with a lovely Romanesque doorway from an earlier church incorporated in the west front.

★Kilcooly Abbey

West from Kilkenny in Co. Tipperary lie the ruins of Kilcooly Abbey (National Monument), a Cistercian house founded from Jerpoint in 1182 (entrance on the west side of the estate). The church, erected in 1445–70 on the site of an earlier building, contains a wealth of sculpture. The screen between the south transept and the sacristy has a whole series of reliefs – the Crucifixion, St Christopher, a bishop, a mermaid with a hand-mirror, followed by two fish, and coats of arms of the Butler family. Notable among the monuments in the choir is the tomb of Piers Fitzjames Og Butler, adorned with the knight's recumbent effigy and panels of saints and Fathers of the Church as weepers. Rory O'Tunney, who carved this tomb about 1526, was also responsible for the monuments of William Cantwell and Margaret Butler and of John Cantwell and Elicia Stouk. In front of the altar is the gravestone of Abbot Philip (d. 1463). One rather unusual feature is a pair of stone seats set against the piers at the end of the nave.

Among the remains of the conventual buildings is a corbel-vaulted circular dovecot.

Killaloe · Cill Dalua   D 3

Republic of Ireland
Province: Munster
County: Clare
Population: 1000

Location

The village of Killaloe (Cill Dalua="Dalua's church") lies inland in the south-west of Ireland, at the point where the Shannon, emerging from the elongated Lough Derg, threads a course between the Arra Mountains and Slieve Bernagh out into the Plain of Limerick.

Killaloe is a good centre for water-sports and a popular stop for hire cruisers.

Sights

St Flannan's Cathedral

St Flannan's Cathedral, built in 1185, occupies the site of an earlier church and incorporates its Romanesque doorway. Beside it is an interesting stone shaft with matching inscriptions in ogham script and Viking runes – a rarity in Ireland – having the meaning: "A blessing on Thorgrim, who made this stone".

St Flannan's Oratory

Elsewhere within the cathedral precinct is St Flannan's Oratory (12th c.; National Monument), a small Romanesque church with a beautiful doorway and a well preserved stone roof.

Also of interest is St Molua's Oratory (11th c.?; National Monument), transferred here in 1929 from an island in the Shannon due to be submerged by the rising waters of a hydro-electric scheme. Re-erected on a site near the Roman Catholic parish church, the little chapel has a nave and stone-roofed chancel.

St Molua's Oratory

Surroundings

To the north of the town extends Lough Derg, a long straggling lough with the boundary between Co. Clare and Co. Tipperary running down the middle. A beautiful road, the R463, skirts the west side of the lough, passing the large fort of Beal Boru, from which King Brian Boru took his title.

Lough Derg

Continue for 8 miles/13km to Tuamgraney, which boasts the oldest church in Ireland still in regular use (parts of it dating from the 10th/11th c.). The East Clare Heritage Centre (open: in summer, Mon.–Fri 9am–5pm, Sat. 9am–1pm) provides information about the region and arranges excursions to Holy Island off-shore.

Tuamgraney

The most convenient access to Holy Island, also known as Inishcealtra, is from the Mountshannon Angler Centre (boats at the landing-stage). In the 7th c. St Caimin founded a monastery on the island, which was still being visited by pilgrims and penitents at the end of the 17th c. It is now a peaceful and charming little spot, with five churches, an 80ft/24m high round tower, a hermit's cell and a churchyard with numerous crosses.

Holy Island

Killarney · Cill Airne

D 2

Republic of Ireland
Province: Munster
County: Kerry. Population: 9600

Killarney (Cill Airne="church of the sloe") is situated close to the coast in the south-west corner of Ireland. Near by lie the well-known Killarney Lakes. Killarney itself has few outstanding sights, but the lake district to the south and east, known as "the Killarney Area", make it a popular holiday destination. Its tourist tradition goes back to the 19th c. when it particularly appealed to prosperous English travellers. Today the town has some 6000 guest beds; crowds of day-trippers swell the numbers during the peak season.

Location

Sights

The Roman Catholic St Mary's Cathedral, a building by Pugin, in the Neo-Gothic Early English style, was erected in 1846–55.

St Mary's Cathedral

Opposite the Franciscan church (1860) near to the railway station stands a monument to the "four Kerry poets" of the 17th and 18th c.: Pierce Ferriter (d. 1653), Geoffrey O'Donoughue (d. 1677), Aodhagan O'Rahilly (d. 1728) and Eoghan Ruadh O'Sullivan (d. 1784).

Kerry Poets monument

In East Avenue Road, leading to the bus station, is the National Museum of Irish Transport (open: daily 10am–6pm). As well as a collection of vintage vehicles including a 1907 "Silver Stream", designed by an Irishman, and the 1910 "Wolseley Siddeley" in which W. B. Yeats toured the area, there are old bicycles and motorcycles and a complete workshop of the 1930s.

National Museum of Irish Transport

★★Killarney Area

Visitors to the Killarney Lakes have a choice between exploring the area independently or taking advantage of the sightseeing tours organised by

N.B.

223

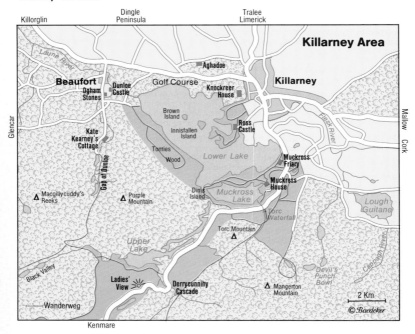

Killorglin
Dingle Peninsula
Tralee Limekick

Killarney Area

Beaufort
Aghadoe
Golf Course
Knockreer House
Killarney
Dunloe Castle
Ogham Stones
Brown Island
Ross Castle
Kate Kearney's Cottage
Innisfallen Island
Muckross Friary
Tomies Wood
Lower Lake
Muckross House
Gap of Dunloe
Dinis Island
Muckross Lake
Lough Guitane
Macgillycuddy's Reeks
Purple Mountain
Torc Waterfall
Torc Mountain
Upper Lake
Devil's Punch Bowl
Black Valley
Ladies' View
Derrycunnihy Cascade
Mangerton Mountain
Wanderweg
Kenmare
Glencar
Laune River
Flesk River
Mallow Cork
Cappagh River
2 Km
© Baedeker

local agencies. The most popular are packages including a trip in a jaunting car (pony and trap), on ponyback and by boat. One such – very much the standard tour – is as follows: by jaunting car from Killarney round the north side of the Lower Lake to Kate Kearney's Cottage; from there by pony, in a jaunting car or on foot over the Gap of Dunloe and down to the Upper Lake; by boat from the south end of the lake by way of the Muckross Lake to Ross Castle; finally back to Killarney by jaunting car. Bicycles are another option (several bicycle hire firms in Killarney).

★★Topography

The lakes, of varying sizes, around Killarney lie in a breathtakingly beautiful landscape of mountains and hills, the legacy of glacial action. The largest of the lakes, the Lower Lake, also known as Lough Leane, lies immediately south-east of Killarney, separated from the smaller Muckross Lake, or Middle Lake, by a narrow isthmus. A long narrow channel links these two lakes to the Upper Lake, the smallest of the three. 4 miles/6km away to the east is Lough Guitane. To the south, where the hills rise to 2700ft/820m, are numerous smaller lakes, mostly mere hill tarns. Due to the mild oceanic climate the shores of all the lakes have a dense covering of woodland – oak, arbutus, bamboos, giant ferns, etc. In early summer the roads are bordered by banks of tall foxgloves and the hillsides covered in brightly coloured rhododendron bushes.

Killarney National Park

Some 23sq. miles/60sq.km of the Killarney area has been designated a National Park. Included are the Lower Lake, Muckross Lake and the Upper Lake together with their shores. The heart of the National Park is the Bourne Vincent Memorial Park around Muckross House. This park was presented to the Irish nation in 1932 by the Bourne family and Senator Vincent of California. Various waymarked paths criss-cross the entire area.

224

In the Killarney lake district

A few minutes' walk westward from the centre of Killarney stands Knockreer House, surrounded by lovely gardens.

Knockreer House

Ross Castle, 1½ mile/2.5km south-west of the town, is a ruined 14th c. castle (open: Apr. daily 11am–6pm; May and Sept. daily 9am–6pm; June–Aug. daily 9am–6.30pm; Oct. daily 9am–5pm). The 16th c. tower house, enclosed by a wall with round corner towers, has been preserved. There was an old prophecy that the castle would only fall to an attack from the water. Taking advantage of this, in 1652 Cromwell's General Ludlow had a large vessel brought up and launched in the Lower Lake, whereupon the defenders, anticipating fulfilment of the prophecy, promptly surrendered.

Ross Castle

From the pier at Ross Castle visitors can be rowed out to the peaceful little island of Innisfallen, with the remains of a monastery (National Monument). Here, at the beginning of the 13th c., were written the "Annals of Innisfallen", now in the Bodleian Library in Oxford. On the north-east side of the island is a small 12th c. church of red sandstone. Innisfallen still preserves the old native woodland of Ireland – rowan, ash, yew and holly.

Innisfallen Island

3 miles/5km south of Killarney in a lovely woodland setting, lies Muckross Friary (15th c.; National Monument), one of the best preserved Franciscan abbeys in Ireland. The church, with a massive central tower, contains a number of tombs. The very beautiful cloister has arcading in different architectural styles, while in the centre grows a huge yew (a tree frequently found in monasteries since its wood is ideal for carving). Three flights of steps lead to the domestic quarters on the upper floor.

★Muckross Friary

About ¾ mile/1km south, in a park with magnificent beds of rhododendrons, stands Muckross House (open: daily 9am–6pm, Jul. and Aug. until 7pm; farms – Mar.–Oct. only). Some of the rooms with their Victorian furniture are open to the public, including those occupied by Queen

Muckross House

Muckross House

Victoria when she stayed here in 1861. In the basement are several workshops (smithy, weaving-room, pottery and saddlery) where visitors can watch craftsmen at work.

In one wing of the house is the National Park Visitor Centre (video presentation).

Kerry Country Life Experience

Another attraction in the neighbourhood of Muckross House is the National Park's recently acquired Kerry Country Life Experience, providing an insight into rural life here in the 1930s. Three typical Kerry farmhouses together with outbuildings have been reconstructed complete with furniture and equipment. The adjoining land is farmed using the methods of the time (open: daily 10am–5pm).

Dinis Island

Further along the north side of Muckross Lake, which has curiously shaped limestone rock formations, lies Brickeen Bridge leading to Dinis Island. Here boats can be hired for trips on the three lakes. The path continues round Muckross Lake to the N71, running between the lake and Torc Mountain (1740ft/530m).

Devil's Punch Bowl

Away to the east of Torc Mountain the River Torc, flowing down from a small clear tarn known as the Devil's Punch Bowl, plunges over a succession of sandstone cliffs 60ft/18m high to form the beautiful Torc Cascade.

Mangerton Mountain

A path passing the Devil's Punch Bowl leads to the top of Mangerton Mountain (2714ft/827m), from the summit of which there are breathtaking views, both near and distant, of hills, lakes, valleys and arms of the sea – at their most impressive when scurrying clouds cast their shadows and showers of rain are gusting by.

Derrycunnihy

The N71, continuing south-west flanked by rocky hillsides, skirts the shores of the Upper Lake before climbing towards Derrycunnihy, a place of enchanting beauty where a waterfall dashes down over rocks in a delightful sylvan setting of dense greenery. To the north-east the old road to Killarney traverses a wildly beautiful valley.

The Kenmare road (N71) climbs higher still to one of the finest vantage points in the district, Ladies' View, so called after Queen Victoria and her ladies-in-waiting stopped here to admire the prospect more than a century ago.

★Ladies' View

From the Upper Lake it is possible to return to Ross Castle by boat, along a narrow tree-lined waterway past the "Eagles' Nest" and Dinis Island.

3 miles/5km north-west of Killarney, on high ground to the right of the R562, stand Aghadoe Church and round tower (National Monument), formerly belonging to a monastery. Built into the south wall of the church is an ogham stone. To the south-west of the church are the ruins of a circular keep (13th c.; National Monument) in a rectangular walled enclosure encircled by a moat.

Aghadoe
★view

From the hill above there are panoramic views of the lakes and their islands against a backdrop of mountains – the twin summits known as the Paps (2248ft/685m) to the south-east, Mangerton Mountain to the south, and Carrantuohill (3360ft/1024m) to the south-west.

Continue on the R562 to the village of Beaufort where turn south through the village in the direction of the Gap of Dunloe. By the roadside stand a group of ogham stones, discovered in 1833.

Ogham stones

The walk (gravelled track) over the Gap of Dunloe west of the Lower Lake promises more delightful impressions of the landscape. The Gap, a wild and rocky defile, separates Macgillycuddy's Reeks (see entry) to the west from Purple Mountain (2689ft/822m) and its northern spurs to the east. It can be reached by car from off the R562 skirting the north end of the Lower

Gap of Dunloe

The lower lake at Aghadoe

Lake. There is parking at Kate Kearney's Cottage. If the 2½ mile/4km walk to the top does not appeal, a pony or jaunting car can be hired instead.

The route ascends past five small lakes fed by swift-flowing mountain streams, the highest being Serpent Lake into which St Patrick is said to have consigned all the snakes he expelled from Ireland (and indeed none are to be found here). The steep walls of the gorge, scarred by glacial action, produce an excellent echo. From the Head of the Gap (784ft/239m) there are superb views of the surrounding hills, valleys and lakes, the greens, yellows and browns of the vegetation flecked with the red of sandstone.

Tomies Wood

Another extremely pleasant walk is through Tomies Wood, a round walk of roughly 4½ miles/7km. As a rule fewer people are encountered here on the west side of the Lower Lake – though the views of the lake scenery are second to none.

Killybegs · Na Cealla Beaga   B 3

Republic of Ireland
Province: Ulster
County: Donegal. Population: 1600

Location

Killybegs (Na Cealla Beaga="the little churches") is a fishing port on the south coast of Donegal in the north-west Ireland. It lies on a natural harbour formed by an inlet of Donegal Bay. Fish-processing amd sail-making are established industries. The arrival of the fishing fleet and the unloading of the catch are a sight not to be missed. Killybegs also produces the famous Donegal hand-tufted carpets which are to be found gracing e.g. Buckingham Palace and aboard Cunard liners. There are guided tours of the workshops.

Surroundings

Dunkineely

5 miles/8km east of Killybegs on the N56 lies Dunkineely, from where a road runs past a ruined castle and along a narrow tongue of land jutting 5 miles/8km into the sea, to St John's Point (excellent fishing and fine beaches).

Kilcar

Kilcar, a picturesque village to the west of Killybegs, is a centre of the Donegal hand-woven tweed industry. South of the village, on Muckross Head, are cliffs and caves which can be reached on foot at low tide.

Carrick

Carrick, 2½ miles/4km further on and a little way inland, is situated just upstream of the outflow of the River Glen into the very attractive Teelin Bay.

★Slieve League

From Carrick a detour can be made via Teelin to Slieve League, where the sea cliffs are the highest in Europe (1936ft/590m). Passing through Teelin, continue for another 2 miles/3km south-west to Bunglass Point, where the asphalt road ends in a car park a few steps from the cliffs.

Here there is a choice between simply enjoying the view or proceeding further on foot. Those sufficiently nimble and with a good head for heights may wish to continue beyond Bunglass Point to the summit of Slieve League, negotiating en route the 2½ mile/4km ridge walk known as One Man's Path, with precipitous slopes on either side. Though not marked, the route is easily followed in the open terrain. Less adventurous walkers can gain the summit by an alternative route – Old Man's Path – signposted from Teelin village. Allow 1½ to 2 hours to the top and back. Both routes are

Slieve League: the highest cliffs in Europe ▶

arduous despite a mere 1300ft/400m of ascent, and neither should be attempted without stout footwear.

Kinsale · Ceann Saile   E 3

Republic of Ireland
Province: Munster
County: Cork. Population: 2000

Location

Kinsale (Ceann Saile="tide head") lies on the south coast of Ireland overlooking the broad estuary of the River Bandon. It is a favourite destination for trippers and holidaymakers. There is still some fishing done from the harbour, mainly for mackerel; also a well-equipped marina. Kinsale's popularity with cruising yachtsmen of many nationalities has led to the appearance of several good restaurants and wine bars.

History

In 1602 Kinsale became an English town from which the Irish were barred as residents until the end of the 18th c. It was once an important naval base. In 1601 a Spanish fleet landed a force of several thousand men with the purpose of supporting the Irish against the English; when the Irish were defeated the Spaniards surrendered. It was this English victory which prompted the "Flight of the Earls" and confirmed Ireland's position as a dependency of England.

William Penn, founder of Pennsylvania, was a native of Kinsale.

★The town

Kinsale still preserves something of its 18th c. charm. Many of its older buildings have been well restored. The gaily painted houses and narrow streets give the town something of a Mediterranean air.

The best views of the town are gained from Compass Hill (south-west of the town centre) or from the road leading to Charles Fort.

In the centre of Kinsale . . .   *. . . the Court House*

St Multose's Church in Kinsale

Sights

Kinsale's most notable building is St Multose's Church, originally 12th c. but several times rebuilt and today the parish church. The sturdy tower (north-west corner) has a Romanesque doorway. Above the west door is a 15th c. statue of St Multose, credited with founding a monastery here. Inside the church is an interesting collection of tombstones (17th c.) and a fine medieval font.

St Multose's Church

Desmond Castle, in Cork Street, a 15th or perhaps 16th c. three-storey tower house (National Monument), was used for a period at the beginning of the 19th c. to hold French prisoners of war – hence its other name, the "French Prison".

French Prison

Kinsale Regional Museum (open: in summer, Mon.–Fri. 11am–1pm and 3–5pm) is housed in the pretty Court House of 1706. In it can be seen several of the black hooded cloaks which were once the traditional dress of the women of the district.

Kinsale Museum

Surroundings

Summer Cove, 2 miles/3km south of the town on the east side of the inlet, is the site of the well preserved star-shaped Charles Fort (1677), the walls of which still stand 40ft/12m high. At the south-west corner there is a light-house and inside the fort ruins of 19th c. barracks (open: guided tours mid Apr.–mid Jun. and mid Sept.–mid Oct. Mon.–Sat. 9am–5pm, Sun. 9.30am–5.30pm; mid Jun.–mid Sept. daily 9am–6pm; admission fee; caution needed when visiting the outworks). The opposite side of the inlet is similarly fortified (James Fort).

Charles Fort

2 miles/3km east of Kinsale lies another inlet, Oyster Haven, with good bathing and, on the east side, the imposing ruins of Mount Long Castle (1631).

Oyster Haven

Ballinspittle   The R600 runs south-west from Kinsale to the village of Ballinspittle, above which stands the Ballycateen Ring Fort, with three deep ditches and an overall diameter of 400ft/120m.

Old Head of   5 miles/8km south of Ballinspittle, the Old Head of Kinsale juts well out to
Kinsale   sea, with a ruined castle and a lighthouse in the midst of superb cliff scenery.

Garrettstown   Garrettstown, west of the promontory, is a quiet little holiday resort with a sheltered bay. Neither Coolmin Castle nor Kilbrittain Castle (north-west) are open to the public.

Bandon   Beyond Kilbrittain the R603 continues to Bandon (on the N71; 9-hole golf course and good trout fishing). The town was established in 1608 to house English settlers. Kilbrogan Parish Church (1610) was one of the first Protestant churches in Ireland.

Letterkenny · Leitir Ceanainn   B 4

Republic of Ireland
Province: Ulster
County: Donegal
Population: 7000

Location   Letterkenny (Leitir Ceanainn="hillside of the O'Cannons"), county town of Co. Donegal, lies on rising ground above the River Swilly in the far north of Ireland, overlooking the outflow of the river into Lough Swilly, a 25 mile/40km-long inlet opening off the Atlantic.
        Although Letterkenny has few notable features it is a good base from which to explore northern Donegal.

Sights

St Eunan's   The principal landmark of Letterkenny, a long straggling town on the
Cathedral   slopes of the O'Cannon Hills, is the 215ft/65m-high spire of St Eunan's Cathedral (1901); the church is finely decorated with Celtic motifs and stained glass by Harry Clarke and Michael Healy.

Donegal County   Occupying a restored mid 19th c. poorhouse used latterly as local authority
Museum   offices, the County Museum documents the history, geology and archaeology of Donegal as well as Donegal life in times past (open: Mon.–Fri. 10am–4.30pm, Sat. 1–4.30pm).

Surroundings

Rathmelton   From Letterkenny the R245 runs north-east to Rathmelton (8 miles/13km), a friendly little anglers' centre with an attractive harbour flanked by fine Georgian houses. The 17th c. Old Meeting House serves both as an exhibition hall and library (open: July and Aug. daily 9am–5pm).

Kilmacrenan   Kilmacrenan, another angling centre, this time on the N56 7 miles/11km north of Letterkenny, once boasted a monastery founded by St Columba. Only the ruins of a 15th c. Franciscan abbey and an old parish church are to be seen today.
        2 miles/3km west is the Rock of Doom, a large flat-topped block of stone on which the O'Donnell princes were crowned. It is well worth clambering up for the sake of the extensive view of the surrounding moorland. At the foot of the rock is the Holy Well, visited by pilgrims on account of its supposed healing powers.

A side road leads from Kilmacrenan to Church Hill, 10 miles/6km north of Letterkenny, reached from there on the R251. A mile west of the village, by Gartan Lough, stands Glebe House, belonging to the English painter and art collector Derek Hill and worth visiting on account of its superb furnishings. The adjoining stables house the Glebe Gallery, not only displaying landscapes and portraits by Hill himself but also a considerable collection of modern painting (works by e.g. Degas, Renoir, Picasso and Yeats and contemporary British and Irish art (open: June–Sept. Mon.–Thur., Sat., Sun. 11am–6.30pm).

Church Hill,
★ Glebe Gallery

The Colmcille Heritage Centre in Gartan (open: May–beginning of Oct. Mon.–Sat. 10.30am–6.30pm, Sun. 1–6.30pm) is devoted to the life, work and times of St Columba the Elder (also known as St Colm Cille – see Introduction Religion). Situated not far to the west of Church Hill, Gartan was Columba's birthplace.

Gartan

Glenveagh Castle

West of Gartan Lough stretches the Glenveag National Park (open: Easter–Oct. daily 10am–6.30pm but closed Fri. in Oct.). The entrance and Visitor Centre are on the northern shore of Lough Beagh, reached via the R251. The 38sq. mile/100sq.km park, an area of impressive mountain and moorland scenery surrounding Lough Beagh, was established in 1986.

★ Glenveagh
National Park

Private cars are not allowed into the park; a shuttle bus runs to Glenveagh Castle, 2miles/3km from the entrance. This Neo-Gothic building, dating from 1870, has lovely grounds with a Mediterranean aspect. The kitchen garden is particularly attractive.

Limerick · Luimneach

D 3

Republic of Ireland
Province: Munster
County: Limerick. Population: 75,000

Limerick (Luimneach="barren spot"), th Irish Republic's third city, lies on the River Shannon in the south-west of the country, at the point where the river begins to open out into its estuary. This was the most westerly point at which the river could be forded and round it, at the junction of busy traffic routes, a considerable town grew up. A number of main roads and railway lines meet here, and Shannon Airport is only 15 miles/2km away.

Location

Limerick has a harbour, not particularly large but kept very busy. The arrival in recent years of various modern industries (optics, electronics medicinal drugs) has increased the importance of the town. The mainstays of the economy however are flour-milling, tobacco, off-the-peg clothing, cement and steel cables. Even so unemployment tends to be high in Limerick and the standard of living low.

Economy

In the 9th c. the Danes established a base at this "barren spot" from which they could plunder the interior of the country. They were driven out by the celebrated Irish King Brian Bou, after which possession of the town passed back and forth between the Irish and the Anglo-Normans. In 1210 King John ordered a bridge and a castle to be built. In late centuries the town grew in size and maintained its allegiance to the English Crown. During the 17th c. it was several times besieged and captured. The last occasion was in

History

1691, the "year of the broken treaty", when, after a valiant defence, 10,000 Irish troops were allowed to march out with full military honours. Under the treaty, signed by William of Orange himself, the Irish nobility were also granted safe passage, but the English Parliament, objecting to the clauses guaranteeing religious freedom, refused to ratify it. The Irish troops thereupon went to France and took service in the army of Louis XIV; in the course of the next 50 years hundreds of thousands of Irishmen followed their example, entering the service of France and of Spain. During the 18th c. the town expanded south-westward along the banks of the Shannon.

Limerick

Many people assume that the limerick, a five-line verse-form with a comic-satirical message, originated in the town of Limerick. In fact its origin is uncertain; evidence points to its having its roots in England. The specific use of the word "limerick" however is often traced to a popular 19th c. Irish song recounting, in numerous verses, the adventures of Irish townspeople. The following is an example of a limerick:

There was a young lady of Wilts,
Who walked up to Scotland on stilts;
When they said it was shocking
To show so much stocking,
She answered, "Well, what about kilts?"

The town

First impressions are of a not especially attractive town; in particular, parts of English Town, the older district north of the confluence of the Abbey River and the Shannon, appear very run down. South of the Abbey River lies Irish Town, the medieval town centre, and south of that Newtown Pery; dating from the 18th c., this has a disinctly more prosperous air. Today Newtown Pery is the commercial and financial quarter, through which runs O'Connell Street, Limerick's principal thoroughfare. Here and in Mallow Street, which branches off it, there are some attractive Georgian houses.

English Town

Treaty Stone

Cross the Shannon by Sarsfield Bridge (1824–35) and turn right along Clancy's Strand, with a fine view of the city, to reach Thomond Bridge, on the site of the original Shannon bridge built on the orders of King John. At the end of the bridge is the Treaty Stone on which the 1691 treaty is said to have been signed (see History).

King John's Castle

On the opposite bank, rising imposingly above the Shannon stands King John's Castle (13th c.; National Monument) a pentagonal fortress with a main block, three round corner towers, a bastion and a twin-towered gatehouse (disfigured by 18th c. additions). It has recently been restored. Parts of the complex are now an interpretative centre with reconstructions of scenes from Irish history and the history of the town, a video presentation, and information on the excavation of Viking houses, defensive works and siege tunnels (open: mid Apr.–Oct. daily 9.30am–5.30pm; Nov.–mid Apr. Sat. and Sun. noon–5.30pm).

St Mary's Cathedral

Turning right at the end of Castle Street, follow Nicholas Street southward to St Mary's Cathedral, which preserves much 15th c. work (west doorway 12th c.). The oak choir-stalls, a rarity in Ireland, with misericords carved with fabulous creatures, date from 1489. There are a number of notable monuments. From the 120ft/36m-high tower fine views may be enjoyed.

Court House

Not far west, in St Augustine's Place, stands the handsome Court House (1764).

Irish Town

Custom House

To the south, beyond Mathew Bridge spanning the Abbey River, is the Custom House (1769), today an art gallery.

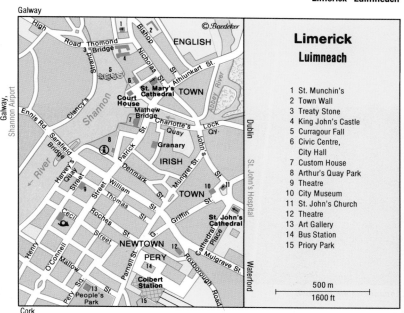

Galway

© Baedeker

Limerick
Luimneach

1 St. Munchin's
2 Town Wall
3 Treaty Stone
4 King John's Castle
5 Curragour Fall
6 Civic Centre,
   City Hall
7 Custom House
8 Arthur's Quay Park
9 Theatre
10 City Museum
11 St. John's Church
12 Theatre
13 Art Gallery
14 Bus Station
15 Priory Park

500 m
1600 ft

The restored Granary in Michael Street, centrepiece of a recently-established conservation area, now accommodates the municipal archives and a library.

The Granary

At the eastern end of Irish Town can be seen St John's Roman Catholic Cathedral (1856–94), boasting the tallest tower in Ireland (275ft/84m).

St John's Cathedral

Adjacent to the cathedral is St John's Square, once an elegant 18th c. residential quarter and now a protected area.

St John's Square

The Limerick City Museum occupies one of the restored buildings in St John's Square (open: Tues.–Sat. 10am–1pm and 2.15–5pm).

City Museum

Newtown Pery

Newtown Pery, the district south-west of Irish Town, came into being with the expansion of the city in the 18th c. Through it runs O'Connell Street, Limerick's main thoroughfare, almost a mile long, and today the heart of the city. At the end of the street stands the O'Connell Monument commemorating Daniel O'Connell, who in 1829 won emancipation for Irish Catholics.

O'Connell Street

Mallow Street is celebrated for its handsome Georgian houses with brightly painted front doors. The easternmost section of the street borders the People's Park in which is situated the Limerick Art Gallery (modern Irish painters).

Mallow Street

Plassey

3 miles/5km from the city centre at Plassey (N7) are the National Institute of Higher Education (NIHE) and a museum, the latter housing part of the Hunt

★Hunt Collection

Limerick on the Shannon

Collection (open: May–Sept. daily 9.30am–5.30pm), principally medieval ecclesiastical art from continental Europe and Bronze Age and Early Christian finds from Ireland. Other parts of the Hunt collection are displayed at Craggaunowen (see Ennis).

Surroundings

Murroe

In the village of Murroe, a good 12 miles/20km east of Limerick at the foot of the Slievefelim Mountains, is Glenstal Benedictine abbey, founded in 1927. Visitors are welcome at the extensive complex (open: Mon.–Sat. 9am–noon and 2–6pm, Sun. 11am–noon and 2–6pm). Highpoints are the terraced garden going back to the 17th c. and the abbey's modern church (1953).

★Lough Gur
Stone Age Centre

15 miles/25km south of Limerick, at Holycross on the crescent-shaped Lough Gur, there is an exceptionally interesting prehistoric site (National Monument). When in the 19th c. the lough was partially drained, evidence was uncovered of occupation since Neolithic times. Numerous finds can be seen in the Interpretative Centre beside the lough, where models, drawings and an audio-visual presentation provide detailed information on what is known as the Lough Gur Stone Age Centre (open: mid May–Sept. daily 10am–6pm).

Highlights on the tour of the site include: No. 4, a wedge-shaped passage grave (*c.* 2000 B.C.); No. 7, a stone fort (8th c.); No. 8, an oval stone fort (Early Christian period); No. 12, a Neolithic burial place surrounded by a double earthwork, with a menhir in the centre; No. 16, a burial mound with a circle of standing stones (*c.* 1500 B.C.); No. 17, a fine double stone circle with an earth rampart and ditch (age uncertain); No. 22, a small stone circle formed from large slabs; No. 23, a crannog (originally a man-made islet but now high and dry); No. 28, an imposing stone circle (*c.* 2000 B.C.), a cult site with an entrance of almost monumental proportions. There are in addition two medieval buildings, Bourchier's Castle (16th c.) and Black Castle (14th c.); also the ruined New Church (17th c.).

Heading south from Lough Gur in the direction of Kilmallock, a detour can be made eastwards to Hospital where the church (National Monument), originally belonging to an establishment of the Knights Hospitallers founded in 1215, contains three very interesting tombs all with effigies.

Hospital

Kilmallock, 21 miles/34km south of Limerick on the R512, is an ancient little country town. The Collegiate Church of St Peter and St Paul (15th c.; National Monument) incorporates 13th c. elements (round tower) and contains fine monuments. King's Castle (14th c.; National Monument) and Blossom's Gate in Emmet Street testify to the importance of the town in medieval times. The Civic Museum has a model of Kilmallock in the 16th c. and a small collection illustrating life in the area in the 19th and 20th c. (open: daily except Sat. 1.30–5pm).

Kilmallock

To the north of the town can be found the ruins of a Dominican abbey (13th–15th c.; National Monument); the church has some good carving, a fine five-light west window, and interesting monuments in the chancel. The 87ft/27m tower is borne on unusually narrow arches.

6 miles/10km south-east of Kilmallock lies the little market town of Kilfinane, at the foot of the Ballyhoura Mountains. Its most striking feature is an unusually large motte surrounded by three earth walls. It is 130ft/39m high with a diameter of 50ft/15m at the base and 20ft/6m at the top. From the summit there is a magnificent view of the great expanse of the Golden Vale.

Kilfinane

In Glenosheen, a beautiful side valley south-west of Kilfinane, stands Castle Oliver, a 19th c. building complete with battlements, towers and bastions, approached along two avenues with curious lodges at the gates. Near the castle can be seen one of the "follies" built to provide employment in times of famine. Castle Oliver is said to have been the birthplace of Marie Gilbert, better known as Lola Montez, mistress of King Ludwig of Bavaria.

Glenosheen

From Kilmallock the R518 and R520 lead westward to Newcastle West, 20 miles/32km south-west of Limerick, a busy market town with the ruins of a 12th c. Templar castle.

Newcastle West

Glenquin Castle (15th c.; National Monument), is a well-preserved six-storey tower house situated 5 miles/8km south of Newcastle West.

Glenquin Castle

2½ miles/4km west of Limerick on the N69 lie the ruins of Mungret Abbey (National Monument), once with an influential monastic school; three of the abbey's original six churches are preserved.

Mungret

4 miles/6km further west stands Carrigogunnell Castle (National Monument), prominently situated on a volcanic crag. An imposing structure with two towers (15th and 16th c.), it is sadly in a poor state of preservation. From the castle there are fine views of the Shannon and surrounding area.

Carrigogunnell Castle

Kildimo boasts the remains of a small Templar church (13th c.) and a parish church of 1705.

Kildimo

On a hill beyond Kildimo is the little Killulta Church (12th c.; National Monument) with an interesting triangular window.

Killulta Church

Kilcornan is the starting point for walks in Curraghchase Forest Park, where can be seen the ruins of an 18th c. mansion, Curraghchase House.

Kilcornan

Replicas of major Irish monuments are a feature of Celtic Park and Gardens. There is also a rose garden, and children especially will delight in the many animals – horses, sheep, deer – and domestic fowl (open: May–Oct. daily 8am–8pm).

Askeaton

Askeaton lies on the banks of the River Deel. On a rocky islet near the bridge stand the ruins of Desmond Castle (15th c.; National Monument), a tower house with a banqueting hall measuring 30×90ft/9×27m, with fine windows, blind arcading and vaulting.

On the east side of the river are the well-preserved remains of a Franciscan abbey (15th c.; National Monument): a church with handsome windows, a lovely cloister with twelve marble arches and a figure of St Francis, and a refectory and other conventual buildings.

Foynes

Foynes, 7 miles/11km beyond Askeaton, is a little port picturesquely situated on the estuary of the Shannon. From the mid 1930s until the end of the Second World War this tiny isolated place was the terminal for the only passenger air service to and from North America. The GPA Foynes Flying Boat Museum (open: Apr.–Oct. daily 10am–6pm) tells the amazing story. On view are the first terminal building, the signal and weather station, and photographs of the first flying boats used on the Atlantic crossing.

From Knockpatrick Hill (565ft/172m), south of the town, there are extensive views over the Shannon estuary. On the summit of the hill are a ruined church and a holy well.

Glin

8 miles/13km west, beautifully situated on the banks of the Shannon (here 1¼ miles/2km wide), lies the village of Glin. Above the harbour rears Hamilton's Tower (19th c.). Outside the town stands Glin Castle, a ruined tower house on the estate of the Knights of Glin, who have been established here in uninterrupted succession for 700 years. The present house, originally Georgian (1780) but remodelled in the Neo-Gothic style in 1820, has handsome rooms with good stucco ceilings (staircase, hall, library). It is furnished in period style (Irish, 18th c.) with family portraits of the 18th to 20th c. (open: May only, daily 10am–noon and 2–4pm; otherwise by arrangement, tel. (068) 34173).

Lismore · Lios Mor Mochuda   D 4

Republic of Ireland
Province: Munster
County: Waterford
Population: 900

Location

Lismore (Lios Mor Mochuda="Mochuda's great hill fort") lies near the south coast of Ireland on the wide Blackwater, a good fishing river spanned at this point by a handsome stone bridge (1775). North of the town the Knockmealdown Mountains rise to heights of up to 2560ft/780m. As early as the 7th c. there was a monastery here renowned for its learning, where in the 9th c. King Alfred the Great is said to have studied.

Sights

Lismore Castle

Lismore Castle, splendidly situated on a tall crag, probably occupies the site of the monastery. Erected in the 12th c., it survived the upheavals of later centuries and in 1602 came into the hands of Richard Boyle, later 1st Earl of Cork, whose son Robert Boyle (1627–91) became the celebrated scientist who formulated Boyle's Law. The castle, which was much enlarged in the 19th c., now belongs to the Duke of Devonshire. The gardens but not the house can be visited (open: mid May–mid Sept. Mon.–Fri. 1.45–4.45pm).

St Carthage's Cathedral (17th c.; National Monument), built by Richard Boyle, incorporates parts of an earlier 13th c. church (chancel arch, windows in south transept). The elaborate MacGrath tomb (1557) has representations of the Crucifixion, an Ecce Homo, and various saints and Apostles. Built into the west wall of the nave are a number of early gravestones. The slender and graceful spire was the work of G. R. Pain (1827).

St Carthage's Cathedral

The history of the town is vividly portrayed in a multi-media presentation at the Lismore Heritage Centre (open: June–Aug. Mon.–Fri. 10am–8pm, Sat. 10am–6pm, Sun. 2–6pm; Sept. and Oct. Mon.–Sat. 10am–5.30pm, Sun. 2–5pm).

Lismore Heritage Centre

Surroundings

4½ miles/7km east of Lismore lies the little town of Cappoquin, charmingly situated on the Blackwater at the point where the river turns sharply south. There is good fishing in the Blackwater and its tributaries. Below Cappoquin the river is tidal.

Cappoquin

Mount Melleray Abbey, in the hills some 4½ miles/7km north of Cappoquin, is a Trappist monastery built in 1833. It has a guest-house in which visitors are accommodated.

Mount Melleray Abbey

Sir Walter Raleigh (1552–1618), credited with having introduced tobacco and the potato into Ireland, is said to have planted the first cherry tree in the British Isles at Affane, a village graced by a handsome Georgian mansion a mile or so south of Cappoquin.

Affane

At Villierstown, south of Affane, can be seen the Dromana Gate, a curious "Indian"-style gateway.

Villierstown

5 miles/8km west of Lismore lies Ballyduff, with Ballyduff Castle, a fortified manor house of 1628.

Ballyduff

Ballysaggartmore Towers stands in pleasant wooded surroundings near Ballyduff. Close by is the elaborate Gothick entrance to Ballysaggartmore Castle (the house was never completed due to lack of funds).

Ballysaggartmore Towers

Londonderry (Derry) · Doire

A/B 4

Northern Ireland
Province: Ulster
District: Londonderry
Population: 70,000

Londonderry, or Derry (Doire="oak wood"), Northern Ireland's second city, lies on the River Foyle just above its outflow into Lough Foyle. It is an important port and industrial town known for its chemical and textile industries, machinery and ceramics.

The partition of Ireland in 1921 cut off Londonderry from much of its natural hinterland. Even so, because of the openness of the border, there has always been a high degree of economic interchange. Many living in the north of the Republic take advantage of the choice of shopping and lower prices Londonderry offers.

Location

A monastery was founded here by Columba the Elder in 546. Later the monastery and the settlement which had grown up around it were several times attacked and destroyed by the Vikings. In 1613 following the "plantation" of Ulster by James I, when mainly English and Scots Protestants were settled in Derry under the auspices of London's wealthy merchant guilds,

History

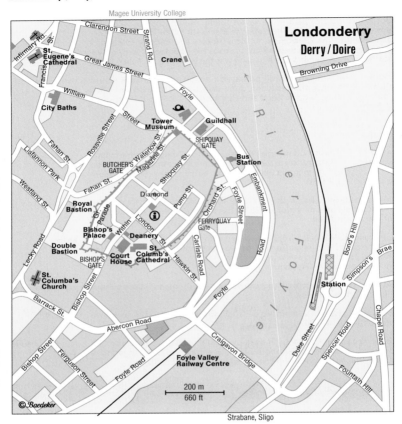

Magee University College

Londonderry
Derry / Doire

Strabane, Sligo

the town and county were declared a "London settlement" and renamed Londonderry. The massive town walls date from this time. When the partition of Ireland took place in 1921, Derry became a frontier town. In recent years it has been one of the main flashpoints for the sectarian violence associated with the conflict between Catholics and Protestants in Northern Ireland.

The town

The political conflict has left its mark on the city. Protestants and Catholics live for the most part segregated, the Protestant districts, protected by elaborate security measures, lying mainly east of the River Foyle. The majority of Catholics live in Bogside, which has recently been redeveloped, and on the Creggan estates.

In the walled Old Town a programme of reconstruction and restoration has been carried out in recent times. One such project is Craft Village, a gallery of shops in a reconstruction of a Derry street at the turn of the century. Shipquay Street, Magazine Street and Bishop Street all have a number of Georgian Houses.

Sights

Londonderry's Old Town is surrounded by the best-preserved town walls in the United Kingdom, still, apart from the addition of three gates of later date, very much as they were in 1618. There is a pleasant walk circling the town on the walls; the best view of the town is from the Walker Monument on the Royal Bastion. The four original gates giving admittance to the old town are Butcher's Gate, Shipquay Gate, Ferryquay Gate and Bishop's Gate, the finest of the four.

★Walls

A tower in the northernmost corner houses a museum documenting the history of Derry from the very earliest times (open: Tues.–Sat. 10am–5pm., later in summer).

Tower Museum

Still in accord with the medieval street plan, Derry's four principal streets, one from each of the original four gates, meet in the central square, known since the 17th c. as the Diamond. The town hall formerly stood here, but after being destroyed during one of the many sieges of the town, it was moved to another site. The principal feature of the square today is a war memorial.

Diamond

In the south of the Old Town in Bishop Street stands the Neo-Classical Court House (19th c.).

Court House

Immediately east of the Court House can be seen St Columb's Protestant Cathedral, built in the 17th c. and Gothicised in the 19th c. The roof is borne on brackets carved with the heads of sixteen bishops of Derry. Eight of the thirteen bells in the bell tower date from the 17th c. Incorporated in the bishop's throne is the throne of Bishop Bramhall, who consecrated the cathedral in 1633. The chapter-house contains documents on the history of the town, also the locks and keys of the four old town gates.

St Columb's Cathedral

To the south-west, outside the walls, is St Columba's Anglican Church, a 19th c. Neo-Gothic building occupying the site of an older church. Nearby is St Columb's Stone, at which the saint is said to have prayed.

St Columba's Church

The Neo-Gothic Guildhall (1912), outside the walls, to the north, has a collection of items to do with Irish history (guided tours by arrangement, tel. (01504) 365151).

Guildhall

From the Guildhall, Strand Road runs north to Magee University College (1865), the grounds of which extend to the banks of the Foyle.

Magee University College

On the west bank of the River Foyle, near the splendid double-decked Craigavon Bridge (1933; 400yd/365m long), is the Foyle Valley Railway Centre, a museum documenting the history of the region's railways. Visitors can enjoy a short trip in a 1934 diesel locomotive (open: June–Aug. Tues.–Sat. 10am–5pm; Sept.–May Sun. 2–6pm).

Foyle Valley Railway Centre

Surroundings

From the east bank of the Foyle the A2 runs by way of two charming villages, Eglinton and Ballykelly, to Limavady (18 miles/29km), an old town in the valley of the river Roe. Less than a mile from Limavady is the Roe Valley Country Park, offering lovely walks, canoeing, fishing and an opportunity to visit old water-mills once used in the process of linen manufacture. (Further information from the Visitor Centre; open: daily 9am–5pm, in summer until 9pm; park open at all times.)

Limavady

From Limavady the A2 describes an arc northward to Downhill on the coast. Here, superbly situated on the cliff edge near the ruined Downhill Castle, stands the Mussenden Temple, a Neo-Classical rotunda erected in 1783 to house a private library.

Downhill Castle, Mussenden Temple

Dunluce Castle

Carrick-a-rede Rope Bridge

Coleraine	Continue inland on the A2 to Coleraine, one of the oldest English settlements in the area. This busy little town on the navigable River Bann is famous for its salmon, distilleries and linen manufacture.
Portstewart	From Coleraine the road heads north again along the coast, coming in 6 miles/10km to Portstewart, with lovely sandy beaches and a picturesque harbour. There is also good bathing at Portrush, 4 miles/6.5km farther east. Offshore lie rocks known as The Skerries.
Dunluce Castle	On the way to the Giant's Causeway the road passes Dunluce Castle (14th c. but altered several times in the 16th and 17th c.), perched on a rocky islet linked to the mainland by a bridge (open: Apr.–Sept. Mon.–Sat. 10am–7pm, Sun. 2–7pm; Oct–Mar. Tues.–Sat. 10am–4pm, Sun. 2–4pm).
Bushmills Distillery	Bushmills boasts the oldest whiskey distillery in the world still in production. Irish monks are said to have been producing "the water of life" here as early as the 13th c., long before the first distiller's licence was granted by James I in 1608. Unlike other Irish producers who use unmalted barley for their pot-still whiskeys, Bushmills follows the method used in Scotland for distilling single-malts. The tour of the distillery ends with a opportunity to sample the resulting light, smokey whiskey.
★★ Giant's Causeway	About 8 miles/13km from Bushmills lies the Giant's Causeway, one of the most extraordinary natural phenomena in Northern Ireland or indeed in the world, a rock formation of volcanic origin consisting of an estimated 40,000 vertical prismatic basalt columns of varying sizes and heights. There is a Visitor Centre at the approach to the Causeway (open: daily 10am–7pm, in winter until 4pm; film presentation; small museum), the Causeway itself being ten minute's walk away (good path; shuttle service). Some of the columnar formations have been given fanciful names – the Lady's Fan, the Giant's Organ, the Horseshoe, and so on. The most impressive, reached by

The Giant's Causeway

way of the Shepherd's Path, is the Amphitheatre, with columns up to 80ft/24m high and numerous blocks of smaller columns like so many giant seats.

According to legend the Causeway was the work of the giant Finn McCool. Falling in love with a giantess from the island of Staffa (in the Hebrides), he began to build the causeway as a means of bringing her to Ulster.

For an alternative route back to the Visitor Centre (30 minutes), go on past the basalt columns and take the first path climbing upwards beyond them. Another option is to continue even further along the coast, on a path which leads to several more unusual rock formations before again doubling back to the Visitor Centre (a round of some 4 miles/7km in all).

13 miles/21km along the coast lies Ballintoy where, during the salmon season (May to September) a 60ft/18m-wide chasm east of the village is spanned by the Carrick-a-rede Rope Bridge (15 minutes' walk from the car park at the Larrybane Visitor Centre). Intended principally for use by salmon fishermen, the bridge has become a considerable tourist attraction, a test of nerves for those daring enough to set foot on the swaying boardway.

Carrick-a-rede Rope Bridge

Ballycastle, 6 miles/10km beyond Ballintoy, is a picturesque little fishing village in wooded surroundings.

Ballycastle

Weather permitting, a boat runs from Ballintoy to Rathlin Island, 6 miles/10km offshore. In earlier times this still inhabited island was used as a base by the Vikings.

Rathlin Island

The road from Ballycastle to Cushendall past the famous Glens of Antrim is one of the most beautiful stretches of coast road in Ireland. At Cushendall either continue down the coast to Belfast (47 miles/76km; see entry) or alternatively head inland through the delightful Glenariff (A43) and afterwards on lovely country roads via Kilrea and Dungiven back to Londonderry.

★Antrim Coast

Longford · Longphort   C 4

Republic of Ireland
Province: Leinster
County: Longford
Population: 4000

Location

Longford (Longphort="fortress"), county town of Co. Longford, lies in the centre of Ireland north-east of Lough Ree.
   The town offers a wide range of leisure activities – golf, tennis, fishing, shooting, horse-racing and greyhound-racing.

Sights

A prominent landmark in the town is the dome of St Mel's Cathedral (1840–93), a Neo-Renaissance building by Joseph Keane. Longford takes its name from a fortress of the O'Farrells of which no trace now remains. The present castle dates from 1627.

Surroundings

Carriglass Manor

4 miles/6km north-east of Longford, on the R194, stands Carriglass Manor, a privately owned house dating from 1837. A costume museum has been established in the stables (open: mid June–early Sept. Mon., Thur.–Sat. 1–5.30pm, Sun. 2–6pm).

Granard

The R194 continues east to Granard, a good place for fishing. Situated close by is a large motte (12th c.; National Monument), possibly the largest of its kind in Ireland. It is topped – though bearing no obvious connection – by a statue of St Patrick, erected in 1932.

Black Pig's
Dyke

About 2½ miles/4km east, beginning at Lough Kinale and extending 6 miles/10km north-west to Lough Gowna, is part of the "Black Pig's Dyke", a long series of earthworks built to protect a network of interconnecting routes. Cutting obliquely across the northern part of Ireland, the individual sections have been dated to between 300 b.c. and a.d. 300. At this particular point the dyke is up to 20ft/6m high and 30ft/9m thick at the base, with a ditch on either side.

Edgeworthstown

About 8 miles/13km south-west of Granard (7½ miles/12km south-east of Longford) lies Edgeworthstown. Edgeworthstown House was the birth-place of the celebrated novelist Maria Edgeworth (1767–1849), whose works depict the social conditions of her time in both castle and cottage. Scott and Wordsworth were among the distinguished writers who visited the house.

Ardagh

En route from Edgeworthstown to Ballymahon on the N55 heading south-west, a short detour can be made (right, on a minor road) to Ardagh, with St Mel's Church (National Monument), said to have been founded by St Patrick.

Ballymahon

Ballymahon is charmingly situated on the River Inny; good fishing.

Lough Ree

From Ballymahon the R392 runs north-west to Lanesborough on the Shannon which here flows into Lough Ree. There is good trout-fishing in both the river and the lough; in summer boats can be hired. Lanesborough is a popular halt for cruising boats on the Shannon (see entry). Near the town, on the east bank of the river, there is a peat-fired power station.

Inchcleraun

On Inchcleraun, an island in Lough Ree, some 6 miles/10km south of Lanesborough, are the ruins of an early monastery (National Monument) including the remains of five churches and other buildings.

Lough Corrib

Republic of Ireland
Province: Connacht
County: Galway

Lough Corrib, north of Galway Bay in the west of Ireland, is nearly 30 miles/45km in length but at some points no more than a few hundred yards wide.

Location

The lough is linked with Lough Mask just to the north by underground streams. The River Corrib, flowing out from its southern end, has barely left the lough before reaching the sea. In summer, excursion boats ply between Galway in the south and Cong in the north. The lough is dotted with numerous islands – said to number 365 in all. They are best seen from a viewpoint on high ground.

The scenery of Lough Corrib is strikingly beautiful. Round the lough's green shores with their clumps of trees and expanses of pastureland, lie countless little bays, promontories and peninsulas, reaching out to tiny islets forming almost a continuation of the land. The countryside east of Lough Corrib is low-lying, while to the west rise hills; in the distance to the north are the mountains of Connemara.

★Topography

Round Lough Corrib

While is possible to drive right round Lough Corrib, with the exception of a short stretch at the north end of the lough the road runs at some distance from its shores. These can only be reached by access roads.

From Galway (see entry) the N59 goes north-west to Moycullen (8 miles/13km), a good fishing centre.

Moycullen

Continue past Ross Lake to where Aughnanure Castle (1500; National Monument) stands proudly on a rocky islet. The castle, a six-storey tower house in an inner and an outer ward with round towers, has been restored (open: mid June–mid Sept. daily 10am–6pm).

Aughnanure Castle

Oughterard, a few miles further on, often dubbed "the Gateway to Connemara", is a pleasant small town in a lovely setting on the River Owenriff. A well-known fishing centre, it is amply supplied with restaurants and accommodation and a good base from which to pursue other activities (9-hole golf course).

Oughterard

From Oughterard a boat can be taken to the picturesque island of Inchagoill, with the remains of two churches (both National Monuments). The smaller of the two dates from the 5th c.; the other (12th c.; restored) is a good example of Irish Romanesque architecture.

Inchagoill

A narrow road running north along the shore of the lough is a dead end; to continue round the lake, rejoin the N59.

From the junction at Maam Cross (see Connemara) the R336 leads north to Maam Bridge. Here the L101 branches off eastwards to Cornamona, a fishing centre in a beautiful location which is also a good base for walking and climbing in the Connemara mountains further west and the hills of Joyce's Country.

Cornamona

From Cornamona a visit can be made to the impressive ruins of Castle Kirke, also known as Hen's Castle (12th c.; National Monument). A large tower enclosed by curtain walls, it takes up virtually the whole of the islet on which it stands.

Castle Kirke

Skirting the lough for much of the way, the road continues for another 5 miles/8km to Clonbur on the isthmus between Lough Mask and Lough Corrib (fine view of Mount Gable to the west).

Clonbur

245

★Ross Abbey

Passing through Cong (see entry), head south on the R346 and R334 to the substantial and exceptionally interesting ruins of Ross Abbey (National Monument), to which, in the little market town of Headford, a signposted road branches off. Also known as Ross Errilly, the abbey, a Franciscan house founded in about 1351, stayed occupied until 1753. Most of the surviving remains, including the tower and the double south transept, date from the 16th c. The cloister has beautiful arcading. To the north of it is an inner court surrounded by conventual buildings, among which are a kitchen with a tank for fish, a bakery complete with oven, and a refectory with a reader's desk. Altogether this is one of the best-preserved ruins of a Franciscan friary in Ireland.

Annaghdown

5 miles/8km south of Headford a narrow road goes off on the right to Annaghdown, with the ruins of Annaghdown Abbey (National Monument). There are some remains of 12th c. work, but the principal church ("cathedral") and the conventual buildings are 15th c.

Lough Erne   B 4

Northern Ireland
Province: Ulster

Location

The extensive and much broken up lake system comprising Lough Erne lies in the far west of Northern Ireland, its northern end being close to the border with the Republic and a short distance inland from Donegal Bay. The lough, some 20 miles/32km long and up to 6 miles/9.5km wide, is a paradise for angling and water-sports. In summer motor launches ply the lake and house boats can be hired. The Shannon–Erne Waterway, opened in 1994, connects Lough Erne to the Shannon (see Carrick-on-Shannon).

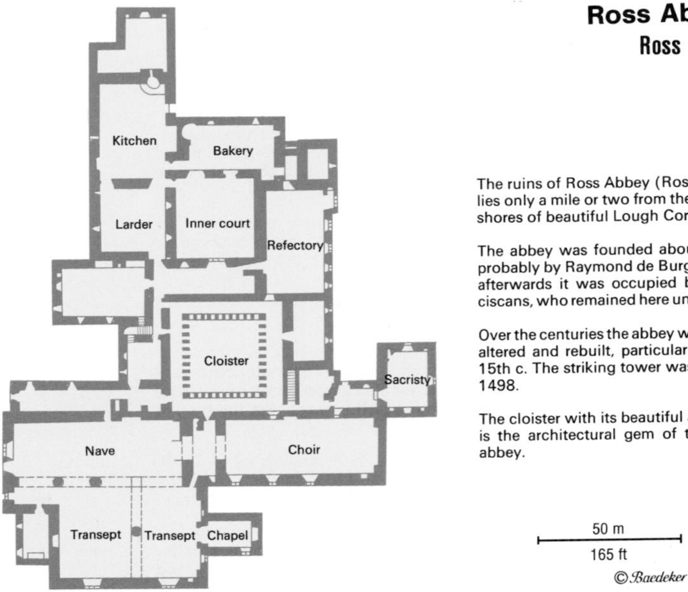

Ross Abbey
Ross Errilly

The ruins of Ross Abbey (Ross Errilly) lies only a mile or two from the eastern shores of beautiful Lough Corrib.

The abbey was founded about 1351, probably by Raymond de Burgo. Soon afterwards it was occupied by Franciscans, who remained here until 1753.

Over the centuries the abbey was much altered and rebuilt, particularly in the 15th c. The striking tower was built in 1498.

The cloister with its beautiful arcading is the architectural gem of this little abbey.

50 m
165 ft
© Baedeker

Enniskillen Castle

The lake, the northern part of which is called Lower Lough Erne and the southern part Upper Lough Erne, is considered the most beautiful in Ireland. Upper Lough Erne is a maze of bays and inlets, its southern half being studded with numerous small islands.

★Topography

Enniskillen

The chief town in the area is the busy resort of Enniskillen, situated between the Upper and Lower Loughs, on the River Erne which links the two.

Of interest in the town is St Macartan's Protestant Cathedral (17th/18th c.), in which the banners of Enniskillen's famous royal regiments hang. Enniskillen Castle (National Monument) now houses a military museum (uniforms, arms, etc.; open: May–Sept. Mon., Sat., Sun. 2–5pm, Tues.–Fri. 10am–5pm; Oct.–Apr. Mon. 2–5pm, Tues.–Fri. 10am–1pm and 2–5pm). Portora Royal School, founded by James I in the early 17th c., claims Oscar Wilde and Samuel Beckett among its former pupils.

Sights

About 1¼ miles/2km south of Enniskillen stands Castle Coole, a magnificent 18th c. mansion by James Wyatt (open: June–Aug. Mon.–Wed. and Fri.–Sun. 2–6pm; May and Sept. Sat. and Sun. 2–6pm).

Castle Coole

Just north of Enniskillen, at the southern end of Lower Lough Erne, lies Devenish Island, with the remains of a monastery founded in the 6th c. by St Molaise, including an impressive and perfectly preserved round tower standing more than 82ft/25m high and tapering towards the top. Parts of St Mary's Abbey and the Great Church (12th c.) also survive together with a particularly fine 6ft/2m-high cross. In summer there is a regular boat service to the island from Trory, 3 miles/5km north of Enniskillen.

Devenish Island

Lough Erne

Tour of the Lake District

Lower Lough Erne Monea

Leave Enniskillen, not on the A46 which keeps close to the lough, but on the B81 heading north-west at some distance from it to Monea, with the ruins of an early 17th c. castle (accessible at any time). The church has a mid 15th c. window from one of the churches on Devenish Island (see above).

Tully Castle

Passing Derrygonnelly, follow the road down again to the shores of the lough. Tully Castle, about 3 miles/5km north of Derrygonnelly, is well worth a visit. Though little remains of the fortified castle (17th c.), the gardens of the same period are very fine (open: Tues.–Sat. 10am–4pm, Sun. 2–4pm, in summer until 7pm).

Lough Navar Forest

Further on, the road skirts, on the left, Lough Navar Forest, where there are a number of small loughs. A side road leads to a viewpoint 985ft/300m above Lough Erne.

Belleek

Continue on the A46 to the small town of Belleek (porcelain manufacture), on the border between Northern Ireland and the Republic.

From here a road runs west to Ballyshannon (see Bundoran). Instead bear sharp right across the River Erne – flowing out of Lough Erne to eventually disgorge into Donegal Bay – and follow the A47 along the north side of the lough. Beyond the Castle Caldwell Forest Reserve (with the ruins of Castle Caldwell on a promontory in the lough), the road branches; ignoring the left-hand fork leading to Pettigo in the Republic, bear right, still on the A47, across a bridge onto the long, narrow Boa Island.

Omagh

From the east end of Boa Island proceed round the foot of the lough to Kesh, where a worthwhile detour can be made north-east to Omagh, at the junction of the rivers Drumragh and Camowen. This is a good base for salmon fishing and for walks in the Sperrin Mountains to the north.

★ Ulster American Folk Park

Just off the A5 about 4 miles/6km north of Omagh is the Ulster American Folk Park (open: Easter–mid Sept. Mon.–Sat. 11am–6.30pm, Sun. 11.30am–7pm; mid Sept.–Easter: Mon.–Fri. 10.30am–5pm), an extensive open-air museum recreating life in Ireland during the period of mass emigration in the 18th and 19th c., also the emigration itself (replica of an emigrant ship), and the emigrants' new life in America. Further graphic illustration of the problems of Irish emigration is presented on video in the Visitor Centre at the park entrance. In the 18th c. alone, 250,000 people left Ulster for an uncertain future in the New World.

Ulster History Park

The Ulster History Park, another open-air museum, is situated on the B48 6 miles/10km north of Omagh. It illustrates by means of reconstructed dwellings, etc. the history of settlement from the Stone Age to the end of the 17th c. (open: Easter–Sept. Mon.–Sat. 11am–6pm, Sun. 1–7pm; Oct.–Easter Mon.–Fri. 11am–5pm).

Castle Archdale Forest

Resuming the circuit of Lower Lough Erne, fork rightwards off the A35 beyond Kesh to follow the B82 along the shores of the lough. After passing a number of marinas, the road comes to Castle Archdale Forest, with a ruined 18th c. mansion of the same name.

From here a boat can be taken to White Island, another of the lough's many delightful little islands, with the remains of a Romanesque church.

Soon afterwards the B82 rejoins the main road (now the A32) leading back to Enniskillen.

Upper Lough Erne

Heading south-west from Enniskillen on the A4, soon branch leftwards onto the A509 to reach, after 5 miles/8km, the popular holiday resort of Bellanaleck (boat hire). Continue to Derrylin, just beyond which take the B127 eastwards across a narrow isthmus in the lough to the fishing centre of Lisnaskea, with the ruins of Balfour Castle. The A509 meanwhile keeps straight on to Cavan (see entry) in the Irish Republic, becoming the N3 south of the border. The hill above Lisnaskea provides extensive views of Upper Lough Erne's deeply indented shoreline. From Lisnaskea proceed north again on the A34 and A4 (or the slightly shorter B514 closer to the loughside), returning by way of Castle Coole (see above) to Enniskillen.

Another delightful excursion from Enniskillen is the drive south-west, at first on the A4 and A32 and then on a side road to the right, to Florence Court, one of the first mansions to be built in the area. The gardens still look much as they did when the house was erected at the end of the 18th c. (house open: June–Aug. Mon., Wed.–Sun. noon–6pm; park daily 10am–an hour before dusk.

Florence Court

Further along the same side road lie the Marble Arch Caves, on the northern slopes of the Cuilcagh Mountains. This limestone cave complex, of which a 766yd/700m section can be visited, features several underground lakes and waterfalls as well as dripstone formations. The guided tour begins with a short subterranean boat trip, passing some impressive stalactites and stalagmites (open: mid Mar.–Oct. 11am–4.30pm).

Marble Arch Caves

Lough Neagh

B 5

Northern Ireland
Province: Ulster

Lough Neagh, at 150sq. miles/388sq.km the largest lake in the British Isles, is situated just to the west of Belfast. It is drained by the River Bann, which flows out at its northern end. The lough is 18 miles/29km long and 11 miles/17.5km wide, with a greatest depth of 40ft/12m. Its waters, sustaining an abundance of fish, are fed by ten tributary streams.
No road or footpath runs close to the shores of the lough, which are low-lying, covered in thick vegetation and in some places marshy. Only gradually are leisure facilities being created – the marinas at Oxford Island and Ballyronan for example.

Location

Antrim

The town of Antrim, from which the magnificent stretch of coast further to the north-east takes its name (see Londonderry, Surroundings), lies at the outflow of Six Mile Water into the lough. Antrim Castle (1622) was several times burned down and rebuilt. The castle gardens were laid out by Le Nôtre, designer of the gardens of Versailles. A mile north-east of the town, in the grounds of Steeple House, stands an excellently preserved round tower, 89ft/27m high.

Loughrea · Baile Locha Riach

C 3

Republic of Ireland
Province: Connacht
County: Galway
Population: 3400

The thriving little town of Loughrea (Baile Locha Riach="town on the grey lough"), episcopal seat of the Bishop of Clonfert, lies in the west of Ireland, at the junction of the N6 and N66 a few miles inland from Galway Bay.

Location

St Brendan's Cathedral, externally a modest and unassuming church, is notable for a magnificent sequence of stained-glass windows which, taken together, illustrate the evolution of Irish stained glass in the 20th c. (work by

St Brendan's
Cathedral

A. E. Childe, Michael Healy, Evie Hone and Sarah Purser, *et al.*). The church has other fine examples of modern art, including a series of Stations of the Cross.

Surroundings

★ Turoe Stone

4 miles/6km north of the town, on the R350 near Bullaun, stands the Turoe Stone (3rd c.; National Monument), an oval granite block 3ft/90cm high with, on the rounded upper half, curvilinear relief ornament in a style characteristic of the La Tène period; this is separated from the otherwise undecorated lower part by a band of meander pattern. The stone formerly stood close to a nearby ring-fort and doubtless served some ritual purpose.

Pallas

South-east of Loughrea, a road at first running along the shores of the eponymous lough, leads to Carrowkeel. Here turn left via Duniry to Pallas with its imposing 16th c. castle (National Monument), a well-preserved tower house in an outer ward. The curtain walls with their parapet walks and towers are largely undamaged.

Portumna

20 miles/30km south-east of Loughrea, at the north end of Lough Derg where the Shannon enters the lough, lies Portumna, with a 9-hole golf course, good fishing and facilities for sailing and rowing (new marina). On the outskirts of the town, in the charming Portumna Forest Park, is Portumna Castle (1618; National Monument), a large fortified mansion with corner towers; also the ruins of a Dominican friary (National Monument) comprising a church with a splendid east window and various conventual buildings.

Athenry

The R349 and then R348 head north-west from Loughrea through an area which becomes steadily more stony and barren, arriving in 11 miles/18km at Athenry, a little town which was a place of some consequence until the end of the 16th c. and has preserved many medieval buildings. Athenry Castle (1235–50; National Monument) is a ruined tower house with roof gables within the remains of curtain walls with two corner towers. The Dominican Friary (National Monument), founded in 1241 and in subsequent centuries much altered and several times destroyed, is represented by a ruined church containing a number of funerary monuments. The Market Cross, of which only the base and the top part survive, has reliefs of the Crucifixion and the Virgin and Child (15th c.). The remains of the medieval town walls (probably early 14th c.) show the extent of the old town; the tower-like north gate is well preserved.

Louisburgh · Cluain Cearban   C 2

Republic of Ireland
Province: Connacht
County: Mayo
Population: 300

Location

Louisburgh (Cluain Cearban="Kerwan's meadow") is a fishing village and holiday resort in the north-west of Ireland, on the south side of Clew Bay. The village is beautifully situated in a coastal plain with good fishing rivers, bounded by Croagh Patrick to the east and the Mweelrea Mountains (2576ft/785m) to the south and fringed on the seaward side by cliffs and sandy beaches. North-east of the village, a promontory called Old Head, from which there are fine views, extends into the bay.

Granuaile Centre

Opened in 1994, Louisburgh's Granuaile Centre commemorates the life and exploits of Grace O'Malley (see below, Clare Island), "Granuaile" being Irish for Grace. Documents and models of castles and ships complement a video film telling the story of this legendary female pirate (open: June–Aug. daily 10am–5pm; May, Sept., Oct. Mon.–Fri. 10am–5pm).

Surroundings

To the east of Louisburgh, Croagh Patrick (2471ft/753m), Ireland's holy mountain, rises abruptly from the plain. It can be climbed from Murrisk (parking on the R335). A small road leads first to the white statue of St Patrick, from where the continuing stony track is clearly seen. The final climb is up a steep slope covered with quartzite scree (strong footwear essential). The ascent is strenuous and takes a good two hours, being rewarded by ever more extensive views. From the top the prospect extends northward over Clew Bay, studded with little islands, to the hills of the Curraun Peninsula and as far north as Nephin – a view which is at its finest at sunset – and southward across the Mweelrea Mountains to the Twelve Bens of Connemara.

★Croagh Patrick

There is a great pilgrimage to Croagh Patrick on the last Sunday in July, commemorating the 40 days of penance which the saint is said to have spent here in the year 441. In the chapel on the flat top of the hill a service is held for the pilgrims, many of whom shed their footwear to complete the final stage of the journey barefoot; the discarded shoes can be seen lying along the wayside.

South of Louisburgh the R335 ascends gradually to Doo Lough, enclosed on either side by steep rock walls. The loughs here offer good salmon and trout fishing, while the beauty of the valley itself is reflected in its name, "Vale of Delphi" (see Connemara).

Doo Lough

A minor road runs south-west from Louisburgh to the River Carrownisky (trout and salmon fishing) and Killeen, an isolated little village with good beaches.

Killeen

Off the coast to the north-west lies hilly Clare Island, today a quiet holiday retreat but in the 16th c. the domain of the legendary Grace O'Malley (see Famous People) by whom the castle beside the small harbour (National Monument; admission free) is said to have been built. The island, which has a population of 140, can be reached by boat from Roonagh Quay, 4 miles/6km west of Louisburgh (no regular service). About 1½ miles/2.5km south-west of the harbour stand the ruins of St Bridget's Church (c. 1500; National Monument). In the choir are medieval frescos with an extraordinary mingling of human figures and animals, the meaning of which is unknown; the only scene which can be understood is a figure of the Archangel Michael weighing souls. On the south side of the island, commandingly situated on the cliffs, is a promontory fort.

Clare Island

Macgillycuddy's Reeks · Na Cruacha Dubha
D/E 2

Republic of Ireland
Province: Munster
County: Kerry

Pronounced "Maclicuddis Reeks", Macgillycuddy's Reeks (Na Cruacha Dubha="the black mountains") lie on the Iveragh Peninsula (see Ring of Kerry) in the south-west corner of Ireland.

Location

Among these ancient red sandstone hills, partly wooded, partly bare, are Ireland's highest peaks, Carrantuohill (3414ft/1040m), Beenkeragh (3262ft/994m) and Caher (3150ft/960m). They offer good climbing, and from the two highest peaks there are far-ranging views over Dingle Bay to the north-west, the Killarney lakes and the south Kerry hills. No less fine are the nearer views of the gorges, green valleys and little lakes glittering far below.

Macgillycuddy's Reeks near Killarney

Ascent of Carrantuohill

The youth hostel on the northern slopes of Macgillycuddy's Reeks or the car park a mile or so from it on the Glencar road both make good starting points for excursions into the mountains.

The climb

The first part of the climb, following a wide path through Hag's Glen, is quite delightful and presents no problems even for less experienced walkers. It takes about an hour and a half to reach Lough Callee, a mountain tarn in a lovely setting at the head of Hag's Glen. From there allow a further two hours to the summit. This second part of the climb involves negotiating the "Devil's Ladder", the name a pointer to its being only for the more experienced.

Alternative route

Carrantuohill can also be climbed from the west by a route starting from Lough Acoose, a picturesque tarn nestling between spurs of the main mountain. This ascent too is only for more seasoned hill walkers.

Macroom · Maghcromtha   E 3

Republic of Ireland
Province: Munster
County: Cork
Population: 2500

Location

Macroom (Maghcromtha="sloping valley") lies on the River Sullane, to the west of Cork in south-west Ireland. It is a busy little town, a market centre for the surrounding area.

The town

In the Square are a number of Georgian houses and the charming Market House. Also of note are the ruins of Macroom Castle (gutted by fire in 1922) with a massive gatehouse. The church is 19th c., by G. R. Pain.

The gatehouse of Macroom Castle

Surroundings

The roads east (to Cork) and west from Macroom are noted scenic routes. The R618 follows a winding course eastward by way of Carrigadrohid Castle, situated on an island, to Dripsey, well-known for its woollen mills.

Dripsey

From the N22 running south-east along the west side of Carrigadrohid Reservoir, a side road branching off to the right after 12 miles/20km leads to Kilcrea, with the well-preserved remains of a Franciscan abbey (15th c.; National Monument) in a delightful setting on the banks of the River Bridge. The remains include the church, with a fine sacristy and bell-tower, and conventual buildings. There is also the keep of an old castle.

Kilcrea

12 miles/20km south of Macroom, beyond a hilly area on the R588 (N22 out of Macroom, then almost immediately right onto the R584 and finally the R585 eastbound), lies Kinneigh. Here, on the site of an early monastery, stands an unusual round tower (National Monument), 65ft/20m high, with the lower 18ft/5.5m hexagonal.

Kinneigh

The R584, branching west off the N22 just south of Macroom, leads to Inchigeelagh, a resort popular with fishermen and artists. It is picturesquely situated at the east end of Lough Allua, a long narrow lough famous for its white water lilies.

Inchigeelagh

Near the west end of Lough Allua is the hamlet of Ballingeary, from which the road climbs to the celebrated Pass of Keimaneigh. Here it runs for almost a mile between sheer rock faces, the severity of which is relieved by ferns and flowering plants clinging to crevices in the cliffs.
    Just before the head of the pass a narrow road branches off on the right to Gougane Barra Forest Park and Lough Gougane Barra. This dark and lonely lough, surrounded on three sides by high hills, is the source of the

Pass of Keimaneigh, Gougane Barra National Park

River Lee, which falls in cascades down the rocky hillside and in times of heavy rain fills the whole valley with the sound of rushing water. In late autumn a pilgrimage takes place here to the site of a monastery founded in the 7th c. by St Finbar, on a little island in the lough connected to the shore by a causeway. There are remains of old buildings and a modern Neo-Romanesque church.

Ballyvourney

From Macroom the N22 continues north-westwards up the valley of the River Sullane, past Carrigaphooca Castle (15th c.; National Monument), to the pilgrimage centre of Ballyvourney. Of the monastery founded by St Gobnat in the 7th c. there remain a circular building with an inner diameter of 20ft/6m and walls 5ft//1.5m thick, a well and the saint's grave.

Moher Cliffs

See Cliffs of Moher

Monaghan · Muineachain   B 5

Republic of Ireland
Province: Ulster
County: Monaghan
Population: 6200

Location

Monaghan (Muineachain="little hills"), county town and agricultural marketing centre of Co. Monaghan, lies in the north of the Republic near the border with Northern Ireland, at the junction of the N2, N12 and N54. The Ulster Canal, which though today in a state of neglect links Belfast in Northern Ireland to the Atlantic coast of Ireland, runs through the town.
   There was a settlement here as early as the 9th c., but the present town dates from the 18th and 19th c.

Sights

Near the Neo-Gothic parish church of St Patrick stands the fine Court House (1829), now occupied by the County Museum and its attached small art gallery (open: Tues.–Sat. 11am–1pm and 2–5pm). Gracing the Market Place is the small and elegant Neo-Classical Market House (1792), while in Old Cross Square are the Old Infirmary (1768) and nearby Market Cross (1714). On the south side of the town stands the Neo-Gothic St Macartan's Cathedral, its slender spire a local landmark.

Surroundings

Glaslough

7 miles/11km north of Monaghan on the R185 lies the pretty little village of Glaslough, on the eastern edge of which extend the grounds of Leslie Castle. Dating in its present form from the second half of the 19th c., and still owned by the Leslie family, it can be visited by arrangement (guided tours). It is also possible to stay overnight in one of the rooms and/or participate in dinner evenings (bookings, tel. (047) 88109).

Castleblayney,
Lough Muckno

Near Castleblayney, 14 miles/22km south-east of Monaghan on the N2, is Lough Muckno, the largest and loveliest of the Monaghan lakes. Like other loughs in the area it offers good fishing.

Carrickmacross

12 miles/20km farther south on the N2 is Carrickmacross, with a convent producing high-quality lace.

Clones

Clones, 13 miles/21km south-west of Monaghan on the Northern Ireland border, boasts the remains of a very early monastery founded by St

Tighearnach. Hand-crocheted Clones lace is also still made here, samples of this superlative handwork being displayed in the Clones Lace Gallery (open: Tues.–Sat. 10am–6pm).

In the Diamond, the main square, stands a 15ft/4.5m high cross (10th c., restored; National Monument) with, on the west side, representations of Adam and Eve, Cain and Abel, Daniel in the Lion's Den and the Arrest of Christ, and on the east side the Adoration of the Magi, the Twelve Apostles (?), the Last Supper and the Crucifixion.

In an ancient graveyard are a 75ft/23m-high round tower and a tomb in the shape of a house, with notable finials (National Monument). In another graveyard nearby can be seen a ruined 12th c. church known as "the Abbey" (National Monument). In both graveyards are a number of unusual 17th and 18th c. gravestones.

Monasterboice · Mainistir Buithe

C 5

Republic of Ireland
Province: Leinster
County: Louth

Monasterboice (Mainistir Buithe="St Buithe's Abbey"), an early monastic site celebrated for its crosses, lies near the Irish Sea coast, on the R168 6 miles/10km north-west of Drogheda.

Location

St Buithe, a little-known saint, founded a monastery here in about the year 500. In 1097 the round tower was gutted by fire, destroying the monastic library. The monastery survived only until the beginning of the 12th c.

History

Monastic Site

Within the old graveyard are preserved two churches, a round tower and three high crosses (all National Monuments), together with two early gravestones and a sundial.

Opening times
Accessible
at all times

The ruins of the two churches are of no particular interest. The round tower stands 108ft/33m high even though the top section is missing. The entrance, 6ft/1.8m above the ground, is now reached by a fixed staircase (closed to the public for reasons of safety).

The most impressive feature, standing near the entrance to the graveyard, is the South Cross or Muireadach's Cross, one of the finest high crosses in Ireland, which takes its name from a donor mentioned in an inscription on the west side. At first it was thought that this was Muireadach II, who died in 922; recent research however has established that the cross probably existed in the first half of the 9th c. Accordingly it could have been commissioned by the first abbot of that name, who died in Monasterboice in 844.

★★Muireadach's
Cross

The monolith, standing 16ft 9in./5.1m high, has reliefs on all four sides which are remarkable both for their form and their execution. A variety of scenes are represented in square panels on the shaft. On the east side are Adam and Eve, Cain and Abel, David and Goliath (?), Moses striking water from the rock (?), the Adoration of the Magi, Christ as Judge surrounded by good and bad souls, and the Archangel Michael weighing souls; on the church-shaped summit of the cross is the meeting of St Paul and St Anthony in the desert. On the west side can be seen the Arrest of Christ (?), Doubting Thomas (?), Christ with St Peter and St Paul (?), the Crucifixion, and an unidentified scene. On the north side are St Paul and St Anthony again, the Scourging, the Hand of God, and interlace ornament and on the south side the Flight into Egypt, Pontius Pilate and more interlace

Muireadach's Cross

Tall Cross

ornament. On the base appear hunting scenes, interlace ornament and meander patterns.

★Tall Cross   As its name implies, the Tall or West Cross is unusually high (21ft/6.4m), in addition to being richly decorated. Not all the 22 scenes represented can be identified. On the east side are David killing the lion, the Sacrifice of Isaac, the Three Young Men in the Fiery Furnace, the Arrest of Christ, the Ascension, and St Michael with the Devil. On the west side are the Vigil at the tomb, the Baptism, the Mocking of Christ, the Kiss of Judas and the Crucifixion. The base has ornamental patterns.

North Cross   Of the North Cross, on the edge of the graveyard, only the upper part and a section of the original shaft survive. The old sundial, enclosed by a railing, is a decorated granite block over 6ft/1.8m high; its age is not yet determined.

Mullingar · Muileann Cearr   C 4

Republic of Ireland
Province: Leinster
County: Westmeath. Population: 8000

Location   Mullingar (Muileann Cearr="Carr's mill"), county town of Co. Westmeath and market centre for this largely agricultural area (mainly stock farming), lies on the River Brosna in north-eastern central Ireland, at the junction of three railway lines and the intersection of two major roads (the N4 and N52). The town is almost completely encircled by the Royal Canal. Mullingar lies between two large loughs, Lough Owel to the north and Lough Ennell to the south. There is fishing for brown trout in both loughs and in the River Brosna.

Sights

The town is dominated by the Roman Catholic Cathedral of Christ the King (1936–39) with its 140ft/42m-high twin towers. Attached to the church is an ecclesiastical museum.

Cathedral of Christ the King

Both the Town Hall and the Court House are handsome 18th c. buildings.

Town Hall, Court House

Pewter, produced in Mullingar for centuries, underwent a revival in the mid seventies; many of the pewter articles made today are based on old patterns. The factory can be visited, the craftsmen watched at their work, and the finished articles purchased.

Mullingar pewter

Surroundings

North of Mullingar on the N4, between Lough Owel and Lough Derravaragh, lies Multyfarnham, with a modern Franciscan college built on the site of a 14th c. monastery, of which the church, with a fine tower, has been restored. In the grounds of the college are life-size Stations of the Cross.

Multyfarnham

The R394 runs north from Mullingar past several small loughs to Castlepollard. En route, 7 miles/11km from Mullingar at Crookedwood, are the ruins of Taghmon Church (15th c.; National Monument) and a four-storey fortified tower house. Both the church and the tower house have vaulted roofs.

Taghmon

At Castlepollard stands Tullynally Castle, still the family seat of the Pakenhams, created Earls of Longford in 1655. A charming 18th c. mansion much altered in the 19th c., Tullynally has associations with the Duke of Wellington and the 18th c. novelist Maria Edgeworth (see Longford).
    The house is set in an attractive park bordering the banks of Lough Derravaragh (open: park all year; house mid July–mid Aug. daily 2–6pm, otherwise by arrangement: tel. (044) 61159).

Castlepollard

2½ miles/4km east of Castlepollard, between two hills, lies Fore, a very ancient settlement where St Fechin founded a monastery in the 7th c. The monastic church (c. 900; National Monument) has been preserved and in the churchyard are a high cross and a tower house known as the Anchorite's Cell, with a 19th c. mausoleum built on to it. The original monastery was superseded in the 13th c. by a Benedictine priory; its fortress-like ruins (National Monument) lie ¼ mile/400m away. They consist of a church, two tower houses, part of a cloister, domestic buildings and a round dovecot. Not far distant, in the fields, are two gates (National Monuments), relics of old town walls.

Fore

Belvedere House and gardens are situated on the N52 a short distance south of Mullingar. The name reflects the lovely view of Lough Ennell enjoyed from the mid 18th c. mansion (park open: Apr.–Sept. daily noon–6pm).

Belvedere House and Gardens

15 miles/24km south of Mullingar the N6 reaches Tyrrellspass, an 18th c. planned village of well-built houses laid out in a crescent round the village green. The village won an award in the 1976 European Architecturel Heritage Year. On the green is an unusual memorial to those who died in the struggle for Irish independence – it shows in stone three children of different ages on their way to school.

Tyrrellspass

Kilbeggan lies on the N6 4 miles/6km west of Tyrrellspass. Here Locke's Distillery, first licensed in 1757, is worth a visit. When its doors closed for the last time in 1954, an industrial museum was planned for the site. In 1987 it was taken over by the Cooley Distillery, whose whiskey continues to be matured here in traditonal fashion in wooden barrels. A winery has

Kilbeggan

recently been added to the museum so that now, on a tour of the distillery, the secrets of producing Irish sherry are divulged along with those of pot-still whiskey (open: Apr.–Oct. daily 9am–6pm, Sun. from 10am; Nov.–Mar. daily 10am–4.30pm, Sun. until 6pm).

Naas · Nas na Ri   C 5

Republic of Ireland
Province: Leinster
County: Kildare
Population: 8500

Location

Naas (Nas na Ri="assembly place of the kings"), county town of Co. Kildare, lies 21 miles/34km south-west of Dublin on the N7. In early times Naas was the seat of the kings of Leinster, the site of whose stronghold was the North Mote (a motte situated in the north of the town). Fortified by the Normans – the remains of one of whose castles are now incorporated in the rectory of the Protestant church – the town was sacked in the 14th c.

Naas is now a thriving industrial town on the edge of the Curragh (see Kildare), a celebrated horse-breeding area. 2½ miles/4km south on the R411 is Punchestown Racecourse (see below), famous for its steeplechases.

Surroundings

Clane

7 miles/11km north of Naas lies Clane, with a Jesuit school, Clongowes Wood College, opened in 1814. The old chapel is a good example of Neo-Classical architecture; the new one has fine stained glass by Evie Hone and Michael Healy.

Maynooth

8 miles/13km north-east of Clane, on the Royal Canal, is Maynooth, a little town best known for its seminary, St Patrick's College, now part of the National University of Ireland. It was established with British approval in 1795, on the site of an earlier college, to enable Roman Catholic priests to be trained in Ireland. It is now the largest seminary for priests in Ireland and in the British Isles, and in recent years has also admitted laymen and women. The handsome college buildings, grouped round lawned courts, are mostly 19th c. They include a church and a small museum with antiquities and works of art illustrating the history of the Church in Ireland and its missionary activity. Adjacent to the college gates can be seen the remains of Maynooth Castle (13th–17th c.; National Monument) – a large keep, a gatehouse and part of the curtain walls.

At the east end of the main street stands Carton House, Classical-style mansion of 1739 by Richard Cassels (not open to the public).

Leixlip

Leixlip (a name of Danish origin meaning "salmon leap") is situated on the N4 4½ miles/7km east of Maynooth. Leixlip Castle dominates the town which in recent years has become a dormitory of Dublin.

On private land a mile south-west of the town stands the "Wonderful Barn", a five-storey conical structure of brick and stone built in 1743 for Lady Connolly of Castletown House. Each storey has a vaulted ceiling and a circular hole in the floor through which goods stored in the barn could be hauled up and down. A spiral staircase winds up round the outside of the building.

★Castletown
House

South-west of Leixlip, on the Liffey, lies the village of Celbridge, 2½ miles/4km upstream from which is Castletown House, a spacious and architecturally important mansion built by the Italian architect Alessandro Galilei in 1722 for the Irish parliamentarian, William Connolly. It consists of a finely proportioned three-storey central block approached up a broad flight of steps, with side wings connected to it by quadrant-shaped colonnades. The interior (open: Apr.–Sept. Mon.–Fri. 10am–6pm, Sat. 11am–6pm, Sun. 2–6pm; Oct.–Mar. Mon.–Fri. 10am–5pm, Sun. 2–5pm)

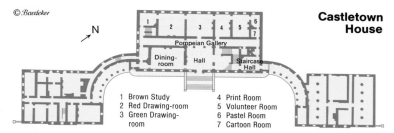

© Baedeker

Castletown House

Pompeian Gallery

| Dining-room | Hall | Staircase Hall |

1 Brown Study
2 Red Drawing-room
3 Green Drawing-room
4 Print Room
5 Volunteer Room
6 Pastel Room
7 Cartoon Room

has superb stucco decoration; the main staircase and the Pompeian Gallery are particularly fine. The house is today the headquarters of the Irish Georgian Society, dedicated to preserving as much as possible of Ireland's Georgian heritage.

Straffan, 4 miles/6km south-west of Celbridge, boasts a railway museum with a collection of rare models (open: June–Aug. daily 11.30am–5.30pm; Sept.–May Sun. 11.30am–5.30pm).

Straffan

From Maynooth the N4/R402 run west to Johnstown, with a large 19th c. mansion, and Carbury, with the extensive remains, commandingly situated on a hill, of Carbury Castle (14th–16th c.), an imposing pile with pointed gables, chimneys and towers.

Less than a mile to the north, also on a hill, can be seen the remains of Carrick Castle (14th c.) and a 13th c. church.

Carbury

North-east of Naas, at Kilteel, are the ruins of a fine Romanesque church and a castle (National Monument). The church (12th c.) has a richly decorated chancel arch, with figures of Adam and Eve, David and Goliath, Samson with the lion, an acrobat, a man with a drinking-horn and an abbot with his crosier.

Kilteel

3 miles/5km south-east of Naas is Punchestown where, near the racecourse, on the Woolpack Road (the medieval road from Dublin to Kilkenny), stands the Lone Stone of Punchestown (National Monument), a huge tapering granite monolith 23ft/7m high. When it toppled over in 1931, a Bronze Age burial place was discovered at its foot.

Punchestown

A mile south-west of Naas on the N7 are the massive remains of Jigginstown House (National Monument), begun by the Earl of Strafford in 1633 as a summer residence for himself and for the entertainment of Charles I, but left unfinished after Strafford's execution in 1641. It was one of the first houses to be built entirely in red brick and with a frontage of 374ft/114m would have been one of the largest mansions in Ireland. As seen at present the most notable features are the groin-vaulted basement and a series of handsome rooms on the ground floor.

Jigginstown House

9 miles/15km north-west of Naas the R409 reaches Robertstown. Here, at the highest point on the Grand Canal (see entry), is the old Canal Hotel, built in 1801 for the convenience of water-borne passengers. The canal frontages of the village and the hotel have been restored to their early 19th c. appearance.

Robertstown

Navan · An Uaimh

C 5

Republic of Ireland
Province: Leinster
County: Meath. Population: 5000

Location	Navan (An Uaimh="the cave") is situated in undulating country north-west of Dublin, at the junction of the River Boyne and the Blackwater. The largest town in Co. Meath, it is a busy market centre and an important road junction.
Sights	The Roman Catholic church (1836) has a fine figure of Christ Crucified (1792) by Edward Smyth. West of the town is a large motte which is a favourite viewpoint.

Surroundings

Donaghmore	A mile north-east of the town on the N51, at Donaghmore, is the site of an early monastery, with a well-preserved round tower and a church (National Monument). St Patrick is said to have founded his first monastery in Ireland here. The tower (10th c.?) has a round-headed doorway 12ft/3.6m above the ground with a relief of the Crucifixion above it and a human mask on either side of the architrave. The church is 15th c. There are early grave-stones in the churchyard. On a hill to the east stands Dunmoe Castle (National Monument): two sides of an originally rectangular structure (16th c.) with round towers at the corners.
Bective	A little more than half a mile beyond the village of Bective, south of Navan on the R161, a path leads off left to the ruins of Bective Abbey (12th c.; National Monument), a Cistercian house founded from Mellifont (see Drogheda). Of the original buildings there remain only the chapter-house and some parts of the church. In the 15th c. the monastery was fortified, and from this period date the beautiful cloister, the tower and the great hall (refectory?).
Rathmore	Rathmore, 7½ miles/12km west of Navan on the N51, has a ruined 15th c. church (National Monument). The nave and chancel are flanked by towers, while the outside of the handsome east window has figural decoration. The interior has fine carving in the apse, on a number of tombs and on a font. On the north side of the church is a cross (1519) with reliefs of St Lawrence, St Patrick and an abbess.
Hill of Ward	Farther along the N51 just before Athboy, the Hill of Ward (384ft/117m; National Monument), an ancient cult site and meeting place, is on the left.

New Ross · Ros Mhic Treoin   D 5

	Republic of Ireland Province: Leinster County: Wexford. Population: 5500
Location	New Ross (Ros Mhic Treoin="wood of Treann's son") lies in the south-east corner of Ireland on the steep east bank of the River Barrow. A market centre for the fertile surrounding area, its chief attraction for tourists are the excursions by boat on the rivers Barrow and Nore.
The town	New Ross is one of the oldest towns in Co. Wexford; its narrow winding streets – some of them stepped and only for pedestrians – still preserve something of a medieval atmosphere. The broad river is busy with small boats.

Sights

St Mary's Church	Of the original St Mary's Church (early 13th c.; National Monument) only the chancel and transepts survive. The nave was pulled down in the 19th c.

to make way for a large new parish church. Notable features are the three fine Gothic windows in the choir and a number of medieval tombs.

The Tholsel (Town Hall), built between 1749 and 1804, is a handsome Neo-Classical building with a cupola-topped bell-tower.

Tholsel

Surroundings

A few miles south of New Ross, on the R733, lies the 620acre/250ha John F. Kennedy Memorial Forest Park, opened in 1968 with funds provided by Americans of Irish descent. The assassinated president's great-grandfather came from the village of Dunganstown not far to the west. 4500 different types of trees and shrubs are found in the park, including 500 varieties of rhododendron and 150 of azalea. There is a good panorama from Slieve Coilte, a hill in the park accessible by car. In the Visitor Centre, in addition to a video presentation, there is a permanent exhibition documenting the flora of the park (open: May–Aug. daily 10am–8pm; Apr. and Sept. until 6.30pm; Oct.–Mar. until 5pm).

★Kennedy Memorial Forest Park

4½ miles/7km farther south on the R733 can be seen the imposing remains of Dunbrody Abbey (National Monument), a 12th c. Cistercian house. The church, in austere Cistercian style, has a chancel, transepts, nave and crossing tower (15th c.). The surviving conventual buildings include the library and chapter-house on the east side and the refectory and kitchen on the south side.

★Dunbrody Abbey

Still further to the south, at Arthurstown, stands Ballyhack Castle (15th c.; National Monument), a fine five-storey stronghold with vaulted rooms, situated at some distance from the road on the banks of the Barrow. The castle has been restored and can be visited (open: July and Aug. daily 10am–7pm; Mar.–June and Sept. Wed.–Sun. noon–6pm). From Ballyhack there is a foot ferry across the broad estuary of the Barrow to Passage East.

Ballyhack

Turning off the R733 at Arthurstown, follow a by-road south to the little fishing village of Duncannon, with a good sandy beach and an old fort on a rocky promontory guarding the entrance to the estuary.

Duncannon

The road continues to Hook Head, at the tip of a long narrow peninsula. On the east side of the peninsula stands Slade Castle (15th–17th c.; National Monument), picturesquely situated beside a small fishing harbour. The 56ft/17m-high tower is battlemented, as are the lower parts of the castle.

Slade Castle

The lighthouse on Hook Head rests on a 700 year-old circular keep.

Hook Head

2 miles/3km back along the road, at Templetown, a righthand fork leads to Fethard-on-Sea, which has good sandy beaches. Not far to the south is Baginbun Head where in 1169 the Anglo-Normans first landed in Ireland.

Fethard-on-Sea

4½ miles/7km north of Fethard the R733 and R734 intersect; a little to the east of the crossroads, a signposted access road branches off on the right to the ruins of Tintern Abbey (11th and 15th c.; National Monument), a Cistercian house. In the 16th c. the tower and chancel of the church were converted into a dwelling-house. The entire complex has now been restored.

Tintern Abbey

Portlaoise · Port Laoise

C 4

Republic of Ireland
Province: Leinster
County: Laois
Population: 4000

Ring of Kerry

Location	Pronounced "Portleesh", Portlaoise (Port Laoise="fort of Laois") lies in south-east central Ireland on the railway line from Dublin to Cork. It is an important road junction where the N7, N8 and N80 meet.
The town	The town was destroyed in the 17th c. and no buildings of that period remain. The Court House and the town gate are both early 19th c.

Surroundings

Emo Court	At Emo, a village about 8 miles/13km north-east of Portlaoise, stands Emo Court, a late 18th c. mansion by James Gandon set in a lovely park. With yew-lined avenues, extensive lawns and rare trees and shrubs, it is a perfect place to walk (open: park daily 10am–6pm; house by pre-arrangement only, tel. (0502) 26110).
Rock of Dunamase	From Portlaoise the N80 runs east, passing in about 3 miles/5km the Rock of Dunamase, an imposing crag 200ft/600m high with the ruins of a large and forbidding 10th–17th c. castle comprising a rectangular keep, a gatehouse, bastioned and turreted walls, curtain walls and a moat. Fine panoramic views.
Timahoe	Timahoe, 7½ miles/12km south-east of Portlaoise, boasts a well-preserved round tower (12th c.; National Monument) nearly 100ft/29m high.
Abbeyleix	8 miles/13km south-west of Timahoe, along minor roads, lies Abbeyleix, an attractive little planned village erected in the 18th c. on the site of an old monastery by the then Viscount de Vesci. The de Vesci mansion, Abbeyleix House (1773), stands surrounded by a lovely park laid out at the beginning of the 19th c. (open: Easter–end of Sept. daily 2.30–6.30pm).
Ballinakill	The Heywood Gardens near Ballinakill, about 3 miles/5km south of Abbeyleix, are also worth a visit. Until 1993 the park was in the care of the Salesians but is now owned by the state (open daily).
Slieve Bloom Mountains	To the west of Portlaoise the Slieve Bloom Mountains rise to 1700ft/520m, with beautiful valleys which are best reached from Mountrath along delightful minor roads.
Mountmellick	7 miles/11km north-west of Portlaoise is Mountmellick, almost completely encircled by the River Owenass. Here in 1677 the Quakers opened their first school in Ireland; and at Rosenallis, 4½ miles/7km north-west at the foot of the Slieve Bloom Mountains, they established their first large cemetery. At Mountmellick, and also to the north of Portlaoise, are found swarms of drumlins, whale-backed mounds of glacial till.

Ring of Kerry D/E 1/2

Republic of Ireland
Province: Munster
County: Kerry

Location	The Iveragh Peninsula is the largest of the peninsulas of Kerry, jutting into the Atlantic in the south-west corner of Ireland. It is bounded to the south by the estuary of the Kenmare River, to the west by the Atlantic and to the north by Dingle Bay. At the east end of the peninsula Macgillicuddy's Reeks (see entry) rise above the Killarney Lakes.
	A scenic road, the famous Ring of Kerry, encircles the peninsula, keeping close to the coastline for most of the way. Starting from Kenmare at the south-east corner of peninsula, the route runs west on the N70 to

Pastoral scene on the Ring of Kerry

Waterville, then north and east to Killorglin; from there it follows the R562 inland to Killarney before returning to Kenmare on the N71. The total distance is 100 miles/158km, to which the detour to Valentia Island in the north-east corner of the peninsula adds at least another 25 miles/40km. In suitable weather the Ring of Kerry is a road of extraordinary scenic beauty; it is not really possible therefore to do it justice in a day. It should also be remembered that at the height of the season traffic can be very heavy.

So as not to be trailing the whole way behind a tourist coach, it is best to start from Kenmare (the coaches set off from Killorglin).

★★Round the Ring of Kerry

From Kenmare (see entry) the N70 proceeds west along the north side of the inlet known as the Kenmare River. On the right can be seen the foothills of Macgillicuddy's Reeks (see entry).

Kenmare

Templenoe's church dates from 1816. Further on, by the ruins of Dromore Castle, there is a viewpoint and car park.

Templenoe

In 4 miles/6km the valley of the Blackwater opens up on the right, the river plunging down to the sea in a deep gorge. A footpath leads down from the road through dense, almost tropical vegetation.

A delightful little road climbs up through the valley and over a 850ft/250m pass to Glencar and Lough Caragh.

River Blackwater

Next along the coast comes Tahilla (sea and freshwater angling), and beyond that Parknasilla, a beautifully situated resort blessed with a climate mild throughout the year, in which palms, pines, bamboos and jasmin flourish.

Tahilla,
Parknasilla

Ring of Kerry

Sneem

The road now loops inland to Sneem, a fishing centre on a narrow inlet. The Protestant church (16th c. but much altered) has an unusual weathervane in the form of a salmon. There is good walking and climbing in hills to the north and west rising to 2166ft/660m.

★ Staigue Fort

At Castlecove, about 8 miles/13km west of Sneem, an extremely narrow road branches rightwards off the N70 to arrive in a little over 2½ miles/4km at a large stone fort, situated on a hill between two valleys. This is Staigue Fort (National Monument), of unknown date, a circular structure of dry-stone walling, 90ft/27m in diameter and over 16ft/5m high, surrounded by a ditch. The walls are 13ft/4m thick with stairways on the inward side and small chambers in the thickness of the wall.

Caherdaniel

The N70 continues for some distance close to the sea, here with many small islands, before turning inland to Caherdaniel (trout fishing, swimming, surfing), near which is a small stone fort similar to Staigue.

★ Derrynane National Historic Park

South-west of Caherdaniel stretches the Derrynane National Historic Park. Nature trails with explanatory signboards conduct the visitor through the dunes which are bordered by a long sandy beach. The tiny Abbey Island offshore can be reached at low tide. Within the grounds stands a fine mansion where "The Great Liberator" Daniel O'Connell (1775–1847) lived. The building now houses a museum (open: May–Sept. Mon.–Sat. 9am–6pm, Sun. 11am–7pm; Apr.–Oct. Tues.–Sun. 2–5pm). The park itself is always open.

Lough Currane

The N70 now climbs to the Coomakista Gap (690ft/210m), from which there are magnificent views, afterwards descending again to Ballinskelligs Bay. To the right, in a beautiful setting, lies Lough Currane. On Church Island in this freshwater lough are a destroyed 12th c. church (National Monument) with a Romanesque doorway, remains of monks' dwellings and a number

Staigue Fort

of gravestones with Christian symbols. From a narrow road which follows the south side of Lough Currane can be seen the ruins of a castle which has been engulfed by the lough. On the west side of the lough are the horseshoe-shaped stone fort of Beenbane and the ruins of a thick-walled beehive hut (both National Monuments).

Waterville (An Coirean="the little whirlpool") lies a good 40 miles/60km west of Kenmare on the narrow strip of land between Lough Currane and Ballinskelligs Bay. The abundance of fish in the local rivers and loughs and in the sea makes this a popular centre for both freshwater and sea fishing.

    From Waterville two lonely, scenically beautiful minor roads, which later unite, traverse the mountainous centre of the Iveragh Peninsula before dropping down to to Killorglin (see below). The more southerly of the two passes a number of loughs well stocked with fish.

Waterville

To the west of Waterville there are good beaches on Ballinskelligs Bay. Across the bay is the village of Ballinskelligs.

Ballinskelligs

Some distance north of Waterville a road branches leftwards off the N70 to Portmagee. Here another delightful but narrow road runs south to the Coomanaspig Pass (1080ft/330m) from where there are splendid views of the bays and bird colonised islands in the Atlantic.

Coomanaspig
Pass

Also at Portmagee a bridge (1970) crosses the narrow strait to Valentia Island. This bare rocky island offers excellent opportunities for sea fishing. From Bray Head (788ft/240m) at the western extremity there are magnificent views of the Atlantic cliffs. At its eastern end is Knights Town from which there is a foot ferry to the mainland.

Valentia Island

The Skellig Experience (near the bridge) is a relatively new tourist attraction on Valentia Island. The Visitor Centre (open: Apr.–Sept. 10am–7pm)

★Skellig
Experience

Valentia Island: starting point for the boats to the Skellig Experience

has a wealth of information about the Skellig Islands and about the life and work of the monks who lived there from the 6th to the 13th c. Another exhibition is devoted to the seabirds and underwater world of the islands. From Valentia Island comfortably equipped excursion boats make regular trips around the Skelligs, which tower above the water like the summits of sunken mountains. In 1987 the little group of islands was designated a bird sanctuary and landing is no longer permitted. Sailings depend on the weather so enquire beforehand (tel. (0667) 6306).

Cahirciveen

Next stop along the Ring of Kerry is Cahirciveen, at the foot of Bentee Mountain (1227ft/374m). Facing Cahirciveen across the broad Valentia River can be seen the ruins of Ballycarbery Castle (15th c.). To the north-east of the castle, reached via a side road off to the left of the N70, are two good stone ring forts – Cahergall (National Monument), 105ft/32m in diameter, with two stone structures within the walls; and commandingly situated on a hill, Leacanabuaile (9th c; National Monument), with staircases and chambers in the thickness of the walls and others underground.

The N70 continues north-east up the wide valley of Kells. On the left rises Knockadober (2230ft/680m), on the right a range of peaks of much the same height. Between them are fine views of the sea and the hills. The road then keeps close to the foot of Drung Hill, at some points high above the sea, passing an old coaching inn with magnificent views of Dingle Bay and the hills of the Dingle Peninsula before descending to Glenbeigh.

Glenbeigh

The delightfully situated little resort of Glenbeigh has good fishing. A mile west is a beautiful sandy beach, Rossbeigh Strand.

Killorglin

From Glenbeigh it is 9 miles/15km through an undulating moraine landscape to the little town of Killorglin, where the famous Puck Fair is held every year on August 10th–12th.

After crossing the River Laune (salmon fishing) the road forks, the N70 going straight on to Milltown, west of which are the ruins of Kilcoman Abbey (13th c.; National Monument), and then Tralee (see entry). The R562 meanwhile turns east and, following the river, continues the circuit of the Ring of Kerry.

Ballymalis Castle

4 miles/6km beyond the fork the road passes Ballymalis Castle (16th c.; National Monument), the picturesque ruin of a four-storey tower on the banks of the river ½ mile/800m off to the right. Extensive views of Macgillicuddy's Reeks.

The route now traverses the Killarney lake district (see entry) then climbs, with fine views to the rear, to Moll's Gap before descending through lovely scenery, with many bends, back to its starting-point at Kenmare (21 miles/34km from Killarney).

Roscommon · Ros Comain   C 3

Republic of Ireland
Province: Connacht
County: Roscommon
Population: 1700

Location

Roscommon (Ros Comain="Coman's wood"), county town of Co. Roscommon, is situated in gently undulating hill country in western central Ireland, at the junction of three main roads (the N60, N61 and N63). It takes its name from St Coman, who founded a monastery here in the 6th c.

Sights

Roscommon
Abbey

In 1253 Felim O'Conor, King of Connacht, founded a Dominican abbey here, which is believed to have occupied the site of a 6th c. monastery. The abbey church (National Monument), altered in the 15th c., still survives; a niche in the north wall contains the founder's tomb (c. 1290) with the figures of eight armed retainers.

Roscommon Castle (National Monument) dates from the same period as the church but subsequently suffered much alteration. An imposing square structure with round bastion towers at the corners and a twin-towered gatehouse, it occupies a commanding position on the hillside.

Roscommon Castle

Surroundings

11 miles/18km north of Roscommon, at Tulsk, where the N5 crosses the N61, are the remains of a castle and a Dominican friary. 3 miles/5km north-west of this, at Rathcroghan, is an area of high ground some 2sq. miles/5sq.km in extent, with a number of earthworks. The site (National Monument) is believed to have been the place of coronation of the kings of Connacht. The earliest feature is a low mound, probably a passage grave. There are also various square, round, oval or irregularly shaped enclosures bounded by earth walls. A standing stone within a stone ring fort is said to mark the grave of Dathi, the last pagan king of Ireland. In the immediate vicinity are other ring forts and megalithic tombs.

Rathcroghan

About 12 miles/19km north-west of Roscommon the R367 branches rightwards off the N60 to Ballintober, with the ruins of a castle built in about 1300 – a square structure with polygonal towers at the corners of its massive walls, two projecting gate-towers on the east side and a moat.

Ballintober

5 miles/8km further north-west on the R60 lies Castlerea, a little town offering a variety of leisure activities (golf, tennis, fishing). Near the town stands Clonalis House, surrounded by its park. The present house dates only from the 19th c. The O'Conors, whose family seat this was, produced in earlier times a number of high kings and kings of Connacht, a period recalled by various documents and other items to be seen in the Victorian house (open: June–mid Sept. Tues.–Sun. noon–5pm).

Castlerea

Roscrea · Ros Cre

D 4

Republic of Ireland
Province: Munster
County: Tipperary
Population: 4200

Roscrea (Ros Cre="Crea's wood"), a small country town with some industry, lies in southern central Ireland at the junction of the N7, N62 and R421. It is a good base for walking and climbing in the Slieve Bloom Mountains.

Sights

The town grew up around a monastery founded by St Cronan in the 7th c. Of the Romanesque St Cronan's Church (12th c.; National Monument), built on the old monastic site, there survives only the west front, with the doorway and blind arcading either side; above the doorway is the figure of a priest. The remainder was pulled down in 1812 to make way for the new parish church. To the north of the church is a high cross (12th c.) with representations of Christ, a bishop and two other figures (possibly the Virgin and St John). The round tower (10th c.; National Monument) is cut off from the church by the modern road which bisects the monastic site. Originally 80ft/24m high, the tower survives today to a height of 60ft/18m.

★St Cronan's Church

Nearby, in Castle Street, are the ruins of Roscrea Castle (13th c; National Monument), with massive curtain walls, several towers and an elaborate

Roscrea Castle, Damer House

system of staircases and passages leading to various defensive stations. The holes in the walls for the chains of the drawbridge can be seen from the street.

In the 18th c., Damer House was erected within the castle walls. After thorough restoration it is now used for periodic exhibitions. Note in particular the staircase with its elaborate carving. Adjoining Damer House is the "Heritage Annexe", a building erected in the 19th c. for military purposes, in which exhibits detailing the history of the region are clearly laid out (open: Mon.–Fri. 9.15am–1pm and 2–5pm, May–Sept. also Sat. 11am–5pm and Sun. 2–5pm).

Franciscan Abbey | In Abbey Street are remains of a 15th c. Franciscan friary – a gateway, the walls of the choir and the bell-tower, the buttresses of which form the entrance to the modern Roman Catholic parish church.

Surroundings

Monaincha | 2 miles/3km east of the town, near the golf course, stands the ruined church (12th–13th c.; National Monument) of the former Monaincha Abbey, founded in the 7th c. on an island in what was then an area of bogland. The church preserves a finely decorated west doorway and chancel arch.

Nenagh | A good 20 miles/30km south-west of Roscrea on the N7, in a fertile plain, lies the town of Nenagh. Its main feature of interest is the massive keep of Nenagh Castle (early 13th c.; National Monument), a five-storey round tower 100ft/30m high with walls up to 20ft/6m thick; the upper part is 19th c. Of the other towers of this pentagonal Norman stronghold of the Butlers, there remains only one of the towers of the gatehouse. An unusual museum can be found in Nenagh – housed in a building formerly used as a prison. The cells and the execution chamber are shown as they were in the 19th c. when prisoners were kept here. Biographical material explains the fate of seventeen men who were hanged. In the adjoining governor's house are reconstructions of a 19th c. schoolroom, shop, smithy and kitchen (open: mid May–mid Sept. Mon–Fri. 10am–5pm, Sun. 2.30–5pm).

Lorrha | 17 miles/27km north of Nenagh, at Lorrha, are three churches (all National Monuments) – a ruined Dominican church with interesting details (13th c., with later alterations); the remains of an Augustinian church (15th c.); and, to the south, another church, part of which is still in use, with sculptural decoration on the doorway, including a pelican, symbol of self-sacrificing love.

Rosguill Peninsula   A 4

Republic of Ireland
Province: Ulster
County: Donegal

Location | The Rosguill Peninsula is one of the small peninsulas on the indented coastline of Co. Donegal in the extreme north of Ireland; it is bounded on the east by Mulroy Bay and on the west by Sheep Haven. The beauty of its scenery attracts many visitors.

Like much of Donegal, this is still a predominantly Irish-speaking (Gaeltacht) area. Hand-woven tweed is also made here.

Atlantic Drive

Carrigart | The Atlantic Drive, encircling the greater part of the peninsula, is one of Ireland's finest scenic roads. The starting-point of the roughly 12 mile/20km circuit is Carrigart, a pleasant holiday resort (golf, tennis, swimming, riding, sea fishing) reached either from the south-east via the N56 from Letterkenny (see entry), along a beautiful stretch of road around Mulroy Bay, or alternatively from the south-west.

From Carrigart a narrow road goes north skirting the west side of Mulroy Bay, after 4 miles/6km bearing west across the peninsula to beautiful Tranarossan Bay (dunes with interesting flora in spring).   Tranarossan Bay

The road now follows the Atlantic coast before winding its way southward, with views of Sheep Haven, to Downings, a holiday resort with a good sandy beach. Visitors can inspect a tweed factory where Donegal tweed can be bought.   Downings

The Rosses · Na Rosa   A/B 3

Republic of Ireland
Province: Ulster
County: Donegal

The much-indented coastal area in north-west Donegal known as the Rosses (Na Rosa="the headlands") extends from Gweebarra Bay in the south to Inishfree Bay in the north – a tract of generally flat countryside of grey rocks, little loughs and tiny fields enclosed by drystone walls. It is a predominantly Irish-speaking (Gaeltacht) area.   Location

Sights

The only place of any size in this still largely unspoilt region is Dungloe on the N56. From here the N56 and another very scenic road further east, run north-east to Gweedore (see Bloody Foreland).   Dungloe

Drystone walls dominate the landscape

269

Lough Anure   Lough Anure, lying to the right of the N56, is of geological interest for its evidence of glaciation.

Crohy Head   South-west of Dungloe is Crohy Head, with fine cliffs and some caves.

Burtonport   From Dungloe the R259 arcs north-west, following the Atlantic coast with its constantly changing views. At the fork in the road just outside Dungloe branch left; keeping close to the coast, with views of the numerous islands offshore, the road next traverses the narrow strip of land between Lough Meela and the sea. To the left can be seen Rutland Island, with the sand-covered remains of a harbour constructed in 1796.

After 5 miles/8km Burtonport is reached, a busy fishing haven where more salmon and lobsters are landed than at any other port in Ireland or indeed the British Isles. Not surprisingly there are several restaurants serving freshly caught lobster and other sea-food.

Aranmore Island   To the west, beyond a number of smaller islands, lies Aranmore or Aran Island (not to be confused with the Aran Islands, see entry), to which a boat runs from Burtonport (hourly in summer), a crossing of about 20 minutes. Some 800 or so people live on the island, only 8 miles/13.5km long and 3 miles/5km wide. Their main sources of income are fishing and tourism.

The island's wild, heather-clad plateau terminates on its western side in cliffs and caves, nesting-grounds of countless seabirds. Lough Shure, a small lough in the centre of the island, has an abundance of rainbow trout. There are sheltered beaches on the east side of the island.

Royal Canal   C 4/5

Republic of Ireland
Length: 90 miles/146km

Course   Like the Grand Canal (see entry), the Royal Canal starts from Dublin and links Dublin Bay with the Shannon (see entry). It follows a course further north than the Grand Canal, joining the Shannon above Lough Ree. Differences in height are overcome by 47 locks.

History   Construction of the Royal Canal was begun in 1792, the culmination of more than 30 years' planning and preparatory work. Each section was brought into use as it was completed; once the link with the Shannon was established in 1817, freight and passenger traffic increased considerably. Branch canals were constructed to link up with towns near the main canal. But, as with the Grand Canal, increasing competition from the railways brought economic difficulties. Finally the canal was purchased by a railway company and a railway line running west was built alongside it (1845). During the second half of the 19th c. traffic on the canal continued to decline, and some of the branch canals and canal harbours were filled in. By the middle of the 20th c. freight transport had stopped completely and in 1961 the canal was officially closed to commercial traffic. The Royal Canal Amenity Group now works for the preservation of the canal as a historical monument and recreational facility.

Pleasure craft   The Royal Canal offers excellent facilities for pleasure craft, the maximum permitted size of vessel – determined by the dimensions of the smallest lock – being as follows: length 75ft/22.9m, beam 13ft/4m wide, draught 4½ft/1.4m. The lowest bridges over the canal have a clearance of 10ft/3.05m.

The canal is well stocked with bream, roach, rudd, tench, pike and the occasional trout.

Shannon (River Shannon)   B–D 3/4

Republic of Ireland
Length: 230 miles/370km

The Shannon, Ireland's longest river, rises in Co. Cavan, flows through the limestone plains of central Ireland and reaches the Atlantic just beyond Limerick. With its loughs, tributary streams and canals it forms a widely ramified system of waterways traversing a fifth of the area of Ireland. The banks of the Shannon, apart from the few places of some size through which it flows, are thinly populated and for much of their length bordered by pastureland. Since there is no industry along the river the light over the water is of unusual clarity. Apart from a short non-navigable stretch on its upper reaches, the gradient down to Killaloe is so gentle that only six locks are required over this considerable distance.

Tourist and recreational facilities are now very well developed on the Shannon all the way from Battlebridge (at its outflow from Lough Allan, a lough well stocked with fish) to Killaloe. Since 1994, when the canal from Leitrim near Carrick-on-Shannon (see entry) to Lough Erne in Northern Ireland, which had lain unused for more than a century, was re-opened after being completely restored, the river has been part of the largest inland waterways cruising area in Europe, a total of 500 miles/800km of interconnected lakes, rivers and canals for pleasure craft to explore!

A leisurely cruise along these peaceful waters is one of the great holiday pleasures that Ireland can offer. Though for the most part sheltered, sudden increases in wind can whip up heavy waves on the two largest lakes on the Shannon waterway, Lough Ree just north of Athlone and Lough Derg just north of Killaloe. There are marinas for boats of all types and sizes on the Shannon at Carrick-on-Shannon, Athlone and Killaloe (see entries). For further information on cabin cruiser hire see pages 305–06.

River area

Tourist development

★Cruising on the Shannon

Boats starting from Carrick-on-Shannon (see entry) are likely to want first to explore the upper reaches of the river; also the River Boyle and its loughs, especially the beautiful Lough Key near the town of Boyle (see entry), with its wooded islands and Forest Park in the demesne of a former mansion (forest trails, bog garden, restaurant, shop).

Carrick-on-Shannon

Downstream from Carrick-on-Shannon, the Jamestown Canal and lock (with detours possible to Drumsna and Jamestown) lead into the delightful Lough Boderg from which there is access via a narrow passage through reed beds to the lonely Corranadoe loughs, a paradise for bird-watchers and anglers.

Jamestown Canal, Lough Boderg

Dromod on Lough Bofin has a pretty little harbour (with correspondingly few mooring places). Roosky, farther south, has a quay.

Lough Bofin

Beyond Roosky a narrow tree-lined stretch of the Shannon leads into Lough Forbes and then on past the junction with the Royal Canal (see entry) to Termonbarry with its large lock. From Termonbarry, or from Cloondara across the river, Strokestown and Longford (see entry) can be visited.

Lough Forbes

Farther downstream is an extensive tract of bogland worked by Bord na Móna, the Irish peat development board. At the little town of Lanesborough (see Longford, Surroundings, Lough Ree), the Shannon is spanned by a nine-arched bridge.

Lanesborough

The river then opens out into the great expanse of Lough Ree (the "lake of kings"). Several islands in the lough, including Inchbofin (National Monument), Inishturk and Inchmore, boast remains of early monastic settlements. On Inchclearaun (also known as Quaker Island after a 19th c. inhabitant), Clothra, sister of Queen Maeve, is said to have been killed by a slingstone hurled from the shore of the lough.

Lough Ree

South of Athlone (see entry) and its lock, the river pursues a quiet winding course through flat countryside until the towers of Clonmacnoise (see

Clonmacnoise

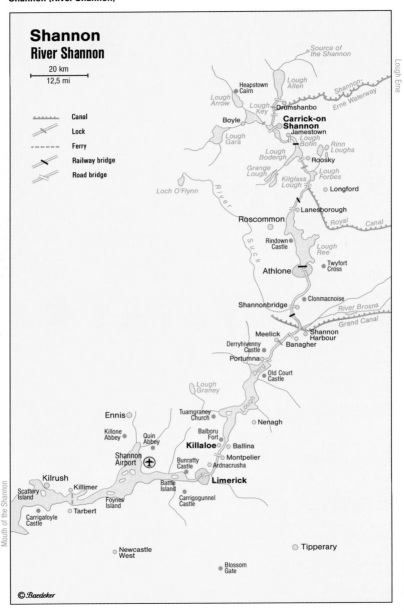

Shannon
River Shannon

20 km
12,5 mi

Canal
Lock
Ferry
Railway bridge
Road bridge

Source of the Shannon
Lough Erne
Shannon-Erne Waterway
Heapstown Cairn
Lough Allen
Lough Arrow
Lough Key
Drumshanbo
Boyle
Carrick-on-Shannon
Jamestown
Lough Gara
Lough Bofin
Rinn Loughs
Lough Bodergh
Roosky
Grange Lough
Lough Forbes
Loch O'Flynn
Kilglass Lough
Longford
River
Lanesborough
Roscommon
Royal Canal
Suck
Rindown Castle
Lough Ree
Twyfort Cross
Athlone
Shannonbridge
Clonmacnoise
River Brosna
Grand Canal
Shannon Harbour
Meelick
Banagher
Derryhivenny Castle
Portumna
Old Court Castle
Derg
Lough Graney
Tuamgraney Church
Ennis
Balboru Fort
Nenagh
Killone Abbey
Quin Abbey
Killaloe
Ballina
Montpelier
Shannon Airport
Bunratty Castle
Ardnacrusha
Kilrush
Battle Island
Limerick
Scattery Island
Killimer
Foynes Island
Carrigogunnel Castle
Carrigafoyle Castle
Tarbert
Atlantic Ocean
Mouth of the Shannon
Newcastle West
Tipperary
Blossom Gate

© Baedeker

River Shannon: popular with holiday boating enthusiasts

entry) appear on the horizon. This is without question the finest way of approaching the ruins of the old monastic settlement (landing-stage).

At Shannonbridge an old sixteen-arched bridge spans the Shannon. The fortifications seen here were built during the Napoleonic era.

Shannonbridge

From Shannon Harbour barges once sailed to Dublin on the Grand Canal (see entry). Nearby ruins of buildings dating from that period still convey some feeling of Regency elegance.

Shannon Harbour

Below Shannon Harbour the river becomes wider, passing the old towns of Banagher (see Birr) and Portumna (see Loughrea) before entering Lough Derg (see Killaloe), the largest of the many Shannon lakes, studded with islands.

Lough Derg

The landscape now changes: the shores become more fertile, farms and villages appear more frequently and there is an air of greater prosperity. The south end of Lough Derg is encircled by hills; ranges of ancient red sandstone mountains mark out the horizon on both sides.

The town of Killaloe (see entry) is noted not only for its remains from the past but also its large marina and water-skiing facilities.

Killaloe

For hire-boats Killaloe marks the end of navigation. Privately-owned craft on the other hand can proceed further, though the lower reaches of the Shannon are considered difficult and hazardous. Over the next 18 miles/29km or so the river, hitherto fairly sluggish, falls rapidly.

At Ardnacrusha ("hill of the cross") there is a huge hydro-electric power-station built in 1925, with a dam at Parteen, a head-race 8½ miles/14km long bringing the water to the power-station, four turbines and two locks. This first and largest of Ireland's power-stations produces some 350,000 mega-watts of electricity annually. Visiting the power-station, reached by road

Ardnacrusha

from Limerick or Killaloe along the north bank of the Shannon, is an impressive experience. In the huge locks vessels are raised and lowered more than 100ft/30m. There is also a fish-lift to ensure that fish – mainly salmon – have access to the upper canal (the lift takes three hours). The waters streaming out of the turbines are fed into the river below Ardnacrusha at a point where it is already tidal.

Limerick

Most of the city of Limerick (see entry) lies on the south bank of the Shannon, with docks and moorings for sea-going vessels of up to 10,000 tonnes.

Beyond Limerick, on the right bank of the river, is Shannon International Airport (see Ennis).

Between here and its outflow into the Atlantic, a distance of some 60 miles/100km, the Shannon opens out into a funnel-shaped estuary. Near Kilkee (see entry) a car ferry operates between Tarbert in Co. Kerry and Killimer in Co. Clare.

Skellig Islands · Skellig Rocks
E 1

Republic of Ireland
Province: Munster
County: Kerry

Location

The Skellig Islands or Skellig Rocks, a group of small rocky islets, lie off the south-west coast of Ireland some 9 miles/14km west of the Iveragh Peninsula. To protect the islands' unique bird life, landing has been prohibited since 1987.

Skellig
Experience

The islands with their curious topography can however be viewed from a distance. Comfortably equipped excursion boats sail to and around the Skelligs from Valentia Island (see Ring of Kerry), where the Skellig Experience Visitor Centre at the landing place provides a wealth of background information on these isolated rocks.

★★The islands

Little Skellig

The boat first passes Little Skellig, an island inhabited by tens of thousands of seabirds of many species, particularly gannets. The dense flocks of birds taking off from their nesting-places, soaring up, swooping down again and all the time uttering their harsh cries form a sight – and a sound – not to be forgotten. Binoculars should be taken.

Skellig Michael

On Skellig Michael, the largest of the islands, the remains of a monastic settlement, said to have been founded in the 6th c. by St Finian, are visible. A total of 670 steps are hewn in the rock leading up to the saddle between the island's two rocky peaks (highest summit 713ft/217m). Below the lower of the two rocky pyramids, the well-preserved monastic remains (National Monument) can be seen laid out on little man-made terraces – six circular beehive huts with rectangular interiors; two boat-shaped oratories built in stone (6th–9th c.); lower down, the remains of a church, probably 12th c.; small areas of garden, a well, gravestones and the remains of a sundial; finally, enclosure walls on the edge of a dizzy precipice.

Until the 13th c. there were always thirteen monks on the island. Since Skellig Michael is without a spring, water had to be collected with considerable difficulty from two small reservoirs. Later many pilgrims came to the island, climbing to the highest point to kiss the ancient stone standing upright in the rock. From 1820 until 1987 a lighthouse keeper kept permanent watch on the island.

Skibbereen · Sciobairin

Republic of Ireland
Province: Munster
County: Cork
Population: 2000

Skibbereen (Sciobairin="little boat harbour"), one of the chief places in Co. Cork, lies near the southern tip of Ireland, charmingly situated on the River Ilen, which a mile below the town opens out into a winding estuary with numerous islands.

Location

Skibbereen is a fishing port and market town, and a good centre from which to explore the surrounding areas.

The town

Surroundings

From Skibbereen the R596 leads south-east to Castletownshend. Here in the middle of the steep and picturesque main street grow a clump of trees. On the south-western outskirts stands Drishane House, home during the last century of Edith Somerville and Violet Martin who, under the pseudonym "Somerville and Ross", wrote novels and short stories vividly describing life in the Anglo-Irish houses of the period. Not far north-west of the village rises the massive Knockdrum Fort (National Monument), a ring fort 95ft/29m in diameter, with stone walls 10ft/3m thick, a narrow entrance protected by a guard-chamber, and chambers underground.

Castletownshend

The R595, heading south-west from Skibbereen, reaches in about 3 miles/5km Creagh Gardens, romantically situated by the sea (open: Apr.–Sept. daily 10am–6pm).

Creagh Gardens

Creagh Gardens near Skibbereen

Baltimore	The R595 terminates at the pleasant holiday resort of Baltimore, a well-known fishing centre also with a sailing school. From here it is possible to visit Sherkin Island and Clear Island, reached either by boat or by the regular ferry to Schull (see below) via Heir Island.
Sherkin Island	Sherkin Island, close offshore, sheltering the town's harbour like a break-water, has the ruins of a castle and a 15th c. Franciscan monastery (daily ferry service from Baltimore in summer).
Clear Island	Farther out, also with a boat service from Baltimore and in summer also from Schull, is Clear Island, whose 150 inhabitants, living off the beaten track as they do, have preserved something of their older way of life and still speak Irish. There are two Irish language colleges on the island. The ruins of a church (12th c.; National Monument) and a cross-slab bear witness to an Early Christian settlement here. The Fastnet Rock, the most southerly point of Ireland away out in the Atlantic, has magnificent cliff scenery.
Lough Ine	On the way back to Skibbereen a detour can be made eastwards on a side road which passes Lough Ine, a clear sea lough whose rich fauna is kept under observation by scientists at a marine biology research station belonging to University College Cork. A waymarked path leads up to Hill Top (a good 20 minutes from the picnic place), from where there are excellent views of the lough and the sea with the outlying islands.
Schull	At Ballydehob 10 miles/16km west of Skibbereen, the R592 branches off south-west to Schull where a planetarium can be visited. In the area around there are a number of old copper mines. From Mount Gabriel (1312ft/400m) there are good panoramic views. Ferries run from Schull to Baltimore and Clear Island.
Crookhaven	From Schull there is an attractive run to Crookhaven, which has a safe, sheltered harbour. A narrow road makes its way to Mizen Head, from the highest point of which (765ft/230m) there is a splendid view of the Atlantic coast.

Sligo · Sligeach   B 3

Republic of Ireland
Province: Connacht
County: Sligo
Population: 17,200

Location	Sligo (Sligeach="river with many shells") lies in the north-west of Ireland, on a well-wooded plain encircled by hills. Most of the town is on the south side of the broad River Garavogue, which flows from Lough Gill (close east of the town) into Sligo Bay.
	Sligo is not only the county town of Co. Sligo but also the chief town in north-west Ireland, and an important road junction at the meeting-place of the N4, N15 and N16. It is also the terminus of a railway line from Dublin, with the most northerly railway station in the Republic. The harbour is of little importance today on account of its shallow water.
	The poet William Butler Yeats (see Famous People) lived for some time in Sligo, and there are many reminders of this famous resident both in and around the town. The Yeats Summer School holds courses every August for Irish and foreign students.
History	Sligo appears in the records for the first time in 537. In 807 it was plundered by Norse pirates. In 1245 Maurice Fitzgerald, Earl of Kildare, took up residence here. Later, rival clans vied for possession of the castle. The town was devastated by Cromwell's troops in 1641 and again in 1645.

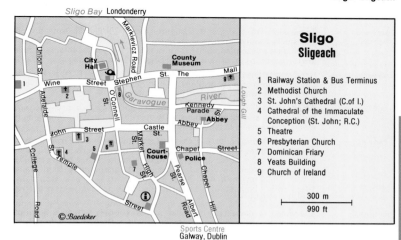

Sligo
Sligeach

1 Railway Station & Bus Terminus
2 Methodist Church
3 St. John's Cathedral (C.of I.)
4 Cathedral of the Immaculate
  Conception (St. John; R.C.)
5 Theatre
6 Presbyterian Church
7 Dominican Friary
8 Yeats Building
9 Church of Ireland

300 m
990 ft

© Baedeker

Galway, Dublin

Sligo, a busy, lively town well supplied with shops and services, has no particularly outstanding sights.

The town

Sights

In Stephen Street, on the north side of the River Garavogue, are the Sligo County Museum and adjoining Art Gallery. The County Museum (open: Mon.–Fri. 10.30am–12.30pm and 2.30–4.30pm), occupying an old rectory, contains material on the history of the region and mementoes of W. B. Yeats, including first editions of his works, letters and family photographs. The Art Gallery (open: Apr. and May Tues., Thur., Sat. 10.30am–12.30pm; June–Sept. Tues.–Sat. 10.30am–12.30pm and 2.30–4.30pm) has pictures by a variety of artists; of particular interest are the works by Jack Butler Yeats, the poet's brother.

County Museum, Art Gallery

From the County Museum a bridge crosses to the south bank of the river. To the left are the oldest buildings in Sligo – the church, cloister and conventual buildings of Sligo Abbey (National Monument), a Dominican friary founded by Maurice Fitzgerald in 1253 and rebuilt in 1416 after a fire. The church has a double-aisled nave and transepts; the choir dates from the original foundation, the transepts from the 16th c. Notable features are the canopied tomb of Cormack O'Crean (1506) on the north side of the nave, with a Crucifixion and other figures in bas relief, and the O'Conor Sligo monument (1624) on the south side. Three sides of the beautiful 15th c. cloister have survived, with the sacristy and chapter-house (13th c.).

★ Sligo Abbey

About 550yd/500m further west are the town's two principal churches, St John's Church (Church of Ireland) in John Street, a Neo-Gothic building of 1812, and the Roman Catholic St John's Cathedral (Neo-Romanesque, 1869–74) in Temple Street.

St John's Church, St John's Cathedral

The Art Gallery in the Yeats Memorial Building beside Hyde Bridge mounts temporary exhibitions; in summer there is an audio-visual presentation documenting Yeats' connection with Sligo.

Yeats Memorial Building

Surroundings

Drive around Lough Gill

To the east of the town lies the delightful Lough Gill, 5 miles/8km long and well stocked with salmon, trout and pike. The 23 mile/37km scenic circuit of the lough is an experience not to be missed. Also very enjoyable in summer are the boat trips on the lough (from Sligo or Parke's Castle).

Hazelwood House

Hazelwood House, a handsome little Palladian mansion (1731; by Richard Cassels) stands on a peninsula at the north-west end of the lough between the lough and the River Garavogue.

Lough Colgagh

Almost immediately north is picturesque Lough Colgagh, above which are found a large ancient burial site, the Deerpark Monument (National Monument), and remains of other early structures.

★Parke's Castle

Proceeding round Lough Gill, Parke's Castle (National Monument), a fine rectangular three-storeyed building with a large 17th c. courtyard is seen on the east shore of the lough. The fortified mansion has been carefully restored and can be visited (unfurnished; open: June–Sept. daily 9.30am–6.30pm; mid Apr.–May Tues.–Sun. 10am–5pm; Oct. daily 10am–5pm). Remnants of an earlier fortified building have been uncovered in the courtyard.

★Dromahair

The circuit continues to Dromahair, an exceedingly attractive place of considerable historical importance. In the 12th c. Dervorgilla, wife of Tiernan O'Rourke, eloped from here with Dermot MacMurrough, King of Leinster. Subsequently outlawed by Ireland's High King, Dermot appealed to Henry II of England who sent his vassals to Dermot's aid. So occurred the first incursion of the Normans into Ireland, landing near Wexford in 1169. The ruins of Breffni Castle, seat of the O'Rourkes, adjoin the Old Hall (1626) on the bank of the river Bonet.

Creevelea Abbey

Across the river from Dromahair are the ruins of Creevelea Abbey (National Monument), a Franciscan house founded in 1508. The remains include a

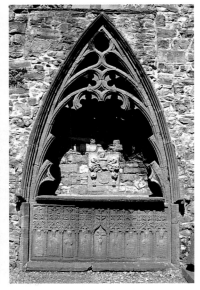

Sligo Abbey

Parke's Castle on the shores of Lough Gill

church with choir and tower, and monastic buildings set around a cloister. The pillars on the north side of the cloister have figural representations including of St Francis with the stigmata preaching to the birds.

The R287 now proceeds west, but after 4 miles/6km turns north along a valley back to the south shore of Lough Gill. Soon Dooney Rock is reached. This much-visited viewpoint is celebrated in a song by Yeats, as also is Inishfree Island situated close to the southern shore.

Dooney Rock

Also to be seen are Church Island with its ruined church (National Monument), and, further on, the smaller Cottage Island. To the north is Cairns Hill on which there are various prehistoric remains. Finally return to Sligo on the N4.

About 17 miles/28km south-east of Sligo lies Lough Arrow. A road turning east off the N4 near Castlebaldwin skirts the lough, leading first to Heapstown Cairn (National Monument), possibly a passage grave, and then, further east, Lough Nasuil. In 1933 this remarkable little lough, roughly 330yd/300m in diameter and normally containing some 1,308,000cu.yd/1,000,000cu.m of water, suddenly emptied, remained dry for three weeks, and then just as suddenly filled up again. To the south, beautifully situated on the shores of Lough Arrow, is Ballindoon Friary (16th c.). After another 6 miles/10km the N4 is regained at Ballinafad, which has a 6th c. castle (National Monument) with massive corner towers.

Drive around
Lough Arrow

About 3 miles/5km north of Ballinafad, on an isolated hill slope in the Bricklieve Mountains, is the Carrowkeel prehistoric site (National Monument), comprising fourteen burial mounds, all circular except for one which is oval, and with various different types of tomb chamber. They date from 2500–2000 B.C. Below the burial site are the remains of 50 circular stone huts, perhaps occupied by those who constructed the graves. From the top of the hill there is a superb view of Lough Arrow.

Carrowkeel

Keshcorran Hill	Keshcorran Hill, a few miles further west (near Kesh, just off the R295), has a number of caves.
Ballymote	6 miles/9km north is Ballymote, with the massive ivy-covered ruins of a castle with six round towers. Built in about 1300, the castle was subject to repeated attack until its fortifications were finally removed about 1700.
Collooney	The R293 continues north to join up with the N17. 2½ miles/4km north-east on the River Owenmore lies Collooney with, near by, the pretty Makree Castle (18th c.).
Ballysodare	At Ballysodare, 1½ miles/2km north, the River Owenmore descends a picturesque series of rapids, with a salmon-ladder by-pass for the benefit of the fish. On the left bank can be seen the ivy-clad ruins of a 7th c. monastery.
Strandhill	Strandhill, situated on a tongue of land jutting out into Sligo Bay 5 miles/8km west of Sligo, is a family seaside resort with good sheltered sandy beaches which also offer excellent surfing.
Knocknarea	On the summit of the easily climbed Knocknarea (1096ft/334m), just to the south of Strandhill, stands a huge cairn (National Monument), 36ft/11m high and 197ft/60m in diameter, popularly supposed to be the grave of Queen Maeve. From the top of the hill there are magnificent views. On the south-west side is a deep chasm between sheer limestone cliffs.
Carrowmore	The Carrowmore burial site (National Monument) can be reached by driving south from Strandhill then turning north-east in the direction of Sligo. Here archaeologists have discovered some 60 graves, many alas destroyed and others severely damaged but comprising nevertheless the largest collection of megalithic graves in Ireland. Most are a mixture of passage graves and dolmens, the oldest dating from between 3000 and 2500 B.C. (open: June–Sept. daily 9.30am–6.30pm).
Rosses Point	Rosses Point is another popular holiday resort situated north-west of Sligo. In addition to a well-known championship golf course it has good sheltered sandy beaches.

Tara · Teamhair na Riogh   C 5

Republic of Ireland
Province: Leinster
County: Meath

Location	25 miles/40km north-west of Dublin, at the village of Tara (Teamhair na Riogh = "Tara of the kings"), a narrow side road leaves the N3 on the left and ascends the famous Hill of Tara, a low grassy hill from which there are extensive views to the north and west.
History	In prehistoric times Tara was already known as a religious centre. From the 3rd c. onwards it became the seat of kings – at first minor priest-kings and later the high kings of Ireland. Every three years popular assemblies were held here at which laws were promulgated and disputes between the clans were settled. With the spread of Christianity Tara lost its importance as a cult site but remained the seat of the high kings of Ireland until its abandonment in 1022. Centuries later, in 1843, Tara was again the scene of a great assembly – a mass meeting at which Daniel O'Connell made a speech calling for the emancipation of Catholics in Ireland.

★Hill of Tara

The Hill of Tara (National Monument) boasts a whole series of grass-covered earthworks. Nothing remains of the timber or wattle-and-daub buildings of the Celtic period, the finest of which were said to have doors set with precious stones and furnishings of gold and bronze. For an appreciation of the importance of the site visitors are referred to the newly produced video film screened in St Patrick's Church.

Ráth of the Kings

The central area of the complex, the Ráth of the Kings, is surrounded by a great rampart, the Royal Enclosure. In the centre of the enclosure are two mounds, Cormac's House and the Royal Seat. Near Cormac's House the coronation stone (the Lia Fail) is supposed to have stood; legend has it that the stone used to sound when the rightful king ascended it. Nearby is a memorial stone (erroneously referred to as the coronation stone) commemorating Irish rebels killed in the 1798 Rising.

To the north, still within the enclosure, is the "Mound of Hostages", a passage grave dating from 1800 B.C. in which were found the remains of 40 cremated corpses. On their accession the kings of Tara were accustomed to take hostages from the noble families of the kingdom as a way of ensuring their loyalty. After their death, which was certainly not always natural, they were buried in the Mound of Hostages.

Tara
Teamhair
na Ríogh
100 m
330 ft

Ráth Gráinne

(Sloping Trenches)

Teach Miodhchuarta (Banqueting Hall)

Ráth of the Synods

Gravestones

St. Patrick's Church

Dumha na Ngiall (Mound of the Hostages)

Ráth na Ríogh

Teach Cormaic (Cormac's House)

Lia Fail Statue

Forradh (Royal Seat)

(Rath of the Kings)

Ráth Laoghaire (Rath of King Laoghaire)

© Baedeker

Adjoining the Royal Enclosure to the north is the Ráth of the Synods (2–4th c.), a living area once surrounded by a ring-wall. Part of it was destroyed at the beginning of this century because it was thought to conceal the Ark of the Covenant.

Ráth of the Synods

Farther north are two parallel earthworks 600ft/180m long and 100ft/30m apart. The depression between them is traditionally known as the Banqueting Hall – there is an old print in existence which depicts a banquet in progress, with the high king's guests seated in order of rank and precedence. Archaeologists however believe that it is more likely to have been the ceremonial approach to a cult site.

Banqueting Hall

To the west of the Banqueting Hall lie other earthworks, firstly Gráinnes Fort, then adjacent to that the so-called Sloping Trenches, probably cult sites.

Ráth Maeve   On a hill 875yd/800m south of the Hill of Tara is the fort known as Ráth
                Maeve (National Monument), 240yd/220m in diameter, surrounded by a
                rampart and a ditch.

Thurles · Durles Eile   D 4

Republic of Ireland
Province: Munster
County: Tipperary
Population: 7400

Location   The little market town of Thurles (Durles Eile="strong fort of Ely") lies in
                the fertile plain of the River Suir in the south of Ireland. It is an important
                road junction (N62, N75, R498) and is on the Dublin–Cork railway line.
                Thurles is the cathedral town of the archdiocese of Cashel and Emly.

Sights   Beside the bridge over the Suir stands the keep of Bridge Castle (12th c.),
                and near the Square the smaller Black Castle (15th c.?). The cathedral
                (1865–72), in Lombard Romanesque style, has a Baroque high altar by
                Andrea Pozzo (17th c.) which came from the Gesù Church in Rome. In a
                mortuary chapel can be found the tomb of Archbishop Croke (1824–1902),
                who took an active part in the struggle for Irish independence and was the
                first patron of the Gaelic Athletic Association (GAA), founded in 1884 and
                now one of Europe's largest amateur sports federations.

Surroundings

Brittas Castle 2 miles/3km north of the town, Brittas Castle, an unfinished 19th c. building
                with an imposing battlemented tower, can be seen from the N62.

★ Holy Cross   Definitely worth visiting is Holy Cross Abbey (13th–15th c.; National Monu-
Abbey   ment), located 4 miles/6km south of Thurles on the right bank of the Suir.
                The Cistercian house, founded in the 12th c., possessed a fragment of the
                True Cross, making it a great place of pilgrimage. The church, re-roofed and
                restored in 1975 as part of European Architectural Heritage Year, has an
                aisled nave and two transepts with a massive tower over the crossing. The
                chancel, transepts and crossing are beautifully vaulted. The choir (15th c.)
                with its east window and stone sedilia bearing coats of arms, is particularly
                fine. In the north transept, partly preserved, is a wall-painting (a feature rare
                in Ireland) depicting a stag-hunting scene in shades of brown, red and
                green. A columned and arched structure situated between two chapel
                recesses in the south transept is probably the shrine in which the relic of the
                True Cross was displayed. From here a staircase leads to the upper floor
                with the monastic living-quarters. On the east side of the attractive and
                well-preserved cloister lies the chapter-house (not open to the public). The
                refectory on the south side has been destroyed.

Ballynahow   About 3 miles/5km north-west of Holy Cross Abbey, Ballynahow Castle
Castle   (16th c.; National Monument) has one of the few circular keeps in Ireland.
                Two out of the five original vaulted roofs are preserved.

Tipperary · Tiobrad Arann   D 3

Republic of Ireland
Province: Munster
County: Tipperary
Population: 5000

Location   Tipperary (Tiobrad Arann="well of Arann") is a market and industrial town
                (dairy products, linoleum, etc.) in the south of Ireland, situated in the fertile

Golden Vale which extends west of Cashel into Co. Limerick. To the south of the town rises the long ridge of the Slievenamuck Hills.

Tipperary became a familiar name to many outside Ireland from the song "It's a long way to Tipperary". A favourite with British troops at the beginning of the century, it became popularised before the start of the First World War.

Little is left of the old town. The most notable remains of the past are the chancel arch of a monastic church (13th c.) and the ruins of a 17th c. grammar school. The Neo-Gothic parish church dates from the 19th c.

Sights

Surroundings

On the N74 about 6 miles/9km east of Tipperary, in the Golden Vale, are the ruins of Thomastown Castle, built in the 17th c. and enlarged in the Neo-Gothic style about 1812. This was the birthplace in 1790 of Father Theobald Matthew, the "Apostle of Temperance" (see Cork). The house fell into disrepair from the end of the last century; the park, which once had a large French-style garden, now forms part of an afforestation scheme.

Thomastown Castle

2 miles/3km farther east where the road crosses the Suir at the village of Golden, a ruined castle stands picturesquely on a rocky islet in the river.

Golden

Beyond the bridge a road on the right leads to the ruins of Ireland's largest medieval monastery, Athassel Priory (13th–15th c.; National Monument), an Augustinian house founded by William de Burgh and dissolved in the mid 16th c. The remains cover an area of 4acres/1.6ha. The church, 213ft/65m long, has an aisled nave, a choir and transepts, with an impressive-looking tower over the crossing. In the choir is the tomb of a Norman knight (13th c.). Practically nothing survives of the cloister, around which are the extensive conventual buildings, surrounded by a high wall. In front of the gatehouse was a bridge giving access to the priory. Until the mid 14th c. there was a little town here, of which no trace remains.

★Athassel Priory

Tralee · Traigh Li

D 2

Republic of Ireland
Province: Munster
County: Kerry
Population: 17,500

Tralee (Traigh Li="bay of the River Lee"), the lively county town of Co. Kerry, lies in the south-west of Ireland, 2 miles/3km above the outflow of the River Lee into Tralee Bay. Despite its relatively small population, Tralee fulfills an important role as the urban centre for Kerry, a particularly large county. In addition to its administrative agencies the town offers a good range of services and shopping facilities. Tralee is the home of the Kerry Group, a dairy co-operative established in 1974, which markets its products (such as butter) under the label "Kerry Gold", exporting them to numerous countries.

Location

For tourists Tralee is above all the gateway to the Dingle Peninsula (see entry), an area steeped in history, and the starting-point for a drive around the famous Ring of Kerry (see entry).

Tralee was twice set on fire by its own garrison (in 1643 and again in 1691) before being given up to the enemy. As a result no older buildings have survived. There are however some fine Georgian houses in the centre of town.

The town

Sights

St John's Church, a 19th c. Neo-Gothic building by the Dublin architect J. J. McCarthy, has fine stained glass by Michael Healy in the sacristy.

St John's Church

283

Court House · The early 19th c. Court House, to the north of the church, in Ashe Street, has an Ionic portico.

Kerry the Kingdom · Housed in the Ashe Memorial Hall (open: Mon.–Sat. 10am–6pm, Sun. 2–6pm, in Aug. until 8pm) are three attractions collectively entitled "Kerry the Kingdom". The first, "Kerry in Colour", is a slide-show introducing visitors to the scenic beauties of the region. The second, "Treasures of the Kingdom", is actually the local museum which brings to life the history of the county from the Stone Age to the present day by means of a series of imaginative scenes and displays; exhibits include various notable archaeological finds and *objets d'art*. The third, "Geraldine Tralee", takes its name from the Desmond Geraldines, one of the Norman families who ruled over Tralee and its surroundings. Eleven "time vehicles" carry visitors through the medieval streets and squares of Tralee in 1450, reconstructed in impressive detail down even to their sounds and smells.

Siamsa Tire · Close to the Ashe Memorial Hall stands Tralee's Siamsa Tire theatre, a new building opened in 1991. The design of the theatre was inspired by Ireland's stone forts. Behind the name Siamsa Tire lies a national people's theatre dedicated to the promotion of Celtic culture. Programmes include music, dance and drama (performances from May to September, 8.30pm).

Biennerville windmill and steam train · From 1891 until 1953 a narrow-gauge railway operated between Tralee and Dingle. In 1993 a section was re-opened with trains running hourly between April and September from Tralee to the restored Biennerville windmill 2 miles/3km away. The mill (open: May–Nov. Mon.–Sat. 10am–6pm), which can also be reached by car via the R559 Dingle road, was erected at the end of the 18th c. and remained in operation until the end of the 19th c.; it was restored in the 1980s. Visitors can watch wheat being ground into flour between the huge millstones. A multi-media presentation recalls the history of the mill and tells the story of its restoration, while a further exhibition is devoted to the mass emigrations of the last

century (in the 18th and 19th c. many ships carrying Irish emigrants sailed from Biennerville Quay).

Surroundings

Fenit · In 1994 "Fenit Sea World" opened on the harbour at Fenit just 6 miles/10km west of Tralee. Visitor are brought face to face with every type of marine creature from tiny crustacea to rapacious-looking sharks (open: daily 10am–8pm).

Ardfert · 5 miles/8km north-west of Tralee on the R551 lies Ardfert, around which can be seen some important medieval remains. St Brendan (483–578), born in neighbouring Fenit, founded a monastery here, to which a group of churches (National Monuments) in the churchyard belonged – the fortress-like "cathedral", with a beautiful 12th c. west doorway and blind arcading and a 13th c. nave and choir (fine lancet windows); to the north-west the little Romanesque church of Temple na Hoe with columns at its outer corners; and the 15th c. church of Temple na Griffin.

A short distance east are the ruins of a Franciscan friary (13th–15th c.; National Monument). The church has cylindrical columns and a fine south window. Two sides of the 15th c. cloister, originally roofed with stone slabs, have survived.

Siamsa Tire Theatre in Tralee

Farther north on the R551 lies the quiet seaside resort of Ballyheige. Near by on lovely Kerry Head, jutting into the Atlantic west of the village, hexagonal quartz crystals from the Kerry Mountains can be found. Banna Beach, extending to the south, is the chief attraction for most holiday-makers however. It was here that in 1916 Sir Roger Casement (see Famous People) landed from a German submarine to take part in the Easter Rising.

Ballyheige

Just off the N21 about 12 miles/20km east of Tralee is found the impressive Crag Cave (open: daily 10am–6pm). Systematically explored for the first time in 1981, it was revealed to be one of the largest cave systems in Ireland, with passages almost 2½ miles/4km long. With lighting and safe gangways installed, Crag Cave was opened to the public in 1989.

★Crag Cave

Trim · Baile Atha Truim   C 5

Republic of Ireland
Province: Leinster
County: Meath
Population: 2100

The little market town of Trim (Baile Atha Truim="town of the elder tree fort") lies on the River Boyne in a fertile plain north-west of Dublin. Here within a small space are gathered remains of a rich past both religious and military.

Location

In 1172 Hugh de Lacy, a vassal of Henry II, built a castle on a site close to the spot where St Patrick had founded a monastery in the 5th c. The castle subsequently changed hands several times, being successively fought over, destroyed, rebuilt and enlarged. In the 14th c. the town which had

History

grown up around the castle was fortified with walls and gates. The Irish Parliament met here several times during the 15th c. In 1649 the town fell into Cromwellian hands.

Sights

Yellow Steeple

Trim's most prominent landmark is the Yellow Steeple (National Monument), the last relic of an Augustinian abbey built on a bare hill above the river in the 14th c. The finely proportioned tower, still over 126ft/38m high, formerly stood on the north side of the church.

Talbot's Castle

Near by is the privately owned Talbot's Castle, built in 1415 but later modernised and converted into a school. Among its pupils was Arthur Wellesley (1769–1852), the future Duke of Wellington. He later lived in Patrick Street, where there is a monument to him.

Sheep Gate

A little way south of the Yellow Steeple (near the river embankment) can be seen the two-storeyed Sheep Gate, the only surviving town gate.

★Trim Castle

Opposite, on the south side of the Boyne in the heart of town, rises a magnificent stronghold, Trim Castle (National Monument), the largest Anglo-Norman castle in Ireland, occupying an area of 3acres/1.2ha. In the very centre of the castle precinct, at its highest point, stands the square keep, with turrets at the four corners and projecting rectangular towers (only three of the original four survive) in the middle of each of the

Trim Castle/ Keep

11ft/3.3m-thick walls, giving the massive structure a cruciform plan. The outer ward is surrounded by a curtain wall with semi-circular towers (five of which remain) and a moat. Entry was via a drawbridge operated from the tower on the south side. The parapet walks originally linked with the town walls.

Butterstream Gardens

On the edge of Trim lie the exceedingly pleasant Butterstream Gardens (open: May–Sept. Tues.–Sun. 2–5pm), consisting of several adjoining gardens separated by box hedges, each with its own individual character.

Surroundings

Newtown Trim

Just over ¾ mile/1km upstream to the east of the town, at an old bridge over the Boyne, lies Newtown Trim, with the ruins of the Abbey of St Peter and St Paul (National Monument). Of the very large cathedral (13th c.; transitional Romanesque-Gothic), built for the see of Meath, there remain only the choir, the crossing and a small section of the nave. On the south side of the church are some remains of conventual buildings. To the east is a smaller church (13th c.) containing a fine late 16th c. double tomb.

Tuam · Tuaim   C 3

Republic of Ireland
Province: Connacht
County: Galway
Population: 4500

Location

Tuam (Tuaim="burial place") is situated in the west of Ireland on the N17 east of Lough Corrib. The little market town has some industry including a sugar factory; it is also a good centre for fishing.

Tuam was from quite early on a place of great ecclesiastical importance. The town's first two Protestant archbishops between them produced the first ever translation of the New Testament into Irish (1602). It is now the see of a Roman Catholic archbishop and a bishop of the Church of Ireland.

Sights

The 19th c. St Mary's Cathedral (Church of Ireland) in Galway Road in-corporates the barrel-vaulted chancel (with beautifully carved chancel arch) and fine east window from the original 12th–14th c. church. In the south aisle is the ornamented shaft of a 12th c. high cross. The choir stalls are Italian Baroque.

★ St Mary's Cathedral

In the Market Square stands another high cross (12th c.; National Monu-ment) assembled from various fragments, with a number of figures and interlace ornament.

High cross

In nearby Shop Street is found the Mill Museum, with a working corn-mill and milling equipment.

Mill Museum

Surroundings

On the N83 some 8 miles/13km north-east of Tuam lies Dunmore, a place of some age with the ruins of a castle and abbey (both National Monuments). The castle (14th c.) consists of a sturdy four-storey rectangular tower with gables. The abbey was an Augustinian friary founded in 1425 by a member of the Bermingham family; all that survives is the church, with a massive central tower borne on arches.

Dunmore

2 miles/3km north of Tuam stands Bermingham House (1730), with good stucco work and fine furniture (open: weekday afternoons).

Bermingham House

Picturesquely situated on a small lough 7 miles/11km from Tuam, reached via the R347 and N63 (the Roscommon road), are the ruins of Knockmoy Abbey (National Monument), a Cistercian house founded in 1190. The nave is undecorated but the choir has some fine carving. On the north wall is one of Ireland's few examples of medieval wall-painting, dating from about 1400. Only the outlines, drawn in black, have survived. The scenes depicted are Christ in the attitude of blessing, the Martyrdom of St Sebastian and the legend of the three dead and three living kings. Under the three dead kings was the inscription: "That which you are, we were; that which we are, you will be". The east wing of the conventual buildings is well preserved but the cloister has completely gone.

Knockmoy

On the site of an old Franciscan friary at Kilbennan, 2½ miles/4km north-west of Tuam, are a partly collapsed round tower and the ruins of a small church (both National Monuments).

Kilbennan

Tullamore · Tulach Mhor

C 4

Republic of Ireland
Province: Leinster
County: Offaly
Population: 8000

Tullamore (Tulach Mhor="great hill of assembly"), county town of Co. Offaly, lies almost exactly in the centre of Ireland at the junction of the N52 and N80 and on the Dublin to Galway railway line. Until 1804 the town was the terminus of the Grand Canal (see entry) from Dublin.
    It is now an important agricultural and whiskey distilling town (Tullamore Dew Irish Whiskey) and the site of the Republic's main radio transmitter.

Location

The town   Having been almost totally destroyed in 1790 – when it was a much smaller
                  place than today – by the explosion of a large crashed balloon, Tullamore
                  has no really old buildings. Noteworthy among those of later date are St
                  Catherine's Church (1818), the Market House and Court House (both like-
                  wise early 19th c.), and various buildings erected in the early years of the
                  Grand Canal. Charleville Castle, off the N52 south-west of the town centre,
                  was built at the end of the 18th c.; the interior has been sympathetically
                  restored by the present owners.

Surroundings

Durrow   4½ miles/7km north of Tullamore is Durrow where in the 6th c. St Colum-
                  cille founded a monastery. It was here in the 7th c. that the famous "Book of
                  Durrow" (now in the library of Trinity College Dublin), was written and
                  illuminated.
                      Also preserved is a 10th c. high cross (National Monument) with figural
                  reliefs of considerable art historical importance: on the east side are the
                  Sacrifice of Isaac and Christ in Glory, flanked by David with his harp on the
                  left and David killing the lion on the right; on the west side the Watching of
                  the Tomb, the Scourging, the Arrest of Christ and the Crucifixion; on the
                  south side Adam and Eve, Cain and Abel, a warrior and a horseman; and on
                  the north side two groups of figures. The cross is in the grounds of the
                  privately owned Durrow Abbey; visitors are therefore asked to behave
                  circumspectly.

Edenderry   22 miles/35km north-east of Tullamore, on the eastern edge of Co. Offaly,
                  lies the pretty little market town of Edenderry, overlooked by Blundell's
                  Castle.

Rahan   On the Grand Canal 6 miles/9km west of the town is Rahan, where from the
                  8th to the 18th c. there was a monastery. Two churches belonging to
                  the monastery (both National Monuments) can still be seen. The larger of
                  the two (Romanesque) has a splendid doorway and good carving on the
                  chancel arch and two windows; the nave is 18th c. on earlier foundations.
                  The smaller church dates from the Early Christian period but has been
                  much altered.

Boher Church   A good 12½ miles/20km north-west of Tullamore, off the R436, the Roman
                  Catholic parish church at Boher preserves the 12th c. Shrine of St Manchan.
                  The yew-wood casket containing the saint's remains is housed within
                  a portable metal reliquary decorated with animal symbols and bronze
                  figures, the latter being later additions.

Waterford · Port Lairge   D 4

Republic of Ireland
Province: Munster
County: Waterford
Population: 40,000

Location   Waterford (Port Lairge="Lairge's landing-place"), county town of Co.
                  Waterford, lies near the south-eastern tip of Ireland on the south bank of the
                  River Suir, some 20 miles/30km above its mouth. The river at this point is
                  broad and deep, and has thus enabled the town to develop into a seaport of
                  considerable importance.

Industry   The town has a variety of industries but is chiefly known for its glass.
                  Waterford glass was already famous in the 18th c. and since its revival in
                  1947 has won acquired international reputation.

History   In 853 the Danes established a settlement here which they called Vadre-
                  fjord. In 1170 Strongbow took the town, and it became second in impor-

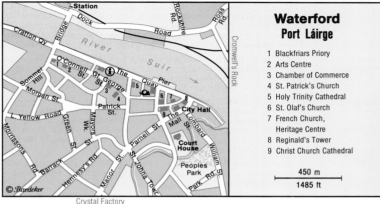

Limerick, Dublin

Waterford
Port Láirge

1 Blackfriars Priory
2 Arts Centre
3 Chamber of Commerce
4 St. Patrick's Church
5 Holy Trinity Cathedral
6 St. Olaf's Church
7 French Church,
   Heritage Centre
8 Reginald's Tower
9 Christ Church Cathedral

450 m
1485 ft

© Baedeker

Crystal Factory
Cork

tance only to Dublin among Anglo-Norman strongholds. Waterford was to remain loyal to Britain well into the 19th c., a loyalty recognised much earlier by Henry VII who, in 1487, granted the town its motto "Urbs intacta manet Waterfordia" ("The Town of Waterford remains intact"), a reference to its refusal on two occasions to bow to rival claimants to the English throne. In 1649 Cromwell too was forced to abandon his siege of Waterford, though the town fell to his troops the following year. Thirty years later, having supported James II, it surrendered to William of Orange.

The town centre still boasts many houses dating from around 1800 when Waterford's glass industry was in its heyday. The Mall in particular is graced by quite a number of Georgian houses. There are also numerous hotels, restaurants and pubs.

The town

Sights

Downstream of the bridge over the Suir a street known simply as the Quay – but in fact comprising Merchants Quay, Meaghers Quay and Parade Quay – runs along the south bank of the river for ¾ mile/1.2km. Most of the principal sights of Waterford can be viewed by venturing down the various streets and lanes opening southwards off the Quay.

The Quay

The church tower seen on the corner of O'Connell Street and Bridge Street is all that now remains of an old Dominican house, Blackfriars Priory (1226–1541).

Blackfriars Priory

The Garter Lane Arts Centre, further along O'Connell Street, exhibits modern Irish art.

Art Centre

O'Connell Street continues into Great George Street, on the right-hand side of which is the Chamber of Commerce, a handsome Neo-Classical building (1795) by John Roberts.

Chamber of Commerce

Near by, in a lane off Broad Street, stands St Patrick's Church (mid 18th c.), with a charming gallery.

St Patrick's Church

Diagonally across from St Patrick's, between Parade Quay and High Street, lies Holy Trinity Cathedral, also by Roberts (1793), with a late 19th c. façade.

Holy Trinity Cathedral

289

Waterford · Port Lairge

French Church

Proceeding along Parade Quay, the ruined French Church (National Monument; in Greyfriars Street) is seen to the right, its 15th c. nave, chancel and tower being all that remains of a monastery founded here in 1240. Between the 17th and the 19th c. the nave was used as a hospice for the poor; the choir served as a church for Waterford's Huguenot refugees, and the Lady Chapel became a place of burial for the leading families of the town.

Waterford Heritage Centre

On display in a building near the church are finds from excavations carried out in Waterford and the surrounding area since 1984 (open: Apr., May, Oct. Mon.–Fri. 10am–1pm, 2–6pm, Sat. 10am–1pm; June–Sept. Mon.–Fri. 10am–8pm, Sat. 10am–1pm, 2–5pm).

★Reginald's Tower

At the far end of the Quay the attractive Mall branches off at a sharp angle rightwards. On the corner stands the imposing circular Reginald's Tower, the walls of which are 10ft/3m thick. It is reputed to have been part of the old Viking fortifications – the date generally given is 1003 – but in its present aspect appears to be Anglo-Norman (13th c.). Today it houses the City Museum (open: daily 10am–5pm).

City Hall

South of the tower, in the Mall, is the City Hall (1788; by Roberts), preserved in very much its original state. Part of the building accommodates the Victorian Theatre Royal.

Christ Church Cathedral

Beyond City Hall can be seen Christ Church Cathedral (1779; by Roberts), Waterford's principal Protestant church, with a spacious interior and two fine tombs, the Rice Monument (1469) and the Fitzgerald Monument, the latter of Carrara marble.

Bishop's Palace

On the south side of the cathedral is the Bishop's Palace (18th c.; restored 1975).

Court House

A short distance away, to the left off the Mall, is found the dignified Court House (1849), from the grounds of which there is access to the wooded People's Park to the south over a little bridge spanning the Johns River.

Making Waterford crystal . . .

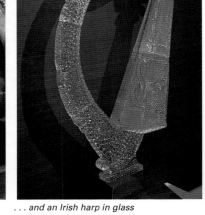

. . . and an Irish harp in glass

In the Ferrybank district, across on the north side of the Suir from the People's Park, can be seen Cromwell's Rock, from which Cromwell is said to have watched the siege of the town (fine view).

Cromwell's Rock

The Waterford Crystal factory is located 1½ miles/2.5km south of the city centre, on the Cork road (N25), the continuation of the Mall. Visitors to the works see glass being blown and cut by hand (guided tours: Apr.–Oct. daily 8.30am–4pm; Nov.–Mar. Mon.–Fri. 9am–3.15pm). Waterford glass can be bought in the Crystal Gallery adjoining the factory (open: Apr.–Oct. daily 8.30am–6pm; Nov.–Mar. Mon.–Fri. 9am–5pm, also Sat. Mar.–Nov.).

Waterford Crystal factory

Surroundings

Passage East lies 6 miles/10km east of Waterford on the R683, at the point where the River Suir flows into the wide inlet known as Waterford Harbour. It was once a fortified town, where in 1170 Strongbow landed with 1200 men before going on to take Waterford. There is a foot ferry to Ballyhack, on the other side of Waterford Harbour.

Passage East

From Passage East, minor roads lead to the southern end of Waterford Harbour where Dunmore East, a pretty little seaside resort, clings to the hillside sloping up from the sea. It has a small-craft harbour and a good beach (diving).

Dunmore East

A detour on minor roads to the west of the R675 (the road from Waterford to Tramore Bay) leads, after 2½ miles/4km, to the very fine Knockeen Dolmen (National Monument). Thought to be 4000 years old, it has a rectangular chamber roofed over with two partly overlapping capstones.

Knockeen Dolmen

The R675 itself continues to Tramore, 8 miles/13km south of Waterford, a popular family resort with a lovely 3 mile/5km-long sandy beach and a wide range of recreational facilities including fishing, horse-racing and golf.
   "Celtworld", Tramore's latest attraction (opened in 1992), utilises all the resources of modern technology (holograms, lasers, computer graphics, etc) in the course of an entertaining presentation, lasting just under an hour, bringing to life the myths and legends of the Celtic peoples (open: Mar.–May and Oct. daily 10am–5pm; June–Sept. daily 10am–11pm).

Tramore

Portlaw, an old Quaker settlement, is reached by following the Suir upstream from Waterford, first heading west on the N25 and then north-west on the R680 (9 miles/15km). The town's tanneries produce a substantial proportion of Ireland's leather.

Portlaw

North-west and just outside Portlaw lies the Curraghmore demesne (open: Easter–Oct. Thur. afternoons and bank holidays only). Here, situated 1¼ miles/2km from the park entrance, in the midst of splendid gardens – among the many attractive features of which is a shell house – is the architecturally notable mansion (1745; by John Roberts) of the Marquesses of Waterford. The house, which boasts fine interior decorations and some famous pictures, is sadly not open to public.

Curraghmore Gardens

A few miles north-west of Waterford, over the county boundary in Co. Kilkenny (N9 then N24), the imposing ruins of Granagh Castle (National Monument) stand high above the north bank of the Suir; they comprise a 13th c. keep, curtain walls reinforced by towers, and a 16th c. great hall.

Granagh Castle

Westport · Cathair na Mart

C 2

Republic of Ireland
Province: Connacht
County: Mayo. Population: 3500

Location

Westport (Cathair na Mart="stone fort of the cattle") is situated in the north-west of Ireland on Clew Bay, in the south-east corner of which the River Carrowbeg flows into Westport Bay.

Before the advent of the railways Westport – a planned settlement established by the Earl of Altamont in 1780, probably to the design of a French architect – was a considerable port. Today it has developed into an angling centre with good fishing in Clew Bay.

★The town

Many people consider Westport one of the prettiest small towns in Ireland. Lime trees line both banks of the little River Carrowbeg which, spanned by attractive old bridges, runs along the middle of the Mall, the town's main street.

The Protestant church (1880) has Art Nouveau carving. At the south end of the Mall is a pleasant square, the Octagon, with an unusual clock-tower erected on the site of a monument destroyed in 1922.

★Westport House

Opening times
Late May–mid Sept.
Mon.–Sat. 2–5pm
(June until 6pm;
July–late Aug.
10.30am–6pm,
also Sun. 2–6pm)

The entrance to Westport House, seat of the Marquesses of Sligo, is reached by following the main road south from the Octagon and turning right towards Westport Quay. The house, built by Richard Cassels in 1730–34 and enlarged by James Wyatt, is one of the finest mansions in Ireland.

Though few of the original furnishings survive, the Long Gallery is hung with portraits of the family, the Dining Room is decorated with good stucco work and on the first floor are a series of paintings of local views.

Installed in the basement are a not very attractive "shopping arcade" and various forms of family amusement.

An unusual feature of the lovely English-style gardens are the fountains which operate by tidal power. Children will entertained by the small zoo.

Westport House

Near Westport House, likewise on Westport Quay, is the Clew Bay Heritage Centre (open: Mon.–Fri. 10am–1pm; Sat. and Sun. 2–5pm) with information about the region's history.

Clew Bay
Heritage Centre

Surroundings

Newport, 7 miles/11km north of Westport, on the N59 leading into northern Mayo, is a fishing centre (sea fishing in Clew Bay, trout in the neighbouring loughs) dominated by an old railway viaduct. The church (1914) boasts a lovely stained glass window ("The Last Judgment", 1930) by Harry Clarke. Swarms of drumlins – mounds of glacial till – abound in the countryside round Newport; many of the islets in Clew Bay are drumlins which have been engulfed by the sea.

Newport

North of Newport, on a quiet bay, are the ruins of a Dominican house, Burrishoole Abbey (15th c.; National Monument). Of the church there remain the nave, choir and south transept (windows), and the squat central tower. There is also a fragment of the cloister.

Burrishoole
Abbey

A few miles further west, on another inlet to the left of the road, stands Carrigahooley Castle (15th c.; National Monument). Formerly called Rockfleet Castle, the turreted four-storey tower once belonged to the notorious Grace O'Malley (see Famous People).

Carrigahooley
Castle

Mulrany, 7½ miles/12km further on, is a little place with a mild climate in which fuchsias, rhododendrons and Mediterranean heaths flourish. The village has facilities for golf and tennis.

Mulrany

From Mulrany the R319 crosses the sizeable Curraun Peninsula to Achill Island (see entry). It is well worth driving round the peninsula; a particularly delightful little road runs along the south side, with constantly changing coastal scenery and fine views over Clew Bay and across to Clare Island. The centre of the peninsula is dominated by the 1815ft/553m Curraun.

Curraun
Peninsula

At the village of Aghagower, on a side road off the R330 4 miles/6km south-east of Westport, can be found the ruins of a round tower and a church (National Monument), relics of a monastery founded by St Senach who St Patrick himself consecrated bishop. The round tower, the top of which is missing, stands 60ft/18m high; the entrance is modern. The church is 15th c.

Aghagower

Wexford · Loch Garman

D 5

Republic of Ireland
Province: Leinster
County: Wexford
Population: 15,000

Wexford (Loch Garman="Garman's loch"), county town of Co. Wexford, lies at the south-eastern tip of Ireland on Wexford Harbour, a sheltered inlet opening off the St George's Channel. Until 1970 the town's economy was largely agriculture-based; today it is mainly industrial (agricultural machinery, electronic metering equipment, submersible pumps, etc.).

Location

Wexford's picturesque historic nucleus with its narrow winding streets is a typical example of Anglo-Norman settlement.
 The principal thoroughfare, Main Street, extends roughly parallel with the town's long harbour quay; almost all the places of interest can be reached with ease via the side streets right and left.

The town

Dublin

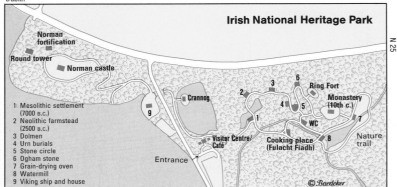

Irish National Heritage Park

N 25

Norman
fortification

Round tower

Norman castle

Crannog

Ring Fort

Monastery
(10th c.)

9

3 6

2

4 5

1

WC

Visitor Centre/
Café

Cooking place
(Fulacht Fiadh)

8

Nature
trail

7

Entrance

© Baedeker

1 Mesolithic settlement
  (7000 B.C.)
2 Neolithic farmstead
  (2500 B.C.)
3 Dolmen
4 Urn burials
5 Stone circle
6 Ogham stone
7 Grain-drying oven
8 Watermill
9 Viking ship and house

Sights

**Westgate
Heritage Centre**

The restored 13th c. Westgate, in the north-west of the town centre, is the
only one of the five original gates to survive. Today it houses the Westgate
Heritage Centre where an audio-visual presentation lasting about half an
hour provides a wealth of interesting information about the town and the
surrounding area (open: May–Dec. Mon.–Sat. 9.30am–1pm and 2–5.30pm,
also Sun. 2–5pm Jul. and Aug.; Jan.–Apr. tel. (053) 3 11 77 for times).

Selskar Abbey

Near by can be seen the ruins of Selskar Abbey, founded in the 12th c. Still
in evidence are a battlemented tower and the remains of St Selskar's
Church (15th c.; National Monument). The abbey was destroyed by Cromwell's troops in 1649.

Bull Ring

At the intersection of Main Street and Quay Street is a little square called
the Bull Ring, recalling the Norman pastime of bull-baiting; in it stands a
bronze memorial to the 1798 rising.

Crescent Quay

Further along Main Street, Henrietta Street leads leftwards to Crescent
Quay, a semi-circular square where stands a statue of Commodore John
Barry (1745–1803), erected by the US Government to commemorate the
father of the American Navy.

Surroundings

**★★Irish National
Heritage Park**

The Irish National Heritage Park, near Ferrycarrig, about 3 miles/5km north-
west of Wexford (reached via the N11, the Dublin road), is an interesting
open-air museum with full-size replicas of dwellings and other man-made
structures (dolmens, a stone circle, ring fort, Early Christian monastery,
crannog, round tower, etc.) illustrating some 9000 years of Irish history. A
nature trail has been laid out inside the park (open: Mar.–Oct. daily
10am–7pm; last admission 5pm).

Wildfowl Reserve

On the northern edge of the wide bay of Wexford Harbour is a wildfowl
reserve (open: mid Apr.–Sept. daily 9am–6pm), notable in particular for the
great numbers of lesser white-fronted geese which winter here every year;
there are also many swans and no fewer than 28 different types of duck.
Entrance to the reserve is from the R741. Facilities include a car park,
screened observation hides, an observation tower and a small Visitor
Centre displaying the various species of bird which frequent the marsh.

In the Irish National Heritage Park

Leaving Wexford by the Rosslare road (N25), a signposted turning on the right not far from the southern exit of the by-pass, leads to Johnstown Castle, a Neo-Gothic edifice built in the second half of the 19th c. incorporating the remains of a Norman fortress. Apart from the entrance hall the castle itself is closed to the public; but the landscaped park with its lakes and over 200 varieties of trees and shrubs is delightful. Farm buildings belonging to the castle have been turned into an agricultural museum, with displays of old implements and machinery and replicas of various workshops and a farmhouse kitchen and bedroom *c.* 1900; also an interesting collection of Irish vernacular furniture (open: park daily 9am–5pm; museum Apr.–Nov. Mon.–Fri. 9am–5pm, Sat. and Sun. 2–5pm; Apr., May and Sept.–Nov. museum closes 12.30–1.30pm).

★Johnstown Castle and National Museum of Agriculture

Proceeding south on the N25, turn left onto the R739 to reach Rathmacknee Castle (15th c.; National Monument). Excellently preserved, it is a good example of a typical 15th c. or 16th c. Irish castle. The five-storeyed keep, battlemented in the manner of the period, stands within an outer ward the walls of which, more than 23ft/7m high and 4ft/1.2m thick, are buttressed by a massive round tower at the north-east corner and a smaller square tower at the north-west corner.

Rathmacknee Castle

From the castle take the minor road leading back to the N25 at Killinick Station. Just beyond the village a road branches off on the left to the little town of Rosslare, which claims to be one of the driest and sunniest places in Ireland. The wide bay boasts several miles of safe shingle and sand beach.

Rosslare

About 3 miles/5km away at the southern end of the bay lies Rosslare Harbour from where there are ferry services to Fishguard (Wales) and Le Havre (France). It has an extensive pier and a car ferry terminal (opened in 1989). Almost all passenger traffic from the European mainland passes

Rosslare Harbour

Johnstown Castle

through Rosslare; the harbour is also important for freight, handling about 10% of Ireland's exports.

Lady's Island Lake

South of Rosslare Harbour, separated from the sea only by a thin strip of land, lies Lady's Island Lake. On an island in the lake, today linked to the shore by a causeway, are the ruins of an Augustinian house and a 12th c. Norman castle with a leaning tower.

Kilmore Quay, Saltee Islands

South of Wexford the R739 leads south-west to Kilmore and Kilmore Quay, a remote and picturesque fishing centre on Forlorn Point. From here a boat can be taken to the rocky Saltee Islands (Little Saltee and Great Saltee). These uninhabited isles are Ireland's largest bird sanctuary, the nesting place of some 30 species including cormorants, puffins, razorbills and fulmers.

Wicklow · Cill Mhantain   D 5

Republic of Ireland
Province: Leinster
County: Wicklow
Population: 5000

Location

Wicklow (Cill Mhantain="St Mantan's church"), county town of Co. Wicklow, lies not far south of Dublin at the southern end of a wide crescent-shaped bay on the Irish Sea coast.

The River Vartry reaches the sea here, first opening out into a 2 mile/3km-long lagoon separated from the sea by a grassy spit (which today is a promenade and recreational area). The Vikings, quick to appreciate the sheltered harbour, established themselves in what was an ancient monastic settlement founded in the 5th c. by St Mantan, which they renamed Wykinglo.

The old town with its narrow streets grew up in the shelter of Black Castle (12th c.), a Norman stronghold on a rocky promontory east of the town. Up until the 17th c. it was subject to repeated attacks as rival clans contended for possession. In the garden of the parish priest's house can be seen remains of a 13th c. Franciscan friary. The 18th c. parish church incorporates a lovely Romanesque doorway.

Sights

Surroundings

Wicklow Head, 2 miles/3km south-east of the town, not only provides fine views but is unusual in having no fewer than three lighthouses on the point. Further south, the sandy beaches of the "Silver Strand", today disfigured by excessive numbers of caravans, extend down the coast to Brittas Bay and Mizen Head.

Wicklow Head

Leaving Wicklow on the R750, follow the N11 north-westwards through Rathnew to Ashford, attractively situated on the River Vartry. Along the banks of the river close to the village are the superb Mount Usher Gardens, with many varieties of rare trees and shrubs, some of them subtropical. The gardens, a modest 1¼ acres/0.5ha at the time, were first laid out by Edmund Walpole in 1868; today, still privately owned, they cover some 20 acres/8ha. About 5000 different species of plants flourish in this quite enchanting demesne. The colours are particularly splendid in May and early June when the azaleas and rhododendrons are in bloom (open: mid Mar.–Oct. daily 10.30am–6pm).

★ Mount Usher Gardens

The Devil's Glen, a noted beauty spot higher up the Vartry valley, is a deep chasm with craggy sides overgrown with trees and shrubs. On entering the glen the river plunges nearly 100ft/30m into the Devil's Punchbowl. There are fine views of the waterfall from well-sited paths in the glen.

★ Devil's Glen

Wicklow Mountains

C/D 5

Republic of Ireland
Province: Leinster
County: Wicklow

The Wicklow Mountains, a range of granite hills, extend for some 40 miles/60km from just south of Dublin southward through Co. Wicklow. Their eastern slopes run down towards the Irish Sea, while their western slopes border the plain of the River Barrow.

Location

Only two passes, the Sally Gap and the Wicklow Gap, offer a route through the mountains from east to west. Until the 18th c. the inaccessible high valleys provided a relatively safe retreat for refugees, outlaws and criminals. Following the 1798 rising, a strategic highway known as the Military Road was constructed, giving greater control of the area.

The Wicklow Mountains are a lonely region of purple-and-brown flecked hills, dark lakes and conical peaks, often shrouded in mist. Moorland alternates with heath, deciduous with coniferous woodland.

★ Topography

Those intending to walk in the hills can obtain information from the Visitor Centre at Upper Lake, Glendalough (open: Apr.–Aug. daily 10am–6.30pm; Sept. weekends only).

Through the Wicklow Mountains

From Rathfarnham (see Dublin) the R115 leads south, climbing steadily. Ahead, half right, can be seen Kippure (2517ft/767m) with its television

Rathfarnham to Laragh

297

tower; to the rear there is a fine view of Dublin. At Glencree, shortly before the Enniskerry road branches off to the left, there is a German Military Cemetery. From here the route continues south, passing two small loughs and traversing a boggy plateau.

On gaining the watershed at the Sally Gap (1657ft/505m), the R115 crosses the R759, afterwards winding its way south over bare moorland, negotiating several streams flowing down from the hills on the right – Gravate (2396ft/730m), Duff Hill (2406ft/733m) and Mullaghcleevaun (2839ft/865m) – before descending the rugged Glenmacnass valley with its splendid waterfall (best seen from the valley side) to Laragh. Here a choice of onward routes presents itself.

Laragh to Hollywood and Dublin

From Laragh the R756 climbs steadily west, past the famous monastic site of Glendalough (see entry) in a side valley to the left, and on up to the Wicklow Gap (1595ft/486m) between Tonelagee (2734ft/833m) to the north and Camaderry (2337ft/712m) to the south. Camaderry lies within the Glendalough Forest Park (nature reserve), the boundary of which the road skirts. About 2½ miles/4km beyond the pass a narrow road branches off rightwards to the Glenbridge Youth Hostel, situated in a lonely valley bottom. 4 miles/6km further on another road goes off on the right, this time leading north to the Lacken Reservoir (or Poulaphuca Lake) which, with a surface area of 8sq. miles/2000ha, both contributes to Dublin's water-supply and is also harnessed to produce electricity.

Athgreany

The R756 meanwhile continues down to Hollywood. Somewhat over a mile south of the village, at Athgreany, there is a large stone circle of uncertain age (National Monument) known as the "Piper's Stones" – "The Piper" being another monolith standing alone outside the circle.

✶ Russborough House

4 miles/6km north of Hollywood, on the left of the N81 beyond the reservoir, lies Russborough House, a Palladian mansion (1740–50) by Richard Cassels and Francis Bindon, now the home of the Beit family. The main house, with a great flight of steps leading up to the entrance, is linked by colonnades to substantial wings. The interior has fine stucco work by Francini and contains Sir Alfred Beit's valuable art collection – including works by Goya, Rubens, Velázquez and Vermeer – and a display of Irish silver (open: Easter–Oct. daily 2.30am–5.30pm). From Russborough House it is 19 miles/30km or so back to Dublin on the N81.

Detour to the Glenmalure valley and Lugnaquilla Mountain

This route ventures into an isolated part of the Wicklow Mountains, where the landscape can appear dark and eerie – though with much impressive scenery. Proceed south from Laragh, turning off rightwards after 1¼ miles/2km to follow the old Military Road into the mountains where it climbs steadily to 1267ft/386m before dropping down again into the Glenmalure valley. At the crossroads in the hamlet of Drumgoff, take a narrow road to the right, soon reaching a car park. From here Lugnaquilla (3095ft/943m) can be climbed (unmarked path; 10½ miles/17km there and back; about 2625ft/800m of ascent).

Laragh to Wicklow and Dublin

From Laragh the R755 makes it way through the charming scenery of the Vale of Clara, running south-east along the Avonmore River to Rathdrum. To the south extends the Avondale Forest Park (see Arklow).

At Rathdrum take the R752 in the direction of Wicklow, but before reaching the town turn onto the N11 and drive north to Ashford, with the truly delightful Mount Usher Gardens (see Wicklow). Here the R764 heads in-land, passing the large Vartry Reservoir. At the junction near the pretty little village of Roundwood, turn right and follow the R755 northwards.

Great Sugar Loaf

Further along, to the right of the road, rises the Great Sugar Loaf (1644ft/501m); it can be climbed in about 45 minutes from the large car park on its south side (689ft/210m of ascent).

Enniskerry

Another recommended stop on this stretch of the route is at Enniskerry (see entry) for a visit to the magnificent Powerscourt Gardens near by. From Enniskerry the R117 leads back to Dublin (9 miles/15km).

At the Sally Gap

The Wicklow Way

Opened in 1983, the long-distance trail known as the Wicklow Way runs for 80 miles/126km from Marley Park, Co. Dublin (car park; bus service from Dublin), to Clonegal in Co. Carlow. A series of parking places conveniently sited within easy reach of the well-signposted Way, make it possible to walk individual sections of the route.

The first section follows the eastern slopes of the hills, ending at Luggala near Lough Tay, on the R759 between Sally Gap and Roundwood. The second section makes towards Laragh, passing the end of Glenmacnass before turning south-west via Drumgoff and Aghavannagh to Moyne. The final section runs south through the Ballycumber and other ranges of hills, by way of Tinahely and Shillelagh, to Clonegal. From there it is possible to continue even further – though of course no longer in the Wicklow Mountains – on the South Leinster Way to Graiguenamanagh in Co. Kilkenny (25 miles/40km). For those who would like more information, a leaflet "The Wicklow and South Leinster Way" is available from the Irish Tourist Board.

Youghal · Eochail   E 4

Republic of Ireland
Province: Munster
County: Cork
Population: 6000

Pronounced "Yaul", Youghal (Eochail="yew wood") is situated on the south coast of Ireland on Youghal Bay. Here the Blackwater River opens out into a sea lough, forming a fine sheltered harbour. Youghal is a popular seaside resort, with good sandy beaches.

Location

Youghal point lace, distinguished by its vivid patterns, is justly renowned.

History

From the 13th c. until its destruction by the rebel Earl of Desmond in 1579, Youghal was a flourishing place. At the end of the 16th c. it was governed by Sir Walter Raleigh, and later by Richard Boyle. In 1649 the town surrendered to Cromwell, who made it the base for his Irish campaigns.

The town

Youghal is an ancient little market town and fishing port with a main street running parallel to the Blackwater embankment. A considerable number of 18th and 19th c. houses still grace the centre of town. There are also remains of old fortifications: on the west side, a section of the old 15th–16th c. town walls, buttressed with towers, extends south-east for a distance of about 650yd/600m.

Sights

North Abbey

Approaching the town from the north, the road passes, in a churchyard on the right, the ruins of North Abbey (National Monument), a Dominican house founded in 1268.

St Mary's Church

William Street, branching rightwards off North Main Street, leads to St Mary's Church, a collegiate church founded in the early 13th c. and subsequently much rebuilt (most recently the choir in 1854). The church has an aisled nave and a detached tower. Notable features of the interior include the oak carving in the nave, the font, and a number of tombs, in particular the elaborately sculpted monument (1619) of Richard Boyle in the south transept, where he lies buried with his two wives and nine of his sixteen children.

Myrtle Grove

North-east of the parish church stands Myrtle Grove, a stately Elizabethan mansion which belonged to Sir Walter Raleigh (not open to the public).

Clockgate Tower

At the south end of Main Street rises the five-storey Clockgate Tower, erected in place of an old town gate in 1771; until 1837 it was the town prison. Today it houses a small museum.

Surroundings

Molana Abbey

North of Youghal a side road branching left from the N25 skirts the west bank of the Blackwater. Passing by the ruins of Rinncru Abbey and Templemichael Castle, it comes to the remains of Molana Abbey, beautifully situated on the river, with church and conventual buildings (chapter-house, refectory, kitchen) laid out round a cloister.

Ballycotton

The fishing village of Ballycotton, about 15 miles/25km south-east of Youghal, has good beaches and splendid cliff scenery.

Cloyne

5 miles/8km north-west of Ballycotton is Cloyne, which in the 12th c. was the see of a bishop. Though dating from 1250, the cathedral has undergone much alteration and modernisation; it contains a number of fine monuments and, by the north door, crude carvings representing pagan symbols. On the opposite side of the street stands a 100ft/30m-high round tower, its original roof replaced by a battlemented top.

Killeagh

Killeagh is situated on the N25 7½ miles/12km west of Youghal. North of the village, extending for some miles up the valley of the River Dissour, lies the Glenbower State Forest which preserves something of the character of Ireland's ancient native woodland. South-east of Killeagh stands the round keep of Inchiquin Castle (13th c.).

Further west, also on the N25, is Castlemartyr where, in the grounds of a Carmelite priory, are the remains of Seneshal's Castle – a 15th c. outer ward with corner towers, a keep of the same period, and 17th c. domestic quarters.

About 6 miles/10km west again is Midleton, a thriving little market and industrial town with a handsome 18th c. Market House and a church designed by the Pain brothers (19th c.).

The principal feature however is the Jameson Heritage Centre, housed in old mill buildings dating from the end of the 18th c. From 1825 to 1975 the premises were in use as a whiskey distillery. Models, lectures and displays explain the process of whiskey production (open: May–Sept. daily 10am–4pm).

Practical Information

Accommodation

See Bed and Breakfast
See Camping and Caravanning
See Country Houses
See Holiday Homes
See Youth Hostels

Air Travel

In the Republic of Ireland there are four international airports (Dublin, Cork, Shannon and Knock). In Northern Ireland the only one is near Belfast (Aldergrove). Regional airports, including Carrickfinn, Kerry and Waterford in the Republic, as well as Belfast City and Londonderry/Derry in Northern Ireland have connections with UK airports as well as operating inland flights. Galway and Sligo in the Republic are used by small aircraft for inland flights and by pleasure aircaft.

Airports
see map p. 304

Aer Lingus flies several times daily from Dublin to Cork and Shannon. There are two services a day to Galway and Kerry (except one Saturday and three Sunday). There is also one service daily to Sligo.
  There are also services by smaller domestic airlines, including Aer Árann, which flies from airports at Caislean, Inverin, Connemare, near Galway to the Aran Islands. (Information: tel. 0 91/9 30 34.)

Internal air
services

Aer Lingus: 40/41 Upper O'Connell Street, Dublin 1, 13 St Stephen's Green, Dublin 2, 12 Upper George's Street, Dun Laoghaire, one number – tel. 01/8 44 47 77; 2 Academy Street, Cork, tel. 0 21/32 71 55; 136 O'Connell Street, Limerick, tel. 0 61/47 42 39; 46/48 Castle Street, Belfast 1, tel. 06 45/73 77 47.

Information

Banks

See Currency, also Opening Times

Bed and Breakfast

For those visitors who would prefer to be free in their choice of route and overnight accommodation the solution is "bed and breakfast" – comfortable rooms in private houses or farmhouses at reasonable prices with a substantial Irish breakfast. Some package tours also include vouchers for bed and breakfast accommodation. Information may be obtained from the Irish Tourist Board and Northern Irish Tourist Board, see Information.

Boating

Ireland has a great many inland waterways where the water is generally clean, and these rivers and lakes are ideal for boating. The best areas are

◀ *Powerscourt Town House Shopping Centre in Dublin*

Air Services in Ireland

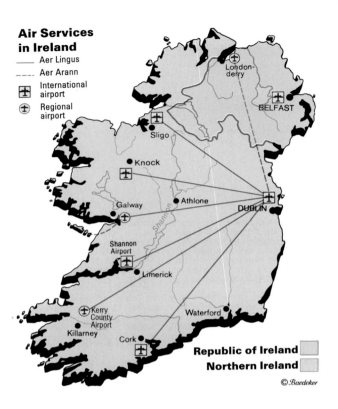

——— Aer Lingus
- - - - Aer Arann
⊕ International airport
⊕ Regional airport

Londonderry
BELFAST
Sligo
Knock
Galway
Athlone
DUBLIN
Shannon
Shannon Airport
Limerick
Kerry County Airport
Killarney
Waterford
Cork

Republic of Ireland
Northern Ireland

© Baedeker

the Shannon, the Shannon–Erne Waterway, Lough Erne in Northern Ireland and the Grand Canal which was once an important route between the east and the west of the Republic.

More than 500 cabin cruisers are available for hire at the numerous marinas; a visitor wishing to hire a boat must be at least 21 years old, but a permit to navigate a boat is not necessary, the only proviso being that at least two persons must be on board. Equipment provided depends on the size of the boat. No provisions are supplied and these must either be ordered in advance from the hirer or bought beforehand. Handling a boat demands considerable commonsense. On each cruiser will be found a copy of the so-called "Shannon Guide"; this contains detailed information about the various stretches of water as well as information concerning facilities for obtaining fuel, water and provisions. Lifebelts, one lifejacket per bed, a first-aid kit and signal rockets in case of emergency must be taken and weather reports heeded.

Basic rules are: always travel on the right, especially when negotiating narrow river passages, always keep black markers (buoys, markers or posts) on the port side – that is on the left.

Shannon

The Shannon has six locks; in general these are operational from April 1st until October 1st weekdays between 9am and 6 or 8pm, on Sundays from 9am until 6pm. At other times delays may be expected. No boat may move after dusk. The cruising season is generally from St Patrick's Day (March 17th) until the end of October because of high winter water levels.

304

Dublin Airport

The 39 mile/62.5km long Shannon–Erne Waterway connects Ireland's two main rivers. This canal was completely restored in 1994 and has six new mooring zones. There are 16 fully automatic locks to negotiate between Leitrim in Ireland and Belturbet in Northern Ireland. There are no passport controls at the border.

Shannon–Erne Waterway

The Grand Canal is an idyllic waterway considerably less used than the Shannon. Since this artificial waterway is never wider than 39ft/12m the large Shannon cabin cruisers cannot use it. Instead of these special "Narrow Boats" between 32ft/10m and 46ft/14m long are in service; of course the internal space is considerably restricted.

Grand Canal

Companies belonging to the Irish Boat Rental Association are listed in the publication "Come Cruise the Irish Waterways" available from the Irish Tourist Board.

Rental companies

Numerous tour operators offer organised holidays in cabin cruisers. Details can be found in "Ireland: A Romantic Blend" published by the Irish Tourist Board.

Package holidays

Business Hours

See Opening Times

Camping and Caravanning

In the Republic of Ireland there are some 120 camping and caravanning sites which are officially recognised by the Irish Tourist Board and classified according to their facilities with from one to four stars. Details can be

Republic of Ireland

found in the brochure "Caravan & Camping Guide" published by the Board. Overnight stays other than on camping sites is generally not permitted. Permission should be sought from the landowner or proprietor before camping on private property.

Northern Ireland — Camping and caravanning is also widespread in Northern Ireland. A list of sites can be found in the brochure "Camping and Caravan Parks" published by the Northern Ireland Tourist Board.

Car Rental

Rental conditions — Irish and international car rental firms are represented in the whole country, especially in the international air and sea ports and in the larger towns. The minimum age for renting a car depends on the firm and type of vehicle but is usually between 21 and 25, the maximum age is 70 or 75. Most firms require a driving licence to have been held for at least one year.

Frontier crossing — Crossing the frontier between the Irish Republic and Northern Ireland must be agreed with the rental firm beforehand; usually there is no objection.

In the Republic of Ireland

Avis

Dublin
1 Hanover Street East; tel. 01/6 05 75 00
Dublin Airport; tel. 01/6 05 75 00

Cork
Emmet Place; tel. 0 21/28 11 11, fax 0 21/28 11 22
Cork Airport; tel. 0 21/28 11 69, 28 11 66

Galway
Higgins Garage, Headford Road; tel. 0 91/6 88 86

Kerry
Tel. 0 64/3 66 55

Knock
Knock Airport; tel. 0 94/6 72 52

Shannon
Shannon Airport; tel. 0 61/47 10 94

Sligo
Sligo Airport; tel. 0 71/6 82 80

Budget

Dublin
151 Drumcondra Road, Ferry Port; tel. 01/8 37 96 11
Dublin Airport; tel. 01/8 44 59 19

Ballygar
Tel. 09 03/2 46 68, fax 09 03/2 47 59

Cork
c/o Tourist Information Center, Grand Parade, Ferry Port; tel. 0 21/27 47 55
Cork Airport; tel. 0 21/31 40 00

Galway
3 Foster Street, Eyre Square; tel. 0 91/56 63 76

Killarney
International Hotel Kenmare Place; tel. 0 64/3 43 41

Roscommon
Tel. 09 03/2 47 77

Shannon
Shannon Airport; tel. 0 61/47 13 61

Waterford
41 The Quay; tel. 0 51/2 15 50

Dublin   Europcar
Baggott Street Bridge; tel. 01/6 68 17 77
Dublin Airport; tel. 01/8 44 41 79

Galway
Headford Road; tel. 0 91/6 22 22

Killarney
Muckross Road; tel. 0 64/3 12 37

Strokestown
Westward Garage; tel. 0 78/3 30 29

Waterford
Sheridan Garage, Cork Road; tel. 0 51/7 31 44

Wexford
Redmond Place; tel. 0 53/2 21 22

Offices also in Rosslare (at the harbour) and at Cork and Shannon Airports.

Dublin   Hertz
Leeson Street Bridge; tel. 01/6 76 74 76
Dublin Airport; tel. 01/8 44 54 66

Cork
Cork Airport; tel. 0 21/96 58 49

Galway
Galway Airport; tel. 0 91/77 00 05

Killarney
28 Plunket Street; tel. 06 04/3 41 26

Shannon
Shannon Airport; tel. 0 61/47 17 39

Sligo
Sligo Airport; tel. 0 71/6 01 11

Waterford
Auto Boland, Newrath; tel. 0 51/7 87 37
Waterford Airport; tel. 0 51/7 89 90

Wexford
Ferrybank; tel. 0 53/2 35 11, fax 0 53/2 24 05

In Northern Ireland

Belfast   Avis
69 Great Victoria Street; tel. 012 32/24 04 04
Aldergrove Airport; tel. 018 49/42 23 33
Belfast City Airport; tel. 012 32/45 20 17

Climbing and Hill-walking

	Coleraine 10 Dunmore Street; tel. 012 65/4 36 54

Larne
Ferry Terminal; tel. 015 74/26 07 99

Lurgan
83 Belfast Road, Dollingstown; tel. 017 62/32 13 22

Budget   Belfast
96 Great Victoria Street; tel. 012 32/23 07 00
Aldergrove Airport; tel. 018 49/42 33 32
Belfast City Airport; tel. 012 32/45 11 11

Europcar   Belfast
Aldergrove Airport; tel. 018 49/42 34 44

Hertz   Aldergrove Airport; tel. 018 49/42 25 33
Belfast City Airport; tel. 012 32/73 24 51

Larne
Ferry Terminal; tel. 015 74/27 81 11

Climbing and Hill-walking

Ireland's inland hills and its coastal cliffs offer ample scope for hill-walking, climbing and rock-climbing.

Good walking country is to be found particularly in the hills of Wicklow, Kerry and Connemara. Guides and maps are readily available, and some long-distance trails such as the Wicklow and South Leinster Way are waymarked.

Before setting out on a long walk climbers should consult the weather forecast.

Further information can be obtained from the Mountaineering Council of Ireland, of which some 40 climbing clubs are members.

Mountaineering Council of Ireland (AFAS)
House of Sport, Long Mile Road, Dublin 12
Tel. 01/4 50 16 33, fax 01/4 50 28 05

Country Houses

Many old country houses and mansions in the Republic have been converted into hotels and restaurants. Establishments of this kind belong to the Irish Country Houses and Restaurants Association, which issues a brochure entitled "Ireland's Blue Book" listing them. They are also included in the list of hotels, restaurants and guest houses published by the Irish Tourist Board.

Some of these houses serve meals only to residents; others cater also for non-residents; and others again are restaurants but have no accommodation for residents.

The "Hidden Ireland"   "Hidden Ireland" is an association of exclusive privately-owned country houses with a limited number of beds. The choice ranges from castles by the sea to luxurious farmhouses. The accommodation list is available from the Irish Tourist Board or direct from The Hidden Ireland, PO Box 4414, Dublin 46, tel. 01/6 68 14 23, fax 01/6 68 65 78.

Crafts

In many parts of Ireland the old, traditional crafts are still practised; these include pottery, weaving, basket-making and glass-blowing. Residential courses are often available.

Information can be obtained from:
Crafts Council of Ireland
Powerscourt Town House Centre,
South William Street, Dublin 2
Tel. 01/6 79 73 68, fax 01/6 79 91 97

Cross Border Routes

Motorists travelling between the Republic of Ireland and Northern Ireland can cross the border at a large number of points, but the following are recommended. At entry or exit you may be required to produce identification and your luggage may be checked.

There are no customs controls between the Republic of Ireland and Northern Ireland.

Recommended route	Republic of Ireland	Northern Ireland
R238–A2	Moville	Londonderry
R238–A2	Buncrana	Londonderry
N13–A2	Letterkenny	Londonderry
R237–B193		
R236–A40	Raphoe	Londonderry
N14–A38	Letterkenny	Strabane
R235–C675a	Castelfin	Castlederg
R232–A35	Donegal	Enniskillen (via Pettigoe)
R230–A46	Ballyshannon	Enniskillen (via Belleek)
N16–A4	Manorhamilton	Enniskillen (via Belcoo)
R202–A32	Swanliba	Enniskillen
R183–A34	Clones	Newtownbutler
R187–B36	Monaghan	Rosslea
N2–A5	Monaghan	Aughnacloy
N12–A3	Monaghan	Armagh
R181–B32	Castleblayney	Keady
R177–A29	Dundalk	Newtownhamilton
R179–B30	Carrickmacross	Newry (via Crossmaglen)
N1–A1	Dundalk	Newry
R173–B79	Carlingford	Newry

Currency

Republic of Ireland

The unit of currency is the Irish pound or punt (IR£) of 100 pence (p). There are banknotes for £5, £10, £20, £50 and £100, and coins in denominations of 1p, 2p, 5p, 10p, 20p, 50p and £1.

Currency

Irish banknotes and coins

Currency
regulations

There are no restrictions on either the import or export of currency.

Northern Ireland

Currency

The unit of currency is the pound sterling (£) of 100 pence (p). There are banknotes for £5, £10, £20 and £50, and coins in denominations of 1p, 2p, 5p, 10p, 20p, 50p and £1.

Currency
regulations

There are no restrictions on either the import or export of currency.

Eurocheques

In the Irish Republic Eurocheques can be cashed up to a limit of IR£140, in Northern Ireland up to £100 sterling; the same limits apply to cash obtained from cash dispensers which often accept valid credit cards.

Credit cards

Banks, larger hotels, good-class restaurants, car-rental firms, petrol stations and a number of shops accept most international credit cards.

Customs Regulations

Allowances
between EU
countries

In theory there is now no limit to the amount of goods that can be taken from one EU country to another provided they have been purchased tax paid in an EU country, are for personal use and not intended for resale. However, customs authorities have issued guide lines to the maximum amounts considered reasonable for persons over 17 years of age. These are: 10 litres of spirits or strong liqueurs, 20 litres fortified wine (port, sherry, etc.) 45 litres of table wine (of which not more than 30 litres may be sparkling wine), 55 litres of beer, 800 cigarettes or 400 cigarillos or 200 cigars). There is no limit on perfume or toilet water.

For those coming from a country outside the EU or who have arrived from an EU country without having passed through custom control with all their baggage, the allowances for goods obtained anywhere outside the EU for persons over the age of 17 are: 1 litre spirits or 2 litres of fortified wine or 3 litres table wine, plus a further 2 litres table wine; 60cc perfume, 250cc toilet water; 200 cigarettes or 100 cigarillos or 50 cigars

Entry from
Non-EU countries

The allowances for goods purchased "duty-free" from airports, on aircraft and ferries are the same as for entry from non-EU countries above.
Duty-free allowances are scheduled to be phased out by January 1st 1999.

Duty-free
goods

Cycling Tours

With its delightfully varied countryside, the relatively short distances and comparatively little traffic Ireland is an ideal country to explore by bicycle.

Many airlines transport bicycles free as they are included in the weight limit of 20kg. There is a surcharge of 25% of the normal fare for taking your bicycle on the train, up to a maximum of 6IR£ (single). A charge is also made on the cross-country buses.

Transport of cycles

There are various cycle hire firms in most cities. As the bicycles are bought new at the beginning of each season they are usually in good condition. Cycles with 3 or 5 gears and also sports cycles with 12 or 18 gears and mountain bikes are all available for hire. In July and August it is advisable to book in advance.
The weekly hire charge (including insurance) depending on the type and the firm is usually between £25 and £50. A deposit is usually required. For an additional charge the cycles can be returned to any hire depot.

Cycle hire

Raleigh Ireland Ltd
Raleigh House, Kylemore Road, Dublin 10
Tel. 01/6 26 13 33, fax 01/6 26 17 70

The Bike Store Limited
58 Lower Gardiner Street, Dublin 1
tel. 01/8 72 59 31, fax 01/8 36 47 63

A list of tour operators who organise cycling holidys can be found in "Europe's Green Holidays" published by the Irish Tourist Board.

Organised
cycling
holidays

The brochure "Cycling Ireland" (obtainable from the Irish Tourist Board) gives information on 23 cycle tours (most between 200 and 300km).

Tours

City Cycle Tours (1A Temple Lane, Dublin 2, tel. 01/6 71 56 10) organises sightseeing tours of Dublin by bicycle.

Dublin
Sightseeing
by bike

Diplomatic Representation

In the Republic of Ireland

Embassy
31 Merrion Road
Dublin 4. Tel. 01/2 05 37 00

United Kingdom

Distances in Ireland

United States of America
Embassy
42 Elgin Road, Ballsbridge
Dublin. Tel. 01/68 87 77

Canada
Embassy
65 St Stephen's Green
Dublin 2. Tel. 01/78 19 88

Australia
Embassy
Fitzwilton House, Wilton Terrace
Dublin 2. Tel. 01/76 15 17

In Northern Ireland

United States of America
Consulate General
Queen's House, 14 Queen Street
Belfast, BT1 6EQ. Tel. 012 32/12 82 39

Canada
Jeanne Rankin, c/o Roscoff
Lesley House, Shaftesbury Square
Belfast 2. Tel. 012 32/33 15 32

Distances in Ireland

The distances between the larger towns in Ireland range, in general, between 60 and 200miles/100 and 320km. Thus from Cork to Limerick it is 65miles/105km, with an average journey time of two hours, while from Dublin to Killarney is 192miles/309km – average time 5½ hours. The greatest distances are, naturally, between the south-west (Killarney) and north-east (Londonderry) of the island.

The table on page 313 shows the distances, in miles and kilometres, between the principal towns in the Republic and Northern Ireland.

Electricity

In the Republic 230 volts (50 cycles); in Northern Ireland 240 volts (50 cycles). Power sockets are of the British type, although two-pin round sockets may still be found in some parts of the Republic; visitors from countries with a different type should take an adaptor.

Emergencies

Throughout Ireland
Police, fire, ambulance: dial 999 (free call)

Breakdown assistance (Automobile Association)
Republic of Ireland (Dublin): 01/2 83 35 55, fax 01/2 83 36 60 or (1800) 66 77 88 (toll-free)

Northern Ireland (Belfast): (0800) 88 77 66 (toll-free)

Events

Events which take place in particular locations will be found in the A–Z section of this guide. In addition, the following events are held at various places in the Republic and Northern Ireland:

Distances in kilometres and miles	Athlone	Belfast	Cork	Donegal	Dublin	Dundalk	Galway	Kilkenny	Killarney	Limerick	Londonderry	Portlaoise	Roscommon	Sligo	Waterford	Wexford
Athlone	•	227	219	183	126	145	93	126	232	121	209	74	32	117	174	188
Belfast	141	•	424	180	167	84	306	284	436	323	117	253	224	206	333	309
Cork	136	264	•	402	257	325	209	148	87	105	428	174	251	336	126	187
Donegal	114	112	250	•	222	158	204	309	407	296	69	257	151	66	357	372
Dublin	78	104	160	138	•	85	219	117	309	198	237	84	146	217	158	142
Dundalk	90	52	202	98	53	•	238	198	352	241	156	151	151	167	243	227
Galway	58	190	130	127	136	148	•	172	193	105	272	150	82	138	220	253
Kilkenny	78	177	92	192	73	123	107	•	198	113	335	51	158	245	48	80
Killarney	144	271	54	253	192	219	120	123	•	111	441	225	264	343	193	254
Limerick	75	201	65	184	123	150	65	70	69	•	328	114	151	232	129	190
Londonderry	130	73	266	43	147	97	169	208	274	204	•	282	211	135	383	378
Portlaoise	46	157	108	160	52	94	93	32	140	71	175	•	106	191	100	114
Roscommon	20	139	156	94	91	94	51	98	164	94	131	66	•	85	208	222
Sligo	73	128	209	41	135	104	86	152	213	144	84	119	53	•	293	307
Waterford	108	207	78	222	98	151	137	30	120	80	238	62	129	182	•	63
Wexford	117	192	116	231	88	141	157	50	158	118	235	71	138	191	39	•

Cavan: International Song Contest   February

Throughout Ireland: St Patrick's Day (17th), with parades in the larger towns   March
Dublin: Feis Ceoil (folk music)

Dublin: Grand Opera Season   April
Tralee: Pan Celtic Festival

Belfast: Lord Mayor's Show (parade with decorated floats and bands)   May
Cork: International Choral Festival
Dundalk: International Drama and Maytime Festival
Ennis: Fleadh Nua (festival of music and dance)

Many places: Music Festival in Great Irish Houses   June
Edenderry: Canal Angling Festival
Kildare: Irish Derby (Curragh Racecourse)
Letterkenny: Donegal International Car Rally
Listowel: Writers' Week
Rathdrum: Guinness International Cartoon Festival

Belfast and 18 other locations in Northern Ireland: Battle of the Boyne Commemorations (Orangemen's Day – July 12th)   July

Fishing

Belfast: International Rose Trials
Clonakilty: Festival of West Cork
Dublin: Dublin International Folk Festival
Galway: Race week (last week in July). Arts Festival
Glenariff: Feis na nGleann (Irish dancing and music)

August
Allihies (Co. Cork): Allihies Sports Day
Ballycastle: Oul' Lammas Fair (popular festival in Northern Ireland)
Clifden: Clifden Pony Show
Dublin: Antiques Fair; Dublin Horse Show
Killorglin: Puck Fair
Kilkenny: International Arts Week Festival (concerts, exhibitions, etc.)
Limerick: Agricultural Show
Stradbally (Co. Laois): Stradbally Steam Rally (for rail enthusiasts)
Tralee: Rose of Tralee International Festival
Wexford: Mussel Festival

In various places: All Ireland Fleadh (pronounced "flah") takes place in a different town each year on the last weekend in August; during this festival not only the official events are worth seeing but also musicians improvising in crowded pubs and hotels and in the streets.

September
Dublin: All Ireland Hurling Final. All Ireland Football Final
Clarenbridge: Clarenbridge Oyster Festival
Galway: Galway International Oyster Festival
Waterford: Waterford International Festival of Light Opera and musical events in the Royal Theatre

October
Ballinasloe: Horse Fair
Dublin: Dublin City Marathon
Cork: Guinness Cork Jazz Festival
Kinsale: International Gourmet Festival (cooking demonstrations, wine tasting, cookery competitions and various other events)
Wexford: Wexford Opera Festival

November
Belfast: Belfast Festival of Queen's (drama and music at Queen's University)

December
Dublin: Dublin Grand Opera Society Winter Season

Fishing

Thanks to its numerous loughs (lakes) and rivers and its extensive coastal waters Ireland is one of the great fishing countries, offering a great variety of angling opportunities – coarse fishing, game fishing (salmon and trout), and deep-sea fishing.

Coarse fishing
Since Irish fishermen are mainly interested in trout and salmon, no licence is required for coarse fishing, either in the Republic or Northern Ireland (only in the area of the north Shannon is a "Share Certificate" required). There is no closed season. Fishing with live bait is not permitted. Fishing with more than one rod at the same time is not allowed. The best fishing is in the Irish "Lake District" which encompasses parts of counties Westmeath, Longford, Cavan and Monaghan; the lake district of County Clare is beautiful. The principal species of coarse fish are pike, bream, tench, rudd, roach, perch, carp and eel. Transfer of roach from one water to another is not permitted. The killing of more than one pike exceeding 6lb/3kg per day is banned.

Game fishing
For game fishing a licence is required; it can be obtained from the office of the fishery board or district concerned and from certain tackle-dealers,

Common Irish freshwater fishes

Rudd
Scardinius erythrophthalmus

Perch
Perca fluviatilis

Brown trout
Salmo trutta

Bream
Abramis brama

Pike
Esox lucius

Salmon
Salmo salar

315

shops and hotels. Most game-fishing waters are privately owned (enquire locally). The commonest species of trout is the brown trout. The best-stocked waters are found in the west of Ireland (Lough Corrib, etc.). Note that the closed season is from the end of August to the beginning of January.

Deep-sea fishing

There are excellent deep-sea fishing grounds off the west and south coasts of Ireland, in the warmer water brought by the Gulf Stream. The fish which can be caught in these waters include shark, ray, cod species, pollack, hake, bass, grey mullet and sea-bream. Tackle can be hired locally. The season is from spring to autumn.

Information

Department of the Marine Fisheries Administration
Leeson Lane, IRL – Dublin 2
Tel. 01/78 54 44

Central Fisheries Board
Balnagowan House, Mobhi Boree
Glasnevin, IRL – Dublin 9
Tel. 01/37 92 06

Food and Drink

Meals

The principal meals of the day in Ireland are breakfast, lunch, tea and dinner. Formerly the traditional Irish evening meal was "high tea", between tea and dinner, but this is now rarely served.

Breakfast

The Irish breakfast is a substantial meal, consisting of corn flakes or porridge, bacon and eggs and sausages, toast, brown bread, butter and jam or marmalade, accompanied by coffee, tea, milk or fruit juice.

Lunch

Lunch is usually a modest meal, often consisting only of sandwiches and tea. Hotels and restaurants, however, offer a full menu; many have a reasonably priced tourist menu.

Afternoon tea

Afternoon tea may be accompanied by cakes, buns or biscuits.

Dinner

Dinner in a restaurant always consists of several courses, with a choice of dishes for each course. Sherry, whiskey or gin may be taken as an aperitif.

Courses

The first course may be smoked Irish salmon, seafood cocktail or egg mayonnaise. This may be followed by leg of lamb with mint sauce, roast rib of beef, gammon steak, grilled sirloin steak, fried fillet of plaice with tartare sauce, or poached or grilled salmon, accompanied perhaps by Brussels sprouts, creamed mushrooms, celery au gratin, carrots Vichy, creamed potatoes or baked potatoes. Among popular desserts are lemon meringue pie, hot apple pie with ice cream and fruit salad with fresh cream.

Irish stew

One celebrated Irish speciality is Irish stew, consisting of mutton, potatoes, onions and seasoning, stewed for several hours.

Drinks

Favourite Irish drinks are beer and whiskey. There is a wide range of beers, from light English ales to the dark Guinness stout with its foaming head, brewed in the celebrated Guinness Brewery in Dublin. A light lager is now also popular.

Irish whiskey

Irish whiskey is quite different from Scotch whisky or American whiskey, in spelling or taste. It is drunk neat or with water.

Irish coffee

Whiskey is also drunk in the form of "Irish coffee" or "Gaelic coffee". To make this warm and comforting drink first warm a glass by washing it out

Jameson Heritage Centre in Midleton: a former whiskey distillery – today a Visitor Centre

with hot water, then pour in a measure of Irish whiskey with a little sugar, fill up with hot black coffee, stir well and, after the mixture has settled, top it up with a good spoonful of fresh or whipped cream.

Irish whiskey is also the basis of a liqueur, "Irish Mist", which is said to have originated in the town of Tullamore, in a process involving the addition of heather honey.

Irish Mist

Among tourist attractions which have become popular in Ireland are the "medieval banquets" held in old castles such as Bunratty, Knappogue (near Quin, Co. Clare) and Dunguaire (Kinvara, Co. Galway). At these events substantial medieval-style meals, with wine, are served by young men and women in contemporary costume to the accompaniment of old ballads and music. (See also entry Medieval Banquets.)

Medieval banquets

Bookings for banquets in the above castles can be made at:
Shannon Castle Tours
Shannon International Free Airport (Co. Clare).
Tel. 0 61/6 17 88

See entry

Restaurants

See entry

Pubs

Getting to Ireland

The Republic of Ireland has four international airports: Dublin, Cork, Shannon and Knock; Northern Ireland has one, Belfast Aldergrove. The Republic's national airline is Aer Lingus, which flies both international and domestic services.

By air

Guinness is Good for You

The heart of Ireland beats in St James Gate in Dublin. Guinness is brewed here, the "wine of the country" as James Joyce in his "Ulysses" calls the almost black beer which everybody in Ireland drinks as medicine, basic food and to raise the spirits. In "Finnigans Wake" Joyce asks "Is Ireland sober, is Ireland stiff".

Soberly considered, Guinness is a dark top-fermented beer, but brewed in a special way. The brewers by the River Liffey make their wort not only from dried malt but also add a little grain, roasted over beech wood but not malted, in order to obtain the dark colour, skilfully mixing several worts and hops to create the unique dry taste. The result is an "Extra Stout", which in spite of its name has an alcohol content of only 4.3%, for nowadays the word "stout" describes the colour and not the strength of the beer. In Ireland draught Guinness tastes strongest and freshest, for here, thanks to the amount consumed, the beer is not pasteurised. Visitors who drink Guinness in their own country will not only be surprised at the taste but also at the colour of the beer in Dublin, much darker and with an almost white head. For every country in which it is sold, Guinness is brewed with a different recipe; the strongest is found in the tropics as "Foreign Extra Stout", the second strongest in Germany.

However, Guinness is not only beer and not only a national drink, it is also the successful history of a family and its product which has become a world-wide legend.

With an inherited £100 in his pocket Arthur Guinness from Celbridge in County Kildare came to Dublin in 1759. He bought a small brewery and produced the "entire beer", a mixture of several worts which at that time was to the taste of customers. Since this strong ale was popular especially with porters it soon acquired the nickname of "porter". When Arthur Guinness I bequeathed the brewery to his son, who, as was customary at the time, was also called Arthur, he already dominated the Irish beer scene and also the cereal market – there were indeed times when almost the entire Irish cereal production found its way into the Guinness brewery. Arthur Guinness II set about capturing English beer drinkers, and straight away even the British upper classes took to the proletarian brew. The continuing thirst for Guinness increased the fame and fortune of the family. Benjamin Lee, the third member of the dynasty, became Mayor of Dublin, distinguished himself as a patron and introduced – what was probably his most important achievement in an international context – bottled beer. His successor, Edward Cecil, who turned the brewery, now the largest in the world, into a limited company, was ennobled and henceforth the head of the Guinness dynasty bore the title of Earl of Iveagh. As if this was not enough, James Joyce brought him literary immortality: in "Ulysses" "Noble Buniveagh" is none other than Edward Cecil. He it was, too, who gave the Australian south-pole explorer Douglas Mawson a few bottles of Guinness; they were buried in permanent ice and when they were found 18 years later they were, of course, perfectly drinkable. Finally Edward Cecil had a tower built near his mansion on his Eleveden estate in Phoenix Park, and each morning he would climb the tower after drinking his early morning tea, in order to see whether the chimneys of his brewery at the far end of the city were still smoking. Even today every member of the Guinness family can climb the tower. After Edward Cecil, his successor Rupert was understandably less charismatic. Although he was a member of the House of Lords he only attended once, on a matter which concerned him personally. When in a debate a complaint was made that his advertisement hoardings with the slogan "Guinness is Good for You" desecrated the countryside, Lord Rupert rose and could only reply truthfully "But Guinness *is* good for you!"

This slogan, invented by Dorothy Sayers, is indicative of the great advertising success of Guinness from the 1920s to the 1940s. As well as well-known authors equally celebrated artists, such as Rex Whistler, H. M. Bateman and the caricaturist "Vicky" worked for Guinness and illustrated the advertising slogans. The most popular was a series featuring a zoo-keeper who was constantly being surprised by the antics of the animals in his charge but who recovered with the aid of a "porter" –"My Goodness, My Guinness". The campaign was so successful that in 1953 at the coronation of Queen Elizabeth II Guinness had advertising posters printed without any text or any reference to beer, only a sealion, a toucan and a kangaroo, for everybody knew to what the posters referred.

If he can say as you can
Guinness is good for you
How grand to be a Toucan
Just think what Toucan do

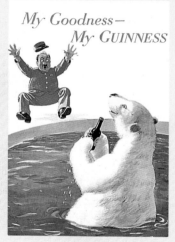

My Goodness—
My GUINNESS

In the course of time "porter" lost its popularity and since 1973 it has no longer been brewed either in Ireland or in England. The last barrel of porter was consumed in a Belfast pub in May 1973 with due obsequies. Guinness, however, had already replaced the stronger "stout" and was successfully filling the gap which "porter" had relinquished. Today, behind the name of Guinness lies not only the largest brewery in Europe but also a group of companies which is active in the automobile and food industries, which owns a fleet of pleasure boats on Ireland's rivers and lakes, and which, of course, publishes the "Guinness Book of Records". Members of the family have married into European aristocracy and for a long time have had no financial worries. For the ordinary Irish people, however, and especially for the men, the dream is to be appointed by Guinness to the post of "test drinker" – and there is, indeed, such a person.

There are regular services from many airports in Britain to the Irish international airports and (less frequently) to certain regional airports (see entry Air Travel); from the United States and Canada to Belfast direct but usually via London Heathrow, Gatwick or Glasgow (Scotland), and to Dublin, Shannon and Knock in the Republic; and from many European cities to Dublin and Belfast. Many visitors from Europe, America and other parts of the world will, of course, fly to a British airport and get a connecting service from there.

The flight from British airports takes an hour or less.

By sea

There are many passenger and car ferry services between British and Irish ports:

From Welsh ports to the Republic: Fishguard/Rosslare and Holyhead/Dun Laoghaire (Stena Line); Holyhead/Dublin and Pembroke/Rosslare (Irish Ferries); Swansea/Cork (Swanse/Cork ferries) – summer only. Crossing times vary from 1 hour 40 minutes to 10 hours depending on type of vessel and the route. From Liverpool to Belfast (Norse Irish Ferries). Crossing time 11 hours.

Liverpool and Holyhead can be reached by direct rail services from London Euston Station, Fishguard and Pembroke from London Paddington Station.

From the Isle of Man to Dublin and Belfast (Isle of Man Steam Packet Company) – summer only. The crossing to Dublin takes 2¾ hours and to Belfast 4½ hours.

From Scottish ports to Northern Ireland: Stranraer/Belfast (Stena Line and SeaCat) and Cairnryan/Larne (P & O). Crossing times vary from 1½ to 3 hours depending on type of vessel and the route.

There are also a number of services from French ports: Le Havre/Rosslare (Irish Ferries) 2–4 sailings weekly, Le Havre/Cork (Irish Ferries) weekly, Cherbourg/Rosslare (Irish Ferries) 1–3 sailings weekly, Roscoff/Cork (Brittany Ferries) spring to autumn 2 sailings weekly, St Malo/Cork (Brittany Ferries) in summer weekly.

Golf

Golf is a popular sport in Ireland, and on summer evenings and at weekends large numbers of people can be seen playing golf, often without any elaborate equipment. There are some 340 golf clubs, and numerous courses, about half of them 18-hole courses. Equipment can often be rented by visitors. There are golf courses near most holiday hotels.

Information

Golfing Union of Ireland
81 Eglington Road
Dublin 4
Tel. 01/2 69 41 11

Golf courses in the Republic of Ireland (Map see page 321)

1 Dublin and surroundings
Balbriggan Golf Club (18)
Ballinascorney Golf Club (18)
Beaverstown Golf Club (18)
Beechpark Golf Club (18)
Carrickmines Golf Club (9)
Castle Golf Club (18)
Clontarf Golf Club (18)
Deerpark Hotel Golf Club Courses (18, 9, 12)
Donabate Golf Club (18)
Dublin and County Golf Club (18)

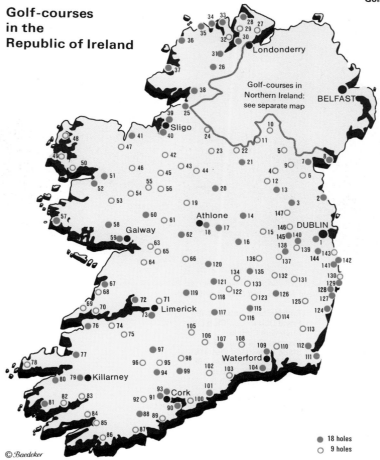

Golf-courses in the Republic of Ireland

Golf-courses in Northern Ireland: see separate map

● 18 holes
○ 9 holes

© Baedeker

Dun Laoghaire Golf Club (18)
Edmonstown Golf Club (18)
Elm Park Golf and Sports Club (18)
Forrest Little Golf Club (18)
Foxrock Golf Club (9)
Grange Golf Club (18)
Hermitage Golf Club (18)
Howth Golf Club (18)
Killiney Golf Club (9)
Lucan Golf Club (18)
Malahide Golf Club (18 and 9)
Milltown Golf Club (18)
Newlands Golf Club (18)
Portmarnock Golf Club (18 and 9)

Beautiful view from Howth Golf Club near Dublin

Rathfarnham Golf Club (9)
Royal Dublin Golf Club (18)
Rush Golf Club (9)
Skerries Golf Club (18)
Slade Valley Golf Club (18)
Stackstown Golf Club (18)
St Anne's Golf Club (9)
Stepaside Golf Club (9)
Sutton Golf Club (9)
The Island Golf Club (18)
Woodbrook Golf Club (18)

2 Layton and Battystown Gold Club (18)
   County Louth Golf Club (18)
3 Royal Tara Golf Club (18)
4 Cabra Castle Golf Club (9)
5 Castleblayney Golf Club (9)
6 Ardee Golf Club (18)
7 Dundalk Golf Club (18)
8 Greenore Golf Club (18)
9 Nuremore Golf Club (18)
10 Rossmore Golf Club (9)
11 Clones Golf Club (9)
12 Virginia Golf Club (9)
13 Headfort Golf Club (18)
14 Mullingar Golf Club (18)
15 Edenderry Golf Club (9)
16 Tullamore Golf Club (18)
17 Moate Golf Club (9)
18 Athlone Golf Club (18)

19 Roscommon Golf Club (9)
20 County Longford Golf Club (18)
21 County Cavan Golf Club (18)
22 Belturbet Golf Club (9)
23 Ballinamore Golf Club (9)
24 Blacklion Golf Club (9)
25 Bundoran Golf Club (18)
26 Ballybofey and Stranorlar
    Golf Club (18)
27 Greencastle Golf Club (9)
    Redcastle Golf Club (9)
28 Ballyliffen Golf Club (18)
29 Buncrana Municipal Golf Club (9)
30 North West Golf Club (18)
31 Letterkenny Golf Club (18)
32 Otway Golf Club (9)
33 Portsalon Golf Club (18)
34 Rosapenna Golf Club (18)
35 Dunfanaghy Golf Club (18)
36 Gweedore Golf Club (9)
    Cruit Island Golf Club (9)
37 Narin and Portnoo Golf Club (18)
38 Donegal Town Golf Club (18)
39 County Sligo Golf Club (18)
40 Strandhill Golf Club (18)
41 Enniscrone Golf Club (18)
42 Ballymote Golf Club (9)
43 Boyle Golf Club (9)
44 Carrick-on-Shannon Golf Club (9)
45 Ballaghaderreen Golf Club (9)
46 Swinford Golf Club (9)
47 Ballina Golf Club (9)
48 Belmullet Golf Club (9)
49 Achill Golf Club (9)
50 Mulrany Golf Club (9)
51 Castlebar Golf Club (18)
52 Westport Golf Club (18)
53 Ballinrobe Golf Club (9)
54 Claremorris Golf Club (9)
55 Ballyhaunis Golf Club (9)
56 Castlerea Golf Club (9)
57 Connemara Golf Club (18)
58 Oughterard Golf Club (18)
    Ashford Castle Golf Club (9)
59 Galway Golf Club (18)
60 Tuam Golf Club (18)
61 Mountbellew Golf Club (9)
62 Ballinasloe Golf Club (18)
63 Athenry Golf Club (18)
64 Gort Golf Club (9)
65 Lougrhea Golf Club (9)
66 Portumna Golf Club (18)
67 Lahinch Golf Club (18 and 18)
68 Spanish Point Golf Club (9)
69 Kilkee Golf Club (9)
70 Kilrush Golf Club (9)
71 Clonlara Golf Club (18)
72 Shannon Golf Club (18)
    Ennis Golf Club (18)
    Dromoland Castle Golf Course (18)
73 Limerick Golf Club (18)
    Castleroy Golf Club (18)

74 Foynes Golf Club (9)
Adare Manor Golf Club (9)
75 Newcastle West Golf Club (9)
76 Ballybunion Golf Club (18 and 18)
77 Tralee Golf Club (18)
78 Ceann Sibeal Golf Club (9)
79 Killarney Golf Club (18)
Mahony's Point Course (18)
80 Dooks Golf Club (18)
81 Waterville Golf Club (18)
82 Parknasilla Golf Club (9)
83 Kenmare Golf Club (9)
84 Glengarriff Golf Club (9)
85 Bantry Golf Club (9)
86 Skibbereen Golf Club (9)
87 Dunmore Golf Club (9)
88 Bandon Golf Club (18)
89 Kinsale Golf Club (9)
90 Monkstown Golf Club (18)
91 Muskerry Golf Club (18)
92 Macroom Golf Club (9)
93 Mahon Municipal Golf Club (9)
Douglas Golf Club (18)
Cork Golf Club (18)
Frankfield Golf Club (9)
94 Mallow Golf Club (18)
95 Doneraile Golf Club (9)
96 Kanturk Golf Club (9)
97 Charleville Golf Club (18)
98 Mitchelstown Golf Club (9)
99 Fermoy Golf Club (18)
100 East Cork Golf Club (18)
Rafeen Creek Golf Club (9)
Cobh Golf Club (9)
101 Youghal Golf Club (18)
102 Lismore Golf Club (9)
103 Dungarvan Golf Club (9)
104 Tramore Golf Club (18)
105 Tipperary Golf Club (9)
106 Cahir Park Golf Club (9)
Rockwell Golf Club (18)
107 Clonmel Golf Club (18)
108 Carrick-on-Suir Golf Club (9)
109 Waterford Golf Club (18)
110 New Ross Golf Club (9)
111 Rosslare Golf Club (18)
112 Wexford Golf Club (18)
113 Enniscorthy Golf Club (18)
114 Borris Golf Club (9)
115 Kilkenny Golf Club (18)
116 Callan Golf Club (9)
117 Thurles Golf Club (18)
118 Templemore Golf Club (9)
119 Nenagh Golf Club (18)
120 Birr Golf Club (18)
121 Roscrea Golf Club (9)
122 Rathdowney Golf Club (9)
123 Castlecomer Golf Club (9)
124 Courtown Golf Club (18)
125 Coolattin Golf Club (9)
126 Carlow Golf Club (18)
127 Arklow Golf Club (18)

Golf courses in Northern Ireland (Map below)

1 Belfast and surroundings
 Aberdelghy Golf Club (9)
 Ballyearl Golf Club (9)
 Balmoral Golf Club (18)
 Belfast Parks Golf Course (9)
 Belvoir Park Golf Club (18)
 Cliftonville Golf Club (9)
 Dunmurry Golf Club (18)
 Fortwilliam Golf Club (18)
 Gilnahirk Golf Club (9)
 Knock Golf Club (18)
 Knockbracken Golf Club (18)

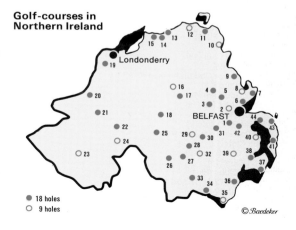

Golf-courses in Northern Ireland

Londonderry

BELFAST

● 18 holes
○ 9 holes

© *Baedeker*

Golf

Malone Golf Club (18 and 9)
Ormeau Golf Club (9)
Shandon Park Golf Club (18)
Holywood Golf Club (18)
Royal Belfast Golf Club (18)

2 Greenisland Golf Club (9)
3 Massereene Golf Club (18)
4 Ballymena Golf Club (18)
5 Ballyclare Golf Club (18)
6 Carrickfergus Golf Club (18)
7 Whitehead Golf Club (18)
   Bentra Golf Club (9)
8 Larne Golf Club (9)
9 Cairndhu Golf Club (18)
10 Cushendall Golf Club (9)
11 Ballycastle Golf Club (18)
12 Bushfoot Golf Club (9)
13 Royal Portrush Golf Club (18, 18 and 9)
14 Portstewart Golf Club (18, 18 and 9)
   Ballyreagh Golf Club (9)
   Benone Golf Club (9)
15 Castlerock Golf Club (18 and 9)
16 Kilrea Golf Club (9)
   Brown Trout Golf Club (9)
   Manor Golf Club (9)
17 Moyola Park Golf Club (18)
18 Killymoon Golf Club (18)
19 City of Derry Golf Club (18 and 9)
20 Strabane Golf Club (18)
21 Newtownstewart Golf Club (18)
22 Omagh Golf Club (18)
23 Enniskillen Golf Club (18)
24 Ashwoods Golf Centre (9)
   Castle Hume Golf Course (9)
   Fintona Golf Club (9)
25 Dungannon Golf Club (18)
26 County Armagh Golf Club (18)
27 Tandagree Golf Club (18)
28 Portadown Golf Club (18)
29 Craigovan Golf Centre (18)
30 Lurgan Golf Club (18)
31 Lisburn Golf Club (18)
32 Banbridge Golf Club (18)
33 Newry Golf Club (18)
34 Warrenpoint Golf Club (18)
35 Kilkeel Golf Club (9)
36 Royal County Down Golf Club (18 and 18)
37 Ardglass Golf Club (18)
38 Downpatrick Golf Club (18)
   Bright Castle Golf Club (18)
39 Spa Golf Club (18)
40 Mahee Island Golf Club (9)
41 Kirkistown Castle Golf Club (18)
42 Scrabo Golf Club (18)
43 Donaghadee Golf Club (18)
44 Bangor Golf Club (18)
   Carnalea Golf Club (18)
   Clandeboyie Golf Club (18 and 18)
   Helen's Bay Golf Club (9)
45 Ashfield Golf Club (18)

Help for the Disabled

The Irish Tourist Board publishes a free booklet, "Discover Ireland", which lists hotels and guest houses with facilities for the disabled and wheel-chair users. The Northern Ireland Tourist Board's booklet "Accessible Accommodation in Northern Ireland" lists places to stay and things to see.

See Insurance   Medical treatment

National Rehabilitation Board   Further
25 Clyde Road, Ballsbridge, Dublin 4. Tel. 01/6 68 41 81   information

Disability Action
2 Annadale Avenue, Belfast BT7 3JH.
Tel. 012 32/49 10 11, fax 012 32/49 16 27

See entry   Sport

Holiday Homes

Self-catering accommodation is available throughout Ireland in cottages, bungalows, chalets, apartments, country houses, even castles. The Irish Tourist Board and the Northern Ireland Tourist Board can provide lists of such holiday homes.

Horse-drawn Caravans

The brightly painted round-topped caravans of the tinkers who used to travel the roads of Ireland and who are thought to be descended from Irish

On the road in a horse-driven caravan

people driven into the west of the country by Cromwell's forces and unrelated to the gypsies of the Continent, are now rarely seen. However, in recent years modern replicas of these picturesque vehicles have become popular with holiday-makers as a means of enjoying a leisurely holiday on the quiet roads of the Republic.

These caravans, drawn by sturdy horses, are some 13ft/4m long by 8ft/2·5m wide and usually have room for not more than four people. They have seats and a table which can be converted into beds and a two-burner cooker working on bottled gas. Bedding and bed linen is provided. The caravan operators have fixed itineraries – there is a choice of routes – with suitable overnight stopping-places. The day's journey is unlikely to be more than 10 miles/16km or so. The horse must be given its nosebag of oats once a day and turned out to graze in the evening.

To rent a caravan, with most companies, it is necessary to put down a damage deposit of IR£200, refundable when the caravan is returned in good condition. Rental charges range from IR£300 to IR£550 a week, varying according to season.

Hotels and Guest Houses

Hotels in the Republic of Ireland

In the Republic of Ireland there is a wide range of hotels, from the castle hotel through modern luxury and medium class hotels to simple accommodation. Popular with foreign guests are the many beautifully situated country house hotels (see Country Houses). In addition to the hotels, guest houses are also available and pride themselves on personal service. Also numerous private houses (see Bed and Breakfast) can generally be recommended, but are not listed in this guide.

Categories

Hotels are officially classified in five categories: luxury hotels have five stars, medium class have two or three and basic hotels have one star. Guest houses are classified into four categories (one to four stars).

Bookings and
Reservations

Visitors are recommended, especially in the main season, to reserve accommodation in advance through a travel agent or direct at a hotel. Bookings in advance can also be made by personal callers to Tourist Information Offices (see Information) for which a small charge will be made. Credit card bookings can be made by telephone: 01/6 05 77 77 (00 353/1/6 05 77 77 from outside the Republic) or by fax: 01/6 05 77 87 (00 353/1/6 05 77 87 from outside the Republic), or for accommodation in the whole of Ireland freephone: 0800 31 71 53, stating your credit card number.

Prices

Prices for hotels and guest houses in Dublin and well-known holiday centres are considerably higher than in the more remote parts of the country. There can also be marked differences in costs depending on the season, and therefore only a general indication can be given of probable prices. In the table below the prices are per person for one night's accommodation with breakfast in a double or single room.

Category	Double room	Single room
H★★★★★	60–110IR£	70–130IR£
H★★★★	40– 80IR£	50– 70IR£
H★★★	25– 50IR£	30– 50IR£
H★★	17– 35IR£	25– 40IR£
H★	15– 30IR£	20– 30IR£

G★★★★	20– 40IR£	25– 50IR£
G★★★	15– 30IR£	20– 30IR£
G★★	12– 20IR£	15– 25IR£
G★	10– 18IR£	15– 20IR£

In the following list of hotels and guest houses the official category and number of rooms is given together with the address, telephone and fax numbers. Some hotels and guest houses are denoted only by the letters "H" and "G" as they have still to be categorised. **Note**

H★★★★★Adare Manor, tel. 0 61/39 65 66, fax 39 61 24, 64r. **Adare**
This neo-Gothic castle hotel combines luxury with good taste.
H★★★★ Dunraven Arms, tel. 0 61/39 66 33, fax 39 65 41, 66r.
The rooms of this hotel, which dates from 1792, contain antique furniture; there is an attractive garden and stables.

G★★★Bay View House, tel. and fax 0 75/4 11 45, 6r. **Ardara**
Situated on the outskirts of town overlooking the sea.

G★★★★Annestown House, tel. 0 51/39 61 60, 5r. **Annestown**
Period house overlooking a sandy bay with private access to the beach.

H★★★Hodson Bay, Roscommon Road, tel. 09 02/9 24 44, fax 9 26 88, 97r. **Athlone**
This recently newly furnished house on Lough Ree has many sports facilities (golf course, tennis, etc.) and is suitable as a conference centre.
H★★★Prince of Wales, tel. 09 02/7 26 26, fax 7 56 58, 73r.
Comfortable and modern town-centre hotel.
H★★Royal Hoey, Mardyke Street, tel. 09 02/7 29 24, fax 7 51 94, 38r.
Modern town hotel with a good restaurant.

F★★Ballindrum, tel. and fax 05 07/2 62 94, 5r. **Athy**
Delicious home baked bread is served by the hospitable owners at this friendly farmhouse.

Adare Manor Hotel

Hotels and Guest Houses

Avoca
G★★Ashdene, tel. 04 02/3 53 27, 5r.
Ideally situated for touring Co. Wicklow.

Ballina
H★★★Downhill, tel. 0 96/2 10 33, fax 2 13 38, 50r.
This comfortable house, situated ½ mile/1km out of town offers the guest every type of sport: fishing, golf, swimming pool, squash, sauna, tennis.

Ballinadee
G★★★★Glebe House, tel. 0 21/77 82 94, fax 77 84 56, 4r.
This lovely old house has beautifully furnished rooms and attractive gardens.

Ballinasloe
H★★★Hayden's, Dunlo Street, tel. 09 05/4 23 47, fax 4 28 95, 48r.
Guests can enjoy the stylish atmosphere in this hotel which has a recognised restaurant and a coffee shop for snacks.

Ballybofey
H★★★Kee's, tel. 0 74/3 10 18, fax 3 19 17, 36r.
Once a coaching inn, this comfortable hotel now has an attractive leisure centre.

Ballyconnell
H★★★★Slieve Russell, tel. 0 49/2 64 44, fax 2 64 74, 151r.
The name Slieve Russell stands for luxury and a pleasant atmosphere. A popular place for golfers to stay (18- and 9-hole course)

Ballycotton
H★★★Bayview Hotel, tel. 0 21/64 67 46, fax 64 60 75, 35 r.
A grandiose location with far-reaching views over Ballycotton Bay.

Ballyhack
G★★★★Marsh Mere Lodge, tel. 0 51/38 91 86, 5r.
Near to the Ballyhack ferry and Waterford Harbour.

Ballyheigue
H★★★The White Sands, tel. 0 66/3 31 02, fax 3 33 57, 75r.
Excellent base for exploring the Dingle peninsula.

Ballylickey
H★★★Sea View, tel. 0 27/5 00 73, fax 5 15 55, 17r.
Surrounded by an extensive park this comfortably appointed hotel is in the luxury price bracket.

Ballymacarbry
G★★★Clonanav Farm, Nore Valley, tel. and fax 0 52/3 61 41, 10r.
Salmon and trout fishing are available at this family-run hotel.

Ballynahinch
H★★★★Ballynahinch Castle, Recess, tel. 0 95/3 10 06, fax 3 10 85, 28r.
This 18th c. castle stands on the Owenmore River.

Ballyvaughan
H★★★Gregans Castle, tel. 0 65/7 70 05, fax 7 71 11, 22r.
This luxury hotel is famous for its splendid country gardens and view over Galway Bay.
G★★★★Rusheen Lodge, tel. 0 65/7 70 92, fax 7 71 52, 6r.
Elegantly equipped rooms at moderate prices.

Ballyvourney
G★★★The Mills Inn (on N22), tel. 0 26/4 52 37, fax 4 54 54, 9r.
Surrounded by extensive grounds which include a museum and a shop, this pleasant inn dates back to the 18th century.

Baltimore
H★★★Baltimore Harbour, tel. 0 28/2 03 61, fax 2 04 66, 30r.
A well equipped new hotel overlooking the harbour, with a relaxing lounge and garden room.

Banteer
G★★★★Clonmeen Lodge, tel. 0 29/5 62 38,fax 5 62 94, 6r.
Ideally situated beside the River Blackwater for fishing and other country pursuits.

Bantry
H★★★Westlodge, tel. 0 27/5 03 60, fax 5 04 38, 90r.
Popular with families.
G★★★The Mill, Glengarriff Road, tel. 0 27/5 02 78, 6r.
A laundry service and bicycle hire are available at this pleasant guest house.

H★★County Arms, tel. 05 09/2 07 91, fax 22 34, 18r.
   Built in 1810, this attractive house has retained many of its Georgian
   features. Fresh fruit and vegetables served in the restaurant are grown in
   the hotel's own garden.
H★★★Dooly's, Emmet Square, tel. 05 09/2 00 32, fax 2 13 32, 18r.
   Modern, pleasantly comfortable hotel.

Birr

H★★★Blarney Park, tel. 0 21/38 52 81, fax 38 15 06, 76r.
   This hotel has an attractive bathing area with a pool and sauna; tennis
   courts.
H★★Blarney Castle, tel. 0 21/38 51 16, fax 38 55 42, 10r.
   Medium-range prices with a restaurant and bar.
H★★★Christy's, tel. 0 21/38 50 11, 49r.
   This hotel forms part of the Blarney Woollen Mills complex and is well
   hidden behind the original 150-year-old façade.
G★★★Sylvanmanor, tel. 0 21/38 19 77, 4r.
   A reasonably priced guest house with well equipped bedrooms.

Blarney

H★★★Downshire House, tel. 0 45/86 51 99, fax 86 53 35, 14r.
   Excellent food and a friendly atmosphere can be found in this small hotel.
   Tennis and lawn croquet are available.

Blessington

H★★Royal, tel. and fax 0 79/6 20 16, 16r.
   A friendly family-run hotel located in the town centre. Coffee shop.
H Forest Park, Dublin Road, tel. 0 79/6 22 29, fax 6 31 13, 12r.
   Pleasant atmosphere, attractive garden.

Boyle

H★★★Royal, Main Street, tel. 01/2 86 29 35, fax 2 86 73 73, 74r.
   Swimming pool, whirlpool, sauna and solarium. Suitable for
   conferences.

Bray

H★★★Fitzpatrick Bunratty Shamrock, tel. 0 61/36 11 77, fax 47 12 52, 115r.
   One of the adantages of this hotel is its favourable location: only
   5 miles/8km from Shannon airport and 9 miles/15km from Limerick.

Bunratty

H★★★Derrynane, tel. 0 66/7 51 36, fax 7 51 60, 75r.
   Well placed on the Ring of Kerry, this hotel offers modern accommodation and amenities.

Caherdaniel

G★★★★Barnagh Bridge Country House, tel. 0 66/3 01 45, fax 3 02 99, 5r.
   An attractive house with sea views.

Camp

G★★★★Richmond House, tel. 0 58/5 42 78, fax 5 49 88, 10r.
   Surrounded by rivers, mountains and woodlands this beautiful Georgian
   house makes a perfect base for walking and angling enthusiasts. There
   are several golf courses and pretty beaches nearby.

Cappoquin

G★★★★Barrowville Town House, Kilkenny Road, tel. 05 03/4 33 24,
fax 4 19 53, 7r.
   Georgian house situated on the outskirts of town.
G★★★Greenlane House, tel. 05 03/4 26 70, 7r.
   Well equipped bedrooms in this purpose built hotel.

Carlow

H★★★★Nuremore, tel. 0 42/6 14 38, fax 6 18 53, 69r.
   Excellent leisure facilities and good food await guests at this popular
   hotel.

Carrickmacross

H★★★★Cashel House, tel. 0 95/3 10 01, fax 3 10 77, 32r.
   The parks surrounding Cashel House have been awarded several official
   prizes. It also has tennis courts, its own riding stables and a small private
   beach.
H★★★★Cashel Palace Hotel, tel. 0 62/6 14 11, fax 6 15 21, 13r.
   In the 18th c. Cashel Palace was the bishop's residence. In the park are

Cashel

Cosy Irish comfort in Cashel House Hotel, Cashel Bay

trees which were planted on the coronation of Queen Anne. Such tradition has its price!

H★★★Zeatland House, tel. 0 95/3 11 11, fax 3 11 17, 19r.
Many of the rooms in this lovely country house have garden or sea views. A wide range of leisure facilities are available including fishing and shooting.

Castlebar

H★★★Breaffy House, tel. 0 94/2 20 33, fax 2 22 76, 62r.
This mansion house set in a large park belongs to the Best Western group of hotels.

H★★Welcome Inn, tel. 0 94/2 22 88, fax 2 17 66, 43r.
The Tudor façade hides a modern town-centre hotel complete with occasional disco.

Castleconnell

H★★★Castle Oaks House, tel. 0 61/37 76 66, fax 37 77 17, 20r.
A very attractive Georgian house surrounded by beautiful grounds and offering many leisure facilities including golf, pony trekking and water sports.

Cavan

H★★★Kilmore, tel. 0 49/3 22 88, fax 3 24 58, 39r.
A comfortable hotel with a good restaurant.

Clifden

H★★★Abbeyglen Castle, tel. 0 95/2 12 01, fax 2 17 97, 34r.
This imposing castle stands in the centre of a romantic park with waterfalls and a panoramic view 0 Clifden.

H★★★Ardagh, Ballyconneely Rd., tel. 0 95/2 13 84, fax 2 13 14, 21r.
A quiet hotel 1 mile/2km outside of Clifden with a good restaurant (lobster and seafood specialities).

H★★★Rock Glen, tel. 0 95/2 10 35, fax 2 17 37, 29r.
This converted shooting lodge offers guests a relaxing stay with traditional hospitality and excellent cuisine.

H★★★Clonmel Arms, Sarsfield Road, tel. 0 52/2 12 33, fax 2 15 26, 31r.   **Clonmel**
Popular with businessmen; restaurant and bar.
H★★★Minella, Coleville Road, tel. 0 52/2 23 88, fax 2 43 81, 70r.
An elegantly appointed mansion house on the River Suir.

H★★★★Fitzpatrick Silver Springs, tel. 0 21/50 75 33, fax 50 76 41, 109r.   **Cork**
Comfortable hotel overlooking the River Lee.
H★★★★Jurys, Western Road, tel. 0 21/27 66 22, fax 27 44 77, 185r.
Situated in the middle of a park, it is only a five minute walk to the centre
of Cork. There are two restaurants to choose from.
H★★★Arbutus Lodge, tel. 0 21/50 12 37, fax 50 28 93, 16r.
This period town house has well equipped bedrooms and a friendly
atmosphere.
H★★★Jurys Inn, tel. 0 21/27 64 44, fax 27 61 44, 133r.
On the east side of the city by the River Lee; purpose built family rooms
are popular.
H★★★Metropole, tel. 0 21/50 81 22, fax 50 64 50, 108r.
A feature of this hotel is the indoor swimming pool which is overlooked
by the Waterside café. A crèche is also available.
H★★Vienna Woods, tel. 0 21/82 11 46, fax 82 11 20, 20r.
An 18th-century house overlooking Cork Harbour.

H★★Courtmacsherry, tel. 0 23/4 61 98, fax 4 61 37, 13r.   **Courtmacsherry**
This former residence of the Earl of Shannon overlooks Courtmacsherry
Bay. Cottages to let.

H★★Courtown, tel. 0 55/2 52 10, fax 2 53 04, 21r.   **Courtown Harbour**
A family-run seaside hotel.

H★★★Skellig, tel. 0 66/5 11 44, 115r.   **Dingle**
Attractively situated near Dingle harbour this hotel has a swimming pool,
playground, tennis courts, sauna, etc.

H★★★Abbey, tel. 0 73/2 10 14, fax 2 10 14, 49r.   **Donegal**
Situated in the centre of Donegal town.
H★★★Harvey's Point Country, Lough Estate, tel. 0 73/2 22 08, fax 2 23 52,
20r.
About 3 miles/5km outside Donegal this hotel is set in beautiful scenery
on the Lough Estate. Excellent French-Swiss cuisine.

H★★★Aran View House, Coast Road, tel. 0 65/7 40 61, fax 7 45 40, 19r.   **Doolin**
This Georgian house is magnificently located with views of the Aran
Islands, the Burren and the Cliffs of Moher.

H★★★Boyne Valley Hotel & Country Club, tel. 0 41/3 77 37, fax 3 91 88, 37r.   **Drogheda**
Country house with lovely gardens.
H★★★The Westcourt, Main Street, tel. 0 41/3 09 65, fax 3 09 70, 27r.
An all-day food service is available at this hotel which also has a shared
indoor car park, free to guests.

H★★★★★Berkeley Court, Lansdowne Road, tel. 01/6 60 17 11, fax   **Dublin**
6 60 23 65, 189r.
A luxury hotel in the exclusive diplomatic quarter of Dublin.
H★★★★★Conrad International, Earlsfort Terrace, tel. 01/6 76 55 55, fax
6 76 54 24, 191r.
This four-star hotel offers the standard of comfort appropriate to this
price category.
H★★★★★Burlington, Upper Leeson Street, tel. 01/6 60 52 22, fax
6 60 31 72, 450r.
Ireland's largest hotel has a cosmopolitan atmosphere.

Hotels and Guest Houses

Dublin: Shelbourne Hotel . . .

. . . entrance to Anglesea Guest House

H★★★★Gresham, tel. 01/8 74 68 81, fax 8 78 71 75, 200r.
Guests are well looked after from the moment they arrive; the hotel concierge parks the car and bags are carried by dilligent hotel porters leaving guests free to enjoy the comfortable foyer lounge or the Aberdeen restaurant.

H★★★★Jurys, Pembroke Road, tel. 01/6 60 50 00, fax 6 60 55 40, 292r.
South of the city centre, this hotel has a range of accommodation including a choice of luxury suites. There are two restaurants and a heated indoor pool.

H★★★★Shelbourne, St Stephen's Green, tel. 01/6 67 6 64 71, fax 6 61 60 06, 164r.
One of the noblest addresses in Ireland. Rooms are furnished with antiques.

H★★★Abberley Court, Belgrad Road, tel. 01/4 59 60 00, fax 4 62 10 00, 40r.
Food is served all day in the comfortable lounge of this well furnished hotel.

H★★★Adams Trinity, tel. 01/6 70 71 00, fax 6 70 71 01, 28r.
Set in the middle of Dublin's entertainment and cultural district.

H★★★Bewleys, Newlands Cross, tel. 01/4 64 01 40, fax 4 64 09 00, 126r.
A brand new hotel with spacious public areas and well equipped bedrooms.

H★★★Doyle Skylon, Drumcondra Road, tel. 01/8 37 91 21, fax 8 37 27 78, 92r.
Conveniently situated for access to the airport and the city cente.

H★★★Doyle Tara Tower, Merrion Road, tel. 01/2 69 46 66, fax 2 69 10 27, 113r.
Purposely designed rooms

H★★★Hibernian, Eastmorland Place, tel. 01/6 68 76 66, fax 6 60 26 55, 41r.
This town-centre hotel features impressive interior decor and delicious food.

H★★★Jurys Christchurch Inn, Christchurch Place, tel. 01/4 54 00 00, fax 4 54 00 12, 183r.
Prices in accordance with standard.

H★★★Longfields, tel. 01/6 76 13 67, fax 6 76 15 42, 26r.
Small, friendly hotel serving good food.

H★★★Stephens Hall, The Earlsfort Centre, tel. 01/6 61 05 85, fax 6 61 06 06, 37r.
A famous Dublin landmark, the hotel offers a wide range of accommodation from single and double suites to penthouses and studios. Underground parking is available.

H★★★Temple Bar, Temple Bar, tel. 01/6 77 33 33, fax 6 77 30 88, 108r.
Centrally situated hotel of upper middle class category.

H★★Harding, Copper Alley, tel. 01/6 79 65 00, fax 6 79 65 04, 53r.
Situated opposite the 12th-century Christchurch Cathedral in the Temple Bar area, near to bars, restaurants and shops.

G★★★★Anglesea 63 Anglesea Road, tel. 01/6 68 38 77, fax 6 68 34 61, 7r.

G★★★Egan's, 7/9 Iona Park, tel. and fax 01/8 30 36 11, 25r
Pleasing antique decor and friendly service.

G★★Othello House, 74 Lower Gardiner Street, tel. 01/8 74 04 42, fax 8 74 34 60, 12r.
Moderately priced hotel in a central location.

G★★St Andrew's, 1/3 Lambay Rd., tel. 01/8 37 46 84, fax 8 57 04 46, 13r.

H★★★★Forte Posthouse Dublin, Airport, tel. 01/8 44 42 11, fax 8 44 60 02, 188r. **Dublin Airport**
This hotel has two swimming pools, sauna and gym.

H★★★Ballymascanlon House, tel. 0 42/7 11 24, fax 7 15 98, 55r. **Dundalk**
Extensive grounds and an 18-hole golf course are particular features of this comfortable hotel.

H★★★Fairways Hotel & Leisure Centre, Dublin Road, tel. 0 42/2 15 00, fax 2 15 11, 48r.

H★★Imperial, Park Street, tel. 0 42/3 22 41, fax 3 79 09, 47r.

H★★★Lawlors, tel. 0 58/4 11 22, fax 4 10 00, 89r. **Dungarvan**
A family-run hotel.

H★★★Royal Marine, tel. 01/2 80 19 11, fax 2 80 10 89, 104r. **Dun Laoghaire**
This comfortably furnished house stands in the middle of magnificent parklands.

H★★★Auburn Lodge, Galway Road, tel. 0 65/2 12 47, fax 2 12 02, 100r. **Ennis**
The rooms are tastefully decorated in keeping with a country mansion.

H★★★Old Ground, O'Connell Street, tel. 0 65/2 12 47, fax 2 12 01, 100r.
Tradition and modern comfort go hand in hand in this ivy-covered hotel.

H★★★Temple Gate, The Square, tel. 0 65/2 33 00, fax 2 33 22, 34r.
A new hotel in the centre of town with lively public areas such as the Bistro and Macauleys Pub.

H★★Queens, Abbey Street, tel. 0 65/2 89 63, fax 2 86 28, 52r.

G★★Magowna House, Inch, tel. 0 65/3 90 09, 10r.
Country house (4 miles/6km outside Ennis) with views of the Shannon.

H★Murphy-Floods, tel. and fax 0 54/3 34 13, 21r. **Enniscorthy**
Hotel with restaurant near the market.

H★★Enniscree Lodge Hotel and Restaurant, Glencree Valley, tel. 01/2 86 35 42, fax 2 86 60 37, 10r. **Enniskerry**
Impressive location; in summer it is possible to eat on the terrace.

H★★★★Glenlo Abbey, Bushy Park, tel. 0 91/52 66 66, fax 52 78 00, 42r. **Galway**
This classy hotel with marble baths and many other luxurious facilities stands in the middle of beautiful private gardens.

Hotels and Guest Houses

Skeffington Arms Hotel in Galway

H★★★★Ardilaun House, Taylors Hill, tel. 0 91/52 14 33, fax 52 15 46, 90r.
This beautiful house stands in lovely grounds halfway between Galway and Salthill.
H★★★Galway Ryan, Dublin Road, tel. 0 91/75 31 81, fax 75 31 87, 96r.
A recently refurbished modern hotel.
H★★★Jurys Galway Inn, Quat Street, tel. 0 91/56 64 44, fax 56 84 15, 128r.
A very popular hotel which offers a "one price" room rate. Located opposite the Spanish Arch in the city centre.
H★★★Victoria, Victoria Place, tel. 0 91/56 74 33, fax 56 58 80, 57r.
Centrally located hotel with friendly staff.
H★★Lochlurgain, 22 Monksfield, tel. 0 91/52 95 95, fax 2 23 99, 13r.

Glendalough

H★★★Glendalough, tel. 04 04/4 51 35, fax 4 51 42, 44r.
Built at the beginning of the 19th c. this hotel has been completely modernised.

Gorey

H★★★★Marlfield House, tel. 0 55/2 11 24, fax 2 15 72, 19r.
Mansion house surrounded by gardens and woodland.
G★★★★Glenbower House, The Avenue, tel. 0 55/2 05 14, 5r.

Kanturk

G★★★★★Assolas Country House, tel. 0 29/5 00 15, fax 5 07 95, 6r.
A beautiful 17th-century manor house surrounded by magnificent rolling countryside on the banks of a tributary of the River Blackwater.

Kells (Meath)

H★★Headfort Arms, tel. 0 46/4 00 63, fax 4 05 87, 18r.
Medium range hotel correspondingly furnished.

Kenmare

H★★★★Park, tel. 0 64/4 12 00, fax 4 14 02, 49r.
Top class hotel surrounded by superb parkland.
H★★★Kenmare Bay, tel. 0 64/4 13 00, fax 4 15 41, 136r.
Purpose-built hotel, many rooms have views of the mountain scenery.

G★★★★Sallyport House, Glengariff Road, tel. 0 64/4 20 66, fax 4 17 52, 5r.
Set in its own grounds, this superbly refurbished house has well
appointed bedrooms and relaxing public areas.
G★★★Foleys Shamrock, Henry Street, tel. 0 64/4 13 61, fax 4 17 99, 10r.
Guest house in the centre of Kenmare with a restaurant.

H★★Halpin's, 2 Erin Street, tel. 0 65/5 60 32, fax 5 63 17, 12r.   **Kilkee**
Centrally situated, privately run hotel.

H★★★Hotel Kilkenny, College Road, tel. 0 56/6 20 00, fax 6 59 84, 80r.   **Kilkenny**
Stylish house in a lovely garden.
H★★★Newpark, Castlecomer Road, tel. 0 56/2 21 22, fax 6 11 11, 84r.
This hotel has a swimming pool, sauna, steam bath and fitness room.
H★★Club House, Patrick Street, tel. and fax 0 56/2 19 94, 32r.
This city-centre hotel is 200 years old and features an elegant Georgian
dining room.

H★★★★Ambassador, tel. 0 45/87 70 64, fax 87 75 15, 36r.   **Kill**
Roadside hotel convenient for Curragh Race Course and Mondello racing
circuit.

H★★★★★Aghadoe Heights, tel. 0 64/3 17 66, fax 3 13 45, 57r.   **Killarney**
Luxury hotel with corresponding level of comfort.
H★★★★Killarney Park, tel. 0 64/3 55 55, fax 3 52 66, 44r.
Warmth from a blazing log fire in the entrance lobby greets weary
travellers at this traditional hotel.
H★★★★Muckross, Muckross Village, tel. 0 64/3 19 38, fax 3 19 65, 27r.
Lovely 18th-century hotel set in the Killarney National Park.
H★★★Cahernane, Muckross Road, tel. 0 64/3 18 95, fax 3 43 40, 14r.
A grand country house in a stunning location between the mountains
and the lake. Roaring log fires and period furnishings create an
atmosphere of elegance and comfort.
H★★★Castleross, tel. 0 64/3 11 44, fax 3 10 31, 110r.
Special facilities on the local champion golf courses are offered by this
welcoming hotel which overlooks Lough Leane.
H★★★Gleneagle, Muckross Road, tel. and fax 0 64/3 18 70, 200r.
Not a particularly attractive building from the exterior but has many
entertainment and sports facilities.
H★★★Lake, tel. 0 64/3 10 35, fax 3 19 02, 72r.
Set in picturesque countryside with beautiful views and woodland walks.
H★★★Royal, College Street, tel. 0 64/3 18 53, fax 3 40 01, 49r.
Small, friendly hotel situated in the centre of town.
H★★★White Gates, Muckross Road, tel. 0 64/3 11 64, fax 3 48 50, 27r.
Stylish decor is a feature of this newly opened hotel with particularly
attractive lounge and bar areas.
G★★★Gleann Fia, Deerpark, tel. 0 64/3 50 35, fax 3 50 00, 8r.
Surrounded by woodland this attractive guest house is just 1 mile/2km
from the centre of Killarney.

H★★★Court, tel. 01/2 85 16 22, fax 2 85 20 85, 86r.   **Killiney**
Victorian mansion with a breathtaking view of the Bay.
H★★★Fitzpatrick Castle, tel. 0 01/2 84 07 00, fax 2 85 02 07, 90r.
Castle hotel, 9 miles/15km from Dublin.

H★★★Trident, Worlds End, tel. 0 21/77 23 01, ax 77 41 73, 58r.   **Kinsale**
This harbourside hotel has its own marina with boats available for hire.
G★★★★The Old Bank House, 11 Pearse Street, tel. 0 21/77 40 75, fax
77 42 96, 9r.
This Georgian building used to house a bank.

H★★★Aberdeen Arms, tel. 0 65/8 11 00, fax 8 12 28, 55r.   **Lahinch**
Patronised by golfers from the famous Lahinch Links Course, this is a
popular and well appointed hotel.

Hotels and Guest Houses

Limerick

H★★★★Castleroy Park Hotel, Dublin Road, tel. 0 61/33 55 66, fax 33 11 17, 107r.
New hotel furnished in traditional style.
H★★★Greenhills, Ennis Road, tel. 0 61/45 30 33, fax 45 33 07, 59r.
Modern hotel with many comforts. Speciality of the restaurant are lamb dishes (the lamb comes from the hotel's own farm).
H★★★Jurys, Ennis Road, tel. 0 61/32 77 77, fax 32 64 00, 95r.
View over the Shannon is included!
H★★★Two Mile Inn, Ennis Road, tel. 0 61/32 62 55, fax 45 37 83, 123r.
Near to Shannon Airport and Bunratty Castle.
H★★Railway, Parnell Street, tel. 0 61/41 36 53, fax 41 97 62, 20r.
Pleasant family atmosphere.
H★★★Royal George, O'Connell Street, tel. 0 61/41 45 66, fax 31 71 71, 54r.
The traditional Irish bar, An Síbín is a popular feature of this city-centre hotel.
H★★Woodfield House, Ennis Road, tel. 0 61/45 30 22, fax 32 67 55, 22r.
A pleasant hotel both inside and out.

Lisdoonvarna

H★★Sheedy's Spa View, tel. 0 65/7 40 26, fax 7 45 55, 11r.
A former farmhouse has been restored into an exquisite hotel.

Listowel

G★★North Country, tel. 0 68/2 12 38, 8r.
Convenient for Shannon Car Ferry.

Loughrea

H★★O'Dea's, Bridge Street, tel. 0 91/4 16 11, 14r.
Family-owned hotel for almost 100 years.

Lucan

H★★★Finstown House, Newcastle Road, tel. 01/6 28 06 44, fax 6 28 10 88, 25r.
Comfortable house about 8 miles/13km west of Dublin with a sauna, Turkish baths and various sports facilities.
H★★★Lucan Spa, tel. 01/6 28 04 94, fax 6 28 08 41, 59r.
Established for over a hundred years, this traditional hotel boasts excellent conference/party facilities.

Macroom

H★★Castle, Main Street, tel. 0 26/4 10 74, fax 4 15 05, 26r.
Centrally located hotel with a good, well known restaurant.
H★★Victoria, tel. 0 26/4 10 82, fax 4 21 48, 16r.
Located opposite the Town Hall with attractively designed lounge bar that features an impressive stone fireplace.

Mallow

H★★★Longueville House, tel. 0 22/4 71 56, fax 4 74 59, 20r.
Elegance abounds in this beautiful Georgian mansion that is set in a country estate.
G★★★★Springfort Hall, tel. 0 22/2 12 78, fax 2 15 57, 24r.
Comfortable accommodation in a woodland setting.

Midleton

H★★★Midleton Park, tel. 0 21/63 17 67, fax 63 16 05, 40r.
Relatively new hotel with a popular restaurant, bar and conference facilities.
G★★★Ballynona House, tel. 0 21/66 76 28, 5r.
Charming Victorian house in a peaceful setting.

Monaghan

H★★★Four Seasons, Coolshanagh, tel. 0 47/8 18 88, fax 8 31 31, 44r.
You can relax by the logfire in the bar, over a good meal in the restaurant, in the pool or in the hotel's own sauna.
H★★★Hillgrove, tel. 0 47/8 12 88, fax 8 49 51, 44r.
Newly opened in 1994 this hotel has live music at the weekends.

Newbridge

H★★★Keaden, tel. 0 45/43 16 66, fax 43 44 02, 37r.

Newmarket-on-Fergus

H★★★Clare Inn, tel. 0 61/36 81 61, fax 36 86 22, 121r.
Reasonably-priced alternative to Dromoland Castle, also surrounded by woods and with an 18-hole golf course.

H★★Old Rectory, Rosbercon, tel. 0 51/42 17 19, fax 42 29 74, 12r.   **New Ross**
Both hotel and restaurant are extremely tastefully furnished.

G★★★The Boat, The Square, tel. 0 91/8 21 96, fax 8 26 94, 11r.   **Oughterard**
Recently refurbished friendly hotel.

H★★★Killeshin, Dublin Road, tel. 05 02/2 16 63, fax 2 19 76, 44r.   **Portlaoise**
A hotel very popular with businessmen.

H★★★Fort Royal, tel. 0 74/5 81 00, fax 5 81 03, 11r.   **Rathmullan**
A period house in a superb setting by Lough Swilly.
H★ Pier Hotel, tel. 0 74/5 81 78, fax 5 81 15, 10r.
A friendly hotel overlooking a safe sandy beach on the western shores of
Lough Swilly.

H★★★★Tinakilly Country House and Restaurant, tel. 04 04/6 92 74,   **Rathnew**
fax 6 78 06, 29r.
Victorian mansion, set in several acres of well-tended gardens, with
breathtaking views of the sea.

H★★★Renvyle House, tel. 0 95/4 35 11, fax 4 35 15, 65r.   **Renvyle**
A log fire and an attractive lounge add to this hotel's charm.

H★★★Abbey, tel. 09 03/2 62 40, fax 2 60 21, 25r.   **Roscommon**
Stylish house with attractively furnished rooms.

H★★★Grants, Castle Street, tel. and fax 05 05/2 33 00, fax 2 32 09, 25r.   **Roscrea**
An attractive hotel opposite the Heritage Centre and 13th-century castle.

H★★★★Kellys Resort, tel. 0 53/3 21 14, fax 3 22 22, 99r.   **Rosslare**
Many visitors return to this extremely hospitable hotel which was
founded in 1895.
H★★★Cedars, tel. 0 53/3 21 24, fax 3 22 43, 34r.
Modern house with spacious family bedrooms.
G★★★★Churchtown House, Tagoat, tel. and fax 053/3 25 55, 11r.
Thoughtful hospitality in this 18th c. house

H★★★Sand House, tel. 0 72/5 17 77, fax 5 21 00, 39r.   **Rossnowlagh**
Comfortable accommodation in a beautiful seaside location.

H★★★Oak Wood Arms, tel. 0 61/36 15 00, fax 36 14 14, 75r.   **Shannon**
Situated on main airport road.

G★★★Fern Lodge, Baltimore Road, tel. 0 28/2 23 27, 6r.   **Skibbereen**
Good location for outdoor activities and ferry trips.

H★★★Sligo Park, Pearse Road, tel. 0 71/6 02 91, fax 6 95 56, 89r.   **Sligo**
Lovely parkland setting with attractive restaurant and comprehensive
leisure centre.
H★★★Tower, Quay Street, tel. 0 71/4 40 00, fax 4 68 88, 58r.
Comfortable town centre hotel.
H★★Ballincar, Rosses Point Road., tel. 0 71/4 53 61, fax 4 41 98, 25r.
It is about 10 minutes' drive to Sligo from this country house, but the
extensive park and well-run facilities (tennis and sauna) compensate for
this.
H★★Silver Swan, tel. 0 71/4 32 31, fax 4 22 32, 29r.
Riverside setting and the Horseshoe Bar make this a popular place to
stay.

H★★★★★Kildare Hotel and Country Club, tel. 01/6 27 33 33, fax 6 27 33 12,   **Straffan**
43r.
One of the most exclusive and expensive hotels in Ireland. It has a golf
course, tennis courts, swimming pool, sauna, etc.

Hotels and Guest Houses

H★★★Barberstown Castle, tel. 01/6 28 81 57, fax 6 27 70 27, 26r.
This 13th c. castle hotel is very comfortably appointed.

Thomastown   H★★★★Mount Juliet, tel. 0 56/2 44 55, fax 2 45 22, 53r.
Guests can choose between the grand 18th c. Mount Juliet House, the sportier atmosphere of Hunters Yard or the Rose Garden Lodges – all of which are expensive!

Tipperary   H★Royal, Bridge Street, tel. 0 62/3 32 44, fax 3 35 96, 16r.
Weekly live entertainment.
G★★Ach-na-Sheen, Clonmel Road, tel. 0 62/5 12 98, 10r.
Friendly family guest house.

Tralee   H★★★Abbey Gate, Maine Street, tel. 0 66/2 98 88, fax 2 98 21, 100r.
Centrally located new hotel with traditional pub and carvery.
H★★★Brandon, Princess Street, tel. 0 66/2 33 33, fax 2 50 19, 160r.
Elegantly furnished house with swimming pool, sauna and restaurant.
G★★★Ballingowan House, Killarney Road, tel. 0 66/2 71 50, fax 2 03 25, 4r.

Tramore   G★★★Sea View Lodge, Seaview Park, tel. 0 51/38 11 22, 5r.
G★★Rushmere House, Branch Road, tel. 0 51/38 10 41, 6r.
Reasonably priced guest house overlooking the sea.

Tullamore   G★★★★Pine Lodge, Ross, tel. 05 06/5 19 27, 4r.

Waterford   H★★★★Waterford Castle, Ballinakill, tel. 0 51/87 82 03, fax 87 93 16, 19r.
This magnificent castle stands on a small island in the River Suir, not far from Waterford. It has a golf course, tennis courts and a swimming pool.
H★★★Bridge, The Quay, tel. 0 51/7 72 22, fax 7 72 29, 96r.
A busy hotel with a variety of bars and restaurants.
H★★★Granville, The Quay, tel. 0 51/85 51 11, fax 87 03 07, 74r.
Although established many years ago this quayside hotel has been tastefully modernised.
H★★★Tower, The Mall, tel. 0 51/87 58 01, fax 87 01 29, 141r.
Modern well equipped hotel.
H★★Dooley's, The Quay, tel. 0 51/7 35 31, fax 7 02 62, 35r.
An excellent seafood menu using freshly caught fish tempts both locals and visitors alike to this quayside hotel.

Waterville   H★★★Butler Arms, tel. 0 66/7 41 44, fax 7 45 20, 30r.
Charlie Chaplin spent many holidays in this stylish hotel.

Westport   H★★★Westport, tel. 0 98/2 51 22, fax 2 67 39, 49r.
Not far from the centre in the middle of a park. Entertainment in the bar in summer.
H★★The Olde Railway, The Mall, tel. 0 98/2 51 66, fax 2 50 90, 24r.
This original old coaching inn enjoys a lovely position overlooking the river.

Wexford   H★★★Ferrycarrig, tel. 0 53/2 09 99, fax 2 09 82, 39r.
A modern hotel near to Ferrycarrig Castle and bordering onto the National Heritage Park.
H★★★Whites, George Street, tel. 0 53/2 23 11, fax 4 50 00, 82r.
This hotel in the centre is part of the Best Western group.
H★★★Whitford House, New Line Road, tel. 0 53/4 34 44, fax 4 63 99, 23r.
Pleasant hotel with comfortable accommodation.
H★★Wexford Lodge, The Bridge, tel. 0 53/2 36 11, fax 2 33 42, 19r.
Quiet location close to the centre.

Wicklow   H★★★Tina Killy Country House & Restaurant, tel. 04 04/6 92 74, 29r.
This elegant house dates back to 1870 and is surrounded by beautiful grounds; some garden walks have been thoughtfully mapped out.

G★★★★Old Rectory, tel. 04 04/6 70 48, fax 6 91 81, 5r.
A Victorian house furnished in antique country style. Restaurant is
renowned for good food.

H★★Devonshire Arms, Pearse Square, tel. 0 24/9 28 27, fax 9 29 00, 10r.   **Youghal**
Pleasant hotel with individually decorated rooms.

Hotels in Northern Ireland

In Northern Ireland the hotels are officially classified according to their   Categories
facilities, ranging from high-standard hotels (★★★★) to modest hotels
(★), while some hotels are unclassified. Guest houses are classified A or B.

Bookings in advance can be made by personal callers to Tourist Informa-   Bookings and
tion Centres (see Information). Credit card bookings can be made by tele-   Reservations
phone (toll-free): 0800 40 40 50 (from the UK), 1850 230 230 (from the
Republic), or for accommodation in the whole of Ireland freefone: 0800
31 71 53, stating your credit card number.

In Belfast hotel prices are markedly higher than elsewhere in Northern   Prices
Ireland. Here they tend to be at the top end of the undermentioned average
prices. In the table below the prices in £ sterling are per person for one
night's accommodation with breakfast in a double or single room.

Category	Double room	Single room
★★★★	£50–75	£90–100
★★★	£30–60	£50– 90
★★	£20–45	£30– 70
★	£18–40	£25– 60
G (guest house)	£13–30	£15– 35

H★★Glassdrumman Lodge, 85 Mill Road, tel. 013 967/6 84 51, fax 6 70 41,   **Annalong**
8r.
An excellent small hotel with magnificent views of the coast and the
Mourne mountains.

H★★Brown Trout Golf & Country Inn, 209 Agivey Road, tel. 012 65/   **Aghadowey**
86 82 09, fax 86 88 78, 17r.
An established family concern with its own 9-hole golf course.

H★★★Ballygalley Castle, 274 Coast Road, tel. 015 74/58 32 12, fax   **Ballygalley**
58 36 81, 30r.
You can dream about the past from the walls of this castle on Ballygalley
Bay.

H★★★★Galgorm Manor, tel. 012 66/88 10 01, fax 88 00 80, 23r.   **Ballymena**
Peacefully located within beautiful grounds beside the River Maine.

H★★★Clandeboye Lodge, tel. 012 47/85 25 00, fax 85 27 72, 43r.   **Bangor**
In a woodland setting adjacent to the Blackwood Golf Course, this hotel is
ideal for enthusiasts.
H★★★Marine Court, 18–20 Quay Street, tel. 012 47/45 11 00, fax 45 12 00,
51r.
Opened in 1995 it offers modern comfort.

H★★★★Culloden, Bangor Road, tel. 012 32/42 52 23, fax 42 67 77, 87r.   **Belfast**
A baronial mansion set in acres of landscaped grounds with views over
Belfast Lough.
H★★★★Europa, Great Victoria Street, tel. 012 32/32 70 00, fax 32 78 00,
184r.
Recently refurbished with new business and conference facilities.

341

H★★★★Stormont, 587 Upper Newlands Road, tel. 012 32/65 86 21, fax 48 02 40, 109r.
Situated on the city outskirts overlooking Stormont Castle grounds.

H★★★Dukes Hotel, 65 University Street, tel. 012 32/23 66 66, fax 23 71 77, 21r.
Situated about 1 mile/2km from the city centre, near to the university.

H★★★Forte Posthouse, Kingsway, Dunmurry, tel. 012 32/61 21 01, fax 62 65 46, 82r.
This hotel is about 5 miles/8km from the centre in gardens and woodland.

H★★★Lansdowne Court, 657 Antrim Road, tel. 012 32/77 33 17, fax 37 01 25, 25r.
This pleasant hotel has an extensive bar and live music most evenings.

H★★★Plaza, 15 Brunswick Street, tel. 012 32/33 35 55, fax 33 00 70, 76r.
A city centre hotel popular with buinessmen.

H★★Balmoral, Black's Road, tel. 012 32/30 12 34, fax 60 14 55, 44r.
Purpose-built hotel with smart, spacious public rooms.

H★★Rayanne Country House & Restaurant, 60 Desmesne Road, tel. 012 32/42 58 59, 6r.
The friendly proprietors extend a warm welcome to visitors at this small country house.

Carrickfergus
H★Dobbins Inn, 6–8 High Street, tel. and fax 019 60/35 19 05, 13r.
This family-run hotel dates back to the 16th century and offers good value accommodation.

Enniskillen
H★★★Killyhevlin, Dublin Road, tel. 013 65/32 34 81, fax 32 47 26, 44r.
This hotel, picturesquely situated on Lough Erne, is suitable for a longer stay.

H★Railway, tel. 013 65/32 30 84, fax 32 74 80, 19r.
A family-run hotel dating back to 1855, popular with locals.

Londonderry/ Derry
H★★★Everglades, Prehen Road, tel. 015 04/4 67 22, fax 4 92 00, 52r.
Modern hotel situated next to the River Foyle on the south side of town.

Newcastle
H★★★Slieve Donard, Downs Road, tel. 013 967/2 36 81, fax 2 48 30, 134r.
Victorian hotel with extensive grounds and views of the Mourne Mountains.

H★★Enniskeen House, 98 Bryansford Road, tel. 013 967/2 23 92, fax 2 40 84, 12r.
This peacefully located hotel enjoys beautiful sea and mountain views.

Omagh
H★★Royal Arms, 51 High Street, tel. 016 62/24 32 62, fax 24 50 11, 19r.
A modern hotel is hidden behind the historic façade.

Portaferry
H★★★Portaferry, 10 The Strand, tel. 012 477/2 82 31, fax 2 89 99, 14r.
Lovely setting by the sea

Portballintrae
H★★Beach House, 61 Beach Road, tel. 012 657/3 12 14, fax 3 16 64, 32r.
Owned by this family for three generations.

Portrush
H★★★Causeway Coast, tel. 012 65/82 24 35, fax 82 44 95, 21r.
Well equipped modern hotel facing the sea and next to the Ballyreagh Golf Club. Some rooms have small fitted kitchens, or there is a wine bar and a formal dining room for a choice of meals.

Hunting and Shooting

Shooting
There is good shooting in Ireland for pheasant, grouse, partridge, snipe and various species of wild duck. A gun licence is required which is issued only against proof that a shooting holiday has been booked. Quarantine regulations mean that visitors are not allowed to take their own dog.

Deer-stalking is not available for visitors.

The shooting season is fixed each year by the Department of Agriculture; it is usually from the beginning of September to the end of January.

For the addresses of shooting clubs and organisers of shoots apply to the Tourist Board.

Fox-hunting is a popular Irish sport for good horsemen, not only for the "gentry", but for any small farmer who possesses a horse. The hunt can also be followed on foot. There are still some 36 hunts in Ireland with the season lasting from the beginning of November to the end of March. Participants must be experienced riders.

Hunting

Information

Ireland

All Ireland Tourism
12 Regent Street
Piccadilly Circus
London SW1Y 4PQ
Tel. (0171) 839 8416/7

Republic of Ireland

Bord Fáilte Éireann
Head Office
Baggot Street Bridge, Dublin 2
Tel. 01/6 02 40 00, fax 01/6 02 41 00

Irish Tourist Board

53 Castle Street, Belfast BT1 1GH
Tel. 012 32/32 78 88, fax 24 02 01

Northern Ireland

8 Bishop Street
Londonderry BT48 6PW
Tel. 015 04/36 95 01, fax 36 95 01

150 New Bond Street
London W1Y 0AQ
Tel. (0171) 493 3201, fax 493 9065

Great Britain

5–8 Temple Row
Birmingham B2 5HG
Tel. (0121) 236 9724

19 Dixon Street, Glasgow G1 4AJ
Tel. (0141) 221 2311

28 Cross Street
Manchester M2 3NH
Tel. (0161) 832 5981

345 Park Avenue
New York NY 10154
Tel. (212) 418 0800, fax 371 9052

United States of
America

Suite 1150
160 Bloor Street East
Toronto, Ontario M4W 1B9
Tel. (416) 929 2777, fax 929 6783

Canada

Information

Australia	5th Level 36 Carrington Street Sydney, NSW 2000 Tel. (02) 299 6177, fax 299 6323
New Zealand	Dingwell Building 2nd floor 87 Queen Street, PO Box 279, Auckland 1 Tel. (09) 79 37 08

Northern Ireland

Northern Ireland Tourist Board	Head office St Anne's Court 59 North Street, Belfast BT1 1NB Tel. 012 32/24 66 09, fax 24 09 60
The Republic of Ireland	16 Nassau Street Dublin 2. Tel. 01/6 79 19 77, fax 6 79 81 63
Great Britain	11 Berkeley Street London W1X 5AD Tel. (0171) 409 0487 or freefone 0800 28 26 62
	135 Buchanan Street, 1st Floor Glasgow G1 2JA Tel. (0141) 204 4454, fax 204 4033
United States	551 Fifth Avenue, Suite 701 New York NY 10176 Tel. (212) 922 0101 or (800) 326 0036, fax (212) 922 0099
Canada	111 Avenue Road, Suite 450 Toronto, Ontario M5R 3J8 Tel. (416) 925 6368, fax 961 2175

Information in the Republic of Ireland

In the Republic information can be obtained locally from Tourist Information Offices, or, in a few cases, from community tourist information offices. Information offices are generally open Monday to Friday from 9am to 6pm and on Saturday from 9am to 1pm. Many offices are closed during the winter months.

Achill Island	See Keel
Adare	Heritage Centre; tel. 0 61/39 62 55 Open: March to October
Aran Islands	See Kilronan
Arklow	Grand Parade; tel. 04 02/3 24 84 Open: all year
Athlone	Athlone Castle; tel. 09 02/9 46 30 Open: May to mid October
Athy	Tel. 05 07/3 18 59 Open: all year
Aughrim	Tel. 09 05/7 39 39 Open: mid April to early October

Cathedral Street; tel. 0 96/7 08 48
Open: mid April to September

Ballina

Tel. 09 05/4 21 31
Open: July and August

Ballinasloe

The Square; tel. 0 27/5 02 29
Open: June to September

Bantry

Rosse Row; tel. 05 09/2 01 10
Open: mid May to mid September

Birr

Tel. 0 21/38 16 24
Open: all year

Blarney

Courthouse; tel. 0 79/6 21 45
Open: May to mid September

Boyle

Shore Front; tel. 0 77/6 26 00
Open: June to August

Buncrana

Main Street; tel. 0 72/4 13 50
Open: June to September

Bundoran

RIC Barracks; tel. 0 66/7 25 89
Open: June to September

Caherciveen

Castle Car Park; tel. 0 52/4 14 53
Open: April to September

Cahir

Cathedral Close; tel. 05 03/3 15 54
Open: all year

Carlow

The Marina; tel. 0 78/2 01 70
Open: all year

**Carrick-on-
Shannon**

Town Hall, Main Street; tel. 0 62/6 13 33
Open: May to September

Cashel

Tel. 0 94/2 12 07
Open: mid April to early September

Castlebar

Farnham Street; tel. 0 49/3 19 42
Open: all year

Cavan

Tel. 0 95/2 11 63
Open: mid April to September

Clifden

Liscannor; tel. 0 65/8 11 71
Open: Easter to September

Cliffs of Moher

Rossa Street; tel. 0 23/3 32 26
Open: mid June to August

Clonakilty

Tel. 09 05/7 41 34
Open: Easter to September

Clonmacnoise

Tel. 0 52/2 29 60
Open: all year

Clonmel

Tourist House, Grand Parade; tel. 0 21/27 32 51, fax 27 35 04
Open: all year

Cork

Information

Dingle
Main Street; tel. 0 66/5 11 88
Open: April to October

Donegal
The Quay; tel. 0 73/2 11 48, fax 2 27 62
Open: all year

Drogheda
Tel. 0 41/3 70 70
Open: mid June to mid September

Dublin
Suffolk Street; tel. 01/6 05 77 55
Open: all year

Baggot Street Bridge; tel. 01/6 02 40 00
Open: all year

Airport; Open: all year

Dundalk
Jocelyn Street; tel. 0 42/3 54 84, fax 3 80 70
Open: all year

Dungarvan
St Mary Street; tel. 0 58/4 17 41
Open: mid June to August

Dungloe
Tel. 0 75/2 12 97
Open: June to August

Dun Laoghaire
St Michael's Wharf; tel. 01/2 80 69 84
Open: all year

Ennis
Clare road; tel. 0 65/2 83 66
Open: all year

Enniscorthy
Castle Hill; tel. 0 54/3 46 99
Open: mid June to August

Galway
Aras Fáilte, Victoria Place, Eyre Square; tel. 0 91/56 30 81, fax 56 52 01
Open: all year

Airport; tel. 0 91/5 52 52
Open: June to mid September

Glengarriff
Tel. 0 27/6 30 84
Open: July and August

Gorey
Main Street; tel. 0 55/2 12 48
Open: all year

Keel
(Achill Island)
Courthouse; tel. 0 98/4 53 84
Open: July and August

Kenmare
Heritage Centre; tel. 0 64/4 12 33
Open: April to October

Kerry County Airport
Farranfore; tel. 0 66/6 43 99
Open: all year

Kildare Town
Tel. 0 45/2 26 96
Open: June to August

Kilkee
O'Connell Street; tel. 0 65/5 61 12
Open: June to early September

Kilkenny
Shee Alms House, Rose Inn Street; tel. 0 56/5 15 00, fax 6 39 55
Open: all year

Heritage Centre, The Bridge; tel. 0 61/37 68 66
Open: June to mid September **Killaloe**

Town Hall; tel. 064/3 16 33, fax 3 45 06
Open: all year **Killarney**

Tel. 0 99/6 12 63
Open: May to mid September **Kilronan**

Town Hall; tel. 0 65/5 15 77
Open: June to early September **Kilrush**

Pier Road; tel. 0 21/77 22 34, fax 77 44 38
Open: March to November **Kinsale**

Village; tel. 0 94/8 81 93
Open: May to September **Knock**

Airport; tel. 0 94/6 72 47
Open: June to September

Derry Road; tel. 0 74/2 11 60, fax 2 51 80
Open: all year **Letterkenny**

Arthur's Quay; tel. 0 61/31 75 22, fax 31 75 22
Open: all year **Limerick**

St John's Church; tel. 0 68/2 25 90
Open: June to September **Listowel**

Main Street; tel. 0 43/4 65 66
Open: June to August **Longford**

Tel. 0 98/6 64 00
Open: June to August **Louisburgh**

Jameson Heritage Centre; tel. 0 21/61 37 02
Open: April to September **Midleton**

Market House; tel. 0 47/8 11 22
Open: all year **Monaghan**

Dublin Road; tel. 0 44/4 86 50, fax 4 04 13
Open: all year **Mullingar**

Connolly Street; tel. 0 67/3 16 10
Open: mid May to mid September **Nenagh**

Tel. 0 41/2 42 74
Open: April to October **Newgrange**

Kennedy Centre; tel. 0 51/2 18 57
Open: mid June to August **New Ross**

Tel. 0 91/8 28 08, fax 8 28 11
Open: all year **Oughterard**

James Fintan Lawlor Avenue; tel. 05 02/2 11 78
Open: all year **Portlaoise**

Tel. 09 03/2 63 42
Open: June to early September **Roscommon**

Information

Rosslare Harbour	Kilrane; tel. 0 53/3 32 32 Open: June to September
	Rosslare Terminal, tel. 0 53/3 36 22, fax 3 34 21 Open: all year
Salthill	Tel. 0 91/6 30 81 Open: June to early September
Shannon Airport	Tel. 0 61/47 16 64 Open: all year
Skibbereen	Town Hall, North Street; tel. 0 28/2 17 66, fax 2 13 53 Open: all year
Sligo	Aras Reddan, Temple Street; tel. 0 71/6 12 01, fax 6 03 60 Open: all year
Thoor Ballylee	Tel. 0 91/3 14 36 Open: June to September
Tipperary	James Street; tel. 0 62/5 14 57 Open: all year
Tralee	Ashe Memorial Hall, Denny Street; tel. 0 66/2 12 88 Open: all year
Tramore	Railway Square; tel. 0 51/38 15 72 Open: mid June to August
Trim	Mill Street; tel. 0 46/3 71 11 Open: mid June to September
Tuam	Mill Museum; tel. 0 93/2 44 63 Open: July and August
Tullamore	Tel. 05 06/5 26 17 Open: July and August
Waterford	41 The Quay; tel. 0 51/87 57 88, fax 87 73 88 Open: all year
Westport	The Mall; tel. 0 98/2 57 11, fax 2 67 09 Open: all year
Wexford	Crescent Quay; tel. 0 53/2 31 11, fax 4 17 43 Open: all year
Wicklow	Rialto House, Fitzwilliam Street; tel. 04 04/6 91 17, fax 6 91 18 Open: all year
Youghal	Heritage Centre; tel. 0 24/9 23 90 Open: June to mid September

Information in Northern Ireland

	In Northern Ireland information can be obtained from Tourist Information Centres.
Antrim	Pogue's Entry, Church Street; tel. 018 49/42 83 31 Open: Easter to September

Old Bank Building, 40 English Street; tel. 018 61/52 18 00   **Armagh**
Open: April to September

Sheskburn House, 7 Mary St.; tel. 012 657/6 20 24   **Ballycastle**
Open: all year

Gateway Tourist Information Centre, 200 Newry Road; tel. 018 206/2 33 22   **Banbridge**
Open: all year

34 Quay Street; tel. 012 47/27 00 69   **Bangor**
Open: all year

53 Castle Street; tel. 0801–232/32 78 88, fax 0802–232/24 02 01   **Belfast**
Open: all year

Belfast City Airport, Sydenham Bypass; tel. 012 32/45 77 45
Open: all year

Belfast International Airport; tel. 018 49/42 28 88
Open: all year (24 hours)

Heritage Plaza, Antrim Street; tel. 019 60/36 64 55   **Carrickfergus**
Open: all year

Railway Road; tel. 012 65/4 47 23   **Coleraine**
Open: all year

48 Molesworth Street; tel. 016 487/6 67 27   **Cookstown**
Open: Easter to October

See Londonderry   **Derry**

74 Market Street; tel. 013 96/61 22 33   **Downpatrick**
Open: all year

Fermanagh Tourist Information Centre, Wellington Road   **Enniskillen**
Tel. 013 65/32 31 10
Open: all year

44 Causeway Road, Bushmills; tel. 012 657/3 18 55   **Giant's Causeway**
Open: all year

6 Newcastle Street; tel. 016 937/6 25 25   **Kilkeel**
Open: all year

Ballygawley Road, Dungannon; tel. 018 68/76 72 59   **Killymaddy**
Open: all year

Narrow Guage Road; tel. 015 74/26 00 88   **Larne**
Open: all year

Council Offices, 7 Connell Street; tel. 015 047/2 22 26   **Limavady**
Open: all year

Irish Linen Centre & Lisburn Museum, Market Square   **Lisburn**
Tel. 018 46/66 00 38
Open: all year

8 Bishop Street; tel. 015 04/26 72 84   **Londonderry**
Open: all year

1 Market Street; tel. 016 62/24 78 31 and 24 07 74 (after hours)   **Omagh**
Open: all year

Insurance

Newcastle	Newcastle Centre, 10–14 Central Promenade Tel. 013 967/2 22 22 Open: all year
Newtownards	31 Regent Street; tel. 012 47/82 68 46 Open: all year
Portrush	Dunluce Centre, Sandhill Drive; tel. 012 65/82 33 33 Open: all year
Strabane	Abercorn Square; tel. 015 04/88 37 35 Open: April to October

Other outlets for information which are not part of the Tourist Information Centre Network include District Councils and Visitor Centres which exist in: Ballymena, Ballymoney, Ballynahinch, Belleek, Benone, Castlederg, Craigavon, Crossmaglen, Dungannon, Hillsborough, Lurgan, Magherafelt, Newry, Newtonstewart, Portadown, Portaferry, Portstewart, Sion Mills, Sperrins and Warrenpoint.

Insurance

General	Visitors are strongly advised to ensure that they have adequate holiday insurance, including loss or damage to luggage, loss of currency and jewellery.
Health	Nationals of other European Union countries, are entitled to obtain medical care when on holiday in Ireland. Treatment can be obtained free of charge, but medicines must be paid for. An E 111 form should be obtained (by British nationals from post offices in the UK, contained inside the booklet T4 "Health Advice for Travellers") before departure. Visitors from non-EU countries are recommended, and nationals of EU countries are advised, to take out some form of short-term health insurance providing complete cover and possibly avoiding delays.
Vehicles	Visitors travelling by car should ensure that their insurance is comprehensive and covers use of the vehicle in Ireland.
	See also Travel Documents.

Language

English is spoken throughout Ireland. Although the old Celtic language of Ireland, known as Irish, Erse or Gaelic (see Introduction, The Irish Language), is an official language of the Republic of Ireland jointly with English; it is the everyday language only in certain of the remoter parts of the country.

The Irish alphabet has fewer letters than the Latin alphabet – no j, k, v, w, x, y or z. An acute accent over a vowel means that it is long. The traditional Irish uncial script will frequently be seen on road signs, etc.

The following list of Anglicised forms of Irish words may help in interpreting place names, etc.

abha	river
ard	hill, high ground
áth	ford
ball	town, settlement

béal	estuary
ben	hill, mountain
bord	office, board
bun	end
burren	stone
cahir	stone fort
cashel	stone fort
cavan	cave
cill	church
clochán	beehive-shaped stone hut
cnoc	hill
croagh	conical hill
derry	oak
drum	chain of hills
dún	hill fort
éireann	Irish
ennis (innis)	island, meadow
gal	river
grianán	palace
lis	stone fort
lough	lake, arm of the sea
mac	son
monaster	monastery
ráth	ring-fort
skerry	small rocky islet
slieve	hill, mountain
tholsel	town hall

A useful English–Irish and Irish–English dictionary, with an outline of Irish grammar, is published by the Talbot Press in the Republic of Ireland.

For a fuller account of the Irish language, see "Teach Yourself Irish", published by the English Universities Press, London.

Maps and Plans

Visitors who propose to drive off the main roads in Ireland should supplement the general map in this Guide with more detailed maps of the areas they want to explore. The following is a selection of suitable maps:

12 miles to one inch/20km to 25mm
Map of Ireland published by the Ordinance Survey, Dublin: a map designed for the visitor, with through routes shown for main cities and towns.

1:250,000
Holiday Maps of Ireland, published by the Ordnance Survey, Dublin: four sheets (North, East, South and West), showing every motorable road, with places of interest marked; additional holiday information on reverse side.

Ireland North Holiday Map, published by the Ordnance Survey of Northern Ireland.

Quarter-inch/7mm maps of Ireland, published by Bartholomew, Edinburgh: five sheets (Antrim–Donegal, Dublin–Roscommon, Wexford–Tipperary, Cork–Killarney, Galway–Mayo), showing relief and much detail.

Quarter-inch/7mm map of Ulster, published by Bartholomew.

1:570,000 (Republic), 1:290,000 (Northern Ireland)
Map of Ireland (motorways and main roads) and map of Northern Ireland, published by Geographia, London.

Medieval Banquets

In a number of old castles medieval banquets regularly take place. During the meal pages and serving girls in period costume serve wine and substantial dishes. To entertain the guests old ballads are rendered and music of the period is played. Generally there are two banquets per evening at about 5.30 and 8.45pm. The inclusive price is about IR£30 per person.

Information and booking

Booking can be made at any tourist office (see Information) or at:

Shannon Heritage and Banquets
Bunratty Castle and Folk Park
Bunrarry, Co. Clare
Tel. 0 61/36 07 88, fax 0 61/36 10 20

Killarney Manor
Loreto Road, Killarney, Co. Kerry
Tel. 0 64/3 15 51, fax 0 64/3 33 66

Castles

Knappogue Castle
Near Quin, Co. Clare
Banquets only from May to September

Dunguaire Castle
Kinvara, Co. Galway
Banquets only from May to September

Irish Nights

In Bunratty Folk Park (Co. Clare) traditional Irish nights ("Céilís") are organised with Irish food, wine, music, singing and dancing (from May to October): daily 5.30 and 8.45pm; cost IR£25.50 per person.

Motoring

The roads in Ireland are generally good, though in country areas minor roads may be narrow and winding.

Roads

In the Republic, apart from a short stretch around Dublin, there are no motorways. Trunk roads are designated as National roads (N) divided into National Primary (N 1–25) and National Secondary (N over 50), and Regional roads (R). Many roads are extremely narrow but traffic is generally light. Drivers must be careful to avoid cattle and sheep on the roads and beware of agricultural vehicles crossing the roads.

Since many roads are not in very good condition average speeds must be reduced (for example, for the 185 mile/300km-stretch between Dublin and Killarney a good 5 hours should be allowed).

The classification of roads in Northern Ireland is the same as in the rest of the United Kingdom, with A (trunk) roads, B (secondary) roads and M for motorways.

Regulations

Throughout Ireland traffic travels on the left, with passing on the right. At a junction of two roads of equal importance, unless otherwise indicated, traffic coming from the right has priority. Other driving regulations and road signs are in line with European standards.

Seat-belts

Seat-belts must be worn by drivers and front-seat passengers and, where fitted, by rear-seat passengers. Children under twelve years of age may travel only in the rear. Motor-cyclists and moped-riders must wear helmets.

Drink-driving

Drink-driving laws are strict. The blood alcohol limit in the Republic of Ireland and Northern Ireland is 0.8 per mille.

On roads with a "no waiting" sign parking is prohibited. A continuous double yellow line means no parking, a single yellow line indicates that parking is permitted only at certain times. — Car Parking

Exceeding the speed limits by up to 19 miles/30km per hour is punished in Ireland by fines between £15 and £150; failing to give priority or failing to obey a "no overtaking" sign incurs a fine of up to £125. Parking tickets for illegal parking incur a penalty of up to £20 and drink/driving offences may cost over £1000. — Fines

At almost all filling stations throughout Ireland in addition to Diesel "Super Plus Unleaded" (98 octane), "Eurosuper Unleaded" (95 octane) and "Super Leaded" (97 octane) can be obtained. — Motor fuel

In the Republic of Ireland the maximum permitted speed in built-up areas is 30 m.p.h./48km p.h., on most country roads 55 m.p.h./88km p.h.; on some stretches of road there may be a 40 m.p.h./64km p.h. limit, indicated by signs. In Northern Ireland the speed limit in built-up areas is 30 m.p.h./48km p.h. unless a higher limit (40 or 50 m.p.h./64 or 80km p.h.) is indicated, on ordinary country roads 60 m.p.h./97km p.h. and on dual-carriageway roads and motorways 70 m.p.h./112km p.h. — Speed limits

AA Headquarters
23 Rock Hill, Blackrock, Co. Dublin
Tel. 01/2 83 35 55, fax 01/2 83 36 60 — Breakdown

AA Breakdown Freephone Service
Tel. 1800 66 77 88

Opening Times

For opening times of post offices see under Post. — Post offices

For opening times of pubs see under Pubs. — Pubs

Republic of Ireland

Mon.–Sat. 9 or 9.30am–5.30 or 6pm, Sun. 11am–1pm. Chemists open outside these hours are displayed in the windows of chemists' shops. — Chemists/ Pharmacies

Opening times vary, but are usually from 9 or 9.30am–5.30 or 6pm. There is an early closing day on Wed. or Thur. (outside Dublin). Shopping centres and supermarkets stay open until 8 or 9pm on Thur. and/or Fri. In some places shops remain open until 8 or 9pm on Sat. and even on Sunday in most places there is one food shop open, plus in urban areas some supermarkets open noon–6pm. — Shops

Banks are open Mon.–Fri. from 10am–12.30pm and 1.30–3pm, in Dublin to 5pm on Thur. and some to 5pm one day a week in larger cities where banks also do not close for lunch. They are closed on Sat., Sun. and public holidays except at Dublin, Cork, Shannon and Knock airports. — Banks

Opening times at international airports:
Dublin: daily 6am–9pm; in winter until 10.30pm, except Tues. and Wed. until 10pm.
Cork: Mon.–Fri. 9am–5.13pm, Sat. and Sun. 11am–5pm.
Shannon: daily 6am–9pm; in winter from 7.30am–5.30pm.
Knock: all year service for scheduled flights.

Money can be changed at the General Post Office in Dublin Mon.–Sat. 9.30am–6pm, Sun. 10.30am–5.30pm.

Post

Petrol (gas) stations	These are usually open from 9am–6pm. On Sun. they have restricted opening times. In Dublin and Cork some petrol (gas) stations are open 24 hours a day.

Northern Ireland

Shops	Shops in Belfast are open on weekdays from 9am–5.30pm (later on Thur. and Fri.). Many large shopping centres on the outskirts of town remain open until 9pm. Outside Belfast they have one early closing day, varying from place to place. Most of the smaller shops close at lunchtime.
Banks	Banks in main towns are normally open Mon.–Fri. 9.30am–4.30pm; elsewhere they may close 12.30–1.30pm. In small places the banks may open on only two or three days in the week.

Post

Opening times	Post offices are usually open Mon.–Fri. from 9am–5.30pm, Sat. 9am–1pm. Small country post offices close at lunchtime. Head Office in Dublin opens longer and on Sundays.
Postage rates	Letters from the Republic of Ireland to Britain and other EU countries cost 32p (44p to non-EU countries in Europe), postcards 28p (37p). Letters to the United States and Canada cost 52p.

Letters and postcards from Northern Ireland cost 20p (second class) or 26p (first class) to Britain, 26p to EU countries (29p to non-EU countries in Europe) and 34p (for 10g air mail) to the United States and Canada.

Post boxes in the Republic of Ireland are green.

Irish post box

Irish telephone box

Public Holidays

Republic of Ireland

January 1st
March 17th (St Patrick's Day)
Easter Monday
First Monday in May (Labour Day)
First Monday in June (Bank Holiday)
First Monday in August (August weekend)
Last Monday in October (Autumn Bank Holiday)
December 25th (Christmas Day)
December 26th (Boxing Day)

Northern Ireland

January 1st
March 17th (St Patrick's Day)
Easter Monday
First Monday in May (May Day Bank Holiday)
Last Monday in May or first Monday in June (Spring Bank Holiday)
July 12th (Orangeman's Day, anniversary of the Battle of the Boyne, 1690)
Last Monday in August (Summer Bank Holiday)
December 25th (Christmas Day)
December 26th (Boxing Day)

Movable holidays in Ireland (known as Bank Holidays) generally fall on a
Monday.

Public Transport

In the Republic of Ireland the public transport authority responsible for
running rail and bus services is the Córas Iompair Éireann (CIE). Modern
trains run between Dublin and the larger towns, and there are bus services
linking the smaller as well as the larger places. The principal routes are
shown on p. 356.
    Visitors can buy an "Irish Explorer" ticket covering rail only or rail and
bus travel (but not in the central areas of Dublin, Cork, Limerick and
Galway). Information about this ticket can be obtained from all CIE offices
and larger railway stations. Information on timetables. Tel. 01/8 36 62 22.

Republic of Ireland

Northern Ireland also has an extensive network of rail and bus services,
with particularly good bus links between towns not served by the railway
system.

Northern Ireland

Special tickets offer substantial savings, such as the "Emerald Card" which
allows unlimited travel by bus and train for 8 or 15 days in a period of 30
days in Ireland and Northern Ireland, while the "Irish Rover" ticket offers
unlimited rail travel for 5 out of 15 days in Ireland and Northern Ireland.
Further information is available from main railway stations (and bus stations in the case of the "Emerald Card") in the Republic and Northern
Ireland.

Special offer
tickets

Pubs

Pubs serve alchoholic drinks of all kinds which are normally ordered at the
bar and paid for immediately. In some pubs soup, sandwiches, salads
and/or snacks or even hot meals can be obtained for about IR£5.00. It is an

Rail, bus and ferry services in Ireland

—— Rail services

—— Buses (all year)

--- Buses (summer only)

--- Ferries

© Baedeker

Republic of Ireland

Northern Ireland

easy matter to get into a conversation with local customers; if a drink is offered it is usual for this to be reciprocated.

Most pubs are open on weekdays from 10.30am until 11.30pm in summer and until 11pm in winter. On Sundays the hours are 12.30–2pm and 4–11pm. In Dublin, Cork and Limerick pubs are closed from 2.30–3.30pm. "Closing time" is strictly enforced.

In Northern Ireland pubs are open on weekdays from 11.30am until 11pm and on Sundays 12.30–2.30pm and 7–10pm.

Singing Pubs

In the so-called "Singing Pubs" singers and instrumentalists perform without pay and customers can join in the songs.

The following is a selection of typical pubs in the Republic of Ireland. In many of the oldest pubs traditional ballads are often heard.

Dublin pubs: International Bar . . .   *. . . and Madigan's*

John M. Keating, 14 Mary Street, Dublin 1

Madigan's, 25 North Earl Street, Dublin 1
Mooney's, 1 Lower Abbey Street, Dublin 1
  (one of the well-known pubs which James Joyce's character Leopold
  Bloom frequented)
Bartley Dunne's, 32 Lower Stephan Street, Dublin 2
Davy Byrne's, 21 Duke Street, Dublin 2
  (another pub mentioned in Joyce's "Ulysses")
Doheny and Nesbitt, 5 Lower Baggot Street, Dublin 2
  (with an interior unchanged from the last century)
International Bar, 23 Wicklow Street, Dublin 2
Kehoe's, 9 South Anne Street, Dublin 2
McDaid's, 3 Harry Street, Dublin 2
Mulligan's, 8 Poolbeg Street, Dublin 2
  (antique furnishing; another pub mentioned by Joyce)
The Bailey, 2 Duke Street, Dublin 2
  (a meeting place for Joyce enthusiasts and for Yuppies)
The Old Stand, 37 Exchequer Street, Dublin 2
O'Connell's, 29 South Richmond Street, Dublin 2
O'Donoghue's, 15 Merrion Row, Dublin 2
  (birthplace of "The Dubliners", therefore much visited)
Palace Bar, 21 Fleet Street, Dublin 2
Stag's Head, Dame Court, Dublin 2
  (interior in turn-of-the-century style)
Slattery's, 129 Chapel Street, Dublin 2
  (well-know for traditional Irish music)
The Long Hall, 51 South Great George's Street, Dublin 2
  (furnished in Victorian style)
Toner's, 139 Lower Baggot Street, Dublin 2
Kitty O'Shea's, 23–25 Upper Grand Canal Street, Ballsbridge, Dublin 4
  (live music daily, also well-known for brunch at the weekends)

Irish Pubs . . .

M.B. Slattery, 62 Upper Grand Canal Street, Dublin 4
(Irish music daily)
Brazen Head, 20 Lower Bridge Street, Dublin 8
(Dublin's oldest pub, dating from the 17th c.)
Lord Edward, 23 Christchurch Place, Dublin 8
(with an atmosphere of a by-gone age)
Abbey Tavern, Howth
Jack O'Rourke's, 15 Main Street, Blackrock
The Purty Kitchen, Old Dunlearuy Road, Dun Laoghaire
(dating from 1728)

County Cavan Derragarra Inn, Butlersbridge

County Clare Monk's Pub, Ballyvaughan
Durty Nelly's, Bunratty
O'Connor's, Doolin
Cloister Bar, Abbey Street, Ennis
One Mile Inn, Lahinch Road, Ennis
The Irish Arms, Main Street, Lisdoonvarna

County Cork Dan Lowrey's, 13 MacCurtain Street, Cork
An Teach Beag, 42 Oliver Plunkett Street, Cork
Lyster's, Baltimore
Skibbereen Eagle, Tragumna (near Skibbereen)
Creole, Kinsale
The Blue Haven, Kinsale
The Spaniard, Kinsale

County Galway Crane and the Clogs, Dominick Street, Galway
King's Head, High Street, Galway
Paddy Burke's, Clarinbridge
Silver Teal, Moycullen

. . . have imaginative façades

Baily's Corner, The Mall, Tralee	**County Kerry**
Danny Mann, New Street, Killarney	
The Laurels, Main Street, Killarney	
Shoemaker's Inn, 31 Main Street, Castleisland	
Collin's Bar, Main Street, Adare	**County Limerick**
Bell Tavern, 11 Broad Street, Limerick	
Nancy Blake's, Upper Denmark Street, Limerick	
The Vintage Club, Ellen Street, Limerick	
Monasterboice Inn, Monasterboice (near Drogheda)	**County Louth**
Asgard, The Quay, Westport	**County Mayo**
Val's, Ballyhaunis	
Hough's Bar, Main Street, Banagher	**County Offaly**
Hargadon's, O'Connell Street, Sligo	**County Sligo**
Mac Lynn's, Old Market Street, Sligo	
Ivy Bridge Bar, Main Street, Newport	**County Tipperary**
The Monk's Bar, Mitchel Street, Thurles	
Katie Reilly's Kitchen, Tramore Road, Waterford	**County Waterford**
Seanachie, Dungarvan	
Laragh Inn, Laragh	**County Wicklow**

Restaurants

The restaurants listed are in three categories according to their charges. The lowest category (Cat. 3) indicates restaurants where a three-course

Menus

Bewley's Café in Grafton Street, Dublin

meal can be obtained for about the equivalent of £10 Sterling; in restaurants of the middle category (Cat. 2) a similar meal costs up to £20 and in the first category (Cat. 1) prices are somewhat higher.

Establishments which offer a comparatively inexpensive tourist menu are indicated by "TM". These places are often indicated by the sign of a chef's hat on the road leading into the town or village. Hotel restaurants are only included in the list if their address has not already been given under Hotels (see entry).

Medieval banquets	In a few old castles so-called medieval banquets (see entry) take place on some evenings.
Pub grub	Modest meals and snacks are served in pubs (see entry) and are designated as "pub grub".
Alcohol licence	It is sensible to note the type of licence held by a restaurant before going in for a meal. "Full licence" means that during the licensing hours a full selection of drinks is on sale. "Wine licence" means that only wine can be served.

Restaurants in the Republic of Ireland

Achill Island	The Boley House, Keel; tel. 0 98/4 31 47; Cat. 2. Sweeney's Siopa Claddaigh, The Bridge, Achill Sound; tel. 0 98/4 52 11; Cat. 3., TM.
Adare	The Inn Between; tel. 0 61/39 62 09; Cat. 2 (in a 200-year-old cottage) The Mustard Seed; tel. 0 61/39 64 51; Cat. 1.

Attractive restaurant façades in Kenmare

Dun Aonghusa, Kilronan, Inishmore; tel. 0 99/6 11 04; Cat. 2, TM. The Old Pier, Kilronan, Inishmore; tel. 0 99/6 12 28; Cat. 2., TM.	**Aran Islands**
Woodhill House; tel. 0 75/4 11 12; Cat. 2.	**Ardara**
Bonne Bouche, 21 Church Street; tel. 09 02/7 21 12; Cat. 2. Jolly Mariner, Abbey Road; tel. 09 02/72 11 13; Cat. 2., TM. Le Chateau, Abbey Lane; tel. 09 02/9 45 17; Cat. 1.	**Athlone**
Swiss Barn Speciality Restaurant, Foxford Road; tel. 0 96/2 11 17; Cat. 2 (specialities: fondues, lobster and steak tartare)	**Ballina**
Mellotte's Restaurant, The Neale; tel. 0 92/4 10 32; Cat. 2.	**Ballinrobe**
Harty – Costello Restaurant & Bar, Main Street; tel. 06 98/2 71 29; Cat. 2.	**Ballybunion**
Annie's; tel. 0 28/3 72 92; Cat. 1.	**Ballydehob**
Danby Restaurant, Rossnowlagh Road,; tel. 0 72/5 11 38; Cat. 1.	**Ballyshannon**
Larchwood House Restaurant, Pearsons Bridge (near Ballylickey); tel. 0 27/6 61 81; Cat. 1. O'Connor's Seafood Restaurant, The Square; tel. 0 27/5 02 21	**Bantry**
Blazers, 36 Main Street; tel. 01/2 86 97 98; Cat. 2. Tree of Idleness, Seafront; tel. 01/2 86 00 34 98; Cat. 1.	**Bray**
Durty Nelly's Loft Restaurant; tel. 0 61/36 48 61; Cat. 1. Durty Nelly's Oyster Restaurant; tel. 0 61/36 48 61; Cat. 1. Mac Closkey's, Bunratty House Mews; tel. 0 61/36 40 82; Cat. 1. (in a Georgian house).	**Bunratty**

Restaurants

Mac's Bar and Restaurant, Bunratty Folk Park; tel. 0 61/36 15 11; Cat. 3, TM.

Cahirciveen   Old School House, Knockers; tel. 06 67/24 26; Cat. 1.

Cashel   Chez Hans; tel. 0 62/6 11 77; Cat. 1 (in a restored 19th c. church).

Castlebar   Davitt Restaurant, Rush Street; tel. 0 94/2 22 33; Cat. 2.
Oriental Restaurant, Main Street; tel. 0 94/2 34 58; Cat. 2.

Castledermot   Doyles' School House; tel. 05 03/4 42 82; Cat. 1.

Castletownbere   The Old Bank Seafood Restaurant, Bank Place; tel. 0 27/7 02 52; Cat. 2.
Murphy's Restaurant, East End House; tel. 0 27/7 02 44; Cat. 2.

Clifden   High Moors Restaurant, Doonen; tel. 0 95/2 13 42; Cat. 2.
O'Grady's Seafood Restaurant; tel. 0 95/2 14 50; Cat. 2.

Clonakilty   Doloree House Restaurant, Lisivaird; tel. 0 23/3 41 23; Cat. 1.
The Sandlighter, 3/4 Strand Road; tel. 0 23/3 32 47; Cat. 1., TM.
An Sugan, Wolfe Tone Street; tel. 0 23/3 34 98; Cat. 2., TM.

Clonmel   The Buttermarket Restaurant "La Scala", Market Street;
tel. 0 52/2 41 47; Cat. 2.
Mulcahy's Restaurant, 47 Gladstone Street; tel. 0 52/2 28 25; Cat. 2, TM.

Cong   Echoes, Main Street; tel. 0 92/4 60 59; Cat. 1.

Cork   Bully' Restaurant, 40 Paul Street; tel. 0 21/27 35 55; Cat. 2.
Cliffords Restaurant, 18 Dyke Parade; tel. 0 21/27 53 33; Cat. 1.
Crawford Gallery Restaurant, Emmett Place; tel. 0 21/27 44 15; Cat. 2.
Flemmings Restaurant, Silvergrange, Tivoli; tel. 0 21/82 16 21; Cat. 1.
Jacques Restaurant, Phoenix Street; tel. 0 21/27 73 87; Cat. 1., TM.
McCarthy's, Blackrock Castle, Blackrock; tel. 0 21/35 74 14; Cat. 2, TM (in a renovated castle on the north bank of the river)
Tung Sing Restaurant, 23a Patrick Street; tel. 0 21/27 46 16; Cat. 1, TM.

Dalkey   Guinea Pig, 17 Railway Road; tel. 01/2 85 90 55; Cat. 1, TM.
La Romana, Castle Street; tel. 01/2 85 45 69; Cat. 2.

Dingle   Armada Restaurant, Strand Street; tel. 0 66/5 15 05; Cat. 2.
Beginish Restaurant, Green Street; tel. 0 66/5 15 88; Cat. 2.
Doyle's Seafood Restaurant, John Street, tel. 0 66/5 11 17;
Cat. 1.
Fenton's Bar & Restaurant, Green Street; tel. 0 66/5 12 09; Cat. 2.
The Forge Restaurant, Holy Ground; tel. 0 66/5 12 09; Cat. 2.
Greany's Restaurant, Holy Ground; tel. 0 66/5 16 94; Cat. 3., TM.
Half Door Restaurant, John Street; tel. 0 66/5 16 00; Cat. 1.
The Islandman, Main Street; tel. 0 66/5 18 03; Cat. 2, TM.

Donegal   Errigal Restaurant, Main Street; tel. 0 73/2 14 28; Cat. 3, TM.
Magee of Donegal, The Diamond; tel. 0 73/2 11 00; Cat. 3, TM.

Doolin   Bruach Na Haille Restaurant, Broadford; tel. 0 65/7 41 20; Cat. 2.

Drogheda   Gateway, 15 West Street Drogheda; tel. 0 41/3 87 28; Cat. 1.

Dublin (centre)   18th Precinct Restaurant, 18 Suffolk Street; tel. 01/71 80 00;
Cat. 2.
Arnotts Restaurant, 12 Henry Street; tel. 01/72 11 11; Cat. 3 (self-service).
Ante Room Seafood Restaurant, 20 Lower Baggot Street; tel. 01/6 61 88 32;
Cat. 2, TM.
Batz Restaurant, 10 Baggot Lane; tel. 01/60 03 63; Cat. 2.

Bad Ass Café, 9/11 Crown Alley; tel. 01/6 71 25 96; Cat. 2., TM (pizzeria).
Bewley's Café, 78 Grafton Street; Cat. 3 (traditional coffee house serving
    snacks).
Brokers Restaurant, 25 Dame Street; tel. 01/6 79 35 34; Cat. 2.
Le Caprice Restaurant, 12 St Andrew's Street; tel. 01/6 79 40 50; Cat. 2.
Chapter One, 18/19 Parnell Square; tel. 01/21 77 66; Cat. 1, TM (belongs to
    Dublin Writers' Museum; Italian and Continental cuisine).
The Cedar Tree, 11a St Andrew's Street; tel. 01/6 77 21 21; Cat. 2 (Arabian
    cuisine).
The Commons, Newman House, 85/86 St Stephen's Green;
    tel. 01/4 75 25 97; Cat. 1.
Le Coq Hardi, 35 Pembroke Road; tel. 01/68 90 70; Cat. 1.
Dillon's Restaurant, 21 Suffolk Street; tel. 01/6 77 48 04; Cat. 2, TM.
Eastern Tandoori, 34/35 South William Street; tel. 01/71 05 06; Cat. 2.
L'Ecrivain Restaurant, 112 Lower Baggot Street;
    tel. 01/6 11 19 19; Cat. 1.
Flanagan's Steakhouse, 61 Upper O'Connell Street;
    tel. 01/73 13 88; Cat. 2, TM.
Gallagher's Boxty House, 20/21 Temple Bar; tel. 01/77 27 62; Cat. 2.
Kapriol, 45 Lower Camden Street; tel. 01/75 12 35; Cat. 1 (Italian cuisine).
Kilkenny Kitchen, Nassau Street; tel. 01/77 70 66; Cat. 3, TM (self-service).
Lord Edward, 23 Christchurch Place; tel. 01/54 24 20; Cat. 1, TM (traditional
    fish restaurant).
Oisins Irish Restaurant, 31 Upper Camden Street;
    tel. 01/75 34 33; Cat. 1.
Patrick Guilbaud Restaurant, 46 James Place; tel. 01/76 41 92; Cat. 1 (well-
    known French cuisine).
The Riverbank Restaurant, 10 Burgh Quay; tel. 01/77 01 82; Cat. 2.
Royal Garden Chinese Restaurant, Claredon Street;
    tel. 01/6 79 13 97; Cat. 2.

Bridgie Terrie Pub & Restaurant on the N25 to Waterford; tel. 0 51/9 13 24;   **Dungarvan**
    Cat. 2, TM.
Merry's, Lower Main Street; tel. 0 58/4 19 74; Cat. 2.

De Selby's, 17/18 Patrick Street; tel. 01/2 84 17 61; Cat. 2.   **Dun Laoghaire**
Na Mara, 1 Harbour Road; tel. 01/2 80 67 67; Cat. 1.
The South Bank Restaurant, 1 Martello Terrace;
    tel. 01/2 80 87 88; Cat. 2.

Ship; tel. 0 51/8 31 41; Cat. 2.   **Dunmore East**
The Wick Restaurant; tel. 0 51/8 32 15; Cat. 2.

Blairs Cove; tel. 0 27/6 11 27; Cat. 1 (elegant restaurant in a Georgian   **Durras**
    mansion).
Brandon's Bar, 70 O'Connell Street; tel. 0 65/2 81 33; Cat. 3.   **Ennis**
Brogan's Bar & Restaurant, 24 O'Connell Street;
    tel. 0 65/2 94 80; Cat. 2.
The Cloister Restaurant & Bar, Abbey Street; tel. 0 65/2 95 21; Cat. 1, TM.

Brannigan's Restaurant, 36 Upper Abbeygate Street;   **Galway**
    tel. 0 91/6 59 74; Cat. 2, TM.
The Brasserie, 19 Middle Street; tel. 0 91/6 16 10; Cat. 2, TM.
Casey's, Westwood Restaurant, Dangan, Newcastle;
    tel. 0 91/2 14 42; Cat. 1.
The Chestnut Restaurant, Eyre Square; tel. 0 91/6 58 00; Cat. 2, TM.
Galleon Restaurant, Salthill; tel. 0 91/2 29 63; Cat. 3.
G.B.C. Restaurant & Coffee Shop, 7 Williamsgate Street; tel. 0 91/6 30 87;
    Cat 2,TM.
Lydons of Shop Restaurant, 5 Shop Street; tel. 0 91/6 40 51;
    Cat. 3, TM.

Restaurants

Restaurant in Kinsale

Malt House Restaurant, High Street; tel. 0 91/6 78 66; Cat. 2 (traditionally furnished restaurant and bar).
Paddy's Bar, Eyre Square; tel. 0 91/6 78 43; Cat. 2.

Howth

Abbey Tavern; tel. 01/8 39 03 07; Cat. 1.
King Sitric The Fish Restaurant, East Pier; tel. 01/32 52 35; Cat. 1.

Kenmare

The Lime Tree Restaurant; tel. 0 64/4 12 25; Cat. 2.
Mickey Neds Coffee Shop, 6 Henry Street; tel. 0 64/4 15 91; Cat. 3.
The Purple Heather Bistro, Henry Street; tel. 0 64/4 10 16; Cat. 3.

Kilkee

Marine Restaurant, Circular Road; tel. 0 65/5 60 93; Cat. 2.
The Pantry and County Cooking Shop, O'Curry Street; tel. 0 65/5 65 76; Cat. 2, TM.

Kilkenny

Kilkenny Design Centre, Castle Street; tel. 0 56/2 21 18; Cat. 3, TM.
Kyteler's Inn, Kieran Street; tel. 0 56/2 10 64; Cat. 2, TM. (14th c. restaurant; see A to Z Kilkenny).
Parliament House, 24–25 Parliament Street; tel. 0 56/6 36 66; Cat. 2, TM (furnished in Victoria style).
Ristorante Rinuccini, The Parade; tel. 0 56/6 15 75; Cat. 1, TM.

Killarney

Dingle's Restaurant, 40 New Street; tel. 0 64/3 10 79; Cat. 1 (charming restaurant with varied cuisine).
Foley's Seafood & Steak Restaurant, 23 High Street; tel. 0 64/3 12 17; Cat. 2.
Fossa Roof Top Restaurant, Fossa; tel. 0 64/3 14 97; Cat. 2, TM.
Kieley's Restaurant, College Street; tel. 0 64/3 16 56; Cat. 2, TM.
The Laurels, Main Street; tel. 0 64/3 11 49; Cat. 2, TM.

Sheila's Restaurant, 75 High Street; tel. 0 64/3 12 70; Cat. 2.
The Strawberry Tree, 24 Plumkett Street; tel. 0 64/3 26 88; Cat. 1.

Bistro Seafood Winebar, Guardwell; tel. 0 21/77 41 93; Cat. 2, TM.   **Kinsale**
Max's Wine Bar, Main Street; tel. 0 21/77 24 43; Cat. 2, TM.
Season's Restaurant; tel. 0 21/77 22 44; Cat. 2.
The Vintage, Main Street; tel. 0 21/77 25 02; Cat. 1.
The White House, Pearse Street; tel. 0 21/77 21 25; Cat. 2, TM.

Pat's Pizza, Market Street; tel. 0 74/2 17 61; Cat. 3, TM.   **Letterkenny**
The Village Inn, Kerry Keal; tel. 0 74/5 00 62; Cat. 2, TM.

Patrick Punches, Punches Cross; tel. 0 61/2 71 49; Cat. 2, TM.   **Limerick**
Restaurant de la Fontaine, 12 Upper Gerald Griffin Street;
   tel. 0 61/41 44 61; Cat. 2, TM.
Shangrila Restaurant, 103 O'Connell Street; tel. 0 61/41 41 77; Cat. 2.
Silver Plate, 74 O'Connell Street; tel. 0 61/31 63 11; Cat. 2.
Texas Steakout Restaurant, 116 O'Connell Street;
   tel. 0 61/41 03 50; Cat. 2.

Captain's Deck, Main Street; tel. 0 65/8 13 85; Cat. 2, TM.   **Liscannor**

Meadow Court Restaurant; tel. 0 91/4 16 33; Cat. 2.   **Loughrea**

Bon Appetit, 9 James Terrace; tel. 01/45 03 14 ; Cat. 1.   **Malahide**
Breaker's Restaurant, The Diamond; tel. 01/45 25 84; Cat. 2.
Roches Bistro, 12 New Street; tel. 01/45 27 77; Cat. 1, TM.

Finins, 75 Main Street; tel. 0 21/63 18 78; Cat. 1.   **Midleton**

Drimcong House Restaurant; tel. 0 91/8 51 15; Cat. 1 (in a 17th c. mansion).   **Moycullen**

Crookedwood House; tel. 0 44/2 21 65; Cat. 1.   **Mullingar**
Gramby Restaurant, 9 Dominic Street; tel. 0 44/4 02 80; Cat. 2, TM.

Lawlor's, Poplar Square; tel. 0 45/9 70 85; Cat. 2.   **Naas**
Manor Inn, Main Street; tel. 0 45/9 74 71; Cat. 2, TM.

China Garden, 58 Brews Hill; tel. 0 46/2 26 21; Cat. 2.   **Navan**
Dunderry Lodge, Dunderry; tel. 0 46/3 16 71; Cat. 1.
The Roadhouse, Rathdrinagh, Beauparc; tel. 0 46/2 43 20; Cat. 2, TM.

Gurthalougha House, Ballinderry; tel. 0 67/2 20 80; Cat. 1   **Nenagh**
   (candlelight dinner in a country house; reservation necessary).

Bali Room Restaurant, The Weaver Inn; tel. 0 61/3 6 81 14; Cat. 2.   **Newmarket-on-**
Cronins Restaurant; tel. 0 61/36 81 57; Cat. 2, TM.   **Fergus**

Ivory House, Rosslare Harbour Road; tel. 0 53/3 13 58; Cat. 2.   **Rosslare**
Oyster Seafood Restaurant, Rosslare Strand; tel. 0 53/3 24 39; Cat. 2.

Windmill Tavern, 46 North Street; tel. 0 28/2 16 06; Cat. 2.   **Skibbereen**

Beezie's, O'Connell Street; tel. 0 71/4 50 30; Cat. 3, TM.   **Sligo**
Mandarin Court, Wine Street; tel. 0 71/4 25 68; Cat. 2, TM.

Kiely's Lounge, 23 Main Street; tel. 0 62/5 12 39; Cat. 3, TM.   **Tipperary**

Chez Jean-Marc, 29 Castle Street; tel. 0 66/2 13 77; Cat. 1.   **Tralee**
Skillet Restaurant, Barrack Lane; tel. 0 66/2 45 61; Cat. 2, TM.

Restaurant Cre Na Cille, High Street; tel. 0 93/2 82 32; Cat. 2.   **Tuam**

The Ring Lyne; tel. 06 67/61 03; Cat. 2, TM.   **Valentia Island**

Restaurants

Waterford	Dwyers of Mary Street, 8 Mary Street; tel. 0 51/7 74 78; Cat. 2, TM. The Reginald, The Mall; tel. 0 51/5 50 87; Cat. 2, TM.
Waterville	Sheilin Seafood Restaurant; tel. 06 67/42 31; Cat. 2., TM. Smugglers Restaurant & Inn, Cliff Road; tel. 06 67/43 30; Cat. 2, TM.
Westport	The Ardmore Restaurant & Bar, The Quay; tel. 0 98/2 59 94; Cat. 2. The Moorings, The Quay; tel. 0 98/2 58 74; Cat. 2.
Wexford	The Bohemian Girl, North Main Street; tel. 0 53/2 44 19; Cat. 2, TM. Granary Restaurant, West Gate; tel. 0 53/2 39 35; Cat. 2. Uncle Sam's Restaurant, 53 South Main Street; tel. 0 53/2 49 75; Cat. 3. Tim's Tavern, 51 South Main Street; tel. 0 53/2 38 61; Cat. 2, TM.
Wicklow	Pizza del Forno, The Mall Centre, Main Street; tel. 04 04/6 70 75; Cat. 2, TM.
Youghal	Aherne's Pub & Seafood Bar, 163 North Main Street; tel. 0 24/9 24 24; Cat. 2.

Restaurants in Northern Ireland

Armagh	Banisters, 143 Railway Street, tel. 018 61/52 21 03; Cat. 1 Mandarin House, 30 Scotch Street, tel. 018 61/52 22 28; Cat. 2 (Chinese and European cuisine)
Ballymena	Confucius, 45 Springwell Street, tel. 012 66/65 16 38; Cat. 2 (Chinese and European cuisine) Grouse Inn, 2 Springwell Street, tel. 012 66/4 52 34; Cat. 2 Manley, State Cinema Arcade, Ballymoney Road, tel. 012 66/4 89 67; Cat. 2 (Cantonese and European cuisine)
Ballynahinch	Woodlands, 29 Spa Road, tel. 012 38/56 26 50; Cat. 1 (open Thur., Fri. and Sat. evenings only)
Belfast	Bewley's, Donegall Arcade, tel. 012 32/23 49 55; Cat. 3 (self-service) Frames Too, 2 Little Donegall Street, tel. 012 32/24 48 55; Cat. 1 Nick's Warehouse, 35–39 Hill Street, tel. 012 32/43 96 90; Cat. 2 Roscoff, Lesley House, Shaftesbury Square, tel. 012 32/32 37 62; Cat. 1 Skandia, 50 Howard Street, tel. 012 32/24 02 39; Cat. 3 Thompson's Garage, 6 Patterson's Place, Donegall Square East, tel. 012 32/32 37 62; Cat. 2 (sandwiches and soup)
Carrickfergus	Northgate, 59 North Street, tel. 019 60/36 41 36; Cat. 2
Coleraine	Macduff's, 112 Killeague Road, Blackhill, tel. 012 65/86 84 33; Cat. 1
Enniskillen	Crow's Nest, 12 High Street, tel. 013 65/32 52 52; Cat. 3 Franco's, Queen Elizabeth Road, tel. 013 65/32 44 24; Cat. 2 (Italian cuisine)
Larne	Kiln, Old Glenarm Road, tel. 015 74/26 09 24; Cat. 2
Londonderry	Bells, 59 Victoria Road, tel. 015 04/31 15 00; Cat. 3 Brown's, 1 Victoria Road, tel. 015 04/4 51 80; Cat. 3 Three Mile House, 21 Drumahoe Road, tel. 015 04/31 16 38; Cat. 3
Newry	Rose Garden, 3 Sugar Island, tel. 016 93/6 87 02; Cat. 3 (Chinese and European cuisine)
Newtownards	Eastern Tandoori, 16 Castle Street, tel. 012 47/81 95 41; Cat. 3 (Indian cuisine)

Gaslamp, 47 Court Street, tel. 012 47/81 12 25; Cat. 3
Roma's, 4 Regent Street, tel. 012 47/81 28 41; Cat. 2

Mellon Country Inn, 134 Beltany Road, tel. 016 626/66 12 24; Cat. 3 **Omagh**

China House, 55 Eglinton Street, tel. 012 65/82 28 89; Cat. 3 **Portrush**
   (Cantonese and European cuisine)
Dionysus, 53 Eglinton Street, tel. 012 65/82 38 55; Cat. 3
   (Greek and English cuisine)
Ramore, The Harbour, tel. 012 65/82 43 12; Cat. 3

Montagu Arms, 68 The Promenade, tel. 012 65/83 41 46; Cat. 3 **Portstewart**

Fir Trees Lodge, Melmount Road, tel. 015 04/38 23 82; Cat. 3 **Strabane**

The Grange, Main Street, tel. 017 62/88 19 89; Cat. 3 **Waringstown**

Riding

Ireland is an ideal place for a riding holiday, whether as a beginner or an experienced rider. Package riding holidays are offered by some travel firms.

Riding-schools organise courses for beginners, with experienced instructors. The horses are accustomed to strange riders and are generally well-behaved. There are also courses in jumping and dressage – usually lasting a fortnight – for more experienced riders.

Another possibility is a pony-trekking holiday, usually lasting a week, with   Pony-trekking
perhaps four hours in the saddle each day. In the Republic the most

Irish Derby: an annual social occasion

Souvenirs

interesting treks are in Connemara, on the Dingle Peninsula, Co. Sligo, and near Killarney.

Riding holidays Addresses and information about riding holidays in the Republic can be obtained from the brochure entitled "Horse Riding Holidays" published by the Irish Horse Board, Naas Road, Dublin 12. Tel. (01) 50 11 60.
The Northern Ireland Tourist Board issues a leaflet on pony-trekking holidays available spring 97 (30p).

Horse-racing Ireland is a great horse-breeding country, and horse-racing is a very popular spectator sport. There are more than 250 race-meetings every year on the country's 28 racecourses. The sport is promoted by the Racing Board and supervised by the Turf Club, a body with a long tradition behind it. Ireland's best-known racecourse is the Curragh in Co. Kildare.

Dublin Horse Show The Kerrygold Dublin Horse Show, run by the Royal Dublin Society every year at the beginning of August, offers a full programme of events. It is also the largest market for Irish bloodstock and attracts numerous foreign buyers.

Horse-drawn caravans See entry

Souvenirs

Among the most sought-after souvenirs of a visit to Ireland are hand-woven tweed, fine lace, hand-knitted jerseys, pipes, china, pottery, silver and hand-cut crystal. Smoked salmon is also a popular buy.
Fine antiques can be found in antique shops, at auctions and in flea markets at Dublin, Cork and Limerick.
Many visitors like to take home examples of the traditional Irish crafts – such as pottery, hand-woven articles, basketwork, glass-blowing, etc. – which are still practised in many parts of Ireland.

Sport

In Ireland sport is an important element in everyday life.

Aero and gliding clubs Aircraft Owners and Pilots Association
A.O.P.A. Ireland
Ms Catherine Leech
Loughlinston Road, Celbridge, Co. Kildare
Tel. 01 088/50 50 55, fax 4 57 15 09

Ballooning Balloon and Airship Association
Aero and Gliding Clubs
c/o 39 Whitebeam Road, Clonskeagh, Dublin 6

Clay Pigeon Shooting Dr Joseph A. Woodcock, Honorary Secretary
Irish Clay Pigeon Shooting Association
20 Butterfield Drive, Rathfarnham, Dublin 14
Tel. 0 91/79 45 27

Gaelic Athletic Association The desire to establish Irish independence of Britain in sport led to the establishment in 1884 of the Gaelic Athletic Association. Gaelic football, which combines features of association football and rugby, was also actively promoted. Football Finals are in Dublin on 3rd Sunday in September.

Greyhound racing: a popular spectator sport

There is also a special Irish form of bowling, fought out with a heavy steel ball on quiet country roads in the south of Ireland between two towns or villages.

Bord na gCon
Irish Greyhound Racing Board
104 Henry Street, Limerick
Tel. 0 61/31 67 88, fax 0 61/31 67 39

Greyhound Racing

Irish Hang-gliding Association (AFAS)
House of Sport, Long Mile Road, Dublin 12
Tel. 01/4 50 16 33, fax 01/4 50 28 05

Hang-gliding

Cork Paragliding/Hang-gliding Club
Mr Mike Tonner
Donemark, Bantry, Co. Cork
Tel. 0 27/5 15 67

The great Irish game, however, and one mentioned in ancient legend and regarded by many as the fastest game played on grass, is hurling, played by teams of fifteen men with hurling-sticks, which are rather like hockey-sticks but with broader blades. The All Ireland Hurling Final at Croke Park in Dublin on 1st Sunday in September is watched by over 80,000 fanatical spectators.

Hurling

National Microlight Aircraft Association
c/o Paul Chamberlain
Old Cottage, Rathdown Road, Greystones, Co. Wicklow

Motor Gliding

Some 40 mountaineering clubs are included in the Federation of Mountaineering Clubs of Ireland.

Mountaineering

369

Telephone

                    Mountaineering Council of Ireland (AFAS)
                    House of Sport, Long Mile Road, Dublin 12
                    Tel. 01/4 50 16 33, fax 01/4 50 28 05

Polo   All-Ireland Polo Club
                    Phoenix Park, Dublin 8, Tel. 01/6 77 62 48

Squash   Irish Squash Racket Association
                    House of Sport, Long Mile Road, Dublin 12
                    Tel. 01/4 50 15 64/4 50 16 33, fax 01/4 50 28 05

Tennis   Tennis Ireland
                    Argyle Square, Morehampton Road, Dublin 4
                    Tel. 01/6 68 18 41, fax 01/6 68 34 11

                    See also Golf, Fishing, Hunting and Shooting, Riding (including horse-
                    racing) and Water Sports.

Sport for the   The Irish Tourist Board produces a guide for the disabled, with the ad-
disabled   dresses of organisations and clubs (including the Irish Wheelchair Associ-
                    ation and the National League of the Blind) which will advise disabled
                    people interested in sport.

Telephone

                    Local, long-distance and international calls can be made from public call-
                    boxes. A reduced rate tariff operate between 6pm and 8am and all day on
                    Saturdays and Sundays. The more modern telephone boxes accept coins
                    of 5, 10, 20, 50p and £1; from others a call-card can be used with 10, 20, 50
                    and 100 units. These are obtainable from post offices and various shops.

International   From Britain to the Republic of Ireland: 00 353
telephone   From the Republic of Ireland to Britain: 00 44
codes   From the Republic of Ireland to Belfast: 08 01232

                    From the United States or Canada to the Republic: 011 353
                    From the Republic to the United States or Canada: 00 1

                    From the United States or Canada to Northern Ireland: 011 44
                    From Northern Ireland to the United States or Canada: 00 1

                    From Australia to the Republic: 011 353
                    From the Republic to Australia: 00 61

                    From Australia to Northern Ireland: 44
                    From Northern Ireland to Australia: 00 61

                    From New Zealand to the Republic: 00 353
                    From the Republic to New Zealand: 00 64

                    From New Zealand to Northern Ireland: 00 44
                    From Northern Ireland to New Zealand: 00 64

                    The international code is followed by the local dialling code followed by the
                    customer's number; if there is a zero at the beginning of the local dialling
                    code this should be omitted.
                        The following are the local codes (with initial zero omitted where applic-
                    able) for some of the major towns and cities in Ireland; others can be found
                    in the international section of your telephone directory:

                    Athlone: 902, Belfast: 1232, Cork: 21, Donegal: 73, Dublin: 1, Galway: 91,
                    Killarney: 64, Killkenny: 56, Limerick: 61, Londonderry: 504, Sligo: 71,
                    Wexford: 53.

Telephone calls to Britain are charged at the rate of 29p per minute, but cheaper calls at 24p per minute are available after 6pm to 8am each day, at weekends and public holidays. Operator assisted calls are calculated for private phones at £2.02 for 3 minutes and public phones at £2.40 per 3 minutes.

Direct Dial

Time

The whole of Ireland observes Greenwich Mean Time, which is five hours ahead of New York time. Summer Time is one hour in advance of Greenwich Mean Time and is in force from late Mar.–late Oct.

Tipping

In most hotels and restaurants a service charge of ten, twelve or fifteen per cent is automatically added to the bill. Otherwise a tip of between five and fifteen per cent can be given.

Traffic Regulations

See Motoring

Travel Documents

British citizens do not, of course, require a passport to go to Northern Ireland and do not need one to enter the Republic if they are travelling direct from Britain. Nationals of other countries require a passport, or in some cases a national identity card.

Visitors driving their own car should carry their national driving licence and car registration document, as well as a "Green Card" (international insurance certificate) obtainable from their normal insurers of the vehicle.
  In Northern Ireland and in the Republic foreign cars must display an oval international distinguishing sign of the approved type and design.

Vehicle documents

Water Sports

The Atlantic Ocean and the Irish Sea offer excellent sailing waters. In addition sailing on the inland lakes is increasing in popularity. Around the Irish coast are numerous sailing centres and schools for both beginners and the more experienced.

Sailing

Sailing packages can be booked. Operators can be found in the "Green Holiday Pages" of the Irish Tourist Board, or can be obtained from the Irish Sailing Association (3 Park Road, Dun Laoghaire, Co. Dublin; tel. 01/2 80 02 39, fax 2 80 75 58).

Boats can be rented at the following sailing centres:

Hiring boats

Baltimore Sailing School,
Baltimore, Co. Cork

Irish National Sailing School
115 Lower Georges Street, Dun Laoghaire, Co. Dublin

Water Sports

Dingle yacht basin

Fingall Sailing School
Upper Strand, Malahide, Co. Dublin

Galway Sailing Centre,
Oranmore, Co. Galway

Glenans Irish Sailing Centre
28 Merrion Square, Dublin 2

International Sailing Centre
5 East Beach, Cobh, Co. Cork

Shannon Sailing
New Harbor, Dromineer, Co. Tipperary

Shannonside Sailing Centre
Killaloe, Co. Clare

Water-skiing
There are opportunities for water-skiing on loughs (lakes) and rivers and especially off flat coastal areas. The necessary equipment and boats can be rented at many places (including Farran, Castleblayney, Macroom, Sligo).

Irish Water-ski Federation
Mr Des Burke-Kennedy
Mount Salus, Knocknacree Road, Dalkey, Co. Dublin
Tel. 01/4 50 21 22/2 85 52 05, mobile 087/5 58 74, fax 01/4 50 21 38

Surfing
Surfing can be practised in Ireland anywhere there is water: the necessary breeze can usually be relied on. Surf-boards can be rented at many places and courses for beginners and the more experienced are offered (for example at Kinsale, Killaloe, Rosslare, Caherdaniel, Schull and Carlingford).

Information:
Irish Windsurfing Association
48 Marlfield Gardens, Cabinteely, Co. Dublin
Tel. 01/2 85 10 31

For experts Ireland's west coast offers excellent conditions for surfing throughout the year. Waves of 3–13ft/1–4m high can be expected (especially at Doolin, Strandhill and Rossnowlagh).

Irish coastal waters offer ideal conditions for scuba diving. The warm Gulf Stream keeps up the temperature of the water so that it is relatively pleasant even at some depth. At some points the coast falls steeply down, offering a variety of submarine fauna and flora. Some diving centres have equipment for rental (e.g. Bay View Hotel on Clare Island, Dolphin Diving in Ballyvaughan, Valentia Diving Centre on Valentia Island, Skellis Aquatic Dive Centre in Caherdaniel).

Scuba diving

Information:
Scubadive Diving School
Coliemore Harbour, Dalkey
Tel. 01/85 03 57

Irish Underwater Council
78A Patrick Street, Dun Laoghaire, Co. Dublin
Tel. 01/2 84 46 01, fax 01/2 84 46 02

Diving Events

Ireland's numerous rivers and loughs (lakes) offer ample scope for rowing.

Rowing

Information:
Irish Amateur Rowing Union
House of Sport, Long Mile Road
Walkinstown, Dublin 12
Tel. 01/4 50 16 33/4 50 98 31, fax 01/4 50 28 05

The Irish loughs (lakes) and rivers offer opportunities both for canoe touring and white-water canoeing. The best rivers are the Liffey, Barrow, Nore, Boyne, Slaney, Lee, Shannon, Suir and Munster Blackwater. Canoes can be rented.

Canoeing

Information:
Irish Canoe Union
House of Sport, Long Mile Road
Walkinstown, Dublin 12
Tel. 01/4 50 98 38/4 50 16 33, fax 01/4 50 28 05

See also Boating

When to go

The best time to go to Ireland is between the end of March and the end of October. July and August, the warmest months, are best for seaside holidays but the popular places may be crowded. Autumn can also be very pleasant, since the weather in September and October tends to be mild and dry. Visitors who can be flexible in their choice of dates should visit Ireland in May or June when there is the greatest chance of sunny days.

Although, thanks to the oceanic climate it is never particularly cold in Ireland, there is a good deal of rain. As a rule, however, it takes the form of showers and does not last long.

See also Facts and Figures: Climate

Youth Hostels

Youth hostels offer overnight accommodation for young people at reasonable cost. In the Republic of Ireland the Irish Youth Hostel Association (An Oige) maintains 37 hostels and in Northern Ireland the Youth Hostel Association of Northern Ireland (YHANI) has 9 hostels (lists are available from the organisations below). An international youth hostel card must be produced; advance booking is advisable. Charges for accommodation depend on the season, location of hostel and the age of the visitor, varying from between IR£3 and 6 (Dublin up to IR£9).

For information and lists of hostels, apply to the relevant association:

Republic of Ireland
Irish Youth Hostel Association (An Oige)
61 Mountjoy Street
Dublin 7
Tel. 01/8 30 45 55, fax 8 30 58 08

Northern Ireland
Youth Hostel Association of Northern Ireland (YHANI)
22 Donegall Road
Belfast BT12 5JN
Tel. 012 32/32 47 33, fax 43 96 99

Index

Index

Principal Sights of Tourist Interest

(continued overleaf)

Principal Sights of Tourist Interest

Imprint

191 colour illustrations, 10 town plans, 12 ground plans, 8 general maps, 8 drawings, 7 plans, 1 special plan, 1 large-scale map

Original German text: Birgit Borowski, Achim Bourmer, Rainer Eisenschmid, Dr Peter Harbison, Wilhem Jensen, Brian Reynolds, Dr Margit Wagner.

Revised text: Baedeker-Redaktion (Birgit Borowski)

Cartography: Franz Kaiser, Sindelfingen, Gert Oberländer, Munich; Mairs Geographischer Verlag, Ostfildern (large-scale map)

Source of illustrations: Anthony Verlag (1), Baedeker Archiv (2), Bildagenteur Schuster (1), Bilderdienst Süddeutscher Verlag (1), Birgit Borowski (62), Ina Brödel (59), Fotoagentur Helga Lade (6), Green Studio Ltd. (1), Klaus Hartmann (7), Historia-Photo (3), Reinhard Hoene (2), Renata Holzbachová (26), IFA Bilderteam (6), Irish Tourist Board, Dublin (1), Irish Tourist Board, Frankfurt (1), Kai Ulrich Müller (8), Klaus Thiele (1), Ullstein Bilderdienst (2), L. Wuchner (1)

General direction: Dr Peter Baumgarten, Baedeker, Stuttgart

Editorial work, revision and additional translation (English language edition): Alec Court

English translation: James Hogarth, David Cocking, Julie Waller, Crispin Warren

Revised text: Wendy Bell, Margaret Court, Julie Waller

3rd English edition 1997

© Baedeker Stuttgart
Original German edition

© 1997 Jarrold and Sons Limited
English language edition worldwide

© 1997 The Automobile Association
United Kingdom and Ireland

Published in the United States by:
Macmillan Travel
A Simon & Schuster Macmillan Company
1633 Broadway
New York, NY 10019–6785

Macmillan is a registered trademark of Macmillan, Inc.

Distributed in the United Kingdom by the Publishing Division of the Automobile Association, Fanum House, Basingstoke, Hampshire RG21 2EA

A CIP catalogue record of this book is available from the British Library

Licensed user:
Mairs Geographischer Verlag GmbH & Co.,
Ostfildern-Kemnat bei Stuttgart

Printed in Italy by G. Canale & C.S.p.A – Borgaro T.se –Turin

ISBN 0 02 861360 0 USA and Canada
0 7495 1405 1 UK